CIRCUMNAVIGATION: SAIL THE TRADE WINDS

VOLUME II—VANUATU TO FLORIDA
by
Sue Moesly

Edited by Julius M. Wilensky

All photos by the author unless otherwise indicated

Copyright© 1995 by Suzanne E. Moesly
Published by Wescott Cove Publishing Company
P.O. Box 130, Stamford, CT 06904

All rights reserved
No part of this book may be reproduced in any form without the permission of the publisher

First Edition — 1995

Library of Congress Card No. 95-61656
ISBN No. 0-918752-20-5
SAN No. 210-5810

TABLE OF CONTENTS

Chapter	Page
Editor's Preface	7
How This Book is Organized	8
List of Sketch Charts in this Book	10

1. Vanuatu 13
- Port Vila, Efate Island 13
- Anchorage at Emae Island 16
- Foreland Anchorage, Epi Island 16
- Anchorage on North Side of Ui Island 20
- Port Sandwich, near SE end of Malekula I., Vanuatu 21
- Vao Island 21
- Anchorage Between Malo and Malo Killikilli 21
- Santo Village, Espiritu Santo 24
- The Copra Plantation 24
- Surundu Bay, Espiritu Santo Island 26
- Hog Harbor, Espirito Santo Island 26
- Passage to Banks Islands 26
- Lakona Bay, Santa Maria Island, Banks Islands 26
- Rigadoon Bay, Vanua Lava Island 28
- Hayter Bay, Tegua Island, Torres Islands 30

2. Solomon Islands 32
- One of the South Pacific's Best Cruising Grounds 32
- Passage from Torres Islands to Solomon Islands 32
- Port Mary, Santa Ana, Solomon Islands 33
- Star Harbor, San Cristobal Island, Solomon Islands 36
- Kirakira, San Cristobal Island, Solomon Islands 38
- Passage to Ugi Island 42
- Selwyn Bay, Ugi Island, Solomon Islands 43

3. Guadalcanal, Solomon Islands 45
- Marau Sound 45
- Honiara, Guadalcanal 47
- Gavutu Harbor, Florida Island 52
- Baranago Island 53
- Return to Honiara 53

4. Russell Islands and Marovo Lagoon 55
New Georgia Group, Solomon Islands
- Russell Islands 55
- Marovo Lagoon 55
- Anchorage off West Shore of Vangunu Island 62
- Viru Harbor, South Coast of New Georgia Island 64
- Rendova Harbor 64
- Anchorage at Mbaeroko Bay 65
- Gizo 67

      Baga Island 67
      Treasury Islands 67
5. **Bismarck Archipelago** 70
      Passage from the Treasury Islands, Solomons 70
        to English Harbor, New Ireland
      English Harbor, between Lambon Island and New Ireland 72
      Passage to Rabaul, New Britain 72
6. **Rabaul, New Britain** 75
      The Gathering Place 75
      Fire Dance 76
      Unseasonal Weather 77
      Getting Away 79
      Passage to Madang 79
7. **Madang, Papua New Guinea** 83
      Taking Stock 83
      Holiday Time 83
      Madang 84
      The Market 86
      Karkar Island's Volcano 87
      Jellyfish 87
      The Salins 88
      Planning Departure 88
8. **Trobriant Islands, China Straits, and Samarai** 90
      Trobriand Islands 90
      Vakuta Island, Trobriands 92
      Passage to Amphlett Group 94
      Wamea Bay 94
      Fergusson Island 94
      Scrub Island, Gomwa Bay 96
      Sewa Bay, Normanby Island 96
      Nuakata Island 96
      Passage to Samarai 98
      Belesana Slipways 98
      Samarai 99
9. **Port Moresby and Torres Straits** 102
      Passage to Hood Bay and Hood Lagoon, Papua New Guinea 102
      Hood Lagoon, Papua New Guinea 105
      Inside Passage to Port Moresby 105
      Tupuselei, Papua New Guinea 106
      Port Moresby 106
      Captains and Crews 108
      Malaria 110
      Finding Bramble Cay, Torres Straits 110
10. **Islands and Harbors, Australia's North Shore** 118
      Passage from Bramble Cay to Dalrymple Island, Cocoanut 118
        Island, Mt. Adolphus and Thursday Island, Australia

    Thursday Island, Australia 118
    Anchorage off Northwest Shore of Horn Island 120
    Passage to Wessel Islands 120
    Anchorage off Northwest Shore of Wessel Islands 122
    Passage to Croker Island and Port Essington, Australia 123
    Passage to Anchorages at Cape Don and Cape Hotham 126
    Darwin, Australia 127
11. **Bali Beckons** 130
    Benoa Harbor, Bali 132
    Shopping in Denpasar 135
    Benoa Village 136
    Our Island Tour 136
    Preparations, Routes, Arrivals and Departures 138
12. **Gales in the Indian Ocean** 140
    Passage to Christmas Island 140
    Flying Fish Cove, Christmas Island 142
    Passage to Pass by Cocos-Keeling 143
    Onward to the Salomons 144
    Autopilot Kaput 146
13. **Extra-Tropical Cyclone** 148
    Water Below and Water Above 148
14. **The Tempest is Over** 154
    Damage Assessment 154
    Passage to Diego Garcia, Chagos Archipelago 154
    Diego Garcia, Chagos Archipelago 157
15. **Egmont and Mauritius Passage** 163
    Passage to Egmont Islands 163
    Egmont Islands Lagoon 163
    Hearts of Palm 164
    The Beachcomber 166
    Passage to Mauritius 168
16. **La Belle Mauritius** 171
    Grand Bay, Mauritius 171
    Port Louis, Mauritius 176
    Cyclone Season 178
    Cyclone Claudette Hits Mauritius 180
    Engine Repair 182
    Back to Grand Bay 183
17. **Side Trip to Cargados Carajos Shoals (St. Brandons)** 185
    Passage to Cargados Carajos Shoals 185
    Coco Island, Cargados Carajos Shoals 188
    School for Terns 190
    Anchorage Behind Reefs Northeast of Coco Island 191
    Anchorage North of Ile de Paul 191
    Ile Raphael 192

	Ilet Raphael	193
	Passage Back to Mauritius	194
18.	**To Reunion and Passage to Turning Point South of Madagascar**	**195**
	Planning our Passage to South Africa	195
	Currents South of Madagascar and Along the Coast of South Africa	195
	Advantages of Richards Bay, South Africa	196
	Preparations for the Passage from Mauritius	197
	Passage to Reunion	198
	Reunion Island	198
	Passage to Madagascar	200
	Backtracking in the Wrong Direction	202
19.	**Passage to Richards Bay, South Africa**	**205**
	Towards Madagascar	205
	Broken Gudgeon	206
	Wrong Way Again!	207
	Passage from Madagascar to Richards Bay, South Africa	208
	Land Ho!	211
	Richards Bay	212
20.	**Zululand**	**214**
	Richards Bay	214
	Ernst Klaar	214
	Umfolozi Game Reserve	216
	Zululand History	218
	Our Visit to a Sugar Cane Farm	218
	Rudder Repair	220
	Time to Leave	220
21.	**Passage to East London, South Africa**	**222**
	Time to Leave Richards Bay	222
	Off We Go	224
	Five Stormy Sou'westers	224
	East London	227
22.	**Agulhas Current to Knysna**	**230**
	Passage to Knysna	230
	Entering Knysna	232
	Knysna	232
23.	**Cape of Storms**	**237**
	Passage to Mossel Bay	237
	Mossel Bay	238
	Passage to Cape Town	241
	Cape Town	246
24.	**Across the Atlantic**	**249**
	Passage to St. Helena Island	249
	Passage to the Equator	254
	Passage to Bequia, St. Vincent, Windward Islands	255

25. Through the Eastern Caribbean 260
    Bequia 260
    Harbor Hopping to Antigua 262
    St. Bart's 262
    St. Maarten 264
    Anegada Passage 264
    Rendezvous at Trellis Bay, British Virgin Islands 264
    St. John 266
    St. Thomas 266
    Rendezvous with Jeanne Moesly 266
    Passage to the Berry Islands, Bahamas 268
    The Berry Islands 268
Appendix I 273
    True Courses and Nautical Miles
Appendix II 279
    Radio Communications
Appendix III 283
    Mail Forwarding Services
Index 285
Mercator Projection 288

Svea anchored off, Poco on the beach, "The Shoals" (St. Brandon), Chapter 17

EDITOR'S PREFACE

This is Volume II of Sue Moesly's account of her circumnavigation with her husband Don, aboard *Svea*, their 38-foot double-ended ketch. We won't repeat the Editor's Preface or Author's Introduction from Volume I, only to reiterate that you're in for a treat.

Don kept track of their courses and notes on charts. From these, Sue made a great set of sketches that Jo Haight turned into the charts you see in these two volumes. These will enable other sailors to follow in the Moeslys' footsteps, but we want to again caution sailors that these charts are not intended for navigation. The Moeslys carried a complete set of official charts covering the countries that they visited, and you should too.

The other thing worth repeating from our Volume I is to call your attention to Sue's descriptions of flora and fauna and weather phenomena. For me, these were some of the high spots for Volume I. Sue is one of nature's children. I have continued to enjoy our conversations and correspondence, learning what was going on among the wildlife in the Moeslys' 12-acre home in Cocoa, Florida. The Moeslys are listed with the National Wildlife Federation as having a Backyard Safe Habitat. They also belong to the Audubon society, the Nature Conservancy, and the National Wildlife Federation.

For more on Sue's background and the Moeslys' boating experience, see the Editor's Preface and the Author's Introduction in Volume I.

Julius M. Wilensky
August, 1995

Photo by Carl Moesly

Girl with bonito, Bali

HOW THIS BOOK IS ORGANIZED
by
Julius M. Wilensky

If you have Volume I of Circumnavigation: Sail the Trade Winds, this page and the route chart on the last page and inside the back cover, and Appendix I giving true courses and distances port to port, are the only duplications that you'll find in Volume II.

We have made two volumes because there are too many pages to bind properly in one volume, or for readers to use easily. The cause of this is so many charts and street maps. There is some minor redundancy among the sketch charts, but we've felt it better to have a few too many than not enough. Some of this redundancy is due to use of different scales to show more detail, and others are due to inability to show all the detail on one chart. You will note that many of these sketch charts are 8½" X 11½", spread over two adjacent pages. You **can** follow in the Moeslys' footsteps, but many of us will only want to know how it was to sail around the world. I learned a lot as I edited this book.

This book picks up where Volume I left off. Volume I left Fiji, en route to Vanuatu. That was Chapter 25 in *Svea's* odyssey. Volume II starts all over again with Chapter I, Vanuatu. This Volume II's 25 chapters take you through the Solomon Islands, to Papua New Guinea, the China Straits, Torres Straits, Australia's north shore, Bali, across the Indian Ocean via many atolls, to Mauritius, then to South Africa, and home to Fort Lauderdale via the South Atlantic, the Eastern Caribbean and the Bahamas.

Refer to our detailed Table of Contents and to Appendix I which records courses and distances for the Moeslys' whole trip. There is also a place name Index in the back of the book, to help you find what you're looking for. Following this page is a list of all the sketch charts in this book, with page numbers to facilitate your finding the chart you want. These sketch charts are not intended for navigation use. Both the author and the publisher strongly recommend that you carry a complete set of navigational charts for the countries that you intend to visit. Neither the author nor the publisher can be responsible for errors or changes on these sketch charts. Author Sue Moesly would love to hear from you regarding any differences that you find. Write to Sue c/o the publisher, address on the title page.

All photos are by the author unless otherwise credited.

Appendix I gives *Svea's* true courses and distances port to port in nautical miles. These are given for the entire circumnavigation repeated from Volume I. Other Appendices are not repeated from Volume I.

Appendix II describes the ever-changing status of Radio Communications. By the end of this century, this will all be via satellite.

Appendix III gives information on Mail Forwarding Services. If you don't have someone reliable at home, this is a necessity for circumnavigators.

Photo by Carl Moesly

Solomon Island boys with canoe. Note no outriggers. These are sheltered waters

LIST OF SKETCH CHARTS IN THIS BOOK

Title	Page
Efate Island, Vanuatu	14
Port Vila, Efate Island, Vanuatu	15
Anchorages at Emae Island and Epi Island, Vanuatu	17
Malekula Island—Ui Island, Port Sandwich, and Vao I. Anchorages, Vanuatu	18 & 19
Espiritu Santo, Village of Santo, Anchorages at Malo, Killikilli I., Aore I., Surundu Bay, and Hog Harbor	22 & 23
Lakona Bay, Santa Maria Island, Banks Islands	27
Detail of Lakona Bay, Santa Maria Island, Banks Islands	28
Rigadoon Bay, Vanua Lava Island, Banks Islands	29
Hayter Bay, Tegua Island, Torres Islands	31
Regional Chart: Solomon Islands, New Ireland, New Britain, East Portion of Papua New	34 & 35
Santa Ana to San Cristobal Island, Approach to Star Harbor	37
Star Harbor, San Cristobal Island, Solomon Islands	39
San Cristobal Coastline from Wanoni Bay Anchorage to Kirakira, to Ugi Island	40 & 41
Guadalcanal Island, Solomon Islands	46
Marau Sound, East End of Guadalcanal	48
Street Map of Honiara, Guadalcanal, Solomon Islands	49
Florida Island, Gavutu Harbor, Baranago Harbor	51
New Georgia Group, Solomon Islands	56 & 57
Russell Islands, Solomon Islands	60 & 61
Passage from the East through Diamond Narrows into Hathorn Sound	63
Gizo Harbor	66
Treasury Islands	69
New Ireland and New Britain, Bismarck Archipelago, Papua New Guinea	71
Rabaul, New Britain, Bismarck Archipelago	74
Regional Chart: Rabaul, New Britain to Bramble Cay, Torres Strait	80 & 81
Madang Harbor, Papua New Guinea	85
Trobriand Islands	91
Amphlett Group and Fergusson Island	95
Normanby Island through China Straits to Samarai Island	97
Papua New Guinea, China Strait to South Cape	101
Papua New Guinea South Shore, Hood Lagoon and Round Head	103
Papua New Guinea South Shore, Round Hill Port Moresby, Inside Passage	107
Port Moresby, Papua New Guinea	109
Regional Chart: Torres Strait to Mauritius	112 & 113

Torres Strait .... 114 & 115
Thursday Island Vicinity, North Australia .... 116 & 117
Wessel Islands, Australia 121
Croker Island, Port Essington, Cape Don .... 124 & 125
   Cape Hotham and Darwin, Australia
City of Darwin, Australia 129
Approaches to Bali 131
Benoa Harbor, Bali 133
Our Tour of Bali 137
Flying Fish Cove, Christmas Island 141
Chagos Archipelago 155
Diego Garcia 159
Egmont Islands 165
Regional Chart: Mauritius to Cape Town, South Africa 170
Mauritius 171
Grand Bay, Mauritius 173
Entry to Port Louis, Mauritius 175
Port Louis, Mauritius 177
Route from Grand Bay, Mauritius to Cargados 187
   Carajos Shoals (St. Brandons) and to Isle de la Reunion
Cargados Carajos Shoals 189
Port des Galets, Reunion Island, Indian Ocean 199
Indian Ocean Passages Through Gales 201
Bonnet's Sketch of SE Coast of South Africa 204
   Showing Continental Shelf and Currents
Zululand, South Africa 209
Area Around Richards Bay 211
Richards Bay 213
East and South Coasts of South Africa 223
East London, South Africa 229
Entrance to Knysna 233
Upper Reaches of Knysna Lagoon 235
Mossel Bay, South Africa 239
Approaches to Cape of Good Hope and Cape Town, South Africa 243
Table Bay and Cape Town 245
Regional Chart: Cape Town, South Africa to .... 250 & 251
   Ft. Lauderdale, USA
Admiralty Bay and South End of Bequia 259
Bequia to Virgin Islands 261
Isles des Saintes, Guadeloupe, and Antigua 263
St. Barts and St. Martin 265
U.S. and British Virgin Islands 267
Eleuthera, Bahamas to Ft. Lauderdale, USA 269
Berry Islands 271
Bimini Islands and Dollar Harbor Anchorage 272

Photo by Carl Moesly

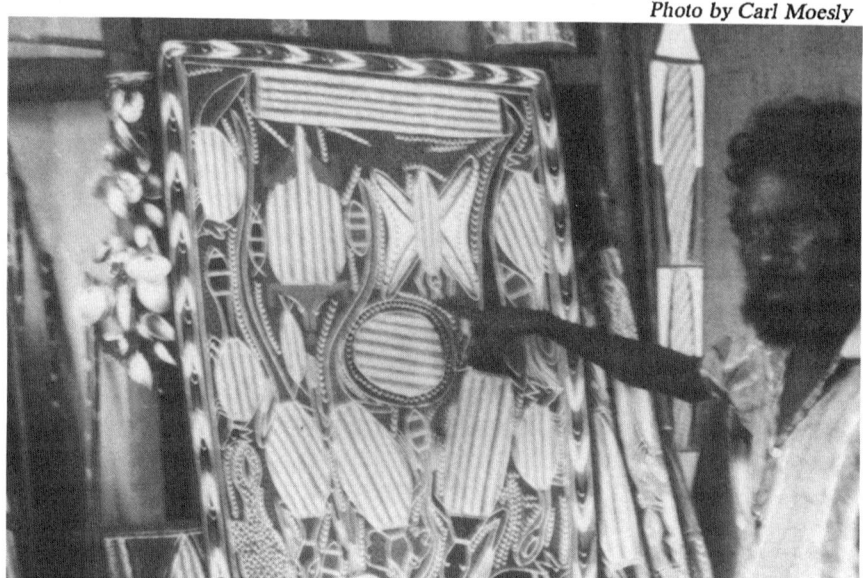

Australian Aborigone with crafts for sale (Chapter 10)

Photo by Carl Moesly

Zulus along the roadside. Many have native crafts for sale (Chapter 20)

CHAPTER 1

VANUATU

Port Vila, Efate Island

After a trouble-free clearance with customs and immigration in the capital city, we milled through Port Vila's shops along the waterfront and the streets behind. Although Vanuatu, the former New Hebrides, was once under a condominium government of both British and French, the town's ambiance was distinctly French. Even the canned goods and various selections of wines in the grocery stores were the same brands we had found in Tahiti. The islands have now gained their independence and their new name of Vanuatu.

Svea was tied stern-to the quay at Port Vila near the native market pavilion. If I arose before dawn, I could always catch the tiny Vietnamese lady as she walked with quick shuffles across the field to her stall. Her fruits and vegetables were loaded in the two baskets that hung from the wooden yoke she bore across her bent shoulders. Not a bean or a cucumber, and not even her coolie hat was dislodged in her clippity-clop pace. Later in the day, I would see her behind neatly arranged piles of produce. She invariably tipped her weighing scales in my favor.

We were now inside Melanesia, which means "the black islands." Fiji provided the door that opened into a new civilization, new cultures and social structures. The care-free Polynesian has been replaced by the more serious and certainly more reserved Melanesian. The "Sailing Directions" warned of bushmen in some of the coastline villages that still might be war-like, but we encountered natives only shy and reticent about extending outward displays of friendship.

Vanuatu consists of three main islands with several outshoots of smaller ones scattered through the group. Efate, the island where Port Vila is located, was of primary importance to the Allied Forces during World War II because of Havannah Harbor, just a bend northwestward around Devil's Point from Port Vila. It became the site of a very large staging area. There was easy access both in and out of the large bay, which gave shelter to the many warships that anchored in the deep waters. On shore was a large airport which handled the air support and communications. Don and I found patches of old cement runways, almost hidden by weeds. North of Efate are the islands of Malekula, then Espiritu Santo at the north end of Vanuatu. From there, the route leads us northwestward through the Banks and Torres Islands and into the Solomon Islands. All of these islands bear the scars and the remnants of World War II. It was like walking through a graveyard in seeing quonset huts and old Marsden tracks that made temporary landing fields.

The memories remain in some of the older natives who recall the days gone by. They are eager to tell the Yanks about their part in the defense of their islands. "I remember when this bay was filled with battleships,"

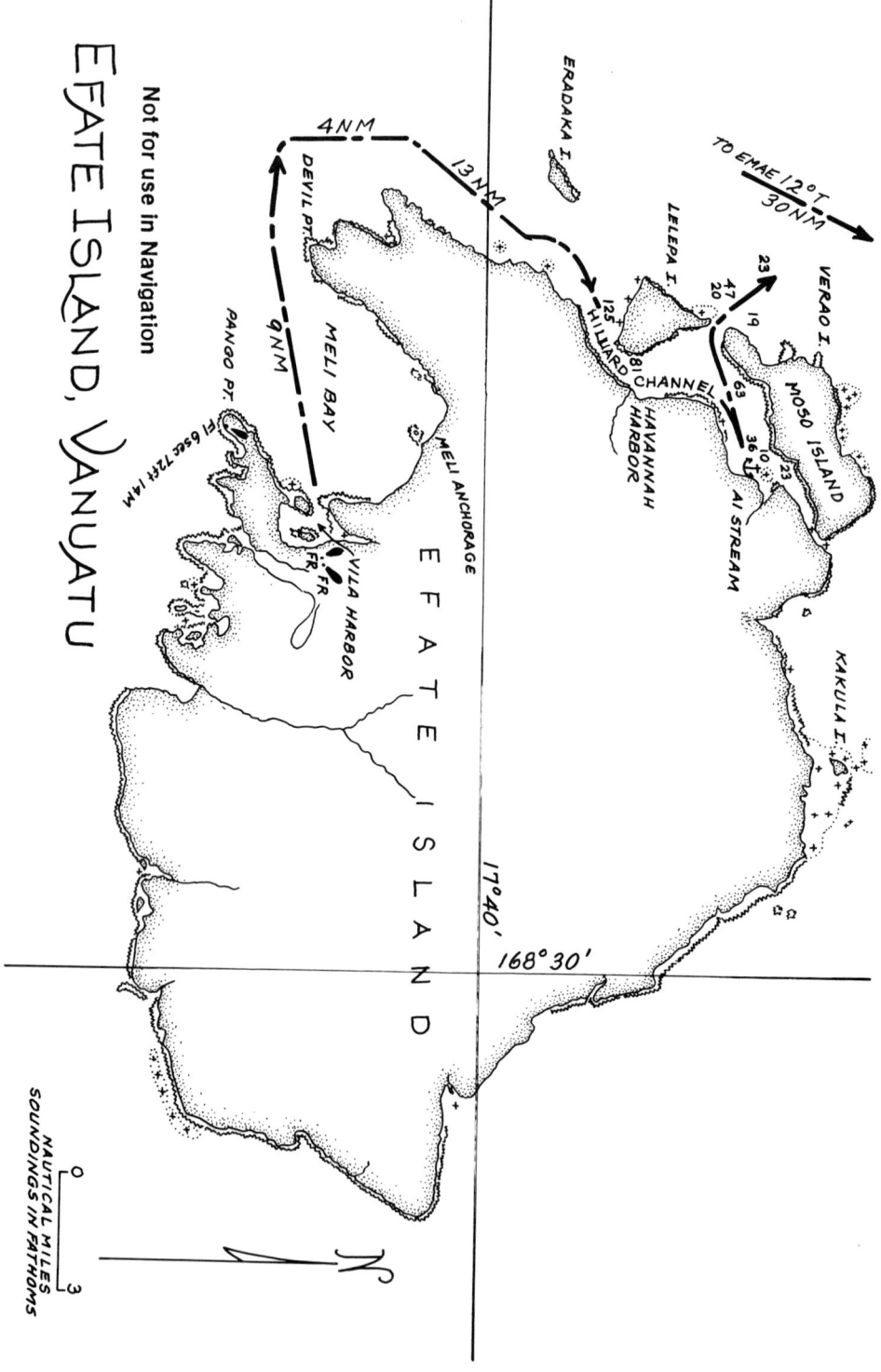

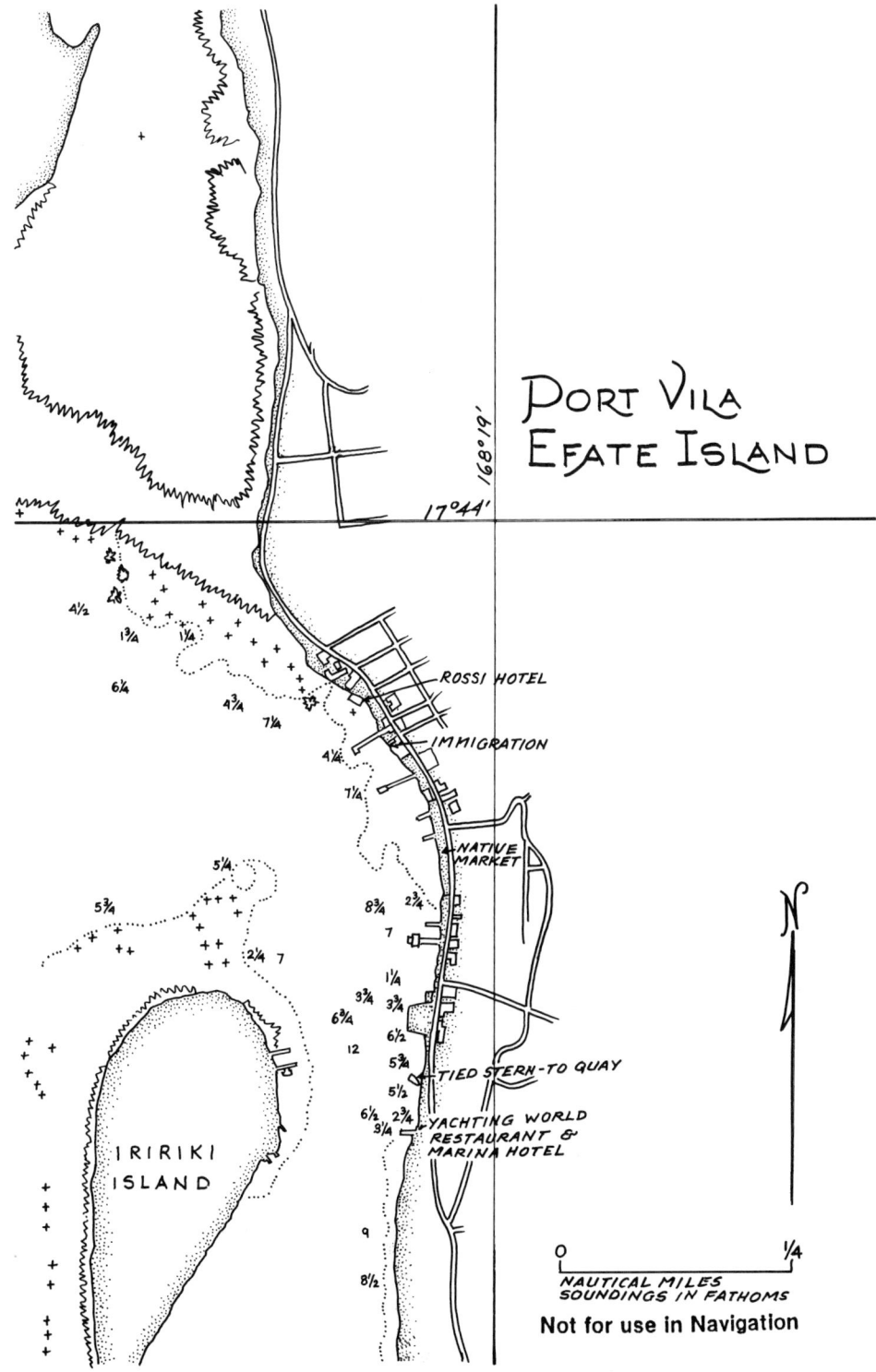

Morris, the elder spokesman from the village of Moso, said when he stopped by to greet us after we had dropped anchor in Havannah Harbor. "We even had aricraft carriers," he continued and smiled when he looked at *Svea*'s American ensign flying from the flagstaff. "I built a sailing canoe for one of the officers and he took it on board the ship when he left," the old man said proudly. He was happy to relive his war years with us Americans.

One day, a young girl pulled her canoe out of the parade of others going to their vegetable gardens on the main island, and paddled towards *Svea*. The others carried on and continued their singing, which they did in perfect harmony, the altos, the sopranos, tenors and basses. I was in the dinghy scrubbing *Svea*'s topsides when she approached and said in English, "Oh, I know this is a good boat. It is so clean!" She blurted out what she really wanted to say, "I don't have a husband!"

Rather taken aback and searching for a reply, I asked her, "How old are you?"

With downcast eyes, the girl, who wore a smock bedecked with ribbons, answered, "Eighteen."

"My, oh my," I smiled. "Girls in America do not marry until they are in their late twenties and into their thirties. They establish careers nowadays before entering into marriage." And then I thought about careers and the native girls who had nothing to do but tend their gardens and have babies. Many of the eligible males in her small village had emigrated to areas where they could earn a living. At least, my words made her smile and she picked up her paddle and carried on for the main island. The ribbons dangling from the puffed sleeves of the girl's smock were explained later. We were told that the women were still as missionary-oriented as their forebears and embellished their Mother Hubbard cover-ups with ribbons and bows and added the more feminine puffed sleeves.

Anchorage at Emae Island

Moving northward towards the chain of islands and away from the more populated areas, we stopped at Emae Island. However beautiful the scenery was there, the roadstead anchorage in front of a group of buildings on the northwest side was not well protected if the wind blew strongly. In a depth of 55 feet, the ground was pocked with coral heads. When the float we tied to the anchor chain dropped suddenly into a pocket, we wondered if we would ever retrieve it the next morning.

Foreland Anchorage, Epi Island

As luck would have it, the anchor did come aboard and we got underway for Epi Island. Leaving behind the rolly anchorage, we were delighted to find more protection at Foreland anchorage in 20-foot depth over a black sand bottom between the house and the mouth of the river. On this northwestern side of the island, the scene before us was a typical copra plantation with symmetrically planted coconut trees waving in the

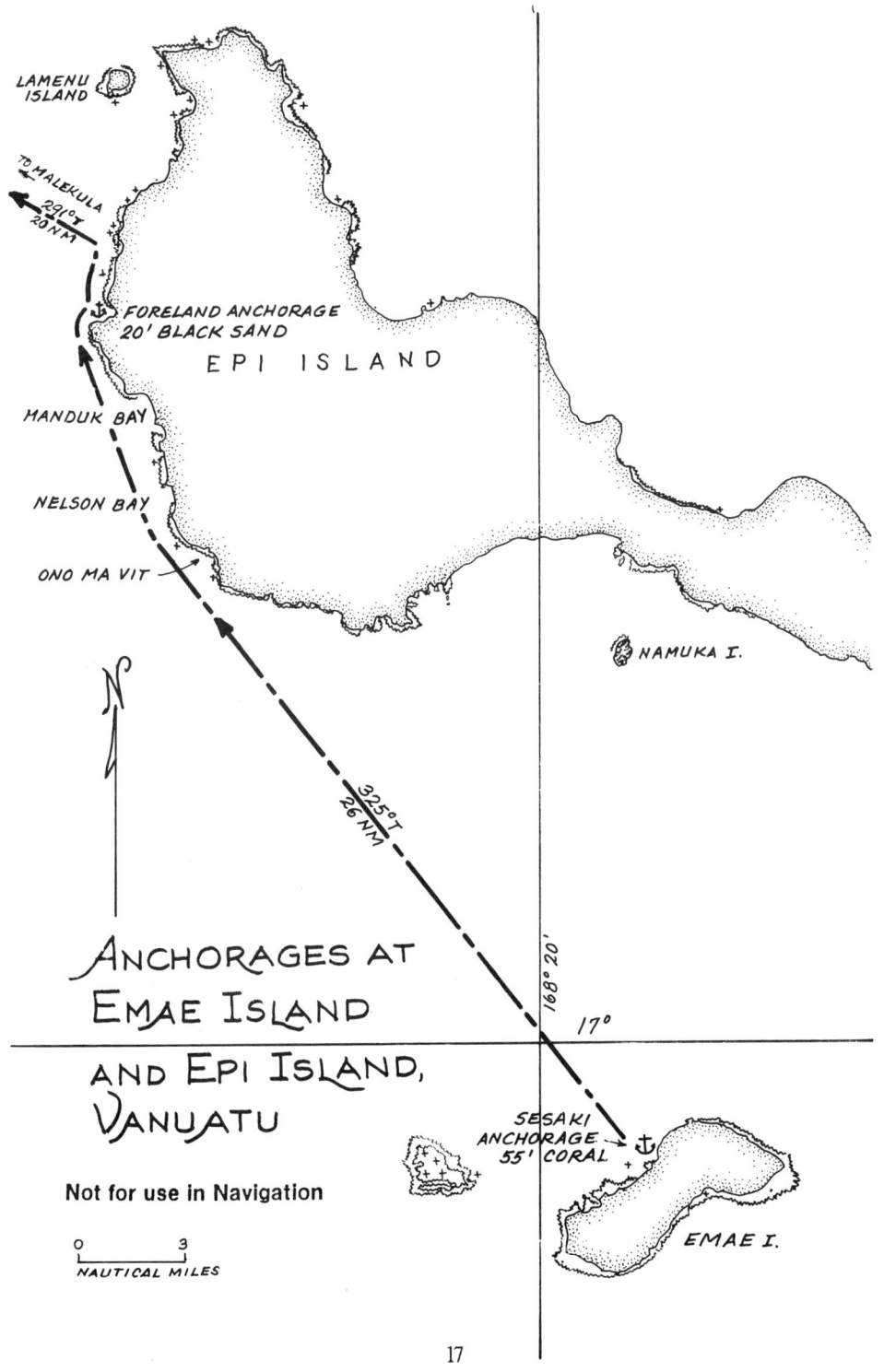

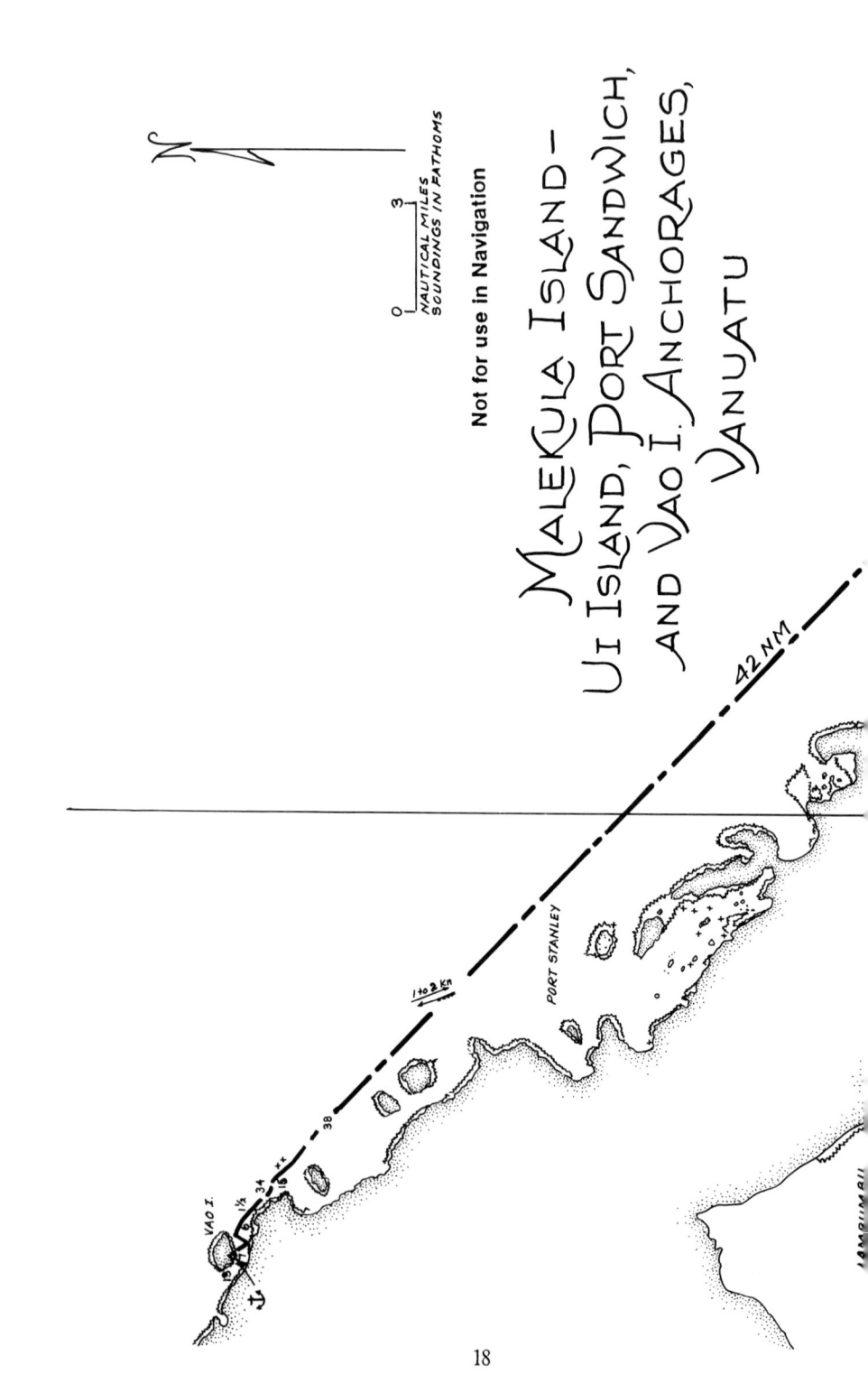

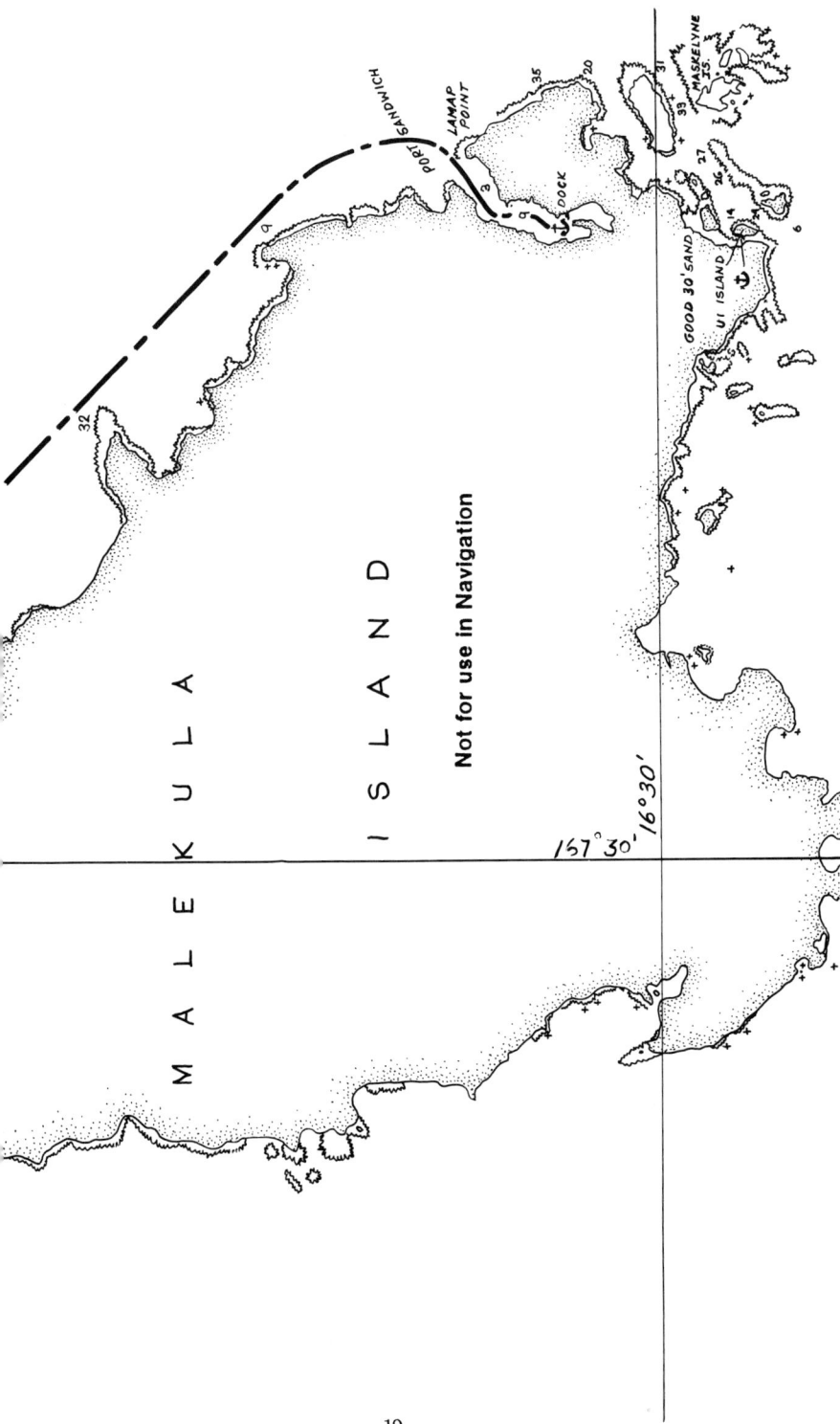

soft breeze. Willie Joseph met us as we came ashore and welcomed us to the village of Bonkovia. As boss of the plantation, Willie had 16 tons of copra waiting for the Burns-Philp boat from Vila. It was due in the next day. "I expect to get $3,000 for this harvest," the friendly man said. Later that night, we welcomed Willie and his gift of a stalk of bananas and three Papayas aboard *Svea*.

Anchorage on North Side of Ui Island

With a light beam wind, we had to motorsail to reach the southeastern end of Malekula where we wound in and around coral heads and islets to find the anchorage on the northwestward side of Ui Island. Although we had yet to encounter any wild bushmen, as the "Sailing Directions" warned, we were most concerned when suddenly we were surrounded by dugout canoes as soon as the anchor hit the sandy bottom. More canoes were coming from around each bend. *Svea* was girdled by big dugouts with men and long spears aboard, and small dugouts with children whose faces bore no smiles, that is, until some one of the group said a few words in English and the spell was broken. The rest all started talking at once in a mish-mash of Pidgin English and their own native language. Like so many other natives, they were only curious. Their spears were used simply for fishing. When the crowd thinned, a family remained and we asked them about the fish we had caught about 3 miles from shore.

"Gutpela, gutpela," the father said and we assumed the words, sounding like good, meant just that. He wasted no time in taking the half we gave him to shore. He started a fire immediately to cook it. We'll hear more about this fish at Marau Sound in the Solomons.

Bushmen approaching us, Malekula I., Vanuatu

Port Sandwich, near Southeast End of Malekula Island, Vanuatu

Port Sandwich was only 5 miles from our anchorage, but as we left the lee of Ui Island and headed northward, once again headwinds and short steep seas greeted us.

"That's the advantage of being a cruising sailor," I said as Don began to check the chart and ponder a way through the winding channel to the protected anchorage. "We always have the right to change our minds. No schedules. No deadlines."

Following the channel markers, we penetrated the channel for 2½ miles until we found an ideal anchorage just opposite a freight dock. Far enough away from land, we were free from mosquitoes.

We walked more than a country mile or two on the road that led to the village of Lamap overlooking the sea. Along the way, we encountered different smaller villages with their pandanus huts painted in very colorful geometric patterns. We found no beers at the local tavern. In swiftly spoken French words, twisted with the native dialect, the barmaid did say something like, "Tomorrow. It will be Bastille Day."

Vao Island

Missing the oncoming festivities, we left Port Sandwich at dawn's early light to make the 45-mile passage farther northward along Malekula's eastern shores to Vao Island. We were learning to notice that the more progressive villages were those established by religious missions. The Seventh Day Adventists appeared to have more followers than any other religion, although the Catholic missions were a close second.

On the island of Vao, where there was a Catholic mission, we counted 55 canoes pulled up on their beach. Canoes in the islands are like automobiles in America. Every family needed at least one, for it was their only means of transportation. There must have been a greater population density on that small island than any other island we had ever seen, except perhaps the San Blas Islands off Panama.

Anchorage Between Malo and Malo Killikilli

As the chart indicates, tide rips do race through the Malo Strait between Malekula and the island of Malo. As expected, it was a rough passage. We were happy to know we could find a lee from the now brisk southeasterly winds between the small island of Malo Killikilli and her larger sister Malo. As we proceeded very cautiously amongst reefs and existing coral heads, we were greeted on the larger island's shoreline by a herd of goats. When times get rough or uncertain, there is always an introduction of a creature, be it bird, fish or mammal, that relaxes the tension. We found a sandy spot in a depth of 22 feet to the northwest of the small island. During the night, the wind veered more northerly, making the anchorage untenable. We had stayed there overnight only to avoid arriving at Santo on a Sunday.

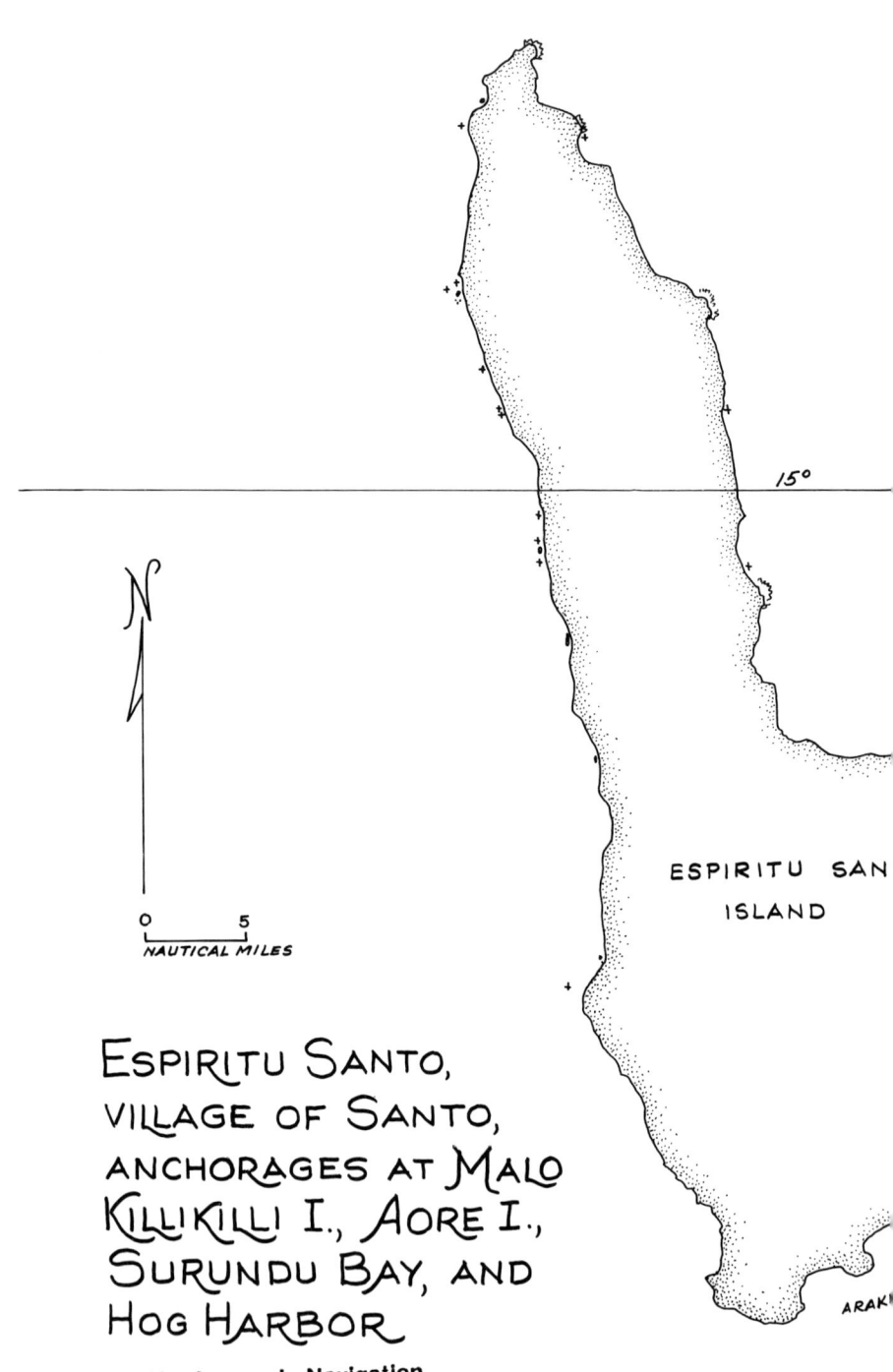

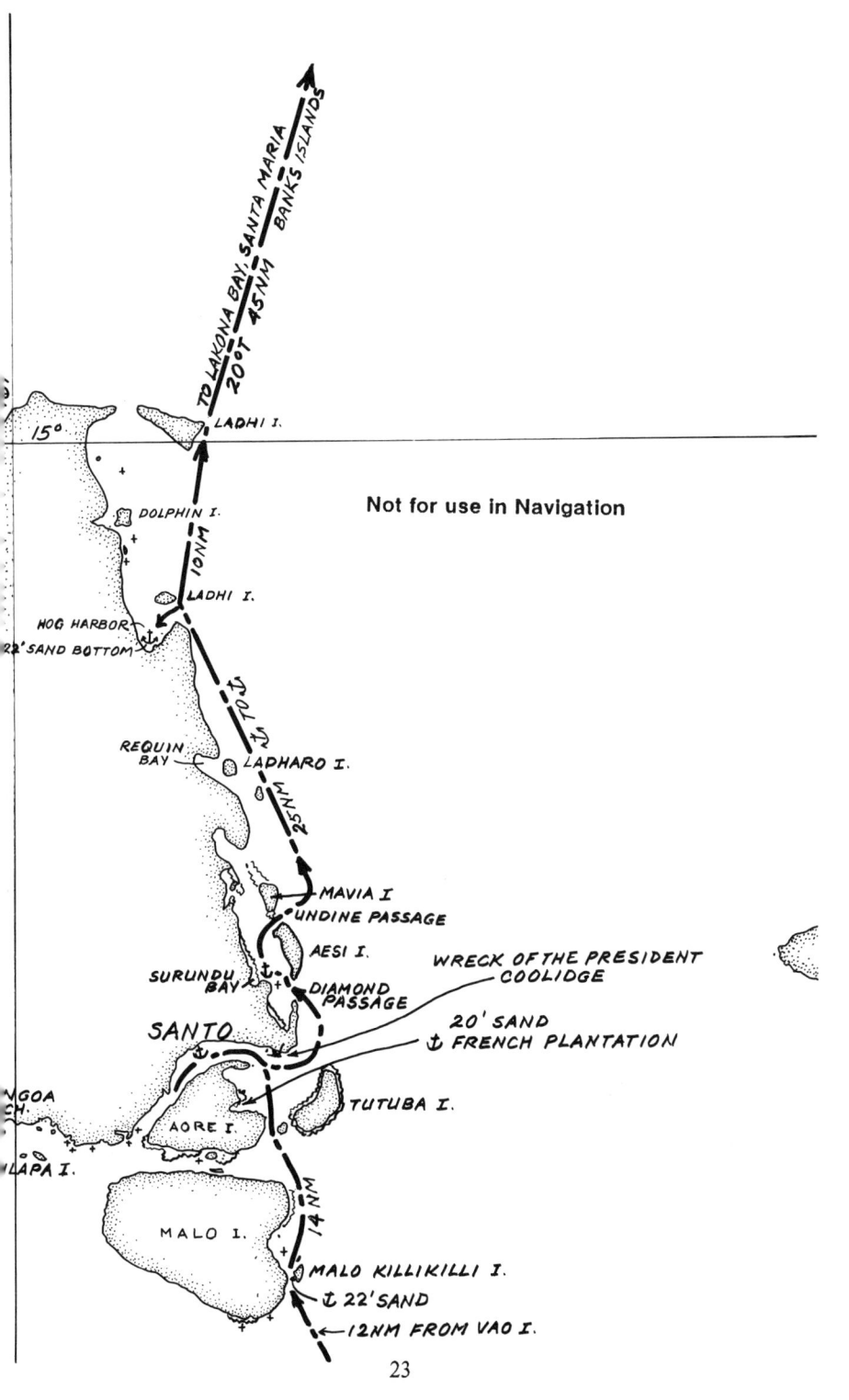

Santo Village, Espiritu Santo

The town of Santo is on the big island of Espiritu Santo. Quonset huts of the World War II days had been converted to dwellings for the population. From a maze of clotheslines, joining the many half-domed buildings together, hung arrays of beribboned smocks, faded lap laps and multitudes of diapers, the sign of domesticity. Across the street another, but larger, quonset hut was the town's Burns Philp supermarket. The local boucherie helped me to restock *Svea*'s freezer with the familiar French cuts of meat.

I left the market and browsed a few of the many Chinese and Vietnamese shops lining the street that led to the city park and the anchorage. In one shop, kerosene lanterns for sale were hanging over the sewing thread cabinet. Beneath that cabinet was the screened-in box for the bread, and under that were baskets of fresh local produce. Scattered on various tables and boxes were articles of clothing, some in neat piles and others in complete disarray. There were so many distractions that you could easily forget what you intended to buy when you first walked in the door. But, some may say, that is a sign of a prosperous shopkeeper. I almost walked out with the purchase of a coolie hat, but I could just imagine the frowns on Don's face when I greeted him at the dinghy landing, so put the hat back on the shelf it shared with the plastic buckets and wash tubs.

The Copra Plantation

We were back on board *Svea* when a powerboat, driven by a white man, approached us. "Saw your flag," said the man with a French accent, "and wanted to invite you over to my bay and plantation, just on the other side of this (Aore) island." He pointed behind us. "It's a well-protected anchorage," the man urged us. Don and I looked at one another and agreed that we should accept the man's invitation, for we had never seen a French plantation before.

Somehow, the picture we had placed in our minds about plantations did not concur with reality. The years and the depressed price of copra were to blame for the changes made to the once prosperous plantation that had produced coffee, cacao and of course, copra. As the price of copra went down, the price of labor went up and there were no profits. There was not even enough money to meet the bare expenses. One by one the buildings fell into disrepair, and the size of the crops fell with the reduction of the work force.

After we had beached *Poco* we climbed the short incline leading to the two-story house that looked barren of life. The windows were tightly shuttered and the only signs of life were the multitudes of flies that swarmed around us. Several out-buildings were in a sorry state of disrepair and seemed to lean against one another for their only support. One collapsed building stood next to a very rusty framework of a former windmill and we surmised that must have been the pump house.

We found our host at the kitchen's back door and he invited us in to the closed house. Inside, it was really a very nice house, one that had seen children and the touch of women in its decorating. All of that was gone. Bob's wife had divorced him many years ago and taken the children back to New Caledonia with her. He was alone with only one native to help him work the small crop of copra.

He looked back over the years and told us, "My father started this plantation when there was nothing at all but bush. His only shelter from the elements was under an upturned dinghy. He used indentured Vietnamese convict labor as his work force." Bob went on to tell us that his father found a couple of wild bullocks to start his herd of cattle and their offspring now ran wild. Only when the generator was running, did the electrified fence keep them away from the small garden patch.

The plantation was thriving at the outbreak of World War II. Bob told about entertaining the Allied officers from the ships that anchored in his bay. "We even had an admiral to dinner one night," he chuckled when he remembered the pleasant days of his life.

Bob paused and looked out over the bay and pointed to a spot where we could just see the yellow color of a reef, lying under the surface of the water. "See that reef?" he asked. "My wife was sitting at the upstairs dormer window when the troop ship *President Coolidge* ran into the American mine fields set in the channel just outside that reef. The ship exploded."

"Oh, my," I said aghast, "You really must have had some casualities in your house."

"No," the man recounted." There were none, except to the ship, for the captain was able to run the ship up onto the reef. The men got off just before the ship foundered, then slid off of the reef into the deep and sank."

One day Bob left work on repairing a wagon he used in the copra grove. He wanted to show us his land: the forests, the citrus and copra groves, the pastures and the areas that were once cleared and bore harvests of vegetables. He warned us ahead of time that nature was reclaiming the land that his father, his brother and he had worked so hard to make productive. We began our tour down by the beach where the big banyan trees stretched out over the water. Bob reached over to pick one of the wild orchids that grew in clusters on the bent limbs. He showed us the point where he stood to do most of his fishing, and the stretch of beach that collected the prettiest shells coming from the reef just in front of it.

We left the water and followed trails, marked by the roaming cattle that led in and around old banyans and mammoth Nawaswas trees, whose huge roots formed cave-like secret enclosures. Small mandarin orange trees fought for survival in the growth of the underbrush and under the shadows of the big trees that dwarfed them. Strangler figs were winning their battles with many of the trees, for their roots had encompassed them in death grips. On the brighter side were the sounds of birds. Brightly-colored lorikeets twittered high notes to their mates in harmony with the lower scale notes of the blue pigeon-type birds.

Bob explained the next scene where the ground was covered with pig tracks and husked coconuts "The wild pigs can tear off the coconut husks, but they can't crack open the inner shell," he said as he picked up a husked coconut. "They let the sun do that for them, and when it starts to crack under the heat, they come back and eat the meat." He noted that the strangest part of the harvest is that one pig will not steal another pig's coconuts.

One night a marauding pig ravaged Bob's pumpkin patch and the following night Bob was waiting for him. That was sure a good roast pork dinner we had aboard *Svea*, and our guest surely enjoyed the pumpkin pie. I even made an extra pie for Bob to take back to the house so he could remember the Americans he had kindly hosted.

Surundu Bay, Espiritu Santo Island

We left Bob, the vanishing breed of French plantation owners, and made an overnight stop in Surundu Bay, westward within the larger bay of Palekula still on Espiritu Santo Island. As we made way through Diamond Passage, we noticed a wrecked boat on the southern shore. A Japanese shipyard was farther into the southern bay and many of the fleet's fishing boats were there as well. Japanese do not fish on the full moon. That night was cause for them to remain in port.

Hog Harbor, Espirito Santo Island

It seems that wherever we anchored in Vanuatu, we were serenaded by mooing cows on shore. Without going ashore we knew they would have their accompanying flies. We did go ashore near Hog Harbor, at the top end of the island. We found not only cattle and flies, but also skeletons of cement roads, ramps and foundations that once were busily traveled by the Allied Forces, during World War II.

Passage to Banks Island

Seas were steep and nasty as we bid farewell to the islands of Vanuatu and set course for the next group of islands, the Banks and then the Torres. The sky was overcast with a filmy haze. Remembering that the "Sailing Directions" had mentioned volcanic disturbances, causing strange clouds that cast stranger still reflections on the water, we assumed the haze to be of a volcanic origin.

Lakona Bay, Santa Maria Island, Banks Islands

We anchored at a roadstead anchorage at the Banks Islands, at Lakona Bay off the west shore of Santa Maria Island. The "authorized yacht greeter," Wores Patteson, paddled out in his canoe and asked us to sign his book. The book's cover was printed with the big letters of his standing in the village. The official greeter wanted to take us to meet his father, who was the chief, and his uncle, who was the customs chief. The customs chief is not the bureaucratic kind, but the man responsible for tribal cus-

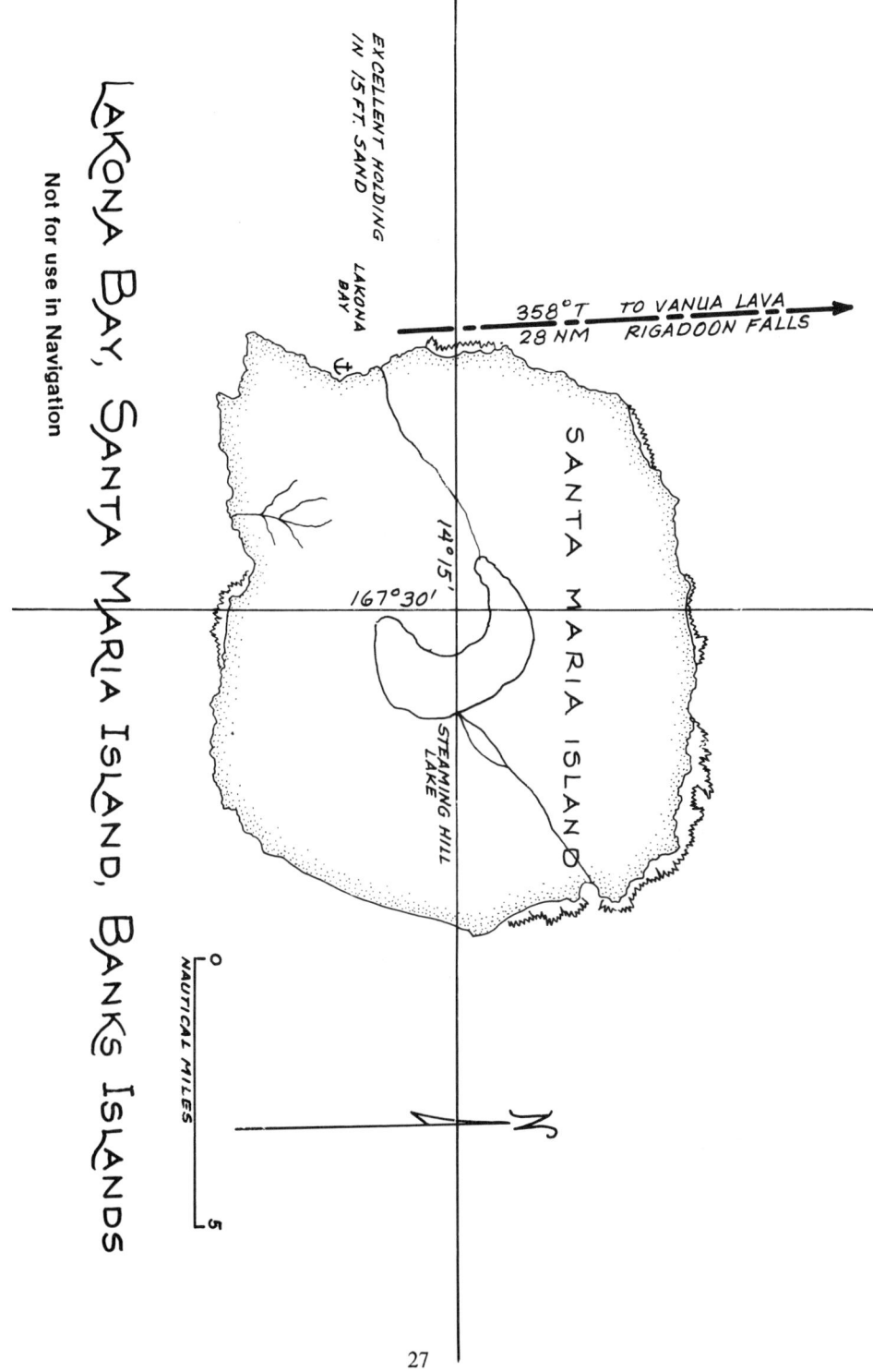

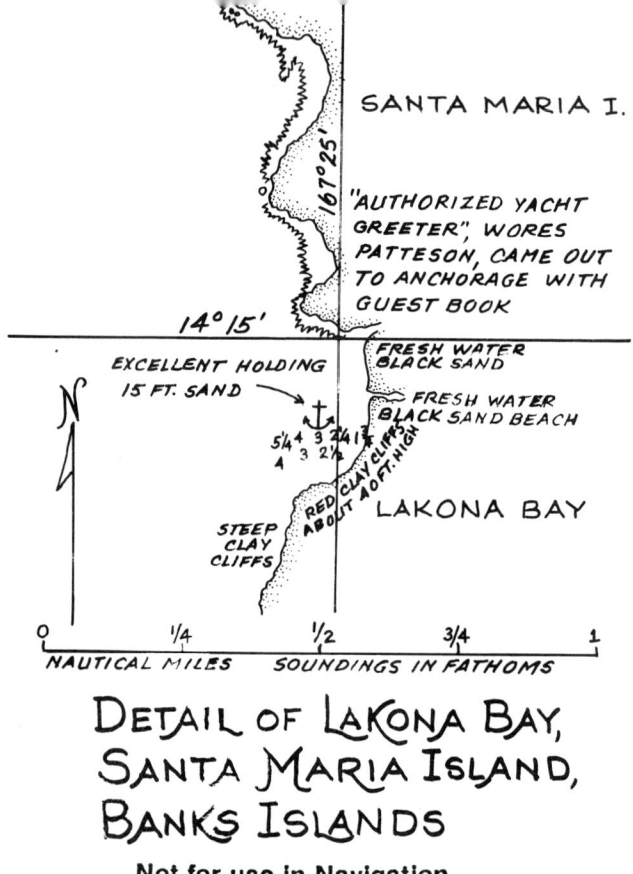

DETAIL OF LAKONA BAY, SANTA MARIA ISLAND, BANKS ISLANDS
Not for use in Navigation

toms and the artifacts belonging to the villagers. Like the Polynesians who had two chiefs for their maraes (houses of worship), so we find that the Melanesians have two chiefs as well.

It is still the tradition of many villages to use custom money in lieu of dollars. Many brides are bought with shells, feather money, cows, chickens, or anything that has a value put on it by legend. Brides on the island of Malaita, in the Solomon Islands, are still bought with custom money. The price one family was paying for a bride of equally high education as their son was nearly $2,000.

Rigadoon Bay, Vanua Lava Island

Working our way northward still in the Banks Islands, we anchored in a small bay on Vanua Lava Island, so small that a name was never given to it by chart makers. It was described by latitude and longitude in the S.S.C.A. bulletins by a cruising sailor, who happened to find the magnificent waterfalls that tumbled off high cliffs into the small cove protected from the rolling swells by an arm of coral reef. Cruising sailors ever since

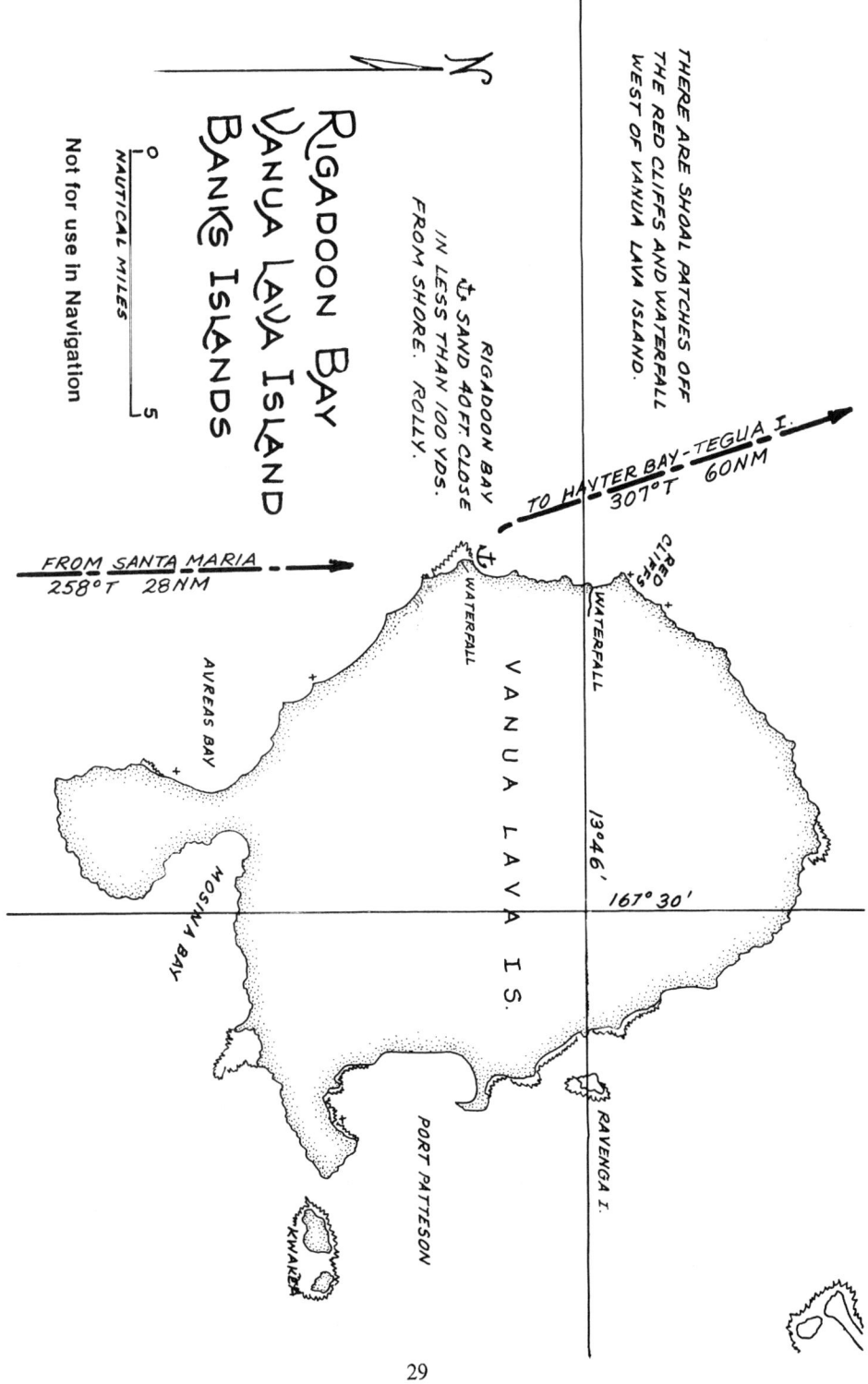

who read the bulletins have called the anchorage Rigadoon Bay. Of course, we had first-hand knowledge of the idyllic setting and made a point to stop at the bay named after Don's brother's boat.

Hayter Bay, Tegua Island, Torres Islands

Cruising up the chain of islands was not so easy as you might expect. Currents raced in and around the islands and ran up on sea mounts, causing dangerous overfalls. Navigating to avoid the charted rises of submarine floors was no simple task. The steep-to seas we were encountering were bad enough, but when the winds reached 25 to 30 knots, we sought the last port of refuge in the Torres Islands at Hayter Bay on Tegua Island before setting out for the 300-mile passage to our next port in the Solomon Islands. Cruising can easily be included in the saying our grandmothers oft-repeated, "If you can't stop along the way in life to take time and pet the cats and smell the flowers, there is no point in living." So, if the hell-bent-for leather-sailor cannot take time to enjoy the scenery, snorkel around the reefs and beachcomb the sandy beaches, or simply listen to the twitterings of the birds, then he has missed the whole point of cruising. He will return to the same mundane life he left, and will never know that life can be beautiful.

On the gentle side of Hayter Bay, away from the wind, sandy knolls, like miniature islands, were separated from one another by small streams of seawater. These were criss-crossing at different angles, as if nature patterned a crazy quilt, using sand for patches and streams for stitching them together. Occasional rocks stood in the streams and diverted the waters to form new designs. Under some of the rocks, I found tiger cowries in pairs and took but one couple, and then was sorry later that I had stolen them.

While I was beachcombing, Don was having his own adventure on the sandy beach that slopes into the head of the bay. For the first time he came upon a coconut crab out in the open on the beach. The creature who can climb coconut trees with ease was efficiently using his formidable claws to tear the husk from a coconut. Don thought he would have some fun with the crab and tried to take the coconut away from him, but instead, Don got the crab as well, for he would not let go. The crab was most unwilling to forfeit all of his laborious work to someone as unworthy as Don, even though 40 times his size. Size does not always measure power, and Don respected the crab's fortitude and dropped the coconut. I found the two of them in a rather stand-off position and when the crab saw me, he only clutched his coconut tighter and showed no signs of retreat. But I did!

"I'm glad we are taking our time to poke into these out-of-the way places and not be in any hurry to go home," I said one evening at dusk when we were sitting in the cockpit with our cocktails and watching breakers pound poor Ethel, the name of the small island that stood as a solitary buttress to the waves threatening Hayter Bay where we were anchored..

"Tomorrow when we pack up and leave with dawn's early light you may have cause to change your mind about the pleasures of the cruising life," Don looked at the sky and the cirrus clouds streaking out in fuzzy wisps above the high cliffs sheltering us.

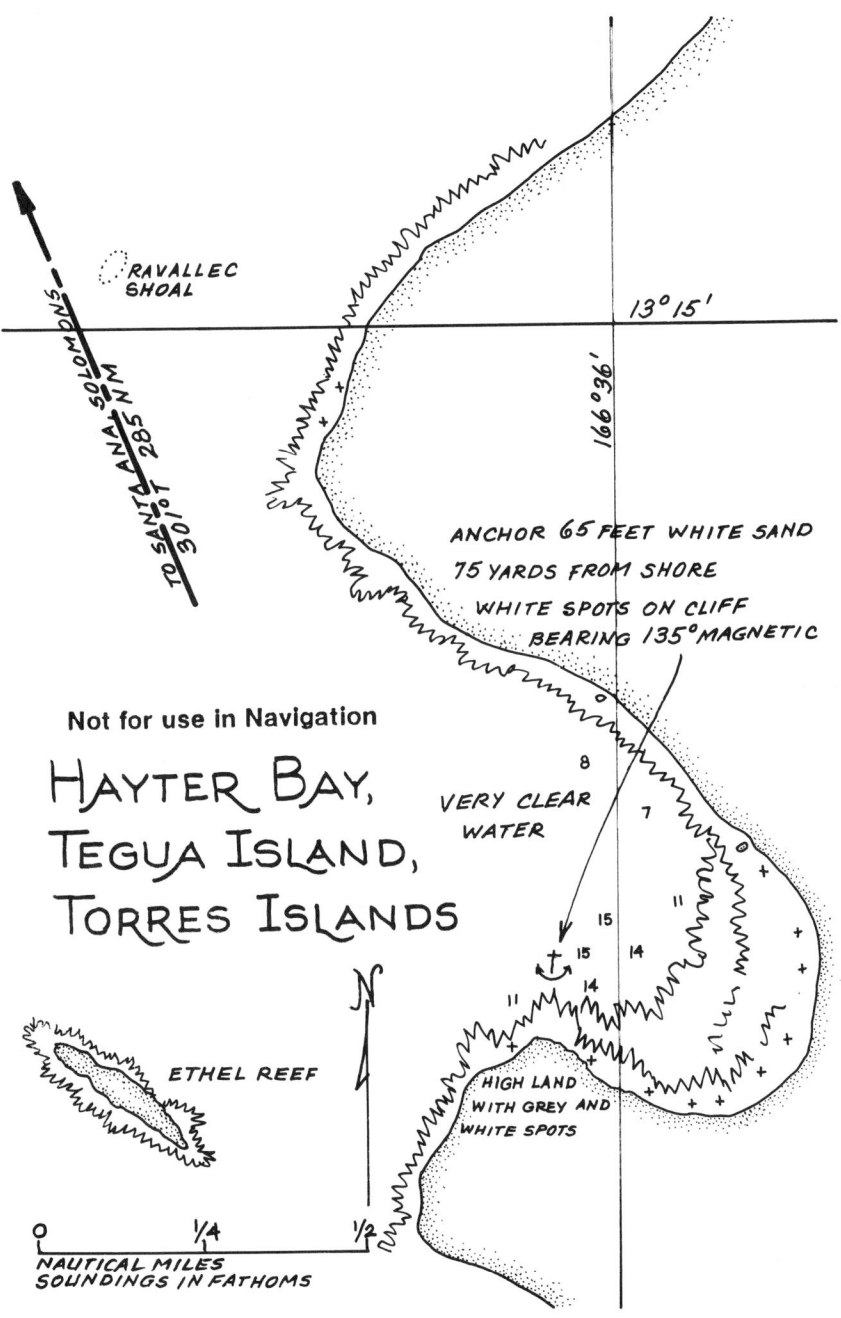

CHAPTER 2

SOLOMON ISLANDS

One of the South Pacific's Best Cruising Grounds

The Solomon Islands are a lovely chain that compare favorably with our still-favorite Bahama Islands. Formerly a British colony, the Solomons are now independent. Their islands stretch for some 600 miles. On outlying isles, natives continue their village ways hoping that they would not be interrupted raising their chickens and rearing their children.

Many of the islands have inland areas that are inpenetrable due to the dense foliage. This is what the natives call the "bush" and it was within those hidden recesses, known only to the natives, where they hid themselves and the downed Allied pilots during World War II.

There are seven major islands in the Solomons and more than 25 smaller islands scattered through the archipelago. This insures easy day-sailing with an island or islet always available to shut out the Pacific swells from anchorages. High mountainous islands with ample freshwater streams blend harmoniously with the lower, calcerous islands, like those that form stepping stones in the wide and clear lagoons. The Solomon Islands provide a wonderful potpourri of marvelous cruising grounds for the passage-weary sailor.

Don plotted a dogleg course that would take us into the Santa Cruz group of islands that stand far to the east of the main contingent of Solomon Islands. It is here where the arm of Polynesia stretches out to engulf these islands, but stops before it reaches the central Solomons. From the Santa Cruz Islands have come the ancient navigators whose legends and lore live still in the natives, who ply the same waters in their outrigger canoes.

Passage from Torres Islands to Solomon Islands

"It's going to be rough out there," Don warned, as we hanked on the twins to their separate forestays and looked at the cirrus clouds streaking a white film across the heavens.

As the lee of Tegua Island fell astern, the wind came at us with full force against the boomed-out twins, straining the mast enough to bow it forward. The back stays were rigid rods of stainless steel combating the pull. Seas were a maze of white cresting rollers. One hit *Svea's* quarter so violently that for the first time, books from the starboard shelves were tossed across the floor. Don's eyeglasses went sailing through the air to end up in the muddle. A reduction of sail was certainly in order, and the smaller storm twins replaced the big blues.

The wind was still increasing when we ended the first leg and considered setting course for the second leg. That course would have put the large seas forward of the beam. "We'll have to beat, won't we?" I asked Don as I resigned myself to a bout of seasickness.

"No," he answered quickly. "It would be foolish if we put those seas forward of the beam. We'll keep them astern and change our plans. We'll head for the main body of the Solomons."

By changing course, we added 250 miles to the passage, but it meant a safer and more comfortable trip. Still it was a miserable night with decks constantly awash. We rolled violently from side to side with the small storm twins offering little effort to stabilize the roll. Flying fish came aboard the catwalks and even down in the cockpit, as their disarranged flight plans combatted the burgeoning seas. Their strong odor and oily bodies with scales that cling to the deck, even after numerous dousings, discouraged us from eating them. Many sailors do eat them, but they never seemed appetizing to us.

By dawn, a misty rain was upon us and the winds abated to a more settled southeasterly trade wind. Don's stomach objected to leaning over the chart table to work out the morning sight. I wasn't too well myself, leaving my bunk only to scan the horizon for traffic. The cockpit was crusted with salt crystals and the lightweight nylon cockpit cushion covers were streaked with white salt stains.

The "Sailing Directions" stressed a strong west-setting current on the eastern approach to the Solomons, which meant our normal 20-mile margin of safety from land was not far enough. We added another 10 miles before we hove-to for the night. Just faintly, we could see the outline of an island against the western setting sun. At dawn, we could see nothing but water and vacant horizons. Steering in a westerly direction towards a cloud bank we figured to be blanketing the island of Santa Ana. We were dismayed when the cover lifted and there was no land underneath. When there was still no land in sight by mid-morning, we knew that unpredictable currents had altered the normal set. When Don took the noon sight, there was nothing on the horizon but sky and water. Yet we were maintaining a good speed of 6 knots.

"It can't be. It just can't be south," I said when Don told me that his plotting figures showed Santa Ana to be south of us. I was basing my theories strictly on woman's intuition. Don did not really believe his figures either, and just at the precarious moment when I began to lower the boom to bring down the twin staysail, I spotted a faint hump on the horizon. "Wait!" I shouted.

Then Don saw it too, and changed his previous order, "Carry on! Maintain course! Land dead ahead!" Very slowly the grey hump took the shape of a wide-brimmed hat, which was the description given for Santa Ana in the "Sailing Directions."

Port Mary, Santa Ana, Solomon Islands

The young boys from the village at Port Mary came out in their dugout canoes to greet us after we had anchored. It was indeed a strange sight to see a dark-skinned Melanesian with a head crowned with bright blond curls.

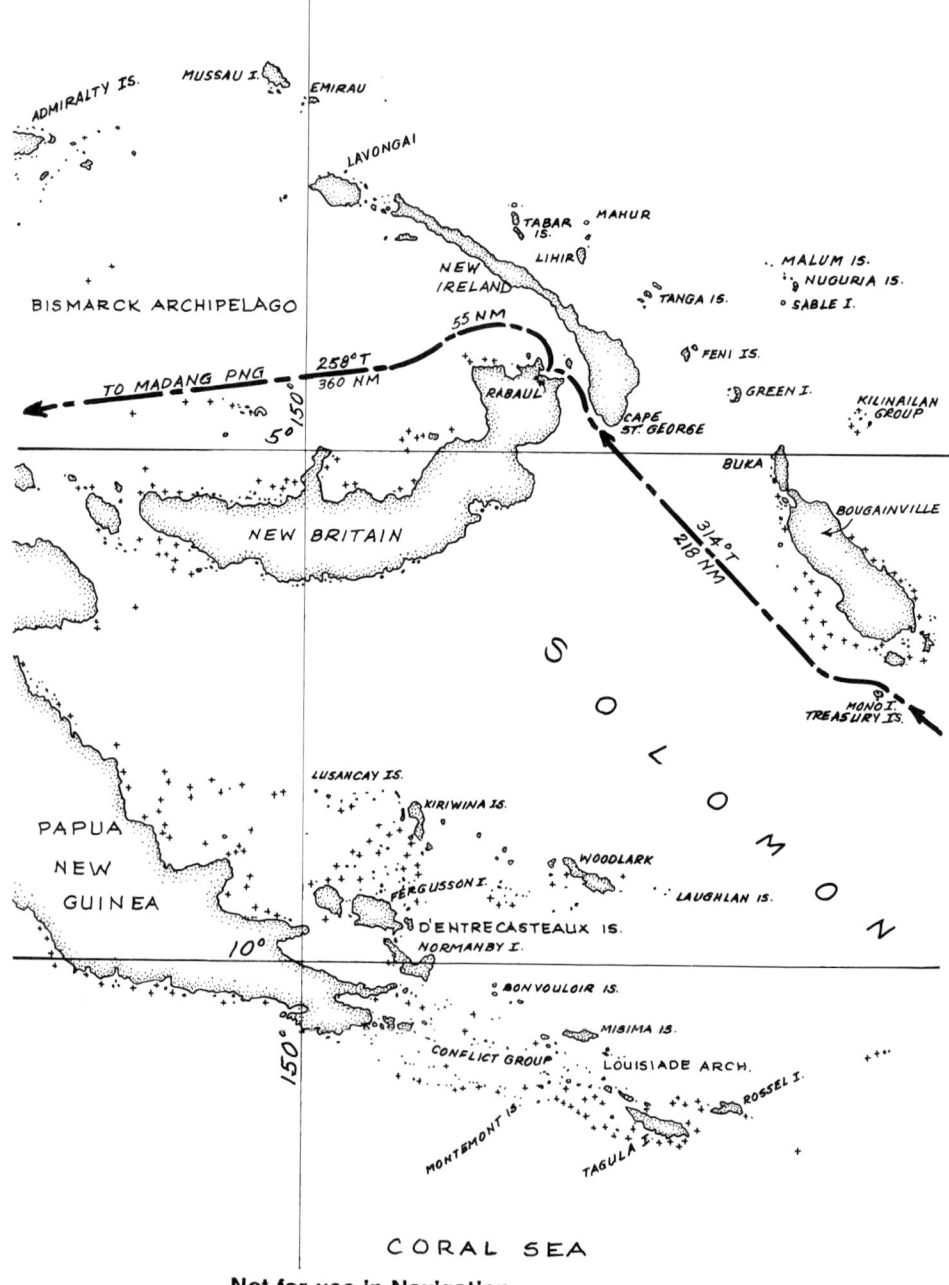
Not for use in Navigation

Not for use in Navigation

Regional Chart – Solomon Islands, New Ireland, New Britain, East portion of Papua New Guinea

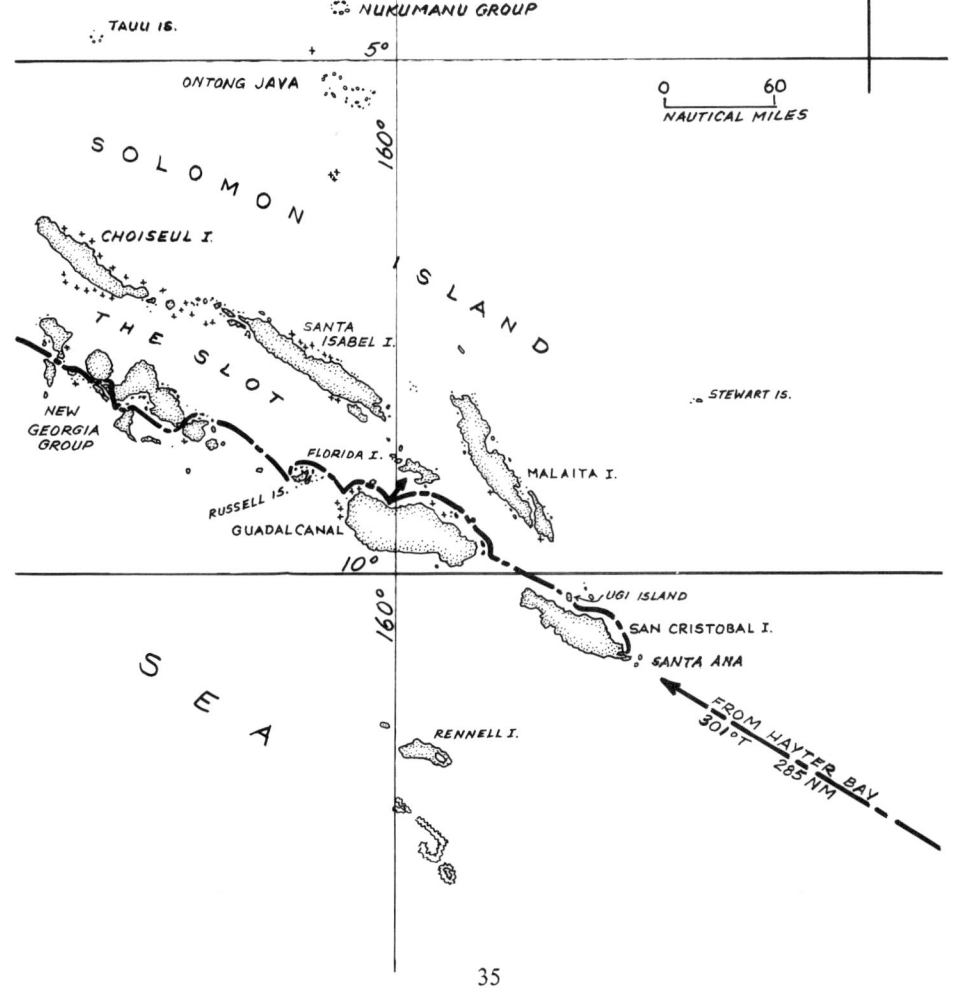

This is a common occurrence for the Solomon Islander who uses lime made from ashes of burnt coral to delouse his hair. We counted 40 children around us when we went ashore to take on water from the faucet that Peace Corps volunteers had piped from a freshwater stream, farther back in the bush and away from the village.

A young boy, acting as guide, proudly showed us his village. He paused when he came to an osprey that was their pet. "We feed him fish," the boy said in English. "Then he won't go after the chickens." Chickens roamed freely in and out of paths that wove among rows of pandanus huts raised some 4 feet off the ground. The floors of the dwellings were a series of large logs tied together with native vines. More logs were incorporated as rafters for the thatched roofs. Using whole logs to construct a floor is an extravagant use of timber, but lumber is plentiful and it a very important industry for the islands. In the Solomons, timber is second in importance to copra for export.

At the edge of the village that fronts the sea, other natives flocked around *Poco* waiting for our return. Many of the women wore nothing but tatoos from their waists up. People were friendly, and their setting was a tranquil one. As we walked along the beach and out towards the reef that was then out of water due to the low tide, we relaxed the tension that is always present for the cruising sailor at sea. It seems we are always on guard, waiting for the unexpected to happen: a sudden squall that could rip a sail, or an encounter with another ship during the night, or a breakdown of equipment. We laid down all of our shields and let the serenity surround us.

Since we had missed the port of entry in the Santa Cruz Islands, we were a bit hesitant to do much exploring until we had cleared customs and immigration. The next port of entry was at Kirakira farther northwest on the larger island of San Cristobal. We needed some overnight stops to make the government port.

Star Harbor, San Cristobal Island, Solomon Islands

After leaving Santa Ana, our first stop was Star Harbor at the southeastern tip of San Cristobal Island. We received instructions for the harbor entrance from several young men at Port Mary, who went over to the larger island to work a patch of copra. The crop on their own island had been devastated by a cyclone which very nearly claimed the entire island. They had new trees, but it takes seven years for a coconut tree to mature enough to produce acceptable fruit.

The scene is totally different from what we had been seeing in the low-lying atolls of the central Pacific. Now we are amongst islands whose mountainous peaks stretch high to reach the sky. The lands are rich with fertile growth, made richer by numerous freshwater streams lacing through the jungle terrains.

We followed one of those mountain streams that fed murky waters into Star Harbor, where *Svea* was anchored behind the village. Webs of vines

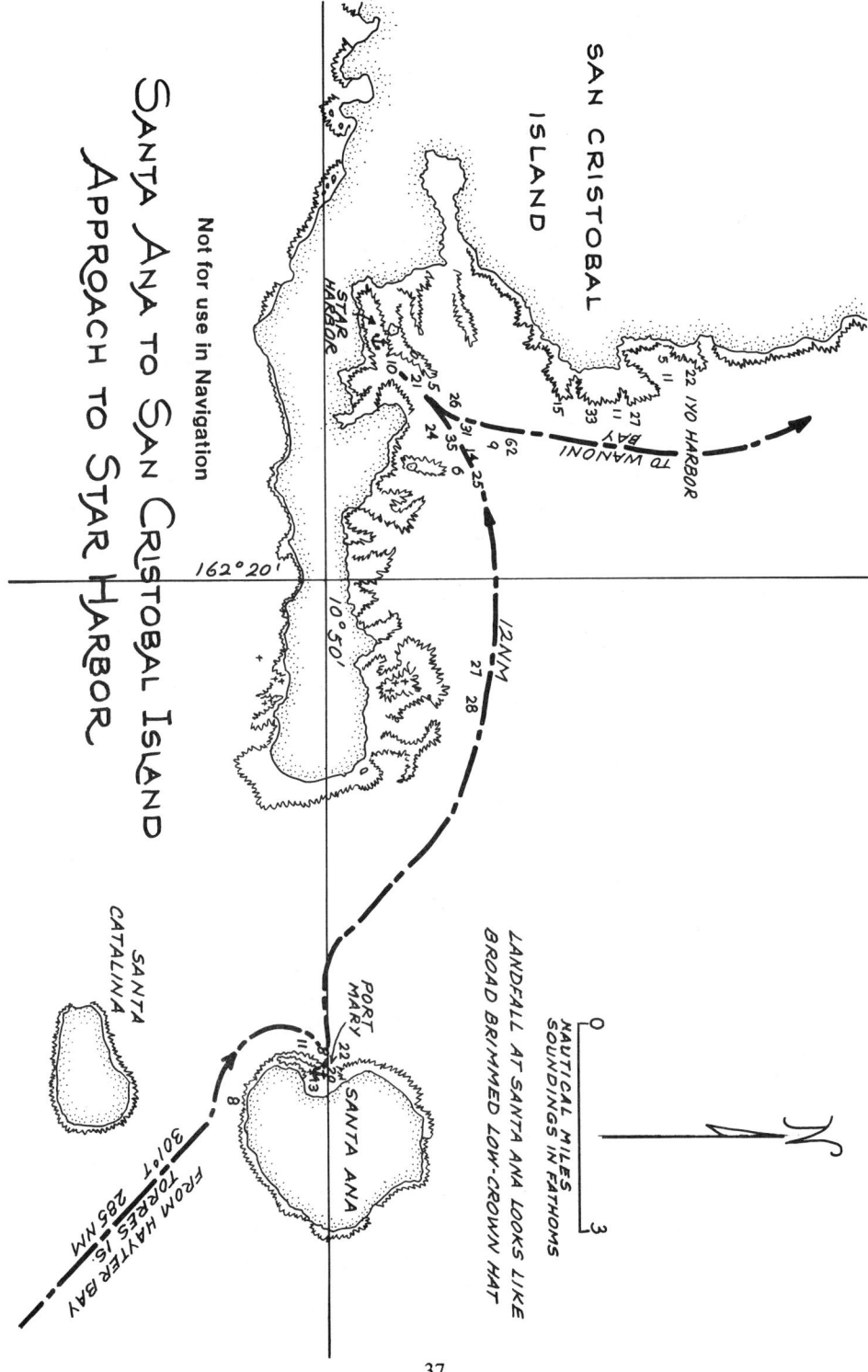

and downed logs threatened *Poco*'s progress many times, but we continued to dinghy into the jungle, which grew thicker and darker as the dense foliage shut out the sun. Somewhere in the tall trees, birds twittered and twaddled. Only their beautiful songs broke through solid greenery as they remained hidden within their sanctuaries.

A young girl in a dugout slowly overtook us, and continued paddling up the narrowing stream. Suddenly the river came to an end at a bank where a well-trodden path continued the mysterious trail. The girl's canoe was pulled up on shore. Rather than intrude upon someone's privacy by following the trail, we turned *Poco* around and returned to *Svea*. We found her surrounded by dugouts and children, eagerly awaiting a chance to sell us some fruits and vegetables, or as they preferred, to trade for any items we had to exchange. They learned quickly that more trips with fewer vegetables produced more articles from the Americans.

It is now difficult to believe that the Solomon Islands witnessed horrendous battle scenes during World War II. Names like Guadalcanal, Tulagi, Bougainvillae, and many others remind us that blood was shed on sandy soils that now show no evidence. Occasionally a ship resting on Iron Bottom Sound turns over in its grave when a tremor rocks the cemetery. Such was the case when we arrived at the Solomon Island capital city of Honiara on Guaudalcanal and ran into oil slicks fouling the clear waters. We blamed the small island freight boats for dumping their oil changes, but found out later it was our own American battle cruiser that had shifted in her coffin and tipped over the ship's fuel bunkers. To cast the blame upon the comely work boats, so admirably crafted from local hardwoods by knowledgeable shipwrights, was most unfair.

Kirakira, San Cristobal Island, Solomon Islands

One such vessel was anchored in the small harbor at Kirakira when we arrived after an overnight stop at Wanoni Bay to check into customs and immigration. Kirakira harbor is exposed to southeasterly swells. Every time a swell entered the harbor it rolled the ship sideways at such a deep angle that her fantail nearly dipped into the water. The ship was in no danger, but the captain's pet rooster that had claimed the fantail for his roost, got his tail feathers soaked with each and every dip. I wondered why the rooster did not move, but then remembered the frigate fledglings that refused to leave their nest when the danger of our presence had threatened them.

When customs officials did not ask for the light fee of $120, which we knew was imposed to foreign yachts of any size, description or nationality, we were surprised. We learned of the levy from the S.S.C.A. bulletins, and it had been a deterrent factor in our deciding whether to cruise Solomon Islands' waters. The tariff caught up with us later when we requested our clearance papers. The officials then asked for the fee, so we did not escape the duty. We followed the policy that if a country did not want us

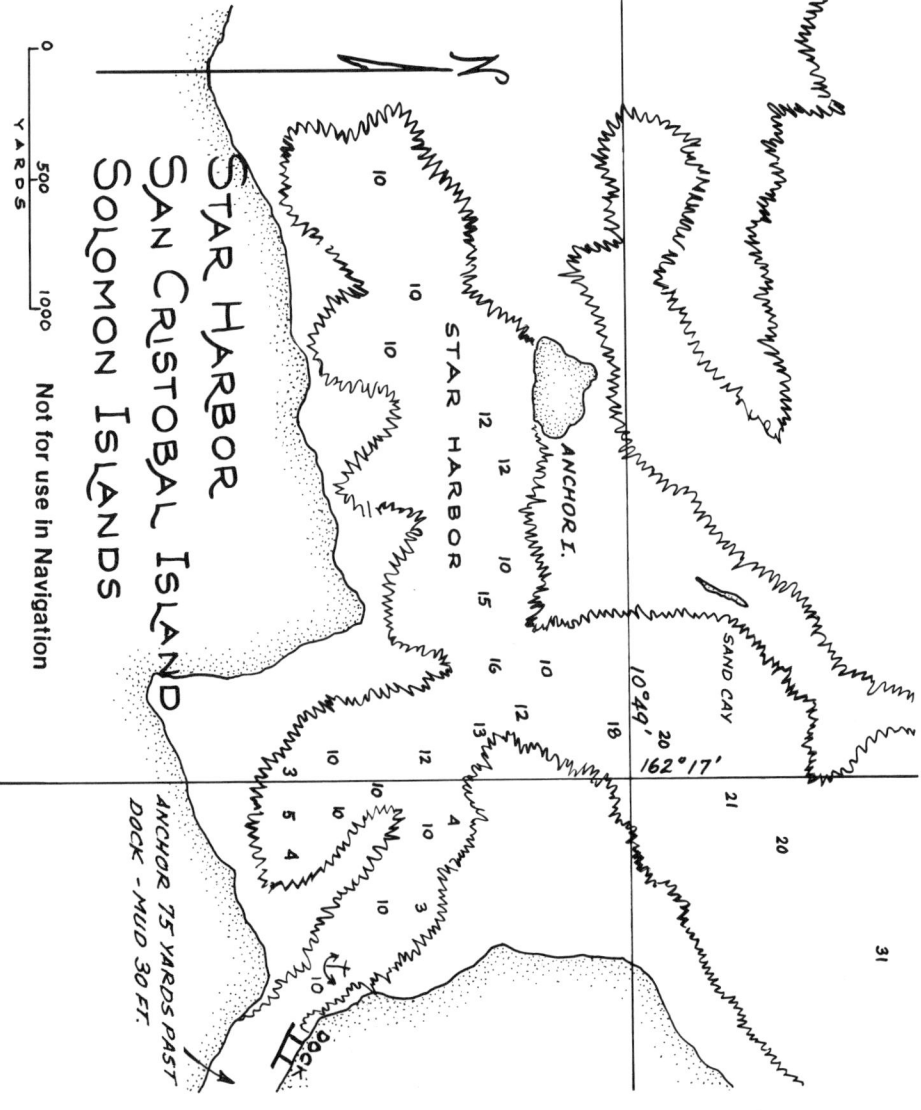

and imposed high duties, we did not want them. However, the Solomons were worth it and we were glad we had chosen to enter their waters.

After the legal entry was accomplished, we walked through the small town of Kirakira in search of the native market. Vendors had already closed their stalls and there was nothing at all left in the open pavilion except blood-red streaks that stained the cement floor. My first thought was of poor chickens that had been in a bloody cockfight. We had never before seen spewed-out sputum from a betel nut chewer, and the streaks were ghastly. The nut comes from the Areca-type palm and is chewed along with lime, made from the ashes of coral rock, and pieces of leaves

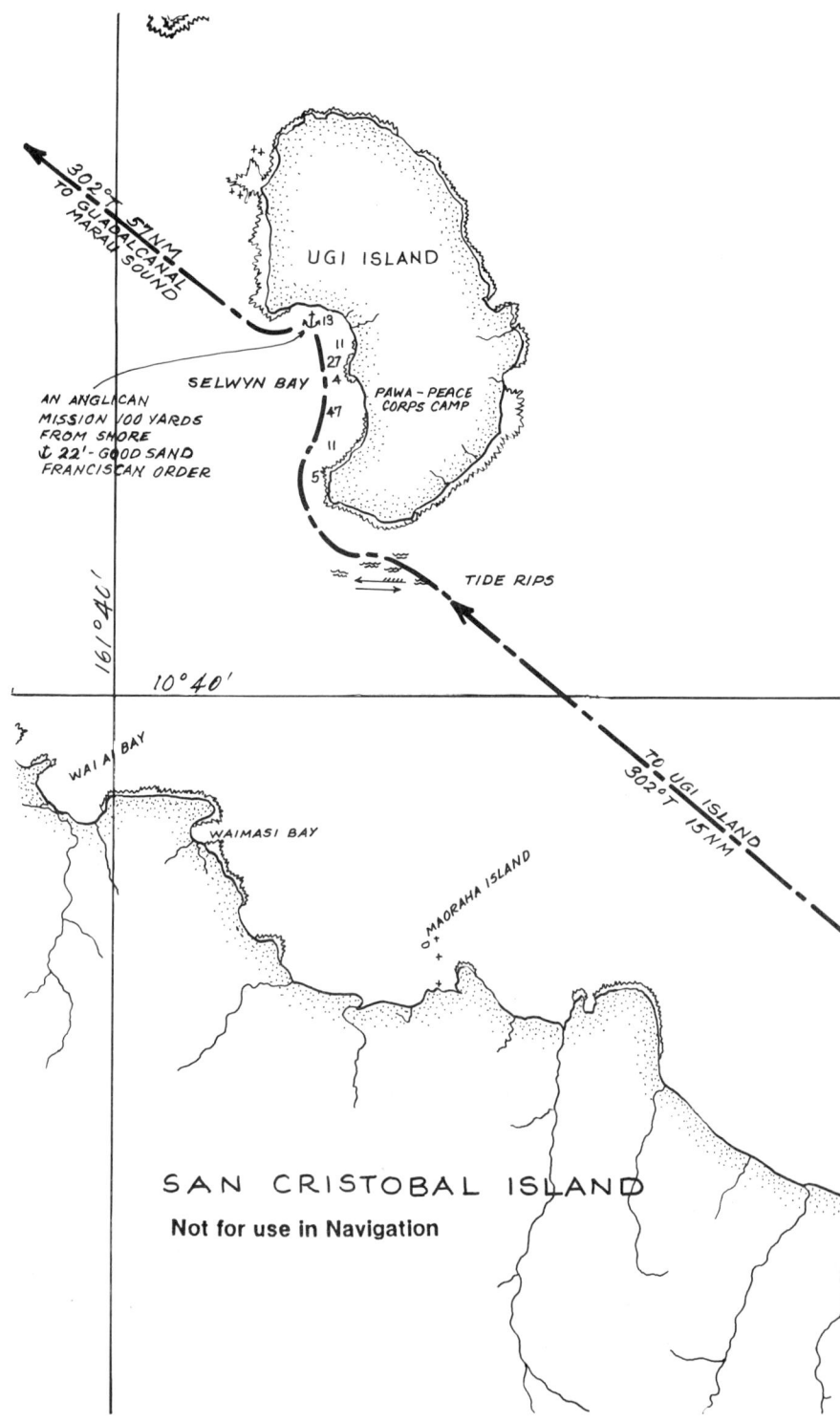

San Cristobal Coastline from Wanoni Bay Anchorage to Kirakira, to Ugi Island

Not for use in Navigation

from the same trees. The combination makes the nut more chewable and effects are a drugged feeling. One young man laughed when he told us it was great fun to watch a novice betel nut chewer, for he became drunk very quickly and did funny things. There is nothing at all funny about the appearance of the chewer whose lips and teeth are permanently stained by their ugly habit. The streets and sidewalks where he walks are fouled with his sputum.

Passage to Ugi Island

Perhaps it was the tranquilizing effect the Solomons evoked, that we relaxed our prudency too much and disregarded former safeguards. We had never considered towing *Poco* behind *Svea* when crossing between islands. Somehow we figured the short 15-mile channel separating San Cristobal from Ugi Island should not be dangerous. Also hoisting the dinghy on board in the rolling swells at Kirakira's harbor could easily inflict injury to us or to *Svea*. We decided to trail *Poco* behind.

Our mistake was compounded when we failed to take note of the markings on the chart that clearly stated the presence of tide rips off the south end of Ugi Island. Winds began to increase sharply when we left the harbor. With only one twin up, *Svea*'s speed was in excess of 6 knots. *Poco* strained painfully at her painter tied to the stern post. Seas were astern, and *Poco* rose with the waves and then jerked back with an agonizing twist if the wave fell out from under her, or rushed towards *Svea* if she rode with the crests. By the time we reached the area of tide rips, the mounting seas ripped into the counter-currents coming out from the island, and the waves stood in high peaks. The sea was a churning cauldron of whitecaps. I was watching *Poco* twist and turn in efforts to stay afloat. Then I heard the line snap and the dinghy was free from her mother ship. I saw the small dinghy flounder like a drowning swimmer, and she fell down into a trough. Another large wave picked her up and the little fiberglass boat turned upside down like a dying belly-up whale. The flotation under her seats had kept her from sinking.

"Get the compass bearing and we'll turn on the reciprocal," Don shouted. The following orders came in rapid-fire succession: "Douse the sail! Lash it to the lifelines! Engage the sailing clutch! Take her off pilot! Grab the tiller! Start the engine! Turn into the seas!"

Somehow, all of the commands were carried out and we followd the compass back to where we thought the dinghy had foundered. "Where is she?" I screamed to Don who was up in the ratlines on lookout for our dinghy, our only lifeline to land. "I can't see her from down here," I shouted.

"I can't see her up here, either. Nothing but white water everywhere," Don shouted back. "Just keep on the same heading," he added.

Svea plunged into the seas and scooped up water on her foredeck, and it ran back and spilled over the cockpit coaming. One time Don looked down and saw nothing of *Svea* or me, as a huge wave of green water had washed over the entire boat.

"I'm all right," I sputtered and spit out the words with the water I had swallowed. I quickly reached down to clear the cockpit drains from the lines that had tumbled down into the cockpit well. The floorboards were awash in the swirling water and *Svea* labored to fight off the burden of water. Thank God none of the water had penetrated any of the closed hatches or portlights, and had spilled off the cabin and decks to return to the sea.

"Do you see her?" I cried frantically. The fear of losing our dinghy was very real and I knew there would not be a replacement for her in the Solomons.

"Yes, I see her," Don shouted down. "But, only just! Thank God she is yellow. We'd never see a boat of any other color in this mess!" Don turned on the narrow step and put his hand to his forehead to shield his eyes from the sun. "I keep losing her as she sinks into the trough."

We made several difficult attempts to get the dinghy alongside *Svea*'s lee side. We reached and grabbed for the dinghy's gunwhales, but the waves jerked *Poco* out of our hands and quickly took her away from us. We searched through cockpit lockers for the stowed line with a snatch hook on the end of it, a line we had used for towing a former small power boat. Again I maneuvered *Svea* into a position to give the dinghy a lee, and this time Don hooked the dinghy's stern handle and we had a bite on it. *Svea* towed the little yellow dinghy upside down and backwards, until we could get away from the tide rips. We needed no extra power, for the speed of the current whipped us right around the island and into its lee.

Selwyn Bay, Ugi Island, Solomon Islands

After we righted *Poco*, we followed the coastline of Ugi Island until we came to the anchorage west of the Anglican mission. The Franciscan brothers welcomed us to the refuge of their cove, and to their freshwater streams behind the mission house. The nearness of God and His missionaries made me bend my head and thank Him for returning *Poco* to us.

The brothers kept us well-informed as to the time of day. They first anounced the new day at 0600 with the sounding of a drum, and 10 minutes later, the ringing of the bells announced morning prayer. The procedure was repeated at eventide vesper services. Father Brian sent out a big loaf of freshly-baked bread and I returned the gesture a few days later with a big batch of homemade oatmeal cookies.

A large Peace Corps enclave, called Pawa, has been established on Ugi Island. We talked with some of the young Americans about our travels and the efforts of the volunteer group to teach the native men animal husbandry and agriculture, and the women more skills of sewing and other home-related projects. The path, following the crooked coast, was often interrupted by logs that spanned the many mountain streams, seeking their outlets in the sea. We also shared the trails with several mother pigs and their shoats, and we stood aside to let them pass.

By now it was the end of August. We expected the southeast trades to hold for another two months before the northwest monsoons set in. We needed the present southeasterlies to get to Madang, New Guinea, where we planned to stop and wait out the oncoming cyclone season. Close to the Equator on the north side of the big island, Madang is out of the tropical cyclone belt and we would be safe from the storms that occur on more southerly latitudes. Two months would give us time to explore more of the islands that, so far, had teased our curiosity and tickled our fancies.

Photo by Carl Moesly

Village of Port Mary, Soloman Islands

CHAPTER 3

GUADALCANAL, SOLOMON ISLANDS

Guadalcanal is the largest of the Solomon Islands and is quite mountainous with peaks often invisible behind their crowns of clouds. One peak reaches over 8,000 feet. The terrain is thick with forests and jungle growth. The capital city of Honiara stares across Iron Bottom Sound to Florida Island. Tulagi, on Florida Island, was formerly the capital of the Solomons, but after World War II, so many buildings, roads and other services remained on Guadalcanal that Honiara became the new seat of government.

Marau Sound

Away from the busy city and the traffic of inter-island freighters, airplanes, cars and trucks, lie the peaceful islands off Guadalcanal's eastern shore in Marau Sound. The islands are a combination of high lands and low lands fringed with tassles of reefs that yielded some of the prettiest shells of my collection. It is here that I saw my first Golden Cowrie. It was in the hands of the reknowned conchologist, Ian Gower, the Australian who makes his home in this shell collector's paradise.

Anchorage between Tavanipupu and Malapa Islands. The very small island of Tavanipupu nestles between other larger islands that protect it. Deep channels lace around its three sides, but the eastern side folds out onto shallow ledges of coral. A small lagoon tucked up against the shallow ledges and between Tavanipupu and Malapa Islands affords one of the pettiest and safest refuges we had ever encountered.

Tavanipupu is privately owned by a gracious British couple, the Charles Humphreys, who extend their hands of hospitality to visiting yachts. Other boats were anchored in the small lagoon with *Svea*. For the first time, she was unseated as the oldest grand lady in the anchorage by the 100-year old *Klaraborg*. Her Swedish owner was more than proud of the 80-foot former Baltic Trader. He had rescued her from anonymity as a derelict in Goteborg, Sweden, and restored her back to life.

Also sharing the anchorage were vast assortments of birds that make their homes in the many jungles on the neighboring islands. Flights of cockatoos and parrots kept us fascinated with their aerial acrobatics, but one day we had a special visitor. "What is that noise?" I shouted to Don as the whirring sound made me think a helicopter was about to land on *Svea's* deck. I looked out the companionway to see a prehistoric bird that must have escaped from an Alfred Hitchcock thriller. The huge wing span of the unbalanced-looking creature with the massive beak cast an ominous grey shadow on the limpid waters of the lagoon. The whirring noise was coming from the fluttering of its large wings. Later I learned the bird was one of a pair of toucans that were frequent guests to Tavanipupu's owners.

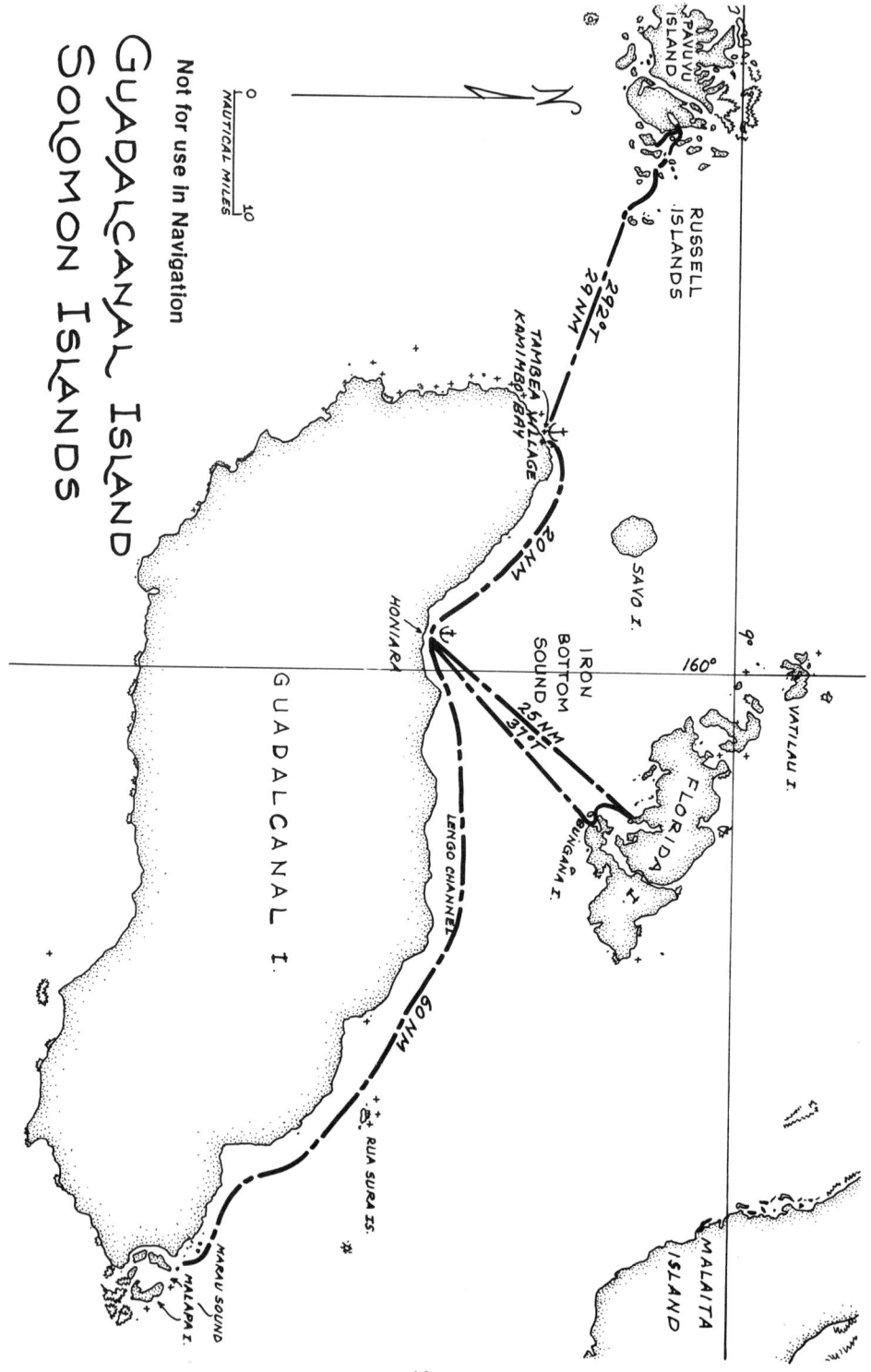

Ciguatera Poisoning. While we were anchored in the placid lagoon, we had our fourth meal of the large jack-type fish, Caranx ignoblis, that we had caught 3 miles offshore in Vanuatu. At that time, we had given half of the fish to a native who assured us the fish was not poisonous. The happy man immediately took his half to shore and started cooking it for his family. Now, a couple of months and many miles later, we ate the fish again. This time we had a stronger attack of diarrhea than we had on previous occasions when eating portions of the frozen fish. We had always blamed the distress on our greedy appetites for fresh vegetables that we always gorge on when we reach land. By morning, we had tingling sensations in our hands and the bottoms of our feet, and the tingling extended to our lips and tongue. We had the classic symptoms of ciguatera poisoning that is so well described in Halstead's book, "Dangerous Marine Animals." The poisoning affects the nerves and is sometimes called "barracuda poisoning" in the Bahamas and Florida.

Lethargy and aching muscles followed the tingling sensation and the Swedish gentleman on *Klaraborg* told us that he knew of one sailor who was hospitalized for nearly six weeks with the poisoning, and others had died from it. Thank goodness our case was a mild one, although we felt miserable for weeks as the the symptoms gradually dissipated. For a long time, it still hurt our tingling fingers to touch an ice cube. Even routine maintenance chores on *Svea* seemed like monumental tasks for our weakened bodies. We realized how accumulative this insidious disease can be, for each meal of the fish had added more poison to our bodies. The fish also had accumulated doses of the poison through his food habits. When the stored poison reached a certain threshold, it errupted into the classic symptoms.

It was not easy leaving Tavanipupu's beautifully clear waters, the wildlife and natives we knew by name who made daily trips to the lagoon with fresh fruits and vegetables. However, we were eager to get our mail in Honiara and exchange our dollars for local currency.

Honiara, Guadalcanal

The scene surrounding Honiara was a far different one from that 7th day of August, 1942 when 10,000 Marines and Allied Forces landed on Red Beach to remove the Japanese forces. The only battles now were in finding places to anchor in the busy harbor. Honiara's harbor was far from adequate for the amount of traffic it served. This very small harbor is better known as Point Cruz. Local island freighters, like the one we had seen at Kirakira, had dropped bow anchors and carried stern lines ashore. There were no proper bollards to tie those lines to, but such things as discarded engine blocks and other scraps of iron and cement blocks took their place. There is only a thin arm of reef protecting the harbor from swells that work their way up the Slot, the name given to the 25-mile wide channel separating one group of the Solomons from another. The Slot became a major naval battlefield.

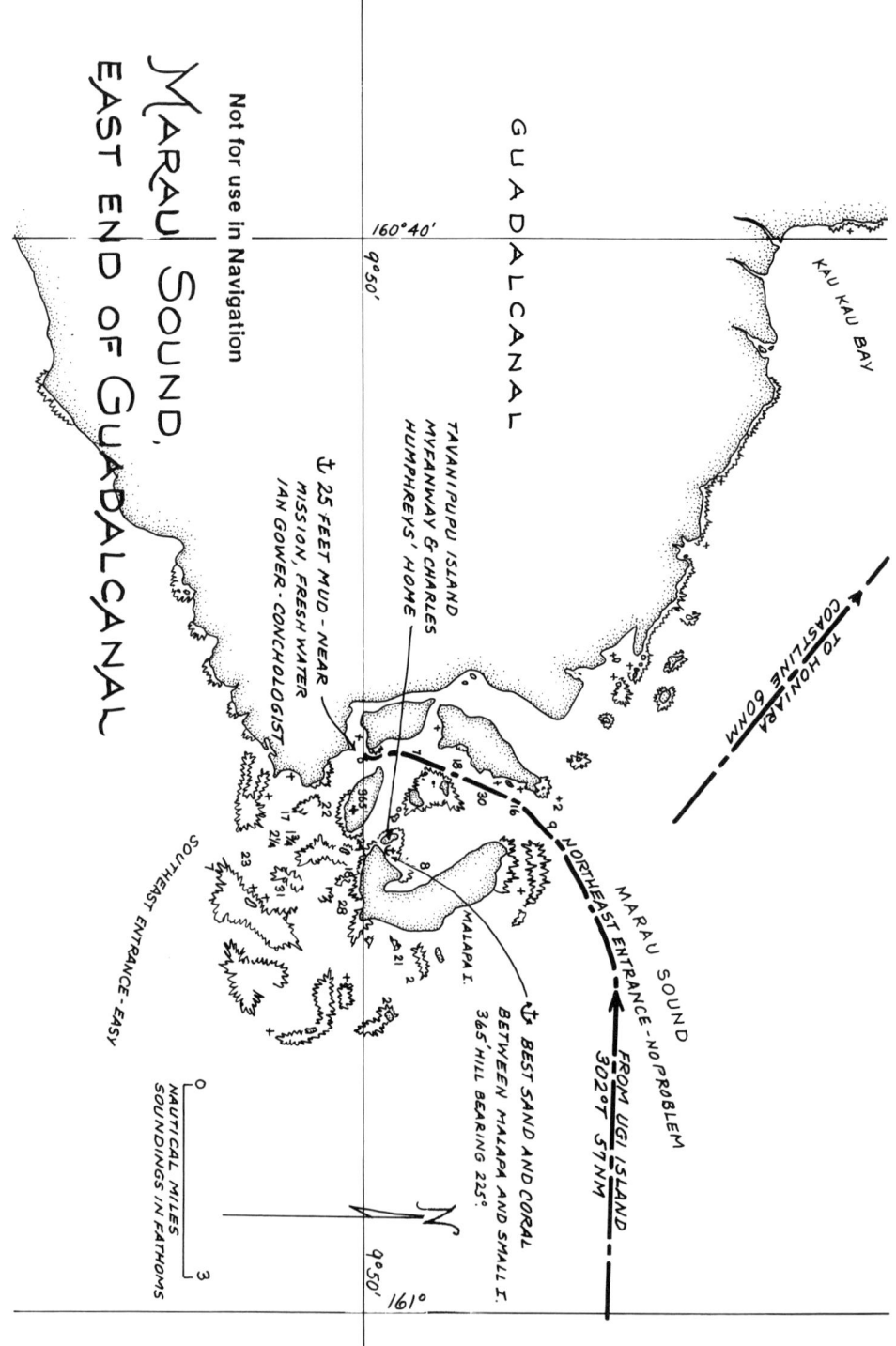

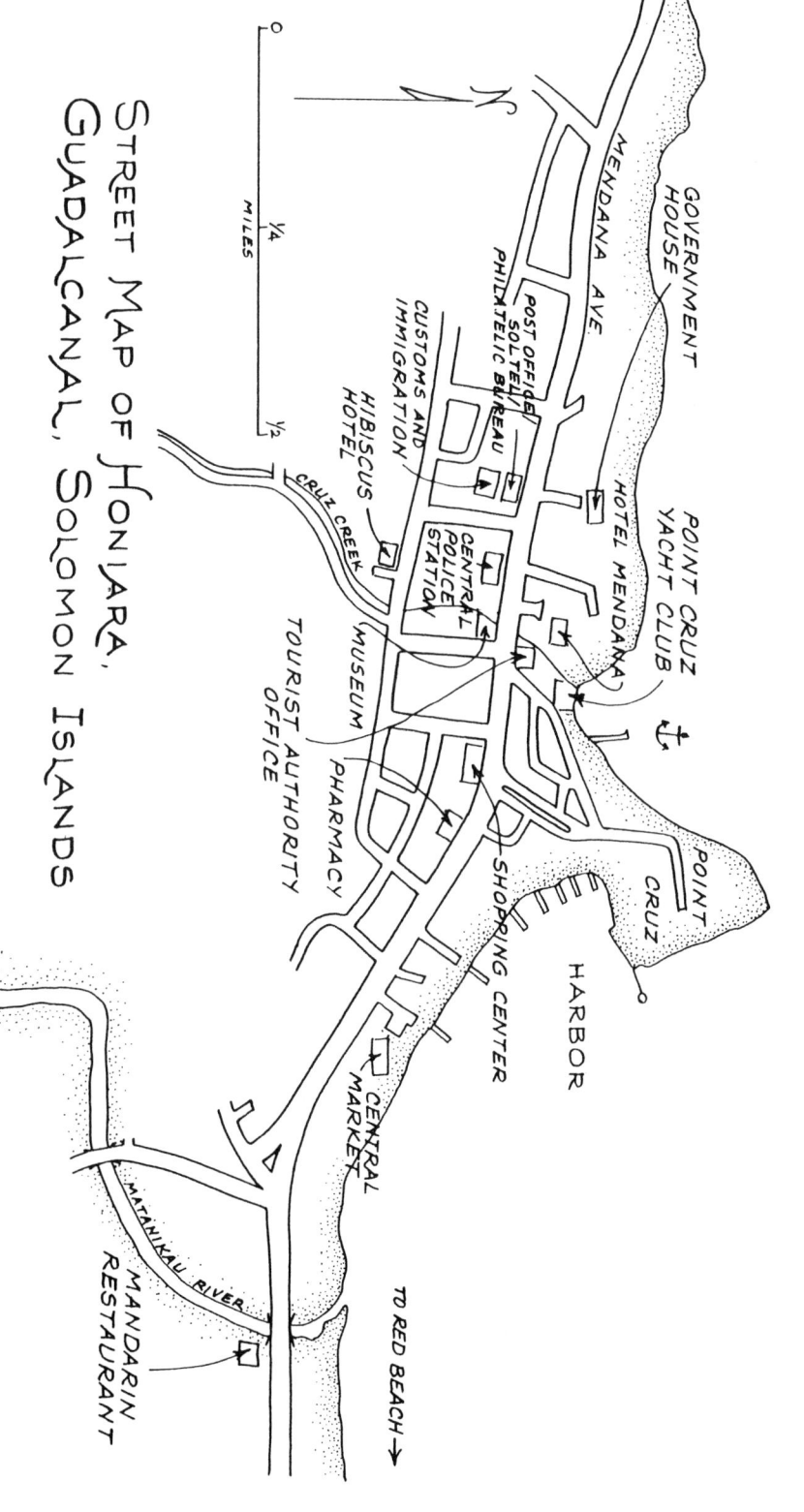

Point Cruz Yacht Club, situated in the middle of the arc of land around the small harbor, had installed some range markers on the club's flagpole yardarm to guide foreign yachts into the cluster of their anchored local sailing craft. Their clubhouse was an open thatched-roof pavilion, but they had the coldest beers in town. Their bar was always busy when members were not working. Most of the members were Australian expatriates, friendly and helpful. As we enjoyed cold beers, it was hard to visualize that the waters of the Slot north of us had been stages for great sea battles between battleships, cruisers and PT boats alike. The men waging war were from lands far removed from the innocent and beautiful land, caught in the middle of the conflict. On clear days, you could see Florida Island where Tulagi was won by the Marines. This happened the same day when the Marines claimed the airport at Honiara still under construction by the Japanese. It was later named Henderson Field.

The scars of history's battles were everywhere and as we walked down Honiara's main street, named for the Spanish explorer Mendana who first discovered the island in 1568. This was another grisly road of warfare. On our island tour at Red Beach, the rusty remains of landing barges stood out as grim skeletons remaining from the battle the amphibious forces faced there. Bloody Ridge was serene and masked in green grass, green bushes and trees. Only the monument that towers skyward above the green valley memorialized the men who shed their blood to give the ridge its name. The valley was quiet. The underground hospital was void of patients, but the tunnels, where no man could stand erect, were mute reminders of the struggle for life that went on beneath the mound of dirt that protected it. Somehow, an American stands out in a crowd. Often the call of, "Hi, Joe," came from a native who remembered those days in the past. This made Don turn his head to look into a smiling black face. Everywhere an American is welcomed and frequently thanked for saving Guadalcanal.

We tried to put the past back into the history books and return to the present, but there were several instances and occasions when the still-primitive ways of many of the natives made us think we had stepped backwards. Such was the case upon entering the native market where every little pile of vegetables or fruit was priced at ten cents. It was easier for both seller and buyer to figure out the total that way, simplifying arithmetic.

Undaunted by pristine social barriers set forth by Puritan forebears in many lands of the world, Solomon Island women were not confused by staid rules. Mothers openly nursed their babies wherever they happened to be. Behind one of the stalls, a woman with grey hair nursed a child of at least three years. While she held the child on one arm, she collected her 10 cents with the other. Tucked in the side of her mouth was her little black pipe, popular with natives who stuff them with rope tobacco. Those who smoke are backsliders, as the popular Seventh Day Adventist religion pronounces smoking to be a sin.

I came very close to buying a baby hornbill bird that one woman was

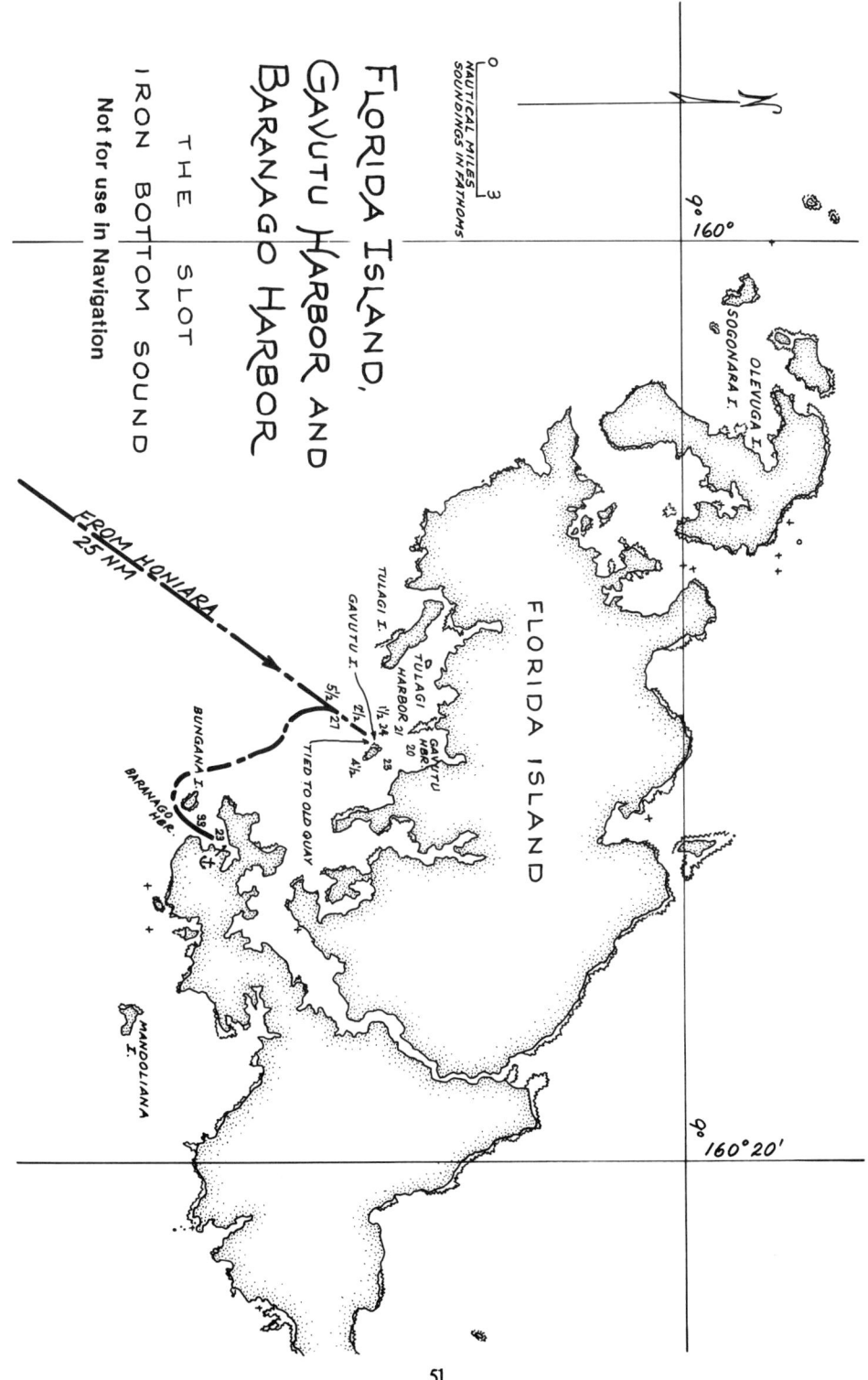

selling, to save it from the inevitable stew pot. I looked at the very large bill on the very small bird and figured the bill would grow even larger and prove to be a lethal weapon against *Svea*'s fine teak interior. A group of women were huddled in a circle, as if preparing signals for the next football play. On further investigation I saw that there was one woman who was the center of attention, and the other women were plucking lice from the woman's head. No wonder the fashionable hairdo is the short-cropped look. On many, the color of black has been bleached to a light yellow by the vast amounts of lime used to kill the lice.

Gavutu Harbor, Florida Island

"Watch out when you go over to Gavatu," Colin, a yacht club member warned us when we talked about sailing across the Slot to Florida Island and its sister island of Gavutu. "You can't anchor. There're so many sunken ships and downed airplanes in those waters, you snag on them and may not get your anchor back. It's best to tie to the old concrete-filled lighter that served as a quay." We did not even take a chance on anchoring and did what Colin had suggested, but by the time we reached the island the wind was beginning to screech and herald a bad weather system. We tied *Svea* to the rusty bollards and had to use our fenderboards to keep her topsides off the deteriorating pilings, as the wind was forcing her against them.

About 200 yards from the quay, and nearly covered with vines and bushes, were the remains of two downed airplanes. There were skeletons under the water as well as on land. We could not escape the graveyards of Guadalcanal and the grey skies and building wind added to the eeriness. We climbed back on board *Svea* and closed the hatches behind us, as if locking out the ghosts that still sat in the cockpits of those airplanes. When a knock rapped on the hull after dark, I nearly jumped out of my skin. Charging back to see who it was, Don quite startled the native, who said simply in very good English, "I've come to welcome you to my island and I have brought you some water grass." The young man was soaked to the skin from the spray that had been tossed into his canoe as he made his way from his village across the choppy water of the small bay.

In the days that followed, Joel became our friend as well as our guide. He was the school teacher in the village, but he smiled and said, "I don't have many students because the parents think their children may learn more than they know, and they would lose respect." Joel took Don for his first ride in a dugout canoe, as he insisted he take the American to shore to show him the flagpole that flew the Stars and Stripes when the battle of Tulagi was won.

James was a wiry old man, bent over and toothless, but a very friendly fellow who wore his green and white lap-lap folded around his skinny hips. James had a daughter he was trying to sell for $75. His greeting was always, "Hello, Joe." He often brought a gift of some sort of fruit or vegetable, and his favorite payment was an invitation to come on board. "You have a number one boat, Joe," he always began the conversation with the same words. Of course, he knew by now that Don's name was not Joe, but he liked the familiarity and the smiles that came to our faces when he called *Svea* number one. We learned that in Pidgin English "nombawan" stands for the "best" and "Nombawan" is the name of Honiara's best butchery.

A flock of red parrots flew over one day while James was aboard. He had to educate us and said, "The red parrots eat yellow bananas. The green parrots eat brown coconuts and the white cockatoos drink the juice from green coconuts." Another day, James came below. When Don told him that we thought the wood carving of the alligator over *Svea's* mast step came from Fiji, the old man looked aghast.

"That not from Fiji, that was carved right here in Gela," he said quite emphatically and used the old name Gela that had been replaced by the white man's name for Florida Island.

Baranago Island

We left Joel and James to move on to another anchorage, one closer to a main body of land and one whose bush was alive with feathered creatures. Way up into the head of Baranago Harbor, we watched villagers tending their gardens and cockatoos flying to and from treetops.

I believe Florida Island has more cockatoos than Florida USA has cattle egrets. Such silly clowns, cockatoos stayed in pairs and would send out constant chitterings and chatterings if they separated. They are really acrobatic comedians as they fly to the highest tops of the trees, grab a limb and hang upside-down for a minute, then twirl around to get right side up.

Cockatoos seem to have the center rings of the circus, but the little willie wag-o-tails take up the side rings with their own aerial acrobatic shows. To us as cruising silors, the shows were free. The only thing missing was a bowl of popcorn! Sometimes I even popped that and we sat back in the cockpit and enjoyed the performing artists.

Return to Honiara

When we sailed back to Honiara, we found a new group of yachties. Among them were Jim and Cheryl Schmidt on the 70-foot motorsailer, *Wind'son*. While we had taken a side trip of 25 miles to Florida Island, Jim and Cheryl had taken theirs to Ontong Java, some 250 miles off the beaten path. It was interesting to compare small *Svea* and the big and fast traveling *Wind'son*, and the life styles imposed by our boats. *Wind'son*'s fuel capacity was 1,280 gallons compared with *Svea*'s 150, which is a large capacity for a boat her size. Range was not the only contrast, for another was the freedom in which Jim and Cheryl could take off for their long jaunts in comfort and safety.

As we left Honiara in company with *Wind'son*, we were on the threshold of yet another door that opened into an even more alluring cruising grounds, Marovo Lagoon, in the New Georgia Group of the Solomon Islands, northwest of Guadalcanal.

Photo by Carl Moesly

Solomon Islanders loading copra into their dugout canoe

CHAPTER 4

RUSSELL ISLANDS AND MAROVO LAGOON, NEW GEORGIA GROUP, SOLOMON ISLANDS

With appetizers behind us, the Solomon Islands had saved the best part of their banquet for the main course—a large casserole of different islands all bound together in land-locked Marovo Lagoon. Each island was within an easy day's sail or less, and yet they were as diverse as the ingredients of any one-pot meal and were spiced with all kinds of good things for the sailor, explorer, skin diver, treasure seeker and artifact collector.

Russell Islands

The lure of yet other islands lying in our path from Guadalcanal to Marovo Lagoon caused us to spend a few days in the Russell Islands. Like a web spun by a very industrious spider, the Russells lie in a haphazard circle with the main islands of Pavuvu and Banika at the center. Smaller islands run out in disconnected strings and are laced together by channels drawn by the not-so-sober spider.

Our main interest was the rumor that at the Lever Plantation off Renard Sound on Banika Island, we could find some fillets for our freezer. That part of the business accomplished, we enjoyed lacing *Svea* through the winding channels. After a couple of nights anchored within the web we departed the Russells at midnight by way of Pepesala Channel.

Marovo Lagoon

By noon we were slipping into Marovo Lagoon through Tongoro Passage, a deep channel between fringing reefs to high coconut palm-bearing islands. Unlike the small body of water at Tavanipupu, Marovo Lagoon is more like the navigable channels in the Society Islands lying between a barrier reef and the main body of the island. Marovo's barriers from the sea, however, are represented by many closely-packed islands, reefs and islets. The islands of New Georgia and Vangunu represent the mainlands.

The lagoon extends more than 30 miles as it wraps itself around the two mainland islands. To the cruising sailor, it is a sheer delight to have so many sheltered islands to sail around.

Wind'son was anchored in a small cove with a backdrop of green trees on the small barrier island behind them. Arriving ahead of us, they had already combed the shores and waters and gave us a dozen oysters they had cut off mangrove roots. Our paths would temporarily separate, but we remained in radio contact. They were avid divers and eager to dive on some of the reported war wrecks lying on the bottom of Marovo Lagoon.

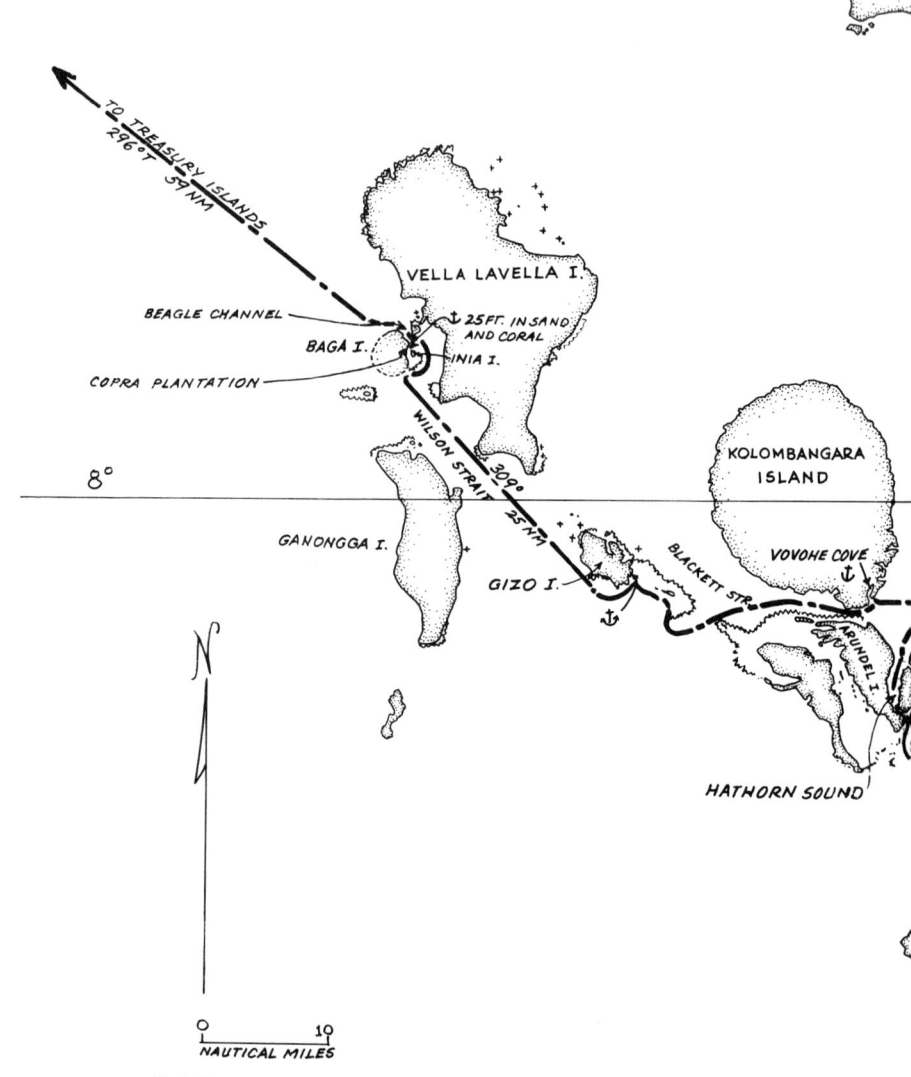

New Georgia Group, Solomon Islands

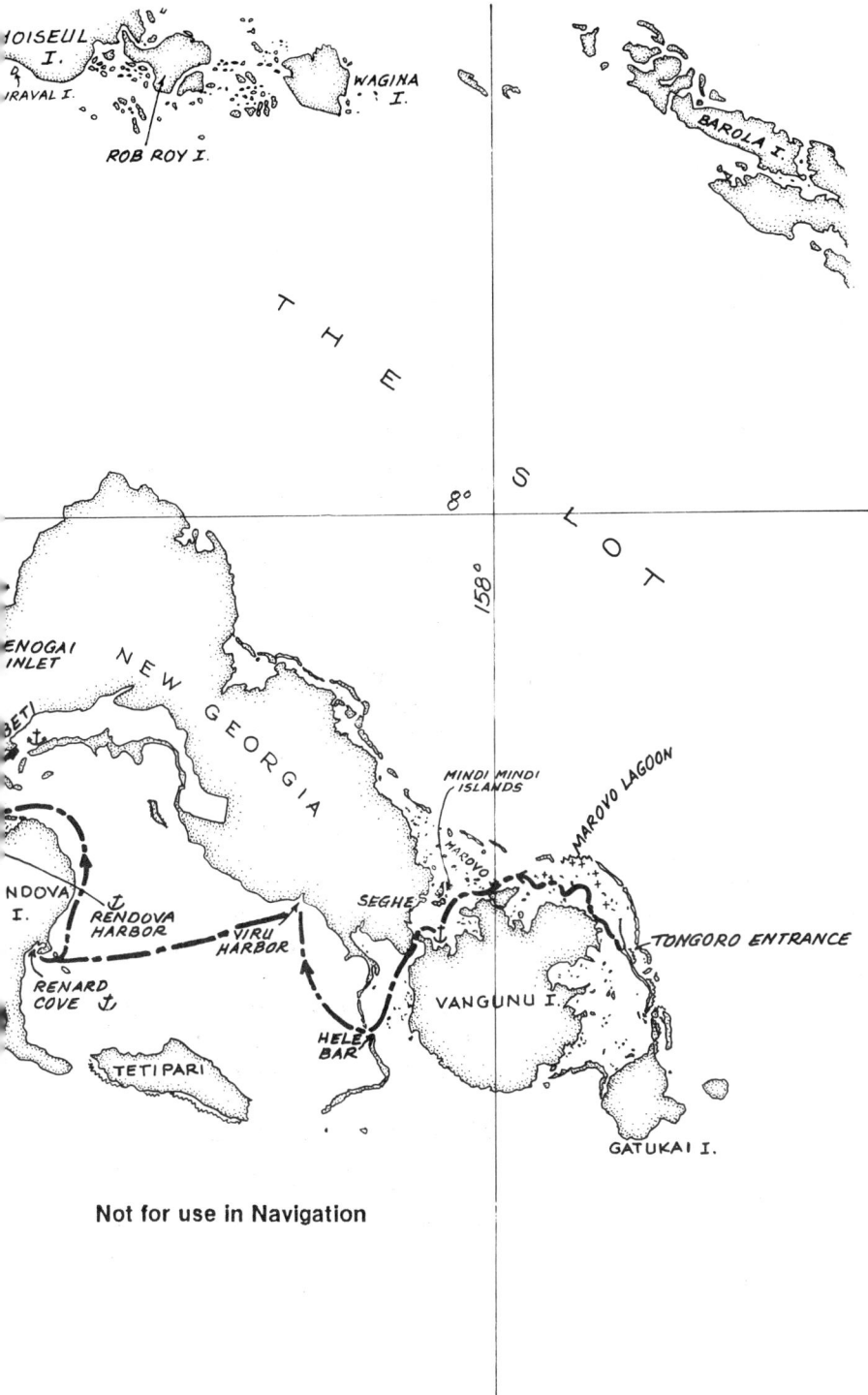
Not for use in Navigation

In a few days, after doing our own looking around, we moved to another site. We were not anchored very long when a local wood carver paddled out to *Svea* to show us samples of his work. The first wood carving was a beautiful model in ebony of a noosa-noosa, (nguzu nguzu). These are intricately carved heads of men, that are inlaid with pearl shells to represent the model's teeth and other embellishments. The original customs pieces were used on the prows of native canoes to signify the paddler's intention. If the carved hands extended from the man's head bore a bird, it meant a sign of peace, but if the hands bore a head, it was a sign of war. Another carving was not of ebony but of indigenous golden-brown kerosene wood. It was of a man with a crocodile tossed over his shoulder. Both pieces were highly polished with shoe polish and wax.

The wood carver turned down every item that I offered in trade. Frustrated, I said, "It looks as if we can't get together on price, for I have nothing you want."

At this, the man exploded into a tirade, "My people are not primitive tribes and do not want cast-off clothing. Furthermore, I am a Seventh Day Adventist and my religion forbids me to wear trinkets and trivia." Neither was the man allowed to drink any form of beer or whiskey, or even tea, and he could not smoke any form of tobacco. To make it harder for him and followers of his religion, he was not permitted to eat the bounty of his waters, no shellfish, which included oysters, clams, turtles and lobster simply available for the taking. He was not allowed to eat pork, and he scoffed at the mirror I wanted to give him for his wife.

I realized I had unintentionally embarrassed this proud man, and his outburst made him more ashamed. Rather than cause further outrage, I purchased his onions at an asking price far above the going rate. He was so startled when I had not given him an argument, that he gave me two beautiful cowrie shells. We both had smiles on our faces when he departed. All men, no matter what color, or what race, or social standing, have an easily bruised sense of pride.

Another wood carver approached us as we island-hopped across the lagoon, but John Wayne was different, as he had left his village to go to Honiara to make some money and returned with a diffrent outlook on life. He was the successful entrepreneur of his village. A Seagull outboard was mounted on his canoe; one of the items he had acquired in a trade with another American cruising sailor for his wood carving. John told us he knew about city life and the lust for women and the greed for money, but he was not happy. He returned to his village and married a girl who could read and write as he could. He said. "I married my wife in the church. I did not buy her. That is still done in Malaita. They cling to the old ways and they are the warlike people." John's carvings were not of the custom style, but rather an independent and original flair that will someday make his art a valuable piece to own. He even encouraged his wife to change the traditional style of her basketry.

Down the chain of islands, still in Marovo Lagoon, we entered Mindi Mindi, a group of some 73 little islets locked together, in some cases, by shallow coral bridges. Here we met another enterprising native, Muven Kuve. He had great plans to turn the islands belonging to his uncle into a resort for tourists. Muven Kuve had worked in the copper mines in Bougainvillae, and had aspirations that surpassed his contemporaries. He was eager to show us the foundation of his dream. The setting was, beyond a doubt, beautiful. All of the islets have massive growths of greenery, trees, bushes and vines. These snake across sandy soils and have brilliant purple blossoms that splash some color to contrast the predominant green. Birds abound and the cacophony of caws, cackles and coos drowned out the sound of a freshening wind.

In *Poco*, the three of us wound in and out of the small passes between the islets. Muven pointed out the one island he had picked for the site of the main building. "Here the yachts could come in and anchor and go ashore for showers and steaks," the bright young man said. He added with a smile, "I know you Americans like your steaks!" We began to think that maybe this young man was an astute business man and was headed in the right direction. However Don pointed out to Muven that the small harbor did not have enough depth for most of the deep-draft cruising yachts. Don suggested another equally pretty cove that could accommodate foreign yachts.

Don added another suggestion, before building up the hopes of the young man too much, "But Muven, don't you think you should find out more about the hotel business before you venture into something you know nothing about?"

"Oh, I'll find a partner who knows all of that," Muven answered positively. "He'll have the money, too." The key word "money" was the answer to his dreams and to many other aspiring men who have the ideas, but not the wherewithal to carry them out. Muven Kuve followed his dream and does indeed now have his resort. It has one leaf house accommodating ten people, and four other huts for couples. I would like to return and shake his hand.

It was a terribly hot day as we wove through the islands, starved for wind as they were packed so tightly together. Muven directed us to a shoreline that has a nice beach and many coconut trees. He grabbed a vine and made a loop in it to tie his ankles together to aid him in climbing the tree. Then, like any trained monkey, he went up the trunk and twisted off six green drinking nuts, three for now and three for later. He wrapped those together with the fibers of the husk.

We were nearing the end of Marovo Lagoon and the month of September. We now started to study the charts and "Sailing Directions" for the next leg of our journey. This would take us to Rabaul, New Britain for Thanksgiving and a look at the Japanese bastion that had served as the headquarters for their Southwest Pacific operations.

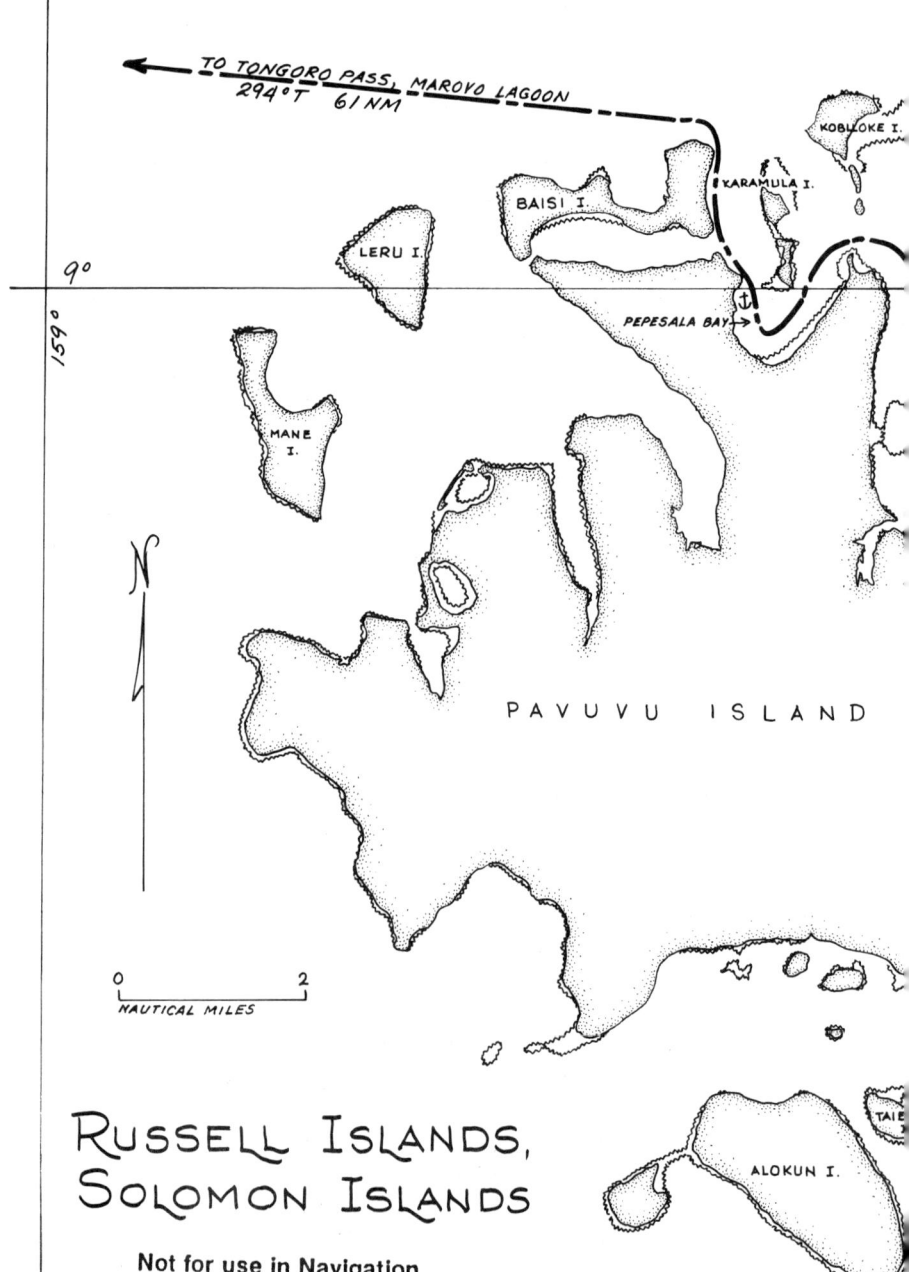

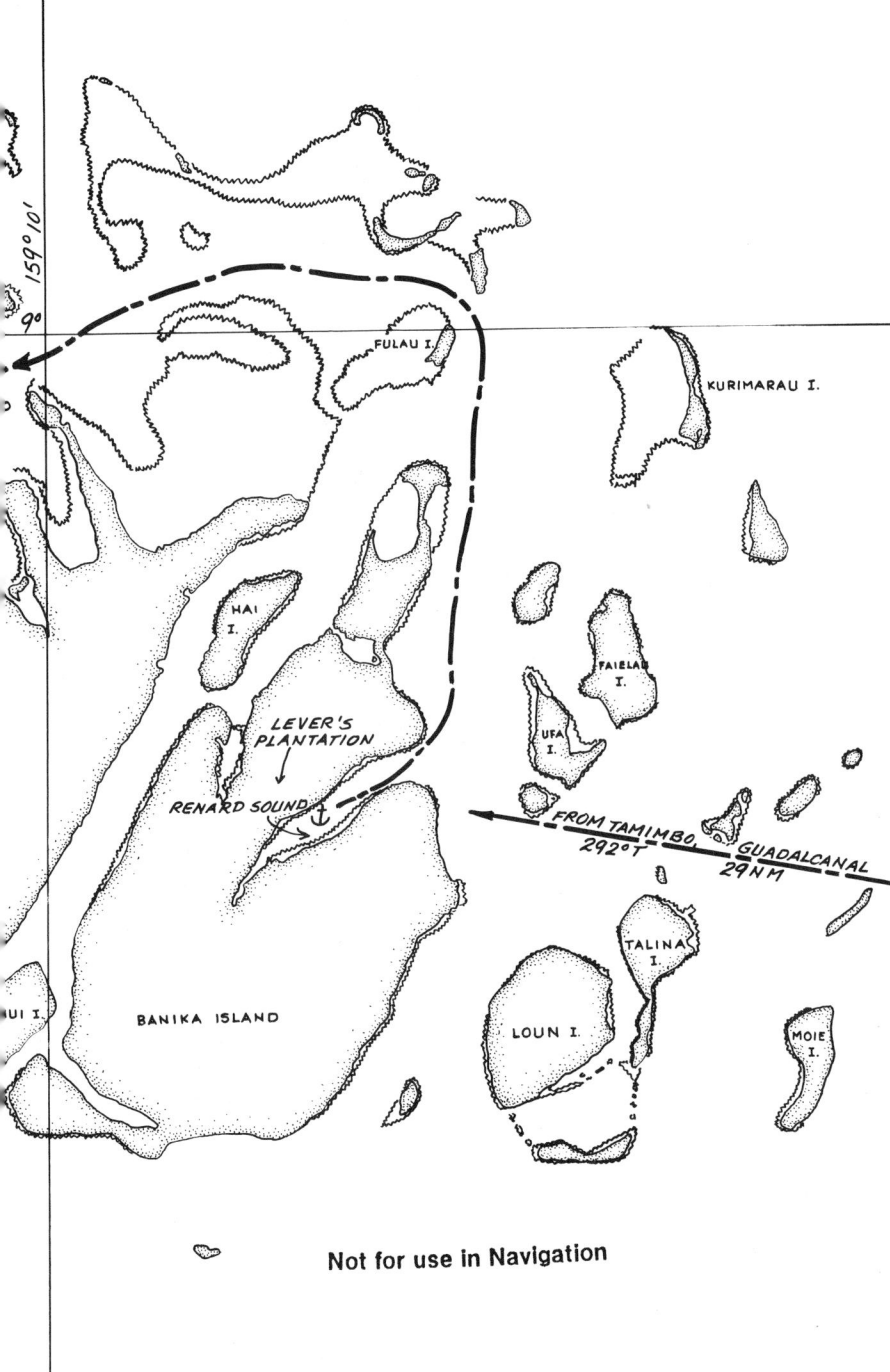

"We found that P-38," Jim said over the radio, "Right off the runway at Seghe in about 20 feet of water."

"Did you find anythng on it?" Don asked, for he knew Jim was an excellent diver and would investigate the wreck thoroughly.

"Sure did," Jim said. "Tell you about it when we see you."

"Roger on that," Don answered. "We're about to leave Mindi Mindi bound for Seghe now."

"We're about to head on up to Kolombangara. Oh," he says, "We heard a call on the ham from *Rigadoon.*"

"They're down in Fiji," Don automatically answered.

"No, they're sailing by on the top end of the Solomons headed for Rabaul, and they want us to be sure to give you the message," Jim said excitedly.

"They were to stay in Fiji. I wonder what changed their minds?" Don questioned.

"Don't know, but I'll relay further messages on the ham until you guys are in receiving distance with your radios," Jim said.

"Thanks Jim," Don answered. "We'll sign off now. We'll see you down the line."

Anchorage off West Shore of Vangunu Island

Naturally we were excited to know that Carl and Jeanne were closer to us, and we began to put out radio calls on our previously scheduled times. We carried on for Seghe and wanted to anchor near the site where Jim found the P-38 and go ashore. Both Muven and John had told us about the big soccer meet there. They were captains of their teams, but the bottom appeared to be too foul. We could not get a good bite with the anchor and questioned, as well, if we might snag on Jim's wreck. Instead, we went over to the mainland island of Vangunu and anchored off a very large mountain stream, and perhaps enjoyed the companionship of nature more than the fellowship of man and his games of soccer.

To leave Marovo Lagoon on its western side, you must cross Hele Bar, which is located at the elbow joint of two large reefs. We needed good light to define the narrow channel between them. The sun was high and clearly outlined the greens and yellows of the treacherous bar that carries only 12 feet depth over its most shallow point. Don was at the bow gauging the breakers and counting their sequence. He shouted back his observations to me at the tiller. I had taken *Svea* off pilot to take a firm hold on our heading.

When a clear space appeared over the reef Don hollered, "Give her more r.p.m.s and let's go!" *Svea* answered her helm well and with more added diesel power we quickly scooted over the bar and gained deeper water.

I looked back at the white rows of breakers that were marching over the path we had just taken. "Whew!" They didn't give us much time, did they?'

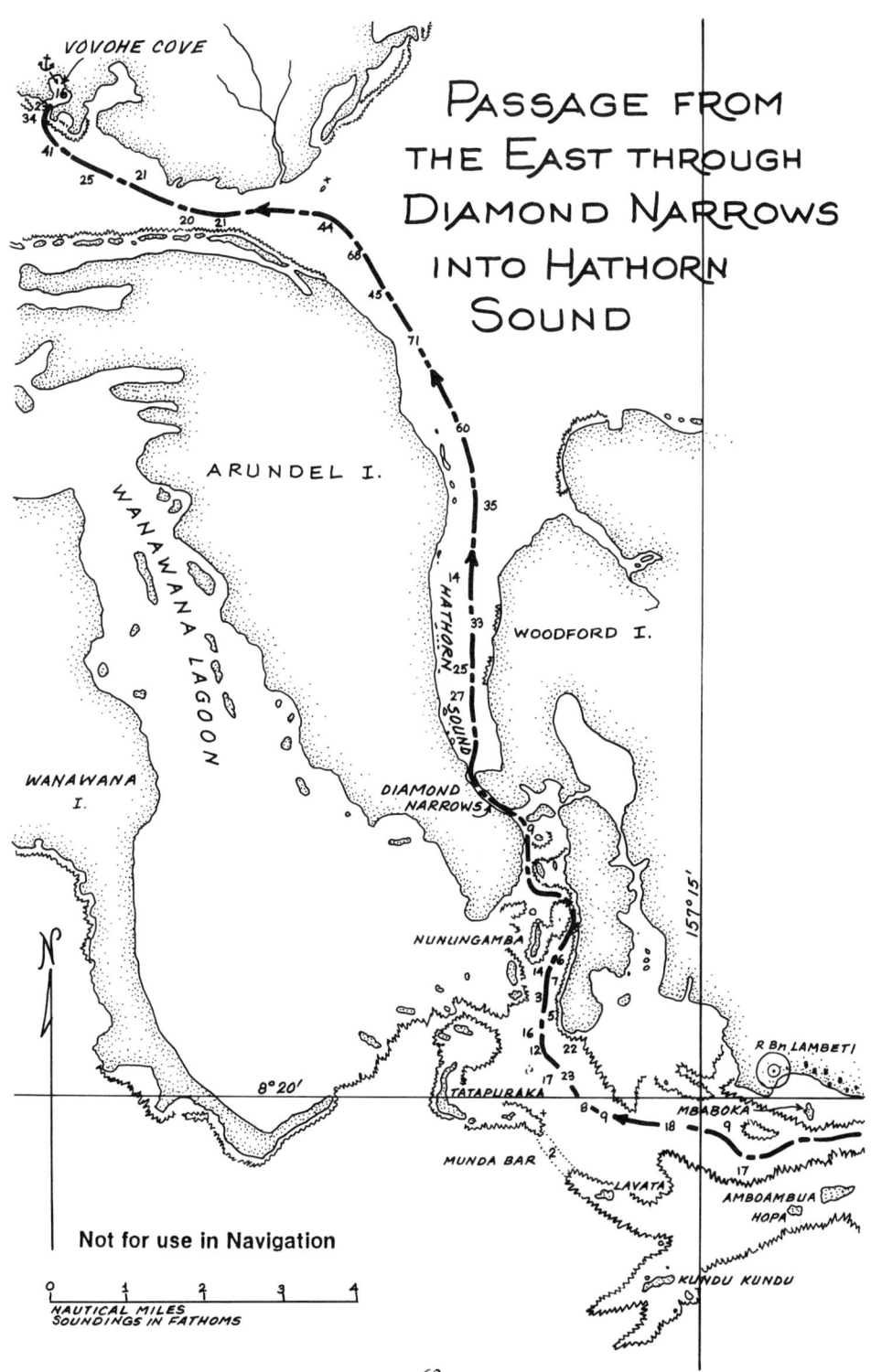

"The Hele Bar is behind us," Don sighed relief as well. "Let's get up the jenny and mizzen. We have a lee from the land and it will be a pleasure to sail in calm waters."

Viru Harbor, South Coast of New Georgia Island

Protected by the high cliffs of New Georgia Island that shut out the sea from the inland valleys, we enjoyed the sail and the scenery. Now we were seeing forests of hardwood trees and rugged coastlines. Our anchorage that night was in Viru Harbor, surrounded by a huge sawmill installation. All of the buildings were painted green by the Lever Brothers company, including the Seventh Day Adventist Church that served the population. Small tugs and ferryboats kept a constant procession of men and tools going from one end of the harbor to the other. It was obvious that Lever Brothers had a busy logging operation going here as well as in other locations in the islands.

We learned that New Zealand was funding a program to teach the natives how to replant the cut forest. We found that the natives in the islands where industry supported them, were more literate and independent. They catered less to their old customs and ways. These more enlightened men were "backsliders" who accepted our rope tobacco.

Although it took us less than a day's sail to reach various anchorages among the remaining Solomon Islands, they seemed a world apart. The natives stayed isolated within the confines of their own islands and villages. Dugout canoes without outriggers are not the most stable of craft and were not seaworthy enough for their paddlers to venture very far from neighboring waters, or to make extended passages. With so many islands close together, and the proliferation of land-locked bays and harbors, the people had little need of craft that would withstand the rigors of the sea. As we travel through the Pacific, we notice how measurably the waters dictate the style of the native craft. The Solomon Islander was surrounded by everything he needed, and there was no need for him to go in search of food or whatever it is that stirs the wanderlust. He had the bush to provide his dwelling and protection from the weather, and the fertile land and sea to provide for his food. He did not need a sail for his canoe, for he never ventured too far to paddle.

Rendova Harbor

At Rendova Harbor on Rendova Island we were once again reminded of World War II and the fact that Solomon Islanders fervently want to talk over those days with an American. A man who paddled up to us repeated what his father had told him, "See over there," Mr. Kingsley pointed to a bunch of small islands on the horizon. "That's where your President Kennedy was rescued by our people when his PT 109 sank out from under him. You know, a Japanese destroyer just cut that boat in two."

We smiled and praised him for his knowledge, but found out later that

Kennedy's Plum Island was closer to Gizo than Rendova Harbor, nearly 30 miles away! Still we realized that although these people appear to be primitive in their ways, they are not ignorant of what is going on in the outside world. Back at Florida Island old James had reminded us that it was our own Neil Armstrong who was the first man on the moon.

Ironically, it was the transgressors, the Japanese, who stole ashore on their islands many years ago, who were now establishing a very successful fish cannery off Hathorn Sound northwest of Rendova Island. They used the waters around Mundi Island to catch and store bait fish for their large tuna-fishing boats. The live bait wells dotting Lambeti's harbor looked like a bunch of strange floating mines. Navigation was difficult enough without having to dodge those obstacles.

After leaving Lambeti's harbor, we were greeted with a maze of reefs and islands through which we had to navigate to reach Hathorn Sound. Markers were located at the twists and turns in the crystal clear waters, but the passage following the western side of New Georgia was still intricate and difficult. The islands of Arundel and New Georgia suddenly close in to form Diamond Narrows, a narrow passage between their high cliffs. Once past Diamond Narrows, we were in Hathorn Sound. We passed by the Taiyo cannery with its unmistakable smell.

We were also passing into the finale of the Solomon's show of shows. We finally made radio contact with *Rigadoon* and reported the news to Jim on our next broadcast with *Wind'son*, "We're going to rendezvous at Rabaul."

Anchorage at Mbaeroko Bay

Jim told us of their anchorage in a bay off Hathorn Sound where Japanese relics rested on the bottom. "And you don't need to anchor," Jim added. "Just tie fore and aft to the sunken Japanese freighter."

We found Mbaeroko Bay at Enogai on New Georgia's west shore mainland. Straddling the bones of the sunken vessel in her graveyard that lay more than 6 feet beneath *Svea*'s keel, we tied bow and stern lines to her masts.

It certainly was a strange sight beneath the surface of the water, as we swam around *Svea* and the graveyard in which she lay. Not only was the freighter under her, but also sunken barges. Fish were in a wonderland of coral-encrusted rigging and frames of the sunken craft. Many different size bullet holes riddled the freighter's smokestack. The yardarm of the ship's mast was the site of nesting willie wag-o-tails. After we first upset the expectant mother by our nearness to her future offspring, she settled into the nest and accepted us.

It was Halloween night, and we thought about the witches and pumpkins as we sat in the cockpit and stared at the star-studded sky through the mast of the sunken freighter. "What is that?" I exclaimed as I pointed to the multitudes of black specks outlined against the red sky of dusk.

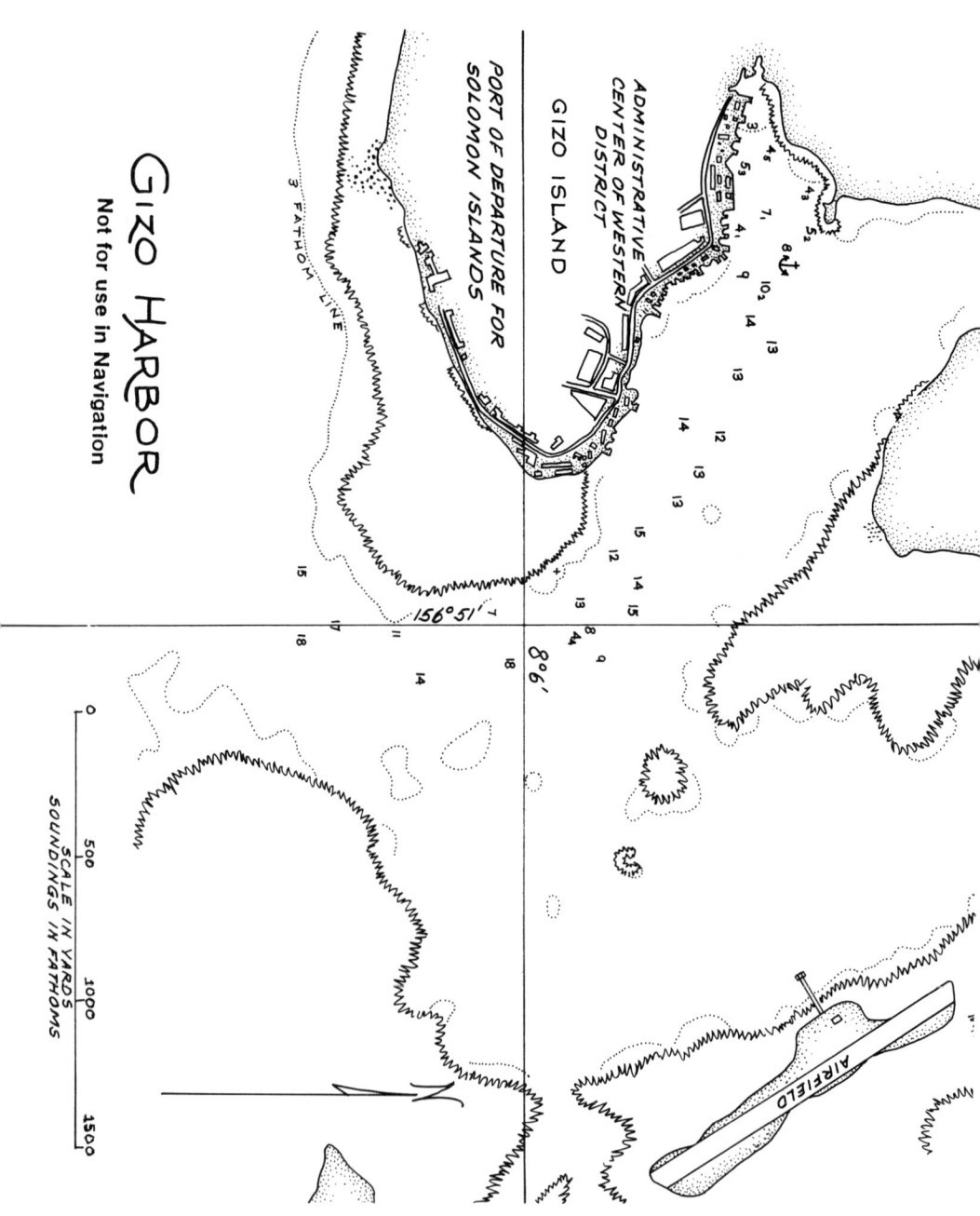

"Witches? Goblins?" My imagination was that of a child, but there was no denying the strange apparition as the specks drew closer and larger, and filled the sky. As they came overhead, we saw that they were only flying foxes, the largest of the bat family. They were heading back to their favorite trees for the night to feast on flowers and fruit. Bats are really quite ugly little creatures, even more so when they appear in their roasted form in the native markets. They are quite a gourmet treat for some, but I couldn't get past the sight of the big-winged and big-eyed critters to consider them as food.

The next morning we headed across the Kula Gulf to Vovohe Cove on the southeastern tip of Kolombangara. Within the growth-shrouded cove we anchored at the mouth of a river in 55 feet depth. Never to let an entreating adventure pass us by, we dinghied up the river as far as we could go until a log footbridge blocked our passage.

Gizo

Gizo was our port of departure from the Solomon Islands. It was at this last port of entry that officials asked us for the "light" fee, named thusly for its intention of being spent to update non-existent navigational lights.

Baga Island

Beyond Gizo lay a few scattered islands that had left that mainstream of the chain of islands to stand alone, rather like dribbles of paint from the paint brush on its way out of the can. The island of Baga may not last much longer as it is slowly sinking into the sea. The owner of the shrinking copra plantation said that after the earthquake of 1963, the island has sunk about 18 to 24 inches, and the sea is creeping towards the main house. Like another plantation in Vanuatu, the one on Baga had seen better days. Only a handful of the Gilbertese Islanders, who served as the labor force, were left on the island.

"In the good days," the owner told us as he sat in *Svea*'s cockpit with a cold beer in his hand, "a man could bring in three bags of copra, each weighing 150 pounds every day. But then, Lever Brothers came along and got their men to bring in 900 pounds a day. That meant the men had to rise at 3 o'clock and work late hours to make their quotas." He went on to tell us that there were no more wild pigs left to shoot, as when his father ran the plantation. Neither were there any crocodiles up the creeks, as they had all been killed off for their valuable skins. It was trouble enough just finding birds to eat. The plantation owners we had met, the individuals like the small businesses back home, were a vanishing breed. The larger conglomerates swallowed them as they gathered in their nets of trapped victims. In every part of the world there are similes to be found.

Treasury Islands

The curtain fell on the last act when we departed from Treasury Islands. These are the two outpost islands of Mono and Stirling, that clasped arms to form a placid lagoon that sheltered a PT fleet during World War II.

Once again, our American flag, brought the friendly villagers out to see the new arrival. They formed a large parade of canoes as they led *Svea* past dilapidated wharves and leaning pilings that had sequestered the fleet of PT boats. Then they led us in and around islands, islets and coral heads to a small cove surrounded on three sides by tall trees.

Once we were securely anchored,, the village elder and leader of the march, John, came aboard to welcome us officially. "Our family hid 10 downed pilots in the bush," the old man recounted the English he had mastered as a 10 year-old youngster. He told of the terror they felt when the Japanese landed on their island, then of the jubilation when the "Joes" came to save them.

George came later with two cucumbers and behind him were Andrew and his nephew Morris with beans and tomatoes. Still others continued the chain of gifts from their gardens. We gave them what we could in return.

We had delayed too long in the Solomons, and the northwest monsoons were overtaking the southeast trades. Winds were northerly of very little strength, bringing upon us the doldrums of convergence zone weather where the two systems waver back and forth until the predominant one overtakes the other. We had 300 miles to reach Rabaul, New Britain. At least the winds were light enough to motor into them. We made way to New Britain, the first island in the Bismarck Archipelago, the beginning of **Papua New Guinea.** We bypassed the island of Bougainvillae which is part of Papua New Guinea, but geographically located within the Solomons.

Photo by Carl Moesly

Children from Port Mary, Santa Ana, Solomons

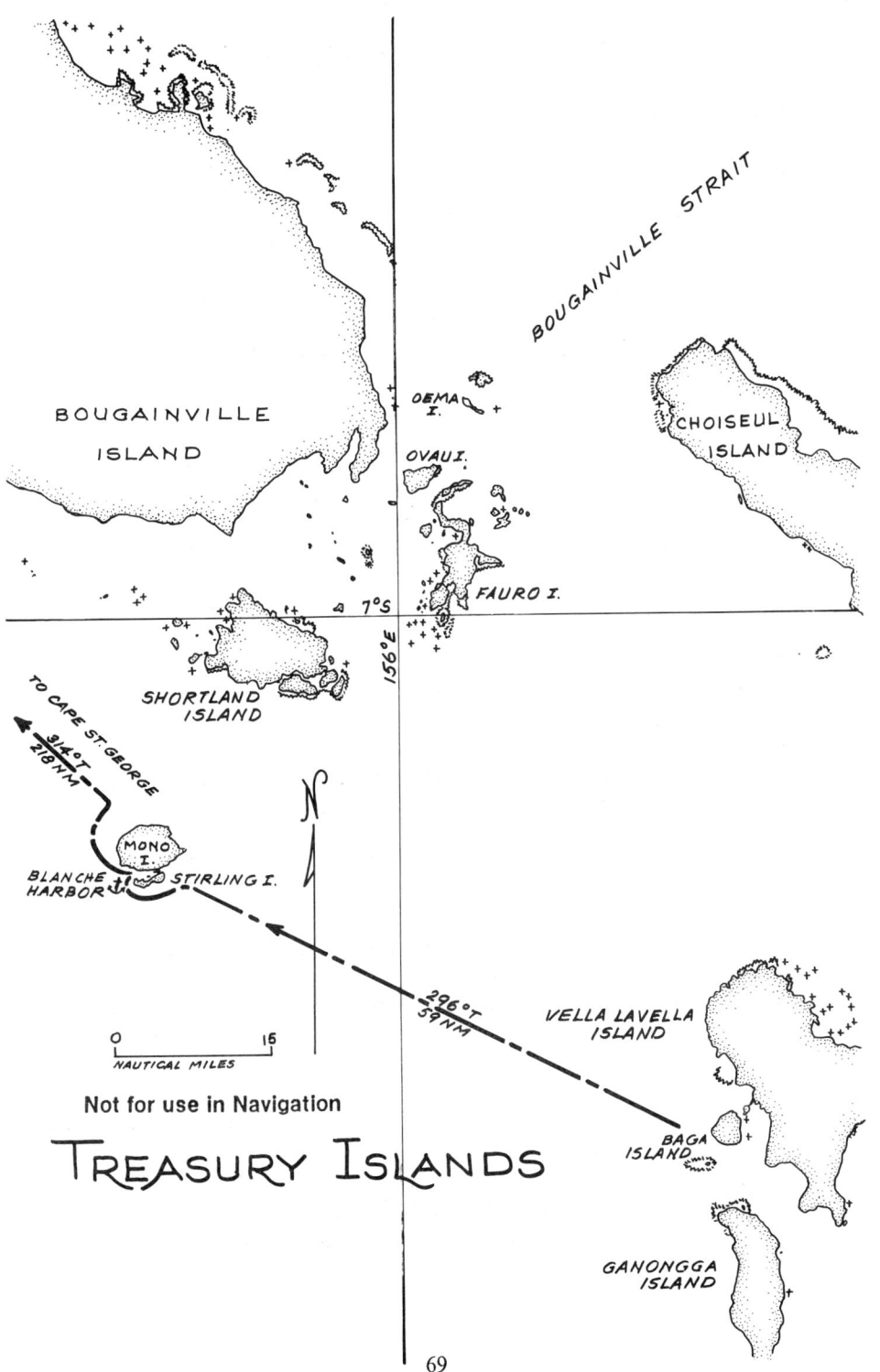

CHAPTER 5

BISMARCK ARCHIPELAGO

Passage from the Treasury Islands, Solomons to English Harbor, New Ireland

Drawing closer to the Equator in the windless days of the convergence zone was like walking a path to the ovens of hell. With the engine running to give us some forward motion, the heat in the closed-up cabin became almost unbearable. Sometimes we could use the main to motorsail and relieve the rolling motion, but nothing relieved the heat. Sleep was a precious commodity. When it did cool down a little at night, we then had to worry about freighter traffic. Our rest was disturbed because we kept uninterrupted watches on deck. Sights were few, for the constant haze blocked the horizons and shut out the sun. After the fourth day out from the Treasury Islands of the Solomons, the skies cleared enough for us to get some good sights, and we found we were near New Ireland.

A bosun bird hovered above the masthead and kept looking down at us as if to say, "Hey you guys, pay attention to me. I know the way to land." Perhaps the heat got to us and our imaginations put words into the mouth of a bird. We welcomed the sight of anything in that haze of nothingness. Pieces of driftwood aimlessly floated by to confirm the nearness of land.

When we finally sighted the island, we were too far away to close with it before darkness descended. We counted on the big lighthouse at Cape St. George to be our guiding light through the night as we remained in a hove-to position waiting for dawn to break. We have conditioned ourselves not to depend upon lights, but still when the light never came on, we were sorely disappointed. The only lights we ever saw during the night were those from passing freighters.

There were many of them pressing on through the night and into the channel, which their radars told them how to find. We worried they would not see our lone masthead light. Many times that night, we turned on all of our navigational lights to be more visible to the ships. As we often do, we pondered how many of those ships had lookouts. So much sophisticated equipment has replaced man on a ship that our worry was not unfounded. It takes a man's eyes to read the radar screens and define what he sees. Some cruising sailors do not display lights at night and the law of averages may someday catch up to them. Ships are welcome to come close to us to investigate our lights. We feel safe in the knowledge that they can see us beforehand to prevent a collision. Some sailors argue that their own lights blind them from oncoming traffic, but it is easy enough to turn them on and off to take bearings.

As dawn cracked, the structure of the lighthouse came into view just where we thought it should be, but it had failed in its duty during the

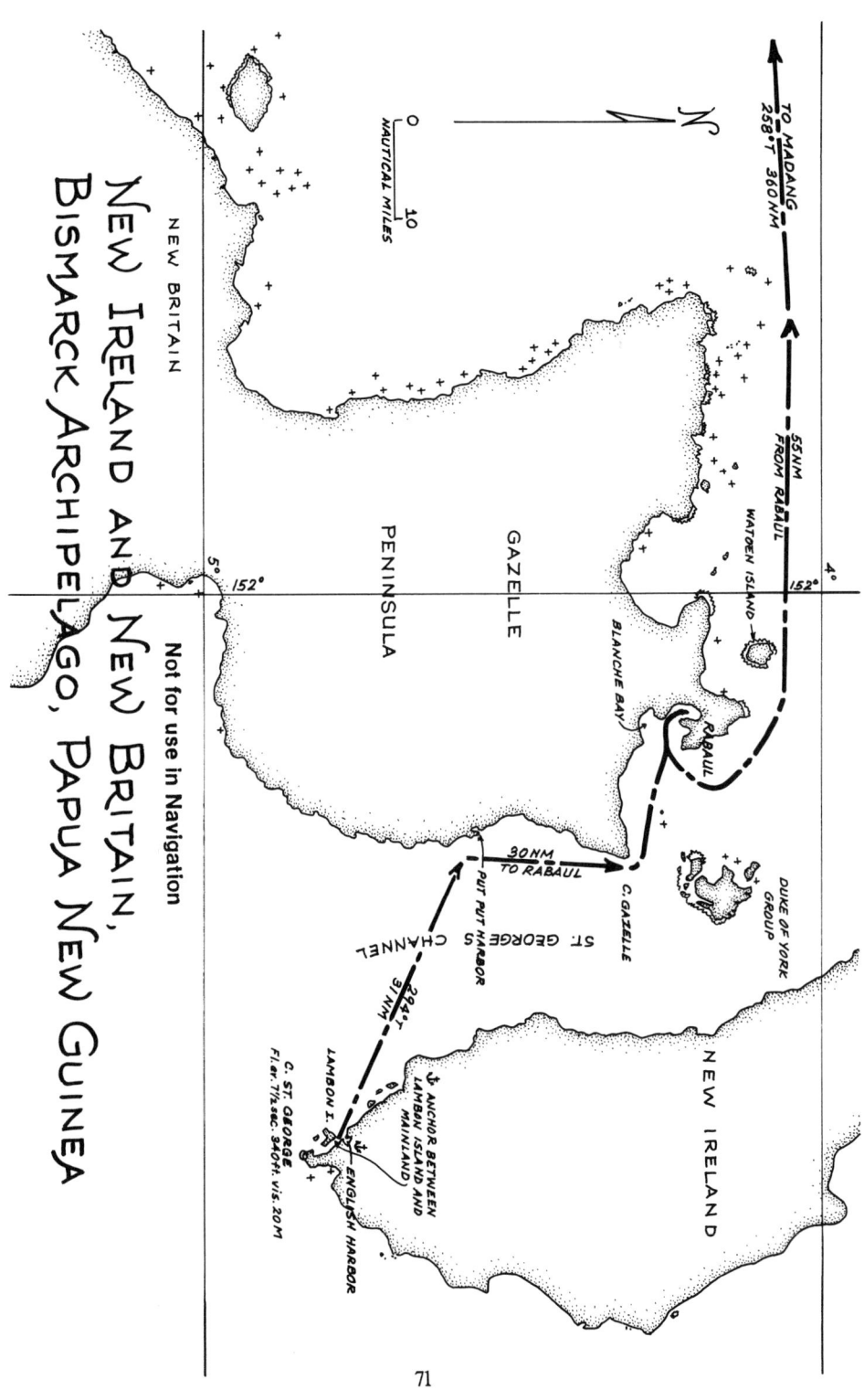

hours of darkness. Jim had reported the same finding when we saw *Wind'son* at Rabaul.

The Bismarck Archipelago, named for the German chancellor, sits like a disjointed arm broken at the elbow. It is located northeast of New Guinea, which is the second largest island in the world, second only to Greenland. The islands were first discovered by British explorers in 1767. A chain of succeeding nations laid claim to them, including their being made a trust territory administered by Australia. The commonwealth of Papua New Guinea gained its independence in 1975 when Michael T. Somare became their first Prime Minister.

Although politically joined, the people of the commonwealth are an extraordinary mixture, socially and culturally. They have from 5 to 6 hundred different languages, Pidgin English being the common one.

English Harbor, between Lambon Island and New Ireland

Nothing is more international than music. Local young people from the village of Lambon came over to English Harbor where we were anchored to watch me do laundry in the fast-moving stream. They broke out in strains of "Comin Round The Mountain!" "Old MacDonald" followed, and they knew the words better than I did. We were accompanied by other songs of the jungle, the birds and a clickety-clack sound that is similar to a katydid. Nature and man blended their tunes in harmony.

The girls wore smock-type blouses with square necklines and puffed sleeves banded with ribbons, but their streamers were not as long as those of the women in Vanuatu. Under the hip-length smocks, they wore the common fathom of cloth, two-yard lengths wrapped around their waists like the Polynesians. However, the younger girls removed their smocks and wrapped their fathoms of cloth around their bosoms and exposed their legs. That display of the woman's anatomy was unusual for the Melanesians, who cover up more than the care-free Polynesians.

Their dugout canoes are different from the Polynesians' version with outriggers, and different from the Solomon Islanders' plain canoes. Sea conditions dictate sturdier craft and New Britain and New Ireland sailors have added higher bulwarks to the sides of their canoes and outriggers for stability.

Passage to Rabaul, New Britain

Burdened rain clouds hung like sodden grey bonnets over the mountain tops, and veils of mist cloaked the jungle that surrounded the small bay. "We're really into the monsoons," Don said as he shook his head when he looked out the companionway hatch. He contemplated our next passage, across St. Georges Channel to the island of New Britain, and then north to Rabaul.

Rabaul was 61 miles away. It meant ever so many things to us: the reunion with Carl and Jeanne Moesly and Thanksgiving dinner together;

and Rabaul's stores, mostly run by Australian ex-patriates. They had supplies to restock our empty lockers.

"It doesn't look like it's going to clear up and get any better," I reported to Don after looking at everything in sight dripping with moisture. "Maybe it's just because we're in a pocket of these high mountains?"

"It's the season, so let's get underway," Don answered. "We'll cross the channel anyway and call in at Put Put Harbor for the night. Then in the morning, we'll head on towards Rabaul."

The best-laid plans of mice and men, and cruising sailors, are subject to change. When we reached Put Put's Harbor at noon, the entrance was blocked by a large freighter. She was taking on a cargo of floating logs, which surrounded the vessel and blocked passage into the inner harbor. Hawsers strung to each shoreline confirmed the fact that we were not going to be able to pass by.

"We're going to have to go on, aren't we?" I asked.

"Rather looks that way and there aren't any more harbors from here along the coastline until we reach Rabaul. Let's hope we can get into Rabaul at night," Don said with disappointment.

"It's about time for our call to *Rigadoon*. Maybe Carl has some suggestions, maybe they got into Rabaul at night," I said with a hope that we could find refuge, for we had precious little space in the channel to try to heave-to.

"Can we enter the harbor after dark?" Don asked the question immediately when Carl answered our scheduled radio call.

His answer was in the affirmative and he described the leading lights and landmarks. He also added that he would stay in radio contact every hour until we grew closer and added that they were having dinner aboard *Intermezzo*. We smiled, as it seemed the flock of cruising sailors was gathering at Rabaul. It would be a time for all of us to give thanks for the blessings of the year that brought us safely together for Thanksgiving.

Following the coastline, we studied landmarks as darkness started to seal them from our eyes. Already, we had in view the volcanic craters that stand as awesome sentinels near the entrance to Rabaul's Simpson Harbor. As we made our turn inward, we turned on the depth sounder to check soundings and searched for the leading lights Carl had described. We had great difficulty in picking them out from the many shore lights. We plugged in the search light and spotted the group of anchored boats. *Wind'son* is here too," I said with excitement. "There's *Rigadoon* and there's *Intermezzo*," I said with glee as the beam of the light moved across the anchored fleet. "Carl's on deck answering with a flashlight."

"He's in the dinghy now and headed this way," Don said as I concentrated on the bearings and Don's instructions for our heading. "Just head as you're going."

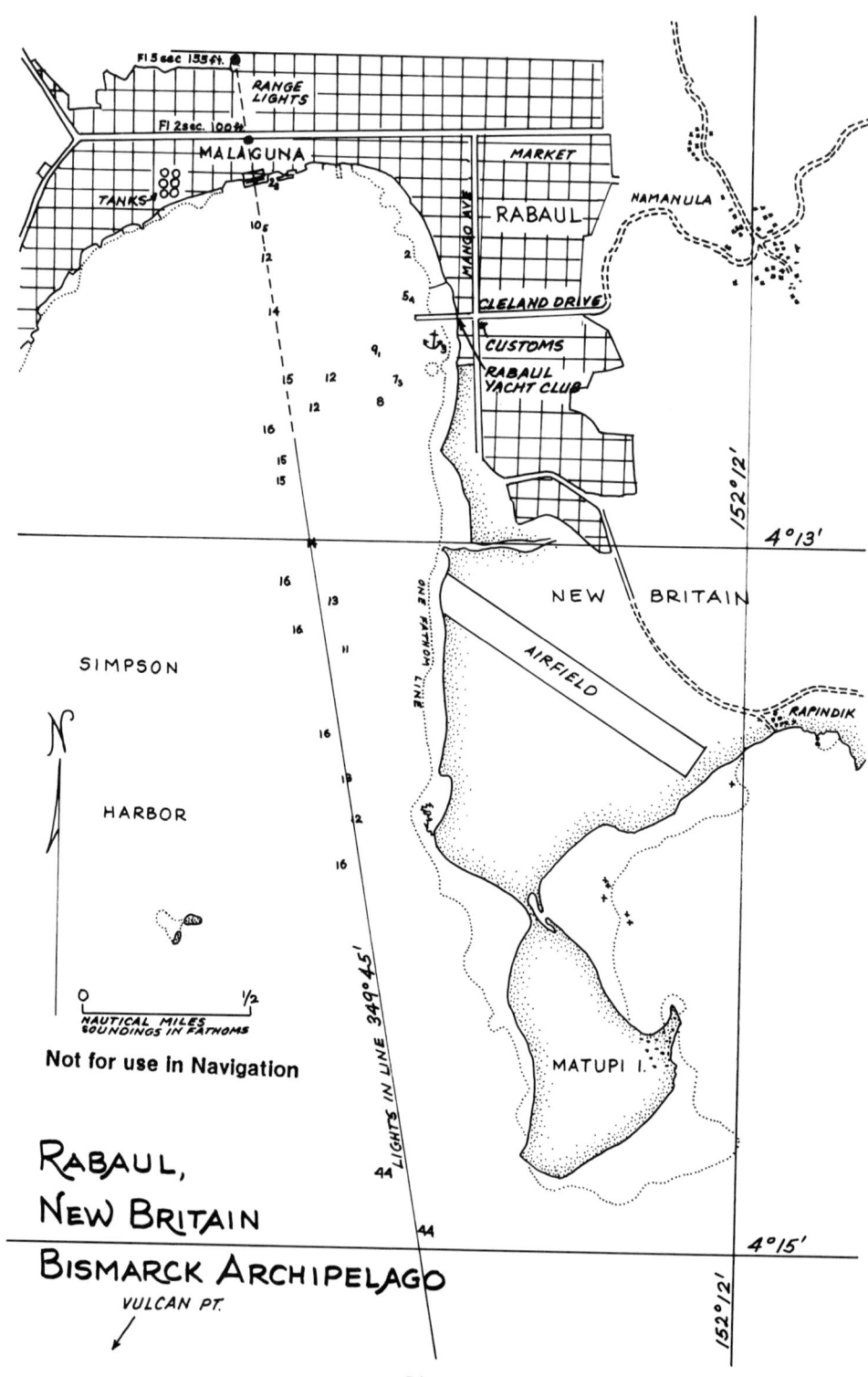

CHAPTER 6

RABAUL, NEW BRITAIN

The Gathering Place

Customs officials at Rabaul were very pleasant, but they did have to take our passports from us to send them to Papua New Guinea's capital city of Port Moresby. Because we had requested a visa for a six-month period, our passports had to be processed at Port Moresby. It was the time of year for voyagers to call a halt to their passagemaking and wait until the cyclone season passed before entering the area of storm tracks. Tropical cyclones occur infrequently within 6 to 8 degrees of the Equator, and are almost unheard of within the 5 degrees on either side of the line that separates the two hemispheres. At the northeast corner of the mainland of New Guinea, Madang is a bare 13 miles from the 5 degrees of latitude and would be a safe distance from the storm belt farther south. The harbor is large, yet protected on all sides by land, providing excellent shelter for visiting yachts. When the season waned in another four months, we would resume our voyaging that would take us south towards Australia. Until then, we would stay within our cocoons until our sails would open once again and carry us into the next stage of our cruising life.

Most of the cruising sailors planned to hole up for the cyclone season, either in Rabaul or Madang. Already in Rabaul, there were eight boats represented from the Seven Seas Cruising Association and those were only the Americans. There were several boats from New Zealand and Australia and one from France. The Royal Rabaul Yacht Club extended all of their membership privileges to their foreign guests, including hot showers and cold beers. The frosting on the cake was the Sunday night barbecues and American movies.

Thanksgiving. Thursday was an off day at the club and the hospitable members opened the kitchen and facilities so we Americans could roast our turkeys and celebrate our day of Thanksgiving. Jeanne was the instigator of the activities that kept growing, along with the list of guests. Volunteers roasted the turkeys in their home ovens. As a result, our feast was more than any Pilgrim could have asked for. To add to the occasion, the cruising ladies rooted through cockpit lockers for impossible to find local items like cranberry sauce. Didi, the artist on *Arion III*, was in charge of decorations and also made pumpkin pies. I also made pies, for the big local pumpkins were only 10 cents in the native market. Kathi of *Sunday Morning* said grace thanking God that we all had made it that far around the world. We showed our Australian guests just how an American is thankful for all blessings and shares the harvests with his friends.

The Market. The Rabaul market was by far the most interesting and complete native market we had ever seen or were yet to see. For only 10 .cents, we could buy avocados as well as pumpkins, bananas, papaya, passionfruit, snake beans, coconuts, soursops and Galip nuts, which were local almonds. Amid the fruit and vegetables were wide selections of shells and native artifacts for sale. Protein was provided by roasted or fresh flying foxes, varieties of fish, smoked or raw, and smoked or charred pig quarters and dried octopi. Those were just a few of the many native foods available in the large market, called the "Bung." We skipped the local source of protein and bought our meat from the frozen food bins in the stores run by Australians.

The big hazard in the native market was trying to dodge the spittle of the many betel nut chewers, as they spewed out the red liquid with intensity, wherever and whenever they wished. The streets were stained with the red sputum. Not even the fallen leaves from the numerous frangipani trees could blot out the scourge of the people.

Volcanic Action. The hardy frangipanis were the first to emerge after the devestating eruption of Mt. Vulcan in 1937 when the entire city was covered in lava and ashen dust. Some 500 people were killed. Mt. Vulcan was originally an island that served as the quarantine station during the German administration, but its eruption joined it to the mainland. Another nearby island, Matupit, still has an active cone and the harbor itself is the inside of an inactive volcano. All of the cruising sailors were aware that we were sitting in a volatile bowl of water with underwater cones that could send us to the heavens if conditions urged them to do so.

We were warned that we might experience tremors in the waters. Don and I remembered the tremors in Pinas Bay when we sailed south along the west coast of Panama.

Fire Dance

Besides volcanoes, eruptions, and tremors, New Britain has a native fire dance that is actually a practised ritual in the villages of the bush, back in the Bainings Mountains. A young boy who has reached puberty is sent out into the bush to live by himself and learn how to survive. He cannot return to the village until he has found a boa constrictor. His homecoming with the snake acknowledges his coming of age and he is honored with the celebration of the fire-walking dance. One of the local Europeans learned of the coming event and asked the cruising sailors if they would like to attend. Permission to invite us had been given by the village chief.

After a bus ride of about 30 miles over paved roads and back and bumpy roads going up and down mountains, we arrived at the village. A fire blazed in the center of the arena, cordoned off by walls of palm fronds. We passed through the small entry, and sat in a wide circle less than 20 feet from the fire. Opposite us on the other side of the fire was a group of scantily-clad men who bonged against a hard surface with bamboo sticks while chanting an eerie six-note dirge. Inciting their spirits with liberal chews of betel nut, the dancers entered the arena one at a time.

The men were clad in capes and anklets of leaves, wearing headdresses made of basketry to look like duck or chicken heads. They first paused in front of the musicians for added stupification from the hypnotizing chants. Added embellishments to their costumes were whirly-gig discs attached that spun around in an array of color every time they jumped up and down, which they did often in erratic hop-skips. Feathers stuck out in all directions from their chicken heads and it was peculiar to watch grown men prancing around the circle in agitated steps. After they were mesmerized by the combination of betel nuts and chants, they fearlessly jumped through the fire, scattering burning embers hither and yon. The fire attendants swept the embers back to the center of the fire with palm fronds and added more to keep the fire ablaze.

Some of the men entered with their own boa constrictors. Some of the snakes were so long that it took an extra man to support the reptile's tail! One snake escaped and all of us hiked up our skirts and trousers, for we could see only what the fire outlined in the dark of the night.

After all of the supporting characters were introduced, including the medicine man who came in with panels of ribbons tied to his arms to simulate the snake, the boy entered. The only difference in his costume from the others was the stately bird of paradise tail that sprouted from his chicken head. It is illegal for any but a native Papua New Guinean to possess feathers from this magnificent creation of nature. Now that the star was introduced, the dancing intensified. Men left the arena for betel nut reinforcement and returned with added vim. Like a bunch of slap-happy drunks, the men danced around and in the fire that was kept blazing by the fire attendants. We lost interest after all of the characters had been introduced, and we were on the first busload back to Rabaul. What did interest us was the fact that rituals are very much a part of the life of the native. Although headhunting is illegal, it is still practiced in parts of the Highlands of the main island of New Guinea. All the missionaries in the world can not stamp out all long-standing customs.

Europeans have colonized this East New Britain Province of Papua New Guinea since 1761, when Philip Carteret sailed through the channel separating New Britain and New Ireland and named it after King George. Despite the legacies of all of the different immigrants, including the loved Samoan Queen Emma, the native people cling to their own ways. Queen Emma started a large plantation on New Britain in 1878.

The Japanese created an elaborate system of tunnels and bunkers when they chose the Rabaul area as their headquarters for the Southwest Pacific Operations during World War II. Some of the tunnels are open to the public as museums. It was a strange feeling to walk down the same narrow hallways that Admiral Yamamoto did when he controlled all naval operations from the Rabaul bunkers.

Unseasonal Weather

It was midnight when the winds began to howl and awaken the fleet of sailors. A very sudden and violent weather system brought all of us back to the awareness that we were of the sea and not the land. A large blue motorsailer, belonging to a local expatriate who was not living aboard, broke from her mooring and dragged down on the reef astern of us. "*Dulcinea* is maneuvering," I cried to Don as I peered out into the darkness and saw the whipped waters of the bay and the sailboat from Australia turned sideways against the intensifying wind.

"She dragged her anchor," Don said as he quickly put on his foul weather suit to check our own anchoring gear. "There's another boat milling around," he called down to me when he got topsides. "You'd better get your foul weather gear on. We could be in for some trouble if any of these boats come down on us," he warned.

"There goes *Intermezzo*," I shouted as I could see the blue ketch dragging past us. "Is Skip on deck?" I asked.

"Not yet, but he soon will be," Don answered.

The wind was not just a sudden squall. It continued to increase and rain spat at us like sharp piercing bullets of water. Sleep was not easy, and at two o'clock we felt a blow to *Svea's* bow. Don raced to the foredeck. It's *Dreamtime*! She's come down on us," Don shouted back to me as I was running and struggling to get my boots on. "Their dinghy is wedged between *Svea* and our anchor chain."

The Australian captain was quite unaware that his dinghy was securely hooked around *Svea's* anchor chain. He poured more r.p.m.s to his engine to pull away from us, but *Svea* kept being towed along. The more power he used, the tighter the wedge became. Our cries to him were of no avail. Finally his crew member sorted out the problem and quickly cut the dinghy's painter from their stern cleat. *Svea* then fell back on her own hook and stopped abruptly.

"Don, is our anchor going to hold? Did it get dislodged? Are we all right?" I asked in staccato-like sentences.

"I think so and we're all right, except for a gouge in our newly-painted topsides where the outboard clobbered the bow," Don answered. I sighed, for it had been such a laborious task to sand and paint *Svea's* topsides, working from the dinghy in busy Rabaul Harbor with active dinghy traffic. Don climbed down in the dinghy and with great difficulty hoisted the outboard on *Svea's* deck for *Dreamtime's* inflatable dinghy had been damaged and air was fast escaping. It was in grave danger of sinking and Don wanted to save the small engine.

The wind continued to increase. I battened down all loose gear on deck, took down all awnings and secured sail covers. What was happening? We were in the belt where storms were not supposed to occur. We later blamed the unseasonable weather on the official change to the northwest monsoons. It lasted two days, similar to the month of March coming in like a lion back home.

By morning, the tempest was still raging and a local broadcast reported winds in excess of 35 knots. A small island freighter came to the aid of the stranded motorsailer, only to become another victim of the reef. Another yacht, not learning by the freighter's abortive mission, tried to save the motorsailer. He failed in his attempt as well, but did mange to anchor just a few feet from the reef to give it another go when the winds subsided. Foolishly, he left his vessel to go ashore with his inflatable dinghy. While he was gone, his boat dragged down on the reef. We now have three boats on the reef. It was almost like watching the first tin soldier of a row fall down and tumbling the rest of the rank and file with him. A tug came to the rescue and pulled all but the original motorsailer off the reef. The crowd of cruising sailors cheered from the cockpits of their boats.

When the wind finally abated enough so we could get to shore, we found the beaches and docks littered with stacks of pumice that had washed up with the extra high tides during the storm. The high winds had really piled the waters of the bay up on one side. The sight of the ashen cinders only increased our apprehension about the question of what strange things the volcanoes under our boats were doing.

Getting Away

Most of the yachts were delayed in Rabaul waiting for their passports to be returned from Port Moresby. One by one, as their visas were processed, boats departed the harbor. Al and Beth on *Sunflower* had left the harbor before the storm. We had been anxious about them as they had sailed north towards the island of Kavieng, where winds had been reported at 70 knots.

Rigadoon was next to leave. Carl plotted his course to Madang with a dogleg towards Kavieng and a planned rendezvous with *Sunflower*, who had survived the strong winds. Gaining their northing, both boats would then head westerly for Papua New Guinea's main island. Carl and Al doubted the strength of the dying southeasterlies and counted on the strength of the newly-born northwesterly monsoons. We doubted the presence of any wind and resigned ourselves to a 400-mile motoring trip to Madang. *Intermezzo* planned to stay in Rabaul. *Wind'son* was off again on another long side trip to Guam, a mere distance of 1,200 miles out of the way! Jim could not resist the temptation to stop at Truk to dive on the many war relics in those waters.

Passage to Madang

Favorable southeasterlies were teasing us when we received our visas and started out. After we had raised all of the working sails in jubilation of wind, all that work was rendered useless by no wind. The heat in the cabin soared to a new high of 102 degrees. We suffered every droning beat of the engine, for we knew it was constantly stoking the inferno below. Watches were set at two hours off and two hours on. I welcomed mine, for

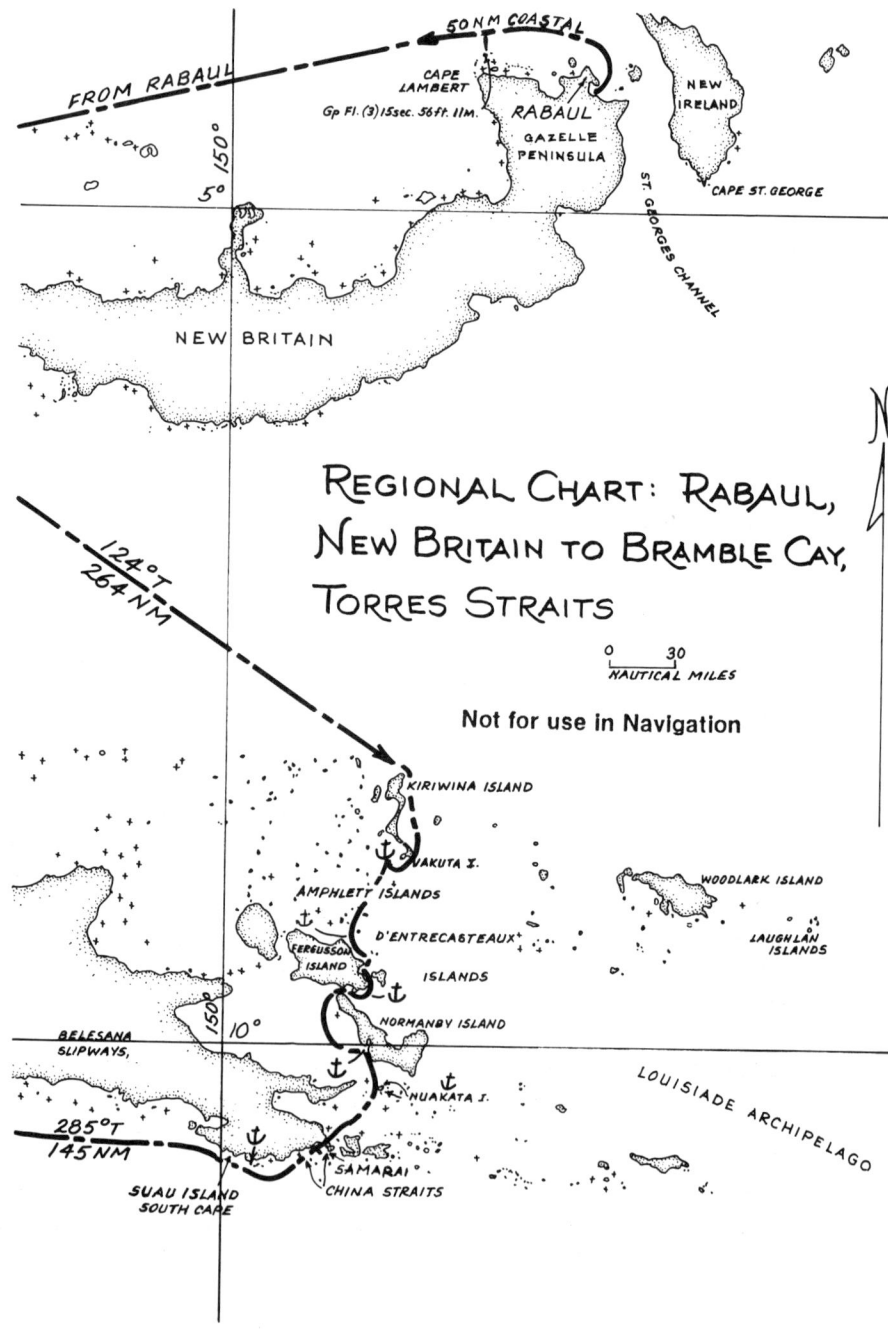

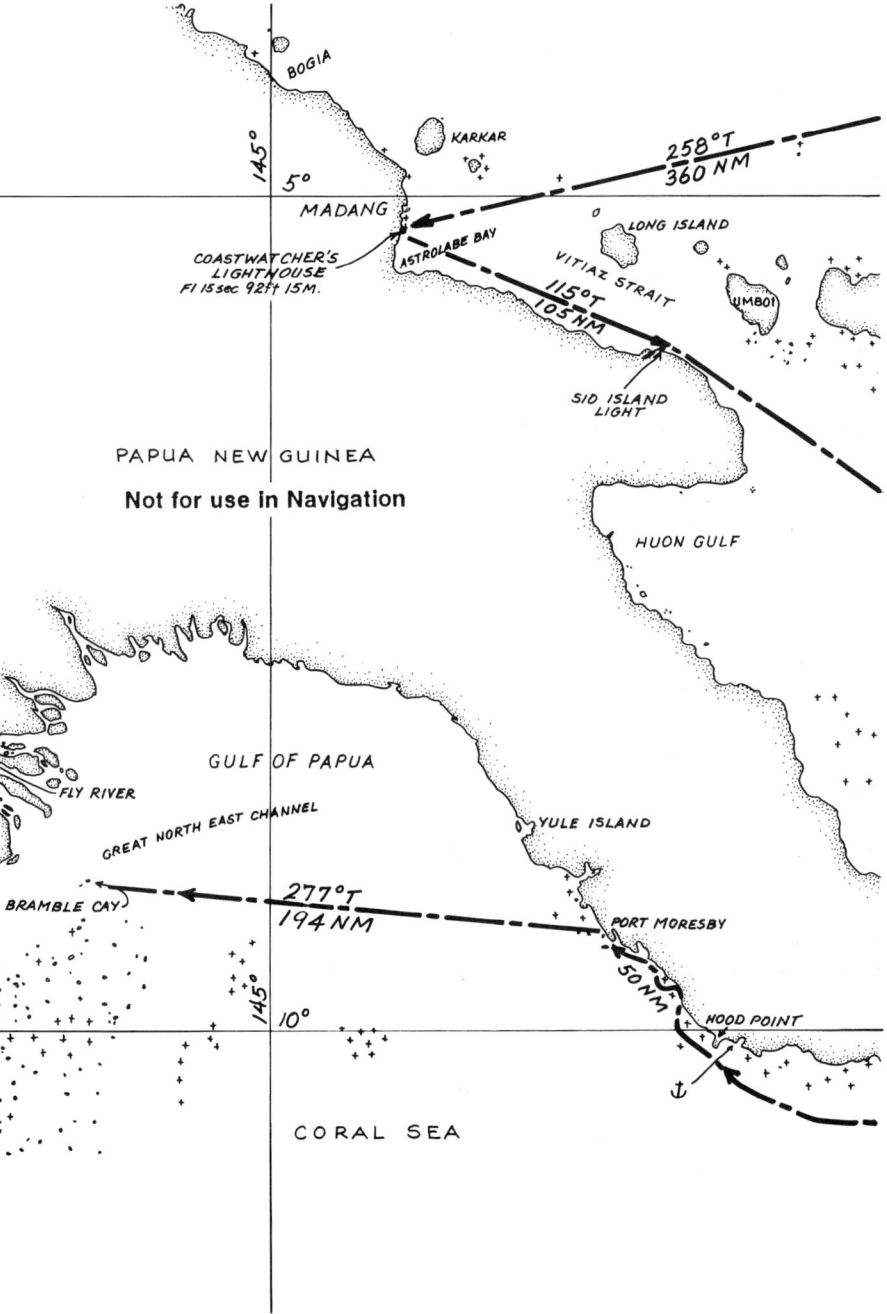

the nighttime offered some relief from the sun that baked the cockpit during the day.

One night while gazing at the sky from the cockpit and collecting my thoughts as I usually do at the end of a day, I saw three falling stars off to starboard. They were followed by a meteor, which paused midway and exploded into a million firey bits that fell into the sea. The strange phenomenon left a trail of smoke drifting aimlessly in the windless sky.

At dawn, a misty rain fell and left in its wake a grey haze. Everything was grey. The sea and sky became one. We could have been sailing up a hill or down into a trough, for there was no horizon to separate up from down. The haze just hung suspended, for there was not a hint of a breeze to chase it away. We powered upon a calm sea into the grey matter. Only the compass gave us direction. By nightfall the grey matter was still there, and there were no stars to tell us where the heavens were. The monotonous drone of the engine hypnotized us into a state of lethargy. Don fell into a drugged sleep just after dinner, and as usual, I took the first watch. I was glad to sit out in the cockpit as cooking dinner had added more heat to the smouldering cabin.

Thunder rumbled on the distant horizon and streaks of lightning slashed through the grey matter. The sky was balling up into dark grey rolls of clouds. I could not believe there was no wind to herald their arrival, but they just rolled over us and, like dump trucks, deposited their heavy loads onto *Svea's* decks. More thunder and more lightning, nature's show was stupendous and Don slept through every act. I crouched in the cockpit to gain some protection from the seats. I did not want to drag soggy foul weather gear down below so many times, for now we were drawing too close to land. Heavy freighter traffic would not allow staying off guard for longer than 10 minutes at a time. I scanned the horizons for any signs of shipping or lights from shore, but nothing except streaks of lightning appeared through the darkness.

Towards midnight on Don's watch, the bright light of Coastwatcher's Memorial Lighthouse at Madang flashed its signal through the mist. With the light in sight, we shut off the engine and turned into our bunks. Every time we peeked through the companionway hatch to look around for traffic, the light blinked a friendly greeting to let us know where we were. Tomorrow would be another day and another beginning. Days are never the same and the anticipation is always exciting.

CHAPTER 7

MADANG, PAPUA NEW GUINEA

Taking Stock

At dawn, we were underway for the rise of land we could see on the horizon. Two hours later, we were in Madang's wide entrance channel. Once inside, waterways go in different directions like fingers from a hand. We did not have to worry about which avenue to follow, for coming up on our bow was *Rigadoon*'s dinghy. Soon Carl and Jeanne Moesly were aboard piloting us to the anchorage. Knowing we were going to be in one place for a length of time was a good feeling. The push to gain miles was relaxed until the end of the cyclone season. Now it was the time to get the chores done that we can not do at sea or in overnight anchorages.

Behind us were not only the miles, but also the best part of the whole voyage, the South Pacific, where islands are many and people friendly and happy. We had shared their joy of life, but now looming before us were long and dangerous passages. Long distances would separate islands and continents. Winds were guaranteed to be stronger and seas would be rougher. Now was the time to separate the men from the boys, for the sailing from here on would be up to the man and not the boat, which was only a vehicle. The boat had to be made ready to withstand the rigors of the Indian Ocean, the unpredictable body of water that could be docile one moment and raging the next. It took more than an idling dreaming sailor to contend with the whims of the Indian Ocean.

Our last stop for rest and relaxation, routines and repairs, had been New Zealand, less than 4,000 miles astern. Ahead lay a distance of over 9,000 miles before we expected to reach our next layover in South Africa, more than twice the distance in the same length of time.

Holiday Time

Passagemaking was almost four months away. Now it was less than a week before Christmas, the time for joy and merriment. We were 14,000 miles from home in an easterly direction, and 17,000 in a westerly direction, but this made no difference to our traditional Christmas festivities. Lacking colored lights, boughs of holly and carols sung by the fire, we launched into the spirit of the holiday season. The cruising women got busy in their galleys to turn out cookies and cakes to exchange. One of them found out that her favorite Christmas fondant would not set in the high humidity of one of the hottest months of southern hemisphere's summer. My sugar cookies of Santas and reindeer seemed out of place for the setting, but brought a tinge of nostalgia to all of us who remembered Christmases past. A hospitable Australian expatriate opened his bayside home to the cruising sailors. While a roasting pig turned on an open spit, all of us enjoyed one of the merriest Christmases we ever had.

New Year's Eve found most of us celebrating on board Didi and Emroy's *Arion III*. When the natives on shore heard us banging on pots and pans and blowing our ship's horns, they took up the chorus banging sticks on empty oil drums lined up on the landing.

After the celebrations were over, we settled into serious efforts to get at our work lists. The dinghy landing in town became the focal point where the yachties exchanged notes about where to get parts, where to take a metal piece to get it welded, or where to get rigging repaired. If the part was not locally available, perhaps another sailor could supply the needed item.

Madang

Madang is not a very large town, although it is an important center for shipping and is the seat for the large province of Madang. This encompasses the coast of the northern half of Papua New Guinea and parts of the interior. There are three large department stores in the small town, a Burns-Philp, Steamships, and Carpenter's. Many domestic products and foreign imports filter through Madang before they reach their ultimate destinations in the interior.

We welcomed the access to supplies, including limited marine items, but we had to send to the States for a replacement part to the hydraulic starter. Our one consolation was in knowing we were not alone in our repair tasks. Al and Beth tried a do-it-yourself boatyard to haul out *Sunflower*. The job had to be aborted when the cutter's cradle got stuck on the railway and very nearly was stranded like the tuna boats in Pago Pago. Emory had a constant task in trying to keep his two Seagull outboards running. Like a one-person dog, they ran only for him and not poor Didi who, out of necessity, became a very accomplished rower for their inflatable dinghy. Another yachtie had his engine dismantled and was waiting for parts while another pulled his engine out by using a dockside crane. One other sailor was not so lucky with his repairs, for the more rotted timber he pulled from his yacht, the more decay he found. He was fighting an almost losing battle, and was not able to leave with the fleet in April.

Still, there were those who had a few chores and left their yachts in care of boatsitters while they traveled inland like ordinary tourists to enjoy the primitive sights and tribal rites. Vivid tales about the Asaro mud men in the Highlands and the topless grass-skirted maidens filtered through our group. We almost felt as if we had been there ourselves from the descriptive travelogues.

Madang lacked a yacht club offering services like the one at Rabaul. We missed the cold beers and hot showers. Instead, we walked to a seaside inn for our beers and took baths in the cockpits of our boats. Rains were frequent enough in that rain forest tropical setting. We caught fresh water in our canvas raincatcher.

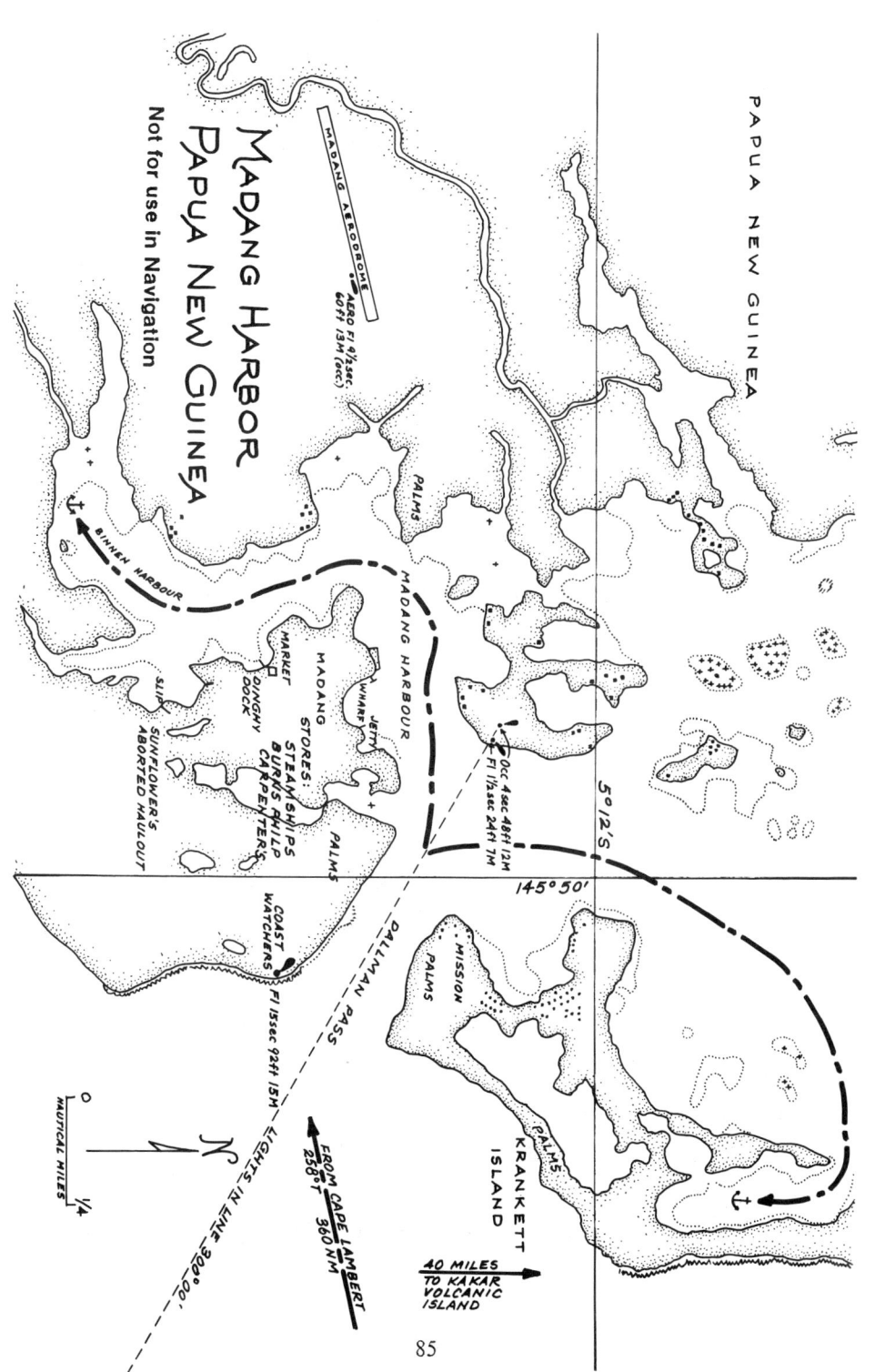

In Papua New Guinea, men as well as the women wear the familiar wrap-around lava-lavas, the fathoms of cloth tied about the waist, but now they are called "lap-laps." In fact, the businessman of New Guinea has tailored grey serge lap-laps with tabs at the waistline to hold his masculine leather belt. He also wears white shirts and ties, and carries an attache case to signify his status as a business man. A man would often complete his stern business attire with the flippant use of a bird of paradise tail stuck into his frizzy-cropped hair. The women's show of adornment was permanent, the intricate tatoos inscribed upon her face in lieu of jewelry. We are asked to call the natives "nationals," as the former title has a primitive connotation and we must be reminded that Papua New Guinea is an independent nation.

The Market

Madang's marketplace offered the usual array of fruits and vegetables, but not in the proliferation as Rabaul's market. Saturday mornings were the busiest selling days. You could buy live birds and cuscus, the small rodent-like marsupials that inhabit trees. They are known to be good pets, but the nationals use their soft fur to decorate their many pieces of art and their tribal costumes. The meat is used as food, for the country lacks a good source of animal protein. Nothing is wasted in a land where everything that grows locally takes precedence over highly-expensive imported tinned foods. The cuscus are nocturnal creatures and those we saw were rolled into tiny balls of fur within their makeshift wire cages.

There was no point in wasting pity on the roasted inert bodies of the flying foxes, but I couldn't help but think about the throngs of them that daily make their trips back and forth over the anchorage. During the day, they slept on the many islands in the harbor. At dusk, they would fly to the mainland and gorge on the bountiful supply of mangoes during the night.

One Saturday, Jeanne and I went to the market together, but she went one way while I the other. The previous Saturday she had purchased a beautiful small parrot they named "Lik-Lik," which means little in Pidgin English. As she came around the snake bean vendor's stall, I saw that she had a brown paper bag in her hand. I thought that strange, for you can't get bags in the market. You must carry your purchases in your own carryalls, or bilums. The nationals carry hand-woven mesh bags that stretch with the size of their contents.

"What's in the bag, Jeanne?" I asked, but knew without looking that inside was a bird of some nature.

"It's a present for Donald," she laughed and opened the small bag to show me the tiny turquoise kingfisher she had purchased for one kina, the equivalent of one and a half dollars.

"Wha-a-ck! Wha-a-ck!" That huge sound could not possibly be coming from that tiny bird, but it was. The poor feathered creature was most unhappy about his entrapment.

"Jeanne, you know that little bird is not at all happy. If he continues with those horrible sounds, Don will not welcome him aboard as a crew member," I said.

"You know he'll end up in someone's stewpot if I take him back," Jeanne warned me.

"I know, but..." I answered and the bird went back to the black woman who had captured him. Papua New Guinea has 26 species of kingfishers, the richest collection in the world.

Another day in the market, I heard a wailing cry, but this time the origin was not from a bird, but from a small baby who had managed to fall down to the bottom of his mother's bilum bag. He was most unhappy about sharing his cradle with snake beans, yams and avocados. The mother carried the bag with its woven string handles across her forehead. Her produce and the baby bounced along on her backsides. Papua New Guinea women tote vast loads like this with the bags strapped across their foreheads, rather than on top of their shoulders like most load carriers. My own neck hurt just looking at the strain that they bear.

When the world was created, and it was time to send down the birds, I am convinced that the packing crates containing the exotic birds, destined for other parts of the world, ruptured and cast their contents over Papua New Guinea. This large island is rich in magnificent feathered creatures. Gorgeous parrots were almost as common flying over the anchorage as mockingbirds in Florida. Cockatoos were numerous and humorous, and kingfishers prolific and proficient. Crows added to the circus of clowns. Their cackles and caws appeared to hawk the events of the carnival's side shows. Nature's creatures were anything but recluses or introverts, for they let the world know their being.

Karkar Island's Volcano

To add to the exciting entertainment, the still-active volcano on offshore Karkar Island belched out frequent displays of fireworks. It was being studied carefully by vulcanologists who felt that if lava flows did occur, they would be confined by the walls of the caldera. However, one day there was cause enough to alert the natives living on the island to be ready to evacuate their villages. That warning did not materialize, but later on two vulcanologists were killed instantly when a chance fireball struck them down as they examined the volcano.

Jellyfish

Another sad accident occurred to one of the Australian expatriates living in Madang. On weekends, she and her husband in their power boat often joined the local and foreign yachts to swim around the beautiful waters surrounding Krankett Island, across from the harbor. This woman swam into sea wasps and very nearly lost her life when she accidently, with a swimming stroke, scooped them up around her face and shoulders. Then she was unable to free herself from their poisonous stings. She lay close to death in the hospital, but by the time we were leaving Madang she had recovered, except for a lingering paralysis in facial nerves. Sea wasps are not common insects that fly through the air, but are actually square jellyfish that swim in pulsating motions under the surface of the water. There are two varieties of sea wasps. Those that frequent the northern waters of Australia and parts of the Indian Ocean are extremely dangerous. When I saw them in the cove at Krankett Island, I thought they resembled yellowish, box-type iridescent blobs in a weird free-form state of suspension, much like an experiment in chemistry class.

The Salins

A lovely national family living on shore behind *Svea* became our friends during the time we stayed in their harbor. There were seven children. The oldest boy, Jack, and his sister Jane, often paddled their beat-up aluminum dinghy around the anchorage. They stopped by *Svea*, but only if we invited them. The children were polite and would always pause at a discreet distance. It was difficult to stay ahead of their many bountiful gifts, for the children loved to give freely. Their mother made a special necklace for me, and Jane made a bilum for me using polypropylene fishing line in the colors of their national flag.

It was number two boy who spotted Don when he slipped on a loose rock while carrying our jerry jugs that he had just filled from the water tank next to a warehouse on shore. The small boy returned home to tell the news to his family, and Jack immediately paddled his dinghy over to *Svea*, "We are very sorry to hear about your accident, Don. My father insists that you come to our house and take water from our tank."

Well, the day came when Don went to the Salin's dock to fill our jugs. We could have given them the world, they were so thrilled to be helping the American. All little hands, down to the two year-old, lined up in the bucket brigade, for Jack had organized the team. I still keep in touch with this lovely family, who educates their children in Catholic schools.

The three oldest children helped us to prepare *Svea* for sea the night before our departure. They untied the lines to the sun awnings, and we folded them carefully and put them in their cockpit lockers. Together we gathered up the clutter of jugs and paraphernalia that seems to accumulate on deck when harbor bound, and stowed them.

Planning Departure

Northwest winds were on the ebb, and southeast trades were just coming in. We still needed the northwest winds to make our way down the eastern coastline of New Guinea towards Port Moresby. At Port Moresby, we would leave our cocoons behind in the tranquil belt around the Equator and, like butterflies, sail off to seek the trade winds farther south. Those are the winds the sailors need for passagemaking. The southern tip of New Guinea introduces us to the Arafura Sea, which then takes us down to Australia and the beginning of the Indian Ocean, where we had more wind at times than we needed.

Rigadoon had already left for the northern shores of New Guinea. Carl and Jeanne were planning to cruise Indonesia. Their first circumnavigation had taken them the southern route that we were planning. Rather than repeat their old tracks, they wanted to sail in Indonesian waters. Then they planned to cross the top end of the Indian Ocean and south through the Chagos Archipelago to the island of Mauritius. *Arion III* was planning the same route across the top end of Indonesia, but they would carry on for the Mediterranean. *Sunflower* was already on her way to Samarai to see if she could be hauled on the railways at Belesana Slipways. *Sunflower* was to be the guinea pig for those of us who had not been able to haul our boats in Madang, and needed to do so.

Just before the general exodus of cruising boats from Madang began, Jim and Cheryl sailed into the harbor from Guam and their last stop at the Hermit Islands. They had enough crayfish in *Windson*'s freezer to bestow the fruits of their labors upon the harbor-bound fleet. *Intermezzo* sailed in from Rabaul where Skip had a bout with dengue fever that had given them some troublesome moments. All of us were taking anti-malaria pills once a week to suppress an attack of an anopheles mosquito. However there is no preventive medicine for dengue, only the safeguard of screens to keep them out.

There will be another episode when Skip tangles with a mosquito. He blames it on his stop at the Belesana Boatyard at Samarai at the east end of the big island of Papua New Guinea. Most of the fleet paused there to haul their boats on their travels south.

Flying foxes, Papua New Guinea

CHAPTER 8

TROBRIAND ISLANDS, CHINA STRAITS, AND SAMARAI

Leaving Madang was no different from arriving. There had been no wind coming, and now there was no wind going. *Svea* powered through slick calm water. Most of the cruising sailors who were heading south towards the capital city of Port Moresby, planned to motor along the coastline. Port Moresby is the jumping-off place for the passage through the Torres Straits and stronger winds. It was rather like a legion of soldiers marching south to do battle with the enemy. All of us knew we would be confronting stronger winds and longer passages. It had all been written down in books, and we had studied our manuals.

Don and I were lured to take another route to Port Moresby, one that would take us through Papua New Guinea's out-lying islands. The stories about free love given by the maidens in the Trobriands was bait enough for Don, who will never turn away anything free. Also by going east rather than due south, we would have a better angle to use the southeast winds if they came in to chase the convergence zone weather away. Our path should join the other cruisng sailors when we reached Samarai. By then, our guinea pig *Sunflower* should know about the haul-out facilities at Belesana Slipways.

Trobriand Islands

With no wind at all, the heat was abominable. Floating islands broken from land moved aimlessly with whichever currents were in command. It was a strange sight to see a detached hunk of land supporting large fallen trees with formidable limbs and roots sticking out in all directions right in the middle of nowhere. At least it looked like it was out of nowhere for a thick haze blotted out the mainland. Our course was set for the island of Kiriwina at the top end of the Trobriands. As the weather willed it, heavy rain squalls arrived the same time as we did at dawn of the next day. We were forced to change plans and abort the idea of taking the channel that runs between the group of islands. Instead, we ended up having to go 30 miles on the eastern weather side of the Trobriands before we could turn inward and find a lee from the persistent squalls. The squalls made it dangerous to close with reef-fringed isles.

"Don, can we make it over that ridge of coral?" I asked anxiously. I had gone below to check the chart and thought the water looked very skinny over the shallow break in the reefs that continued southwestward from the island of Vakuta. Skies were overcast and, to me, the idea of crossing doubtful patches of reefs in poor light was far from appealing.

"Yes, I do, or we wouldn't by trying it," Don said rather curtly. "We could go clear around that reef, but then it would be nighttime," he added. "Just pay attention to me, and we'll get over that bar."

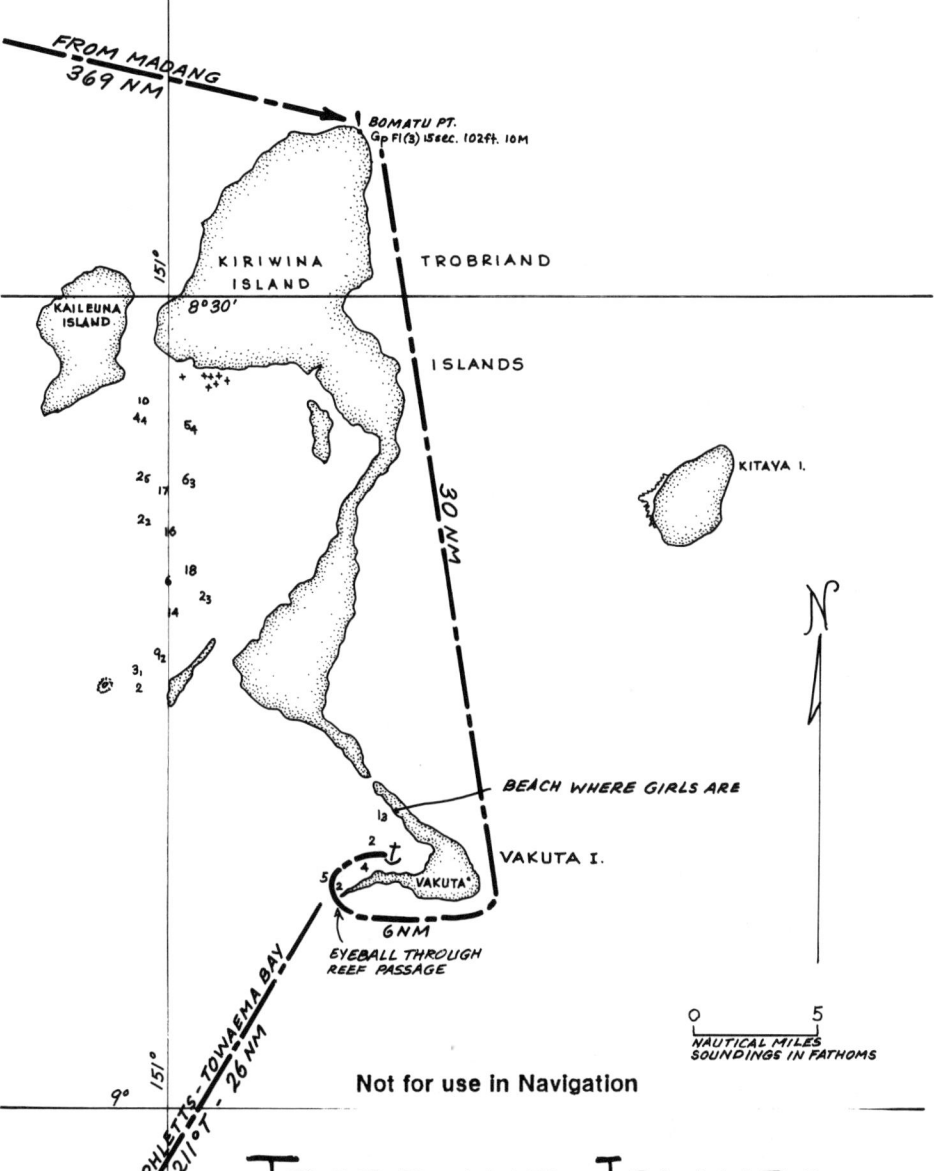

"If you say so, dear," I let go with my pat answer.

Vakuta Island, Trobriands

As it worked out, we skimmed across the bar and *Svea*'s keel never touched, but my heart was in my throat when I looked over the side to see yellow water underneath us. We rounded the southwestern tip of Vakuta Island and came up in the western bight of the sickle-shaped island. There was no doubt that *Svea*'s anchor would hold in the sandy bottom. We relaxed the tension that had tied us in knots. After months being harbor-bound, we had grown soft. We needed to toughen up, if we were to be in condition for the passages ahead.

The squalls continued. Never one to miss an opportunity to do laundry, I used the bountiful supply of water coming from the heavens. *Svea*'s lifelines and rigging were festooned with clothes and towels. In another day, when the rains stopped and the clouds came out like puffs of cotton across a field of blue, the natives came out from holes in the dense mangroves to start their day of fishing. Seeing an American yacht in their bay waters was a most unusual sight and one by one they paddled near to wave a welcome.

Two young men came alongside and introduced themselves as Moses Thomas and Elijah Moses. We knew the boys were eager to come on board, so with our invitation they swung their legs over the lifelines and joined us in the cockpit. Elijah was the spokesman and began to tell us about a New Zealand cruising sailor who had anchored in their bay and they became great friends. Elijah and Moses had learned English in their village school and they invited us to pay them a visit. World War II had reached even into the Trobriands, and Elijah repeated the tale told him by his father.

The boy began, "The skies overhead were thick with airplanes, Japanese and American," Elijah waved his hand across the skies as if to paint a picture of doom. The boy's eyes grew bigger as the tale ensued, "They were diving on one another and the Japanese were dropping bombs on our village. An American G.I. with his mission gun shot one of the bombs in mid-air and then down came the Japanese planes." The story continued to grow as it has through the years, but I'll bet it was a Texan who originated the tall tale. I must explain that the mission gun was, of course, a machine gun, although the former word does sound better.

It was not easy finding the boys' village in our dinghy. Each opening into the mangroves seemed to bring us into winding channels leading us around islands to dead ends or back to our point of origin. One mangrove bush looks just like any other. We were going in circles when we saw a canoe break through the bushes and we hailed it to ask for help. Giggling, like young girls always seem to do, the two teenagers managed between their shy chuckles to lead us into the main channel that gained the small bay.

Native craft lined the muddy shoreline of the only high ground around.

For the first time, we saw big war canoes that were ornately painted in vivid reds, yellows, blacks and whites. Their high gunwhales were trimmed with rows of white egg cowrie shells. Something else was different than other native canoes we had seen, and that was the very practical addition of seats and a raised shelf at the prows of the always leaking dugouts. The paddlers could keep themselves, as well as their produce, out of the water. Where the Solomon Islanders used half-coconut shells for bailers, these natives used bailer seashells. Now, as we draw closer to Australia, this huge shell is more commonly found. Besides the decorations of paint and cowrie shells, the canoes had raised prows that were carved to look like crocodiles. Sometimes the ends were made to look like the tails of the water-borne reptiles.

Small children gathered at the landing to help us beach *Poco*, but one older woman paused in her ascent of the embankment, gazed at us, then scurried off up the hill. Clothed only in a grass skirt, called "ass grass," the old woman kept looking back over her shoulder to see if we were after her. The children, the innocents, knew little of anxiety. Soon we were like the Pied Pipers with a line of children strung behind us. One little fellow, with a stick full of freshly caught fish flung over his shoulder, led us around the village. At each hut a new child came out to join the procession. "One of these little people should have a fife and drum," I laughed to Don, who in his humble way, was actually enjoying the role of a celebrity. We marched in and out of the well-trodden paths and dodged the many chickens, pigs, cats and dogs that used the routes as well.

The humble living quarters were in direct contrast to the ornately decorated sheds that held the supply of yams. We later learned that the natives consider their yams more than just food. They stand as a symbol for fertility, and each year they have festivals to commemorate their crops. By the numbers of children in that one village, I would say they had bountiful harvests.

We left the village of Vakuta to find the legendary spot near the north end of the island, where the women bestow their pulchritudes upon the men who come into their waters. As we drew closer to the beach, we could hear the whoops and hollers coming from the girls lining the shoreline. "Perhaps there is more to this than just a fairy tale," I laughed at Don. "I think I'd best go along to protect your virtue."

Like taking a sandwich to a banquet, Don took me along in *Poco* because I had promised to stay at a discreet distance and look only for shells. The girls quickly grabbed the dinghy's gunwhales as we approached the shoreline, but I stopped them from taking her up onto the beach. "We'll anchor the dinghy here. I'm going to look for seashells," I said.

The girls understood enough English to know what I meant, and immediately put their ardors into helping me look for shells. "I think they've forgotten what they're famous for," I chuckled to Don. Prematurely excited about seeing the maidens remove their blouses, he forgot all about free-love when the girls dunked themselves in the water and started picking lice from one another's frizzy black hair. He started looking for shells. End of that story.

Passage to Amphlett Group

The rains continued and what little wind there was kept switching directions. The convergence zone was still upon us as we departed the Trobriands and headed for the Amphlett Islands. These islands are noted for their pottery. The clay they use is brought from the nearby island of Fergusson.

Wamea Bay

As we approached Wamea Bay, we knew from the chart we would have difficulty finding shallow water for the anchor. The problem seemed less when two men in their dugout came alongside to welcome us. As all natives are prone to do, they led us near their village where we would be closer to the pottery vendors. It was much too deep to anchor so we chose another spot in 72 feet depth, still too deep for comfort. The distance we put between us and the village did not stop the sudden invasion of friendly people. One very old, topless lady in her skirt of grass was very much like a barker in a circus side show. We did purchase one of her pots, but declined the offer of another villager's pet rooster.

"It would be very difficult for me to kill and clean that chicken aboard our little boat. Take your pet back home," I told the young man, holding the rooster in his arms as one would a loved puppy.

As we left the Amphletts bound southward, we were still under the influence of the convergence zone weather. Rain was all around us and we watched as a water spout spawned from a low-hanging black cloud. The pendulous pimple grew longer as it extruded from the cloud to reach out like an arm to the sea beneath it. When the sea and the spout joined hands, water spun up in a funnel and danced crazily with whirling and twirling pirouettes in erratic directions. Fortunately, the route of the water spout fell away from *Svea*'s and we stayed on course.

Fergusson Island

As we approached the high volcanic island of Fergusson, we looked at the patches of bare red clay that blighted the otherwise verdant hillsides. Villages were in every glen and valley and atop the land-eroded plateaus where they looked as if they would topple into the sea. With difficulty we made way to the southeast end of the island, picked our way through the reefs towards Scrub Island, then took up a course bearing 243 degrees past the south end of Dobu Island where we headed north into Gomwa Bay for the night.

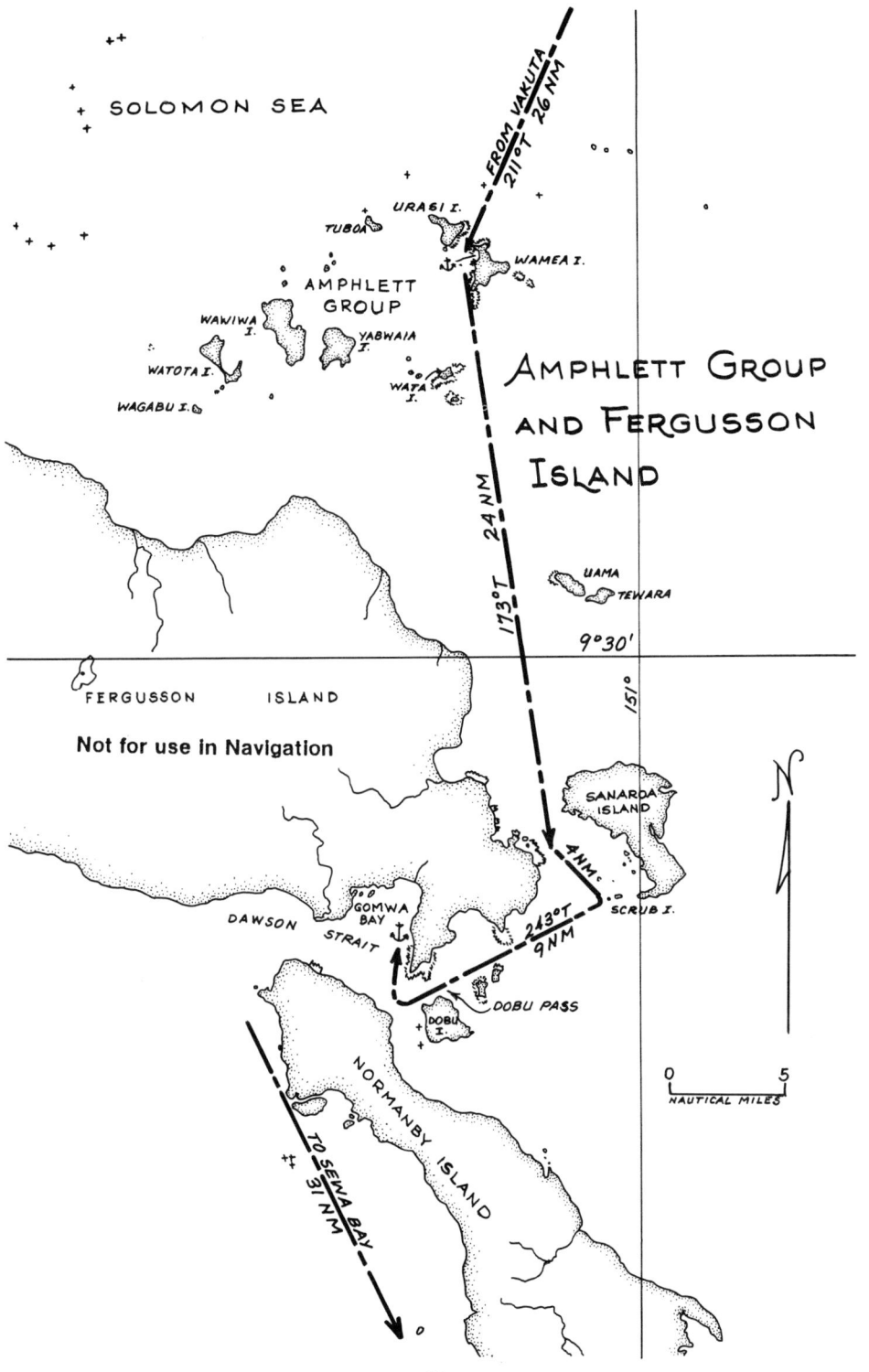

Scrub Island, Gomwa Bay

Our visitors this time were young girls in their dugouts. They brought their younger brothers and sisters as well as the shells they wanted to sell us. Then at 1800 the drums began from the villages. They continued for 15 minutes, stopped, then started anew at 1900. Fortunately they stopped for the rest of the night.

Sewa Bay, Normanby Island

In the morning when we had good light, we departed Gomwa Bay and headed south again along the western side of Normanby Island. Since we were never in a hurry to put miles behind us and we needed good light to navigate these island-packed waters, we decided to turn into the anchorage at Sewa Bay. We learned soon to regret the choice. One man came alongside with his son at the bow of his dugout. "I want some whiskey. Have you got some whiskey for me?" he asked as his son cringed.

"No," I answered rather abruptly. Then the man asked for tobacco and I repeated my answer. I did not tell him further that we never gave away any liquor or cigarettes, that we never encourage bad habits or do anything that may harm them or their family life.

Children came around to peer into *Svea's* portholes and to hang over her low sides to gawk into the cockpit and down through the companionway. Regretfully with the heat, we closed the doors and curtained the portholes.

We were now closing with the mainland of New Guinea as we left Normanby Island. We headed south towards Nuakata Island, our last stop prior to navigating the China Straits. These straits would take us to Samarai, then across to the mainland where the Belesana Slipways was located.

Nuakata Island

All of the young and able men in the village at Nuakata were out fishing when we arrived, but the chief sent his granddaughter out to welcome us. The only canoe left on the beach was a sad derelict. As the girl came alongside and started to talk with us, we could see her chin getting closer and closer to *Svea's* cap rail. "My God, Don, do something," I shouted as I looked over the side. "Her canoe is sinking and she's going right down with it."

"Get her on deck," Don said, as calmly as he could, and we both grabbed the smiling girl's arms and pulled her over the cap rail and onto the deck. Don lowered himself into the sinking canoe. Using *Svea's* deck bucket, he started scooping out the water. I ran below for an empty plastic bottle and cut the end out of it to make a bailer for the girl for her homebound journey.

"Bail with one hand and paddle with the other," I instructed the girl who was embarrassed by causing us so much concern. The young girl knew what we had said. Like a fire boat squirting out water, the canoe

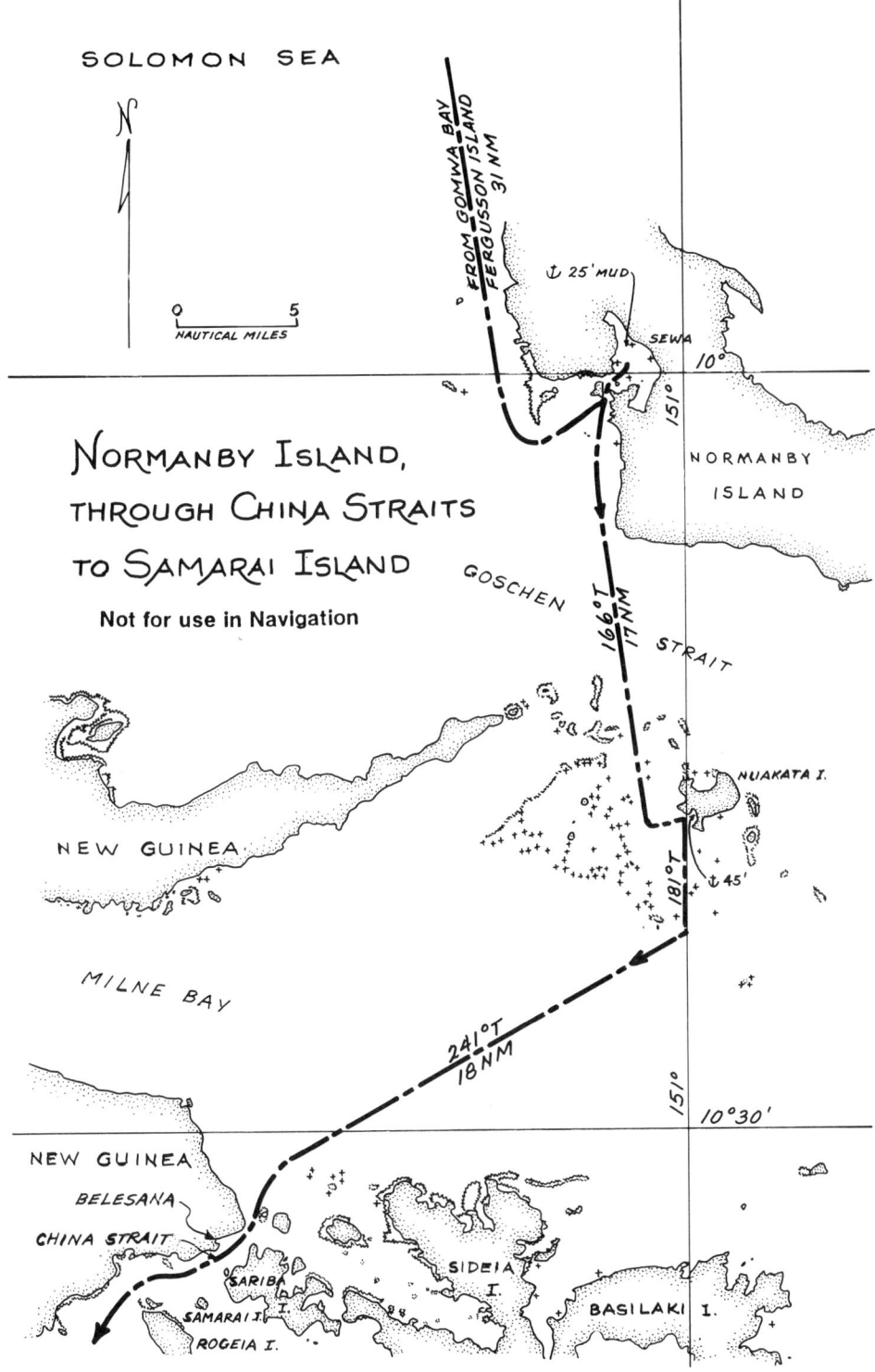

barely made it back to shallow water near shore where the villagers rescued her.

Wishey came by at dusk. He had been out fishing and admiring *Svea's* lines, and he had to paddle by to tell us so. "I'm the shipwright around these parts and I just had to come by and look at your beautiful wooden vessel." Always proud of *Svea*, we graciously thanked him and invited him on board. That turned out to be a providential encounter, for Wishey knew the local waters well. He showed us the intricate passage through the reefs and into the channel of the China Straits.

By the time he left it was really quite dark and there were no lights ashore. "Wishey," I asked with puzzle. "How come there are no lights on in your village?"

"Oh, we ran out of kerosene a few days ago and no one has come with supplies. I don't have a boat able to get over to Samarai to get any," the grey-haired man said.

"Just you wait a minute," I told the man and went below for another empty plastic bottle and filled it with *Svea's* supply of kerosene. "Here you go," I handed the man the bottle, "and thank you Wishey for marking our chart." I was still amazed that Wishey actually knew how to read a chart. Most of the natives we had met would swear they could read a chart, but as often as not, they looked at it upside-down rather than right-side-up .

After Wishey landed his canoe, we could tell his path as a lamplighter. His trail left a light in every place he stopped where he shared his gifts with his neighbors. Wishey returned later to shower us with his gifts of shells and papayas.

Passage to Samarai

China Straits and clipper ships, the two go together like salt and pepper. As we made our way across the current-ridden rough waters, the clipper ships remained only as a figment of my imagination. Some of those majestic sailing vessels had sailed on past Samarai to seek the riches of the east, while others stopped to disembark prospectors in search of gold in the nearby islands of the Woodlarks and Laughlans.

Belesana Slipways

With Samarai off the port bow, we headed instead for the mainland where the familiar masts of *Sunflower* and *Dreamtime* stood out above the treetops. Both boats were on the two ways when we anchored in the bay and launched *Poco* to go ashore. Beth and Al, were pushing sandpaper across *Sunflower's* bottom. "Hey, you guys," Beth called out. "You missed a super barbecue last night. "Had a pig on a spit."

"Is that so?" I queried.

"The managers are a young couple and really go all out to help the yachties," Beth said and Al nodded agreement.

It was a good feeling to know that cruising sailors were welcome at Belesana Slipways. The managers had run a long pipe to connect up to a mountain stream, so we could have plenty of freshwater to wash down our boats and to take showers. *Svea* didn't complain about the cold water touching her hull. That is not saying the same for me when the first blast of mountain water hit me! However, it was more than invigorating after a hot day's work in the high humidity of the tropical climate.

Early every morning, strange bird calls awakened us to a new day, but they were so well-camouflaged by their jungle environment that we could never see them. Always cloaking the mountains behind the boatyard were heavy grey mists. Never did the haze lift enough to disclose who lived within its rain forest.

Sunflower came down from the ways and *Svea* went up and up, higher than most of the boats the yard had ever handled. They were used to hauling steel work boats and *Svea*'s deep keel did not quite fit their cradles. We had to use heavy timbers to shore her. Then she was so high that I could not reach her topsides to paint them without scaffolding. "Scaffolding?" The manager looked at me with a blank face when I asked him if he had any. Don and I finally found a half-sunken houseboat with loose siding. We started carting the boards back to *Svea*, in hopes we could work out some arrangement where I could reach the topsides to paint them.

Our folly was not in getting the boards but in getting rotten ones. When I was half-way between the long plank that spanned the distance between the bow and the beam, I heard the terrifying sound of splintering wood. CR-A-A-C-K! The sound rang through the yard and I fell 7 feet to the ground.

The manager called out, "Is *Svea* all right? I heard the crack."

"She's fine, Peter, just fine," I answered from my ground floor position with little hurt but my dignity and a wrenched shoulder.

Samarai

To go to Samarai aboard the boatyard's launch was a fun trip. Don never ceased to be amazed at the sturdy reliable Gardner diesel that fired to action when Peter turned the hand crank to start it. "Chug! Chug!" The noise of the four-cylinder engine drowned out any chance of a conversation. The excitement was in the way the helmsman maneuvered the many tide rips criss-crossing the channel. The engine never missed a beat to keep the launch headed in the right direction. To stay out of the mainstream of the fast current, the pilot hugged the shoreline, so closely at times that I thought the overhanging rocks would catch on the plywood top of the launch. Once clear of the worst of the turbulence, he headed the launch across the current-ridden China Straits towards Samarai. One chance falter or missed stroke of the engine, and the boat could easily get caught in the twisting eddies, or perhaps worse yet be spit out of the channel with the speed of a bullet. There was no room for pilot error.

With only sails as their power, the captains of the clipper ships of old had to be masters at their trades. Even with power to aid us, we had great difficulty in overcoming the tumbling water in the tide rips. The ancient mariners had to be able to work the tides. They had to know where and how the currents ran through the body of water that narrowed at Samarai to squeeze between the mainland of New Guinea and its off-shore islands.

Samarai was only a legend of the past as she was reduced from a bustling prospecting town, and later a provincial seat, to a mere ghost's existence, like so many towns in western USA that died when the gold did. Past prosperity was in evidence in the decaying filigree-decorated houses and boarded-up shops, but new life was not in the making. A Burns-Philp store still served the dwindling population, but the frames of the community were rotting with time. Like Madang, Samarai had suffered heavy bombardment during World War II. The town had made a comeback from the ravages of war, but when the provincial seat was moved to Alotau on the mainland, progress went with it and left behind a ghost town.

When the work was finished and *Svea* was done-up in her new coat of paint, it was time to start the serious passagemaking. All of the cruising sailors prepared for the rough seas ahead.

Trobriand woman with a pot on her head and "ass" (grass skirt)

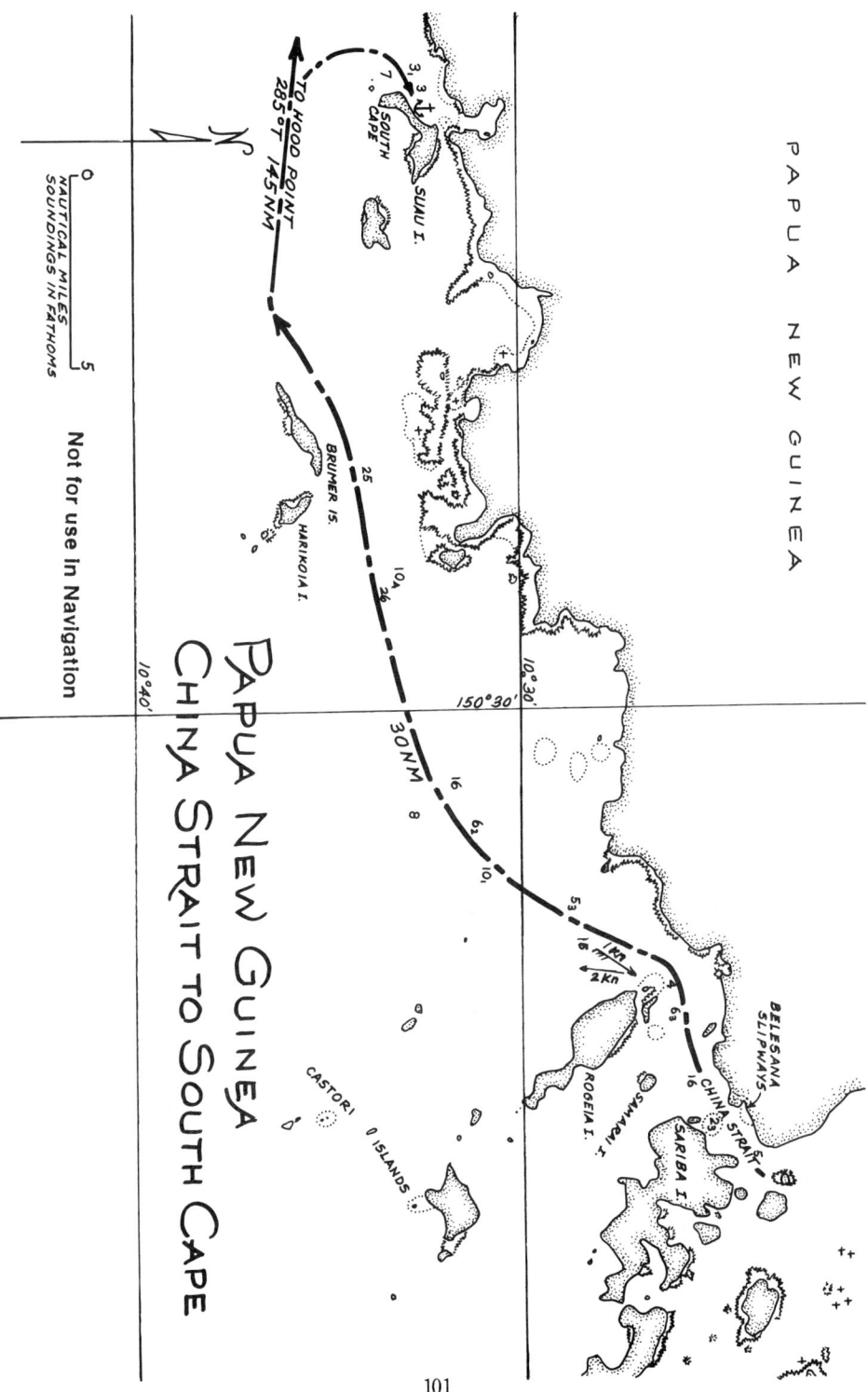

CHAPTER 9

PORT MORESBY and TORRES STRAITS

When we put *Svea* on the same course that the Belesana Slipways launch had taken across the current-riddled China Straits, some of the cruising sailors were already bound for Port Moresby. Still others were waiting their turns on the ways. Winds were a mixture of light southeast to non-existent. After rounding South Cape, the southern tip of Papua New Guinea, rather than motor all the way to Port Moresby, we stowed our sails and anchored for the night in the bight off the west shore of Suau Island.

Passage to Hood Bay and Hood Lagoon, Papua New Guinea

In the morning, the southeast trades were in so we hoisted the big blues (twin staysails) to sail the downwind course to Papua New Guinea's capital city. We were in the Coral Sea, sailing the same course as the Japanese fleet attempted in May 1942, to attack Australian-protected Port Moresby. A combined Allied fleet forced them to turn back to Rabaul. Had their mission succeeded, Port Moresby would have fallen into their hands, serving as a staging center for the threatened invasion of Australia, less than 400 miles farther south.

"What happened to the gentle trades?" we asked ourselves as the winds began to increase further. When a large black cloud appeared astern, we should have taken the big blues down, but we disregarded the adage sailors often repeat, "When you think it's time to reef, do it then." We all tend to wait until it's too late. We were scudding along briskly at 6 knots. The squall line drew closer, bringing only a little extra wind before it. But when the cloud was directly overhead, all hell broke loose. Gusts reached 30 to 35 knots and I screamed down to Don, "Hit the decks!" We immediately released the sheets to dispell as much wind as we could from the big sails which ballooned out. *Svea* sped on regardless and water poured over the catwalks and swirled back to exit off the stern.

"We've got to get them down!" Don shouted, but his words were almost inaudible above the howling wind.

"I know, I know," I cried as I grabbed for the winch handle to be ready to crank in the booms. Oh, how I hate to bring in those voluminous sails when so much wind has them packed so solidly. I wondered if we would ever again find the reliable trade winds and eliminate these Chinese fire drills everytime the wind switched direction or force.

"Are you ready?" Don shouted as he began to lower the halyard, thus giving the wind an ever bigger balloon to inflate and resist further turns on the winch.

"Yes," I gasped, "but don't give me any more sail than I can get down on a turn." I cranked and tailed, gasped, cranked and tailed the small bit

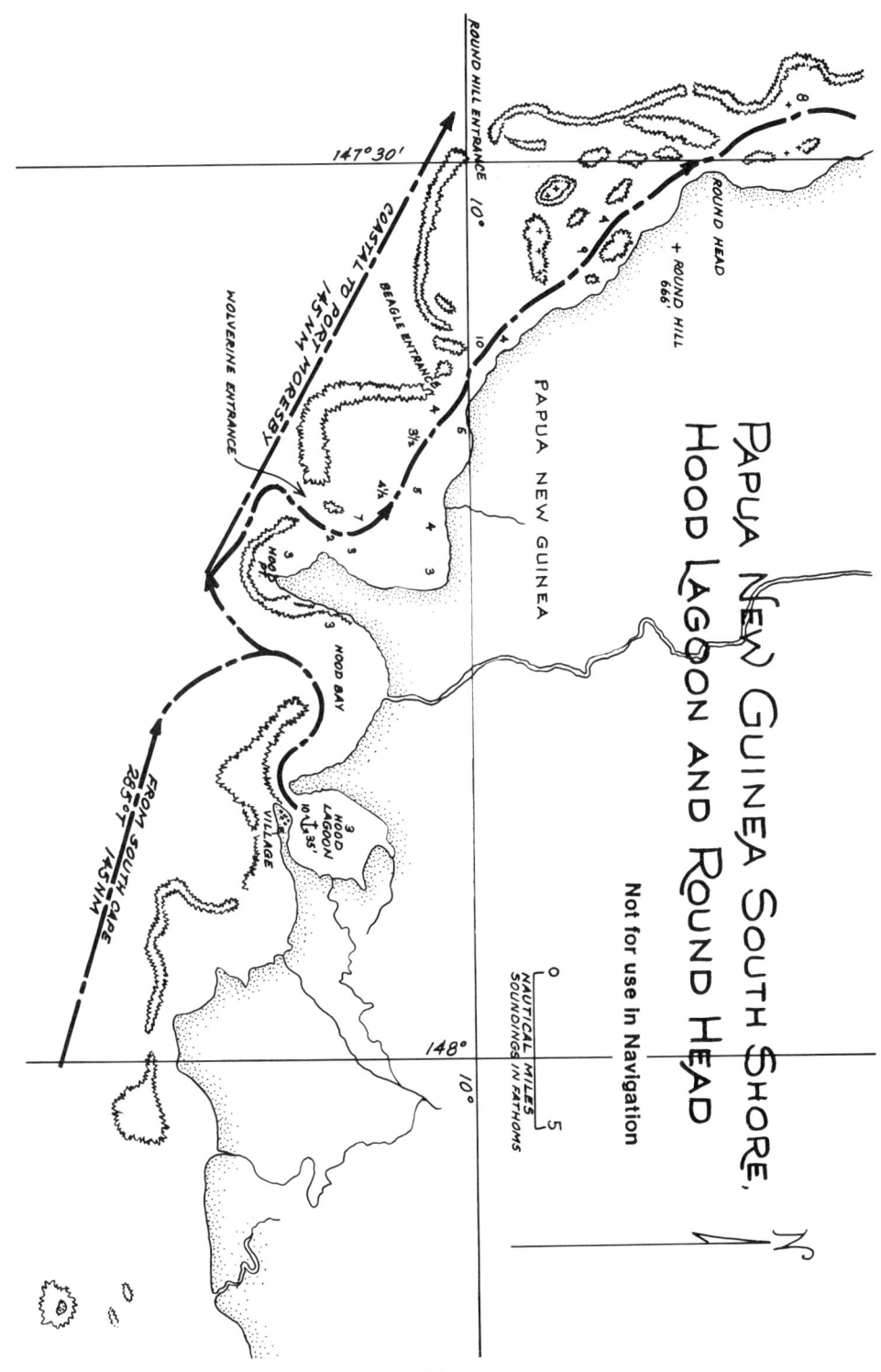

of line I had mastered to gather around the winch. Finally the sail came down and we bagged it. The other twin had to come down, and we repeated the exercise. I should have the biceps of a pugilist if I did many more of these sail changes. We bagged both sails, sodden with saltwater that had been scooped up in their bit pockets of cloth. "Take them below," Don shouted as he coiled lines and looked around.

"But, my clean carpets!" I protested. My objections were overruled. Don grabbed the dripping sail bags and took them below, leaving in his wake a trail of saltwater standing out like an angry snake on my freshly-shampooed carpets.

Don grabbed the storm twins from the forepeak and we returned to the bubbling foredeck, which looked like an overflowing storm drain, so much water was coming over the bow. Even without any raised sails, *Svea* was scudding along under bare poles. The pilot was handling the steering with no effort. We hanked on the storm twins, but I had to stop after we raised the first twin. "Wait a minute!" I shouted to Don, threw a hitch around the cleat and ran for the lee rail.

"We certainly didn't expect this kind of weather, did we Susan E.?" Don called me his pet name in trying to comfort my miserable self. All I could do was shake my head in agreement as I bent over the lifelines. We had to get the other sail up to balance the helm, for *Svea* was yawing badly in the big seas. Somehow I managed my duty, and *Svea* straightened her course, but nothing straightened my stomach. I took the first watch after a dinner of nothing for me and crackers for Don. I was glad to sit out in the cockpit for some fresh air, even though constant spray shot across me. Intermittent rain squalls only added to my distress. I went below for a few minutes to wash up with fresh water and don some dry clothes. I always felt better with a clean face and dry underwear, even though I knew it might soon be wet with seawater.

"I can't sleep anyway," Don muttered from his bunk. "Get on your back and I'll continue the watch." He knew how utterly miserable I was, but I realized that he did not feel so well himself. I appreciated his offer to relieve me even more. We were both below when the crash of the outboard pole slammed against the rigging. This time the cringle in the storm twin pulled loose and sent the sail down to the deck to flop around the lifelines like a freshly decapitated chicken. Another sodden sail was added to the wet salty pile.

Fortunately, the cringle held in the remaining storm sail, but so did the force of the wind. The pilot managed the unbalanced helm far better than we could have done. With each passing squall, stars came out to let us know they were really up there but had been playing a game of hide and seek with the rain clouds. The barometer remained steady, so we put aside the thought of a brewing storm. Again Don repeated the explanation of unseasonable weather, "Must be getting the reinforced trades!"

"Hmm, must," I answered in agreement.

Dawn brought forth no changes in the weather, certainly not for the better. "Let's head into land," Don suggested. "I've checked the chart and we can get into the lee of this weather at Point Hood."

"I'm ready," I quite agreed, but the sail changes necessary to alter course sent me to the rail again.

"Go below and rest," Don said after the work was done. "I don't trust that noon sight, and I'll stay topsides to look out for land. We're getting close and I want to be out here to look for sudden breakers." I grabbed the chance and was soon prone on my bunk and did not even stir when Don shouted out, "Land Ho!"

Don had the engine running to charge the battery and he put it in gear and motorsailed. The added mechanical power gave him more positive control of the heading. When I heard the abrupt drop in r.p.m.s, I knew something was wrong and bolted for the companionway. "Breakers ahead!" Don shouted. "We're going to jibe!" He shoved the tiller hard over and I pulled down on the sheet line to the main, to lessen the swing of the boom as it slammed over on the opposite tack. Directly in front of us stood a line of breakers that charged defiantly against the fringing reef, extending some 7 miles out from the point of land. We were in awe of how easily a ship could come to grief on outlying reefs that stand so far out to sea. Don had become suspicious of the presence of reefs when he spotted two freighters closer in towards shore. They were not underway, and he realized they were wrecks. The cresting waves of the wind-tossed waters had completely camouflaged the breakers piling up on the reef. White caps and breakers melded into one white maze of curling water.

Hood Lagoon, Papua New Guinea

With our hearts pounding, we headed back to sea and thrust *Svea's* bow headlong into the waves. Inch by inch, we gained enough sea room away from the reef. Then we followed its outline down to the non-distinct pass leading into the calmer water of Hood Lagoon. The village nestled snugly behind a grove of coconut trees. If the trees had not been bent by the force of the wind, we would never have believed a sea was raging on Point Hood's windward side. My stomach graciously accepted the placid waters.

For two days, the wind screeched and howled to lock us into that tranquil setting. We gained a new look at still another design of native craft, for in these parts, the weather dictated a stronger and sturdier canoe. So if one canoe is good, two are better. The natives on the wind-swept reaches of New Guinea's southern shores built catamarans using two canoes with high freeboards. They used their paddles as steering rudders and outboard motors for power.

Inside Passage to Port Moresby

It was only 50 nautical miles from Point Hood to Port Moresby and we had a choice of two different routes. The open seas were still agitated from the strong winds. Therefore, we took an inside passage by way of a navigable channel that ran between the barrier reef and the mainland. We used the Wolverine Entrance just west of Point Hood. Although the route was certainly more scenic as we followed the coastline, I wondered how sage our decision had been when reefs appeared that were not marked on the chart, and those marked on the chart were non-existent. Our charts were old and certainly inaccurate. We had no other recourse than for Don to stay in the ratlines to pilot us through the reef-entangled passage. Straining his eyes for reefs and shoals, Don did well in the morning finding obstacles, but when the afternoon sun lowered in the western sky to reach his eye level, it blinded him. We were in for some trouble.

"Neutral! Hard to starboard!" Don shouted.

"I felt the keel touch!" I cried out as I shoved the tiller hard over.

"I don't think so," said Don, "Not from up here we didn't."

"Well, I'm back here at the stern and I felt it," I said curtly. Looking back at the yellow patch of water we had just skitted over sent shivers down my spine. *Svea* had found deeper water, but I was frightened that still another shadowed coral head lay in wait for her around the next bend.

"Don, we've got to stop! You can't see with the sun in your eyes! It's too late in the day and you're tired, besides!" I chided with no uncertain terms.

"I know! I know!" he retorted. "But we've got to find a lee and more shallow water. We just can't drop anchor right here. Now, grab a hold of yourself, and let's get this turkey moving!" Don's eyes were blood-red from hours of staring at the sun and we were both exhausted. The tension wrought from the anxiety of our situation, and not the hours at the helm, was reaping fatigue. We seriously doubted that we would be able to make Port Moresby before dark.

Tupuselei, Papua New Guinea

Don went below to look at the chart for a place to anchor. Due to his fatigue, he doubted what he saw, a village charted as being over water. There was no mistake, for around the next bend stood the village of Tupuselei, high and dry, built upon stilts imbedded in the fringing reef, that was underwater, just like the chart had drawn it.

Port Moresby

After a night of rest, we weighed anchor early in the morning and easily made the remaining 15 miles into Port Moresby. Seeing our cruising buddies already anchored there was a most welcome sight.

While at Port Moresby, most of the cruising sailors had been having their life rafts serviced. It was quite frightening to learn that many of

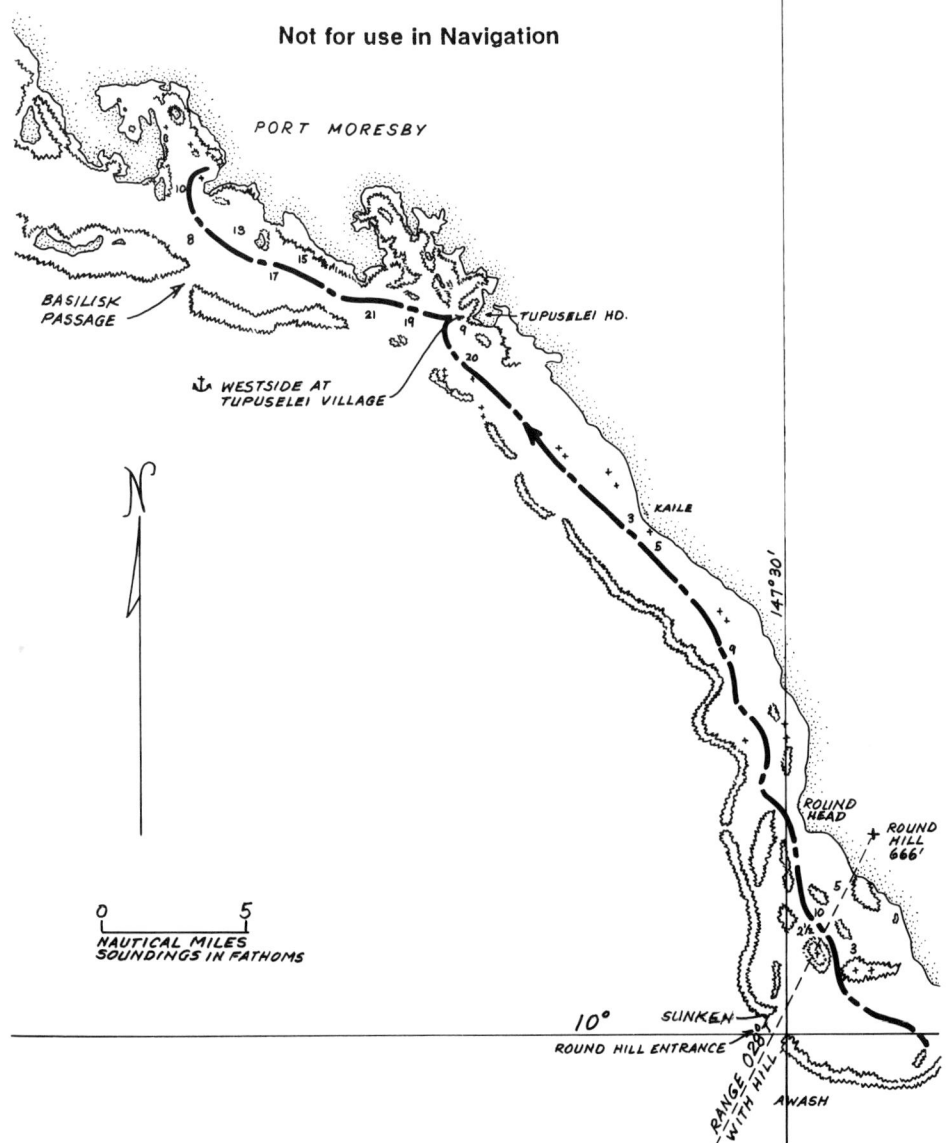

those life rafts would never have inflated should the emergency arise when they most needed them. ***Editor's note:*** *Life rafts should be serviced before making long ocean passages.*

Port Moresby was a busy place for all of us. Those planning to stop at Bali had already set the bureaucratic wheels in motion in Madang to obtain Indonesian cruising permits. Now in Port Moresby, we followed through with applying for visas at the Indonesian Embassy. We also obtained our visas for Australia at that Embassy, for Thursday Island would be our next port o'call, then we would go south to Darwin before heading north again towards Bali.

The Royal Papua Yacht Club served as genial hosts for the foreign yachts. We enjoyed their lunches, showers and cold beers. One day while crossing the road that separates the dinghy landing from the club, we had to pause for the entourage of uniformed motorcycle policemen. They proceeded the sleek black Rolls Royce carrying his honor, the prime minister of Papua New Guinea.

Captains and Crews

Our Australian friends were drawing closer to their home waters. When some of them returned home, they were jumping ship to get on with their lives in land-based operations. One sailor was to leave his wife in Sydney to carry on alone as a single-hander and complete his long desire of sailing around the world. He planned to take on crews as the passages dictated, but after his first trip with non-skilled mates, he pleaded for his wife to join him once again. Like a good mate she left her grandchildren and knitting to join her sailor husband.

The love men feel so fervently and ardently for their boats, and their life of the sea, is so often challenged by a homebound wife who thinks him foolish and selfish. But who is to judge which is the more selfish mate? I was lucky, for I shared my husband's dream and the rewards have been many.

Don often told men who put the blame for their not cruising upon the lack of interest from their wives, "There are plenty of girls in every port who will gladly serve as crew, and some of them look pretty good." My espoused mate encouraged the dreamers, pulling out from under them their usually one and only excuse.

Unfortunately, many hell-bent-for-leather novice sailors introduce their timid wives to sailing by frightening the wits out of them by choosing days of bad weather. They sail the boat's lee rail under the water, then guilefully ask, "Isn't sailing fun?" The fool's seamanship tactics further terrorize her. The confidence she once felt in him as a skipper, and perhaps as a husband, is sorely damaged. Confidence is gained only in the secure knowledge that a competent captain is in control, not only of the helm and the boat, but of the many unexpected challenges that come upon the most seasoned sailors.

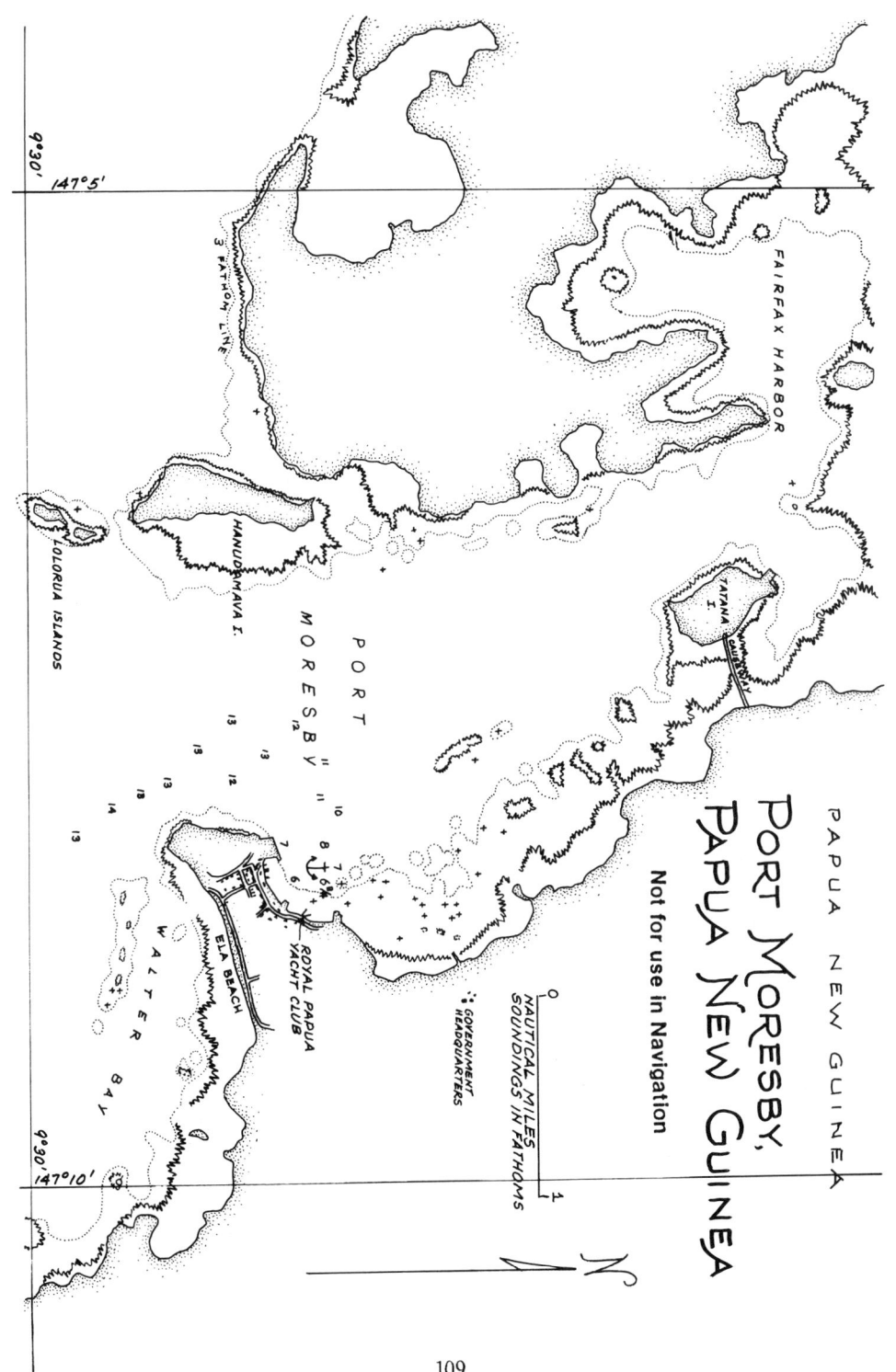

Malaria

It was one of those unexpected happenings that befell *Intermezzo*'s captain. Skip was stricken with the often fatal falciparum malaria. Most all of the cruising sailors had remained in good health, for we were careful to take precautionary measures and medications. However there was no suppressant for cerebral malaria. Had Skip not been in Port Moresby where he was hospitalized with intensive tests and several physicians working on the case to define his uncommon type of malaria, he most likely would have succumbed to the bite of that anopheles mosquito. To this day, he still says the mosquito found him at Belesana Slipways, but he can not vouch for killing the guilty one. Some parts of the world would not have been able to identify the strain, but malaria is no stranger in New Guinea.

Of concern to all of us was Skip's health, but we also worried about Linda and their two young daughters. *Wind'son*'s VHF channel stayed open and tuned to the same open station on *Intermezzo*, so they could monitor any possible needs the girls would have. Skip recovered, but his attack made us keenly aware of our own chances with malaria, and we sought the advice of a local pharmacist who updated our medications. We found it most important to check with local pharmacists on what was taken in their area to suppress malaria. When we reached Australia's borders, the cruising sailors coming from Papua New Ginea were thoroughly tested at the local hospital to avoid the threat of carrying malaria into their country. We all passed their test.

Finding Bramble Cay, Torres Straits

There was no letup in the reinforced trades. We left Port Moresby in much the same blustery weather conditions we had when we arrived. This heavy weather had torn out sails on a couple of the cruising yachts and caused some of the race boats coming up from Australia to lose men overboard. Ahead of us now lay the Torres Straits, reef-strewn islands and islets with crazy unpredictable currents that form a broken necklace strung out from Australia's northern shores.

The question asked by all the cruising sailors at the yarning sessions at the Royal Papua Yacht Club was, "How're you going to find Bramble Cay?" Bramble Cay is a very tiny spot on the chart, but its importance is great. The small island marks the only eastern gateway into the Torres Straits and it has a navigational light. If you miss this tiny low-lying island you can find yourself in a maze of unmarked reefs that wall off the islands inside the Straits. Bramble Cay is so small and low-lying that it's easy to miss. We thought our best chance to find Bramble Cay was at night, when the light would be visible for a greater distance than the land would be during the daytime. We planned our passage accordingly.

What we did not consider was the continuation of strong winds that set our speed beyond our expectations. Overcast skies allowed us only poor sights. We spent a fitful first night pondering our too-fast speed, lack of sights and the probability of heavy freighter traffic using the same elusive gateway. Their advantage was radar.

At dawn, skies were still overcast and there were no hopes for sights to pinpoint our position. Our apprehension mounted new heights. Don honed his keen sense of dead reckoning navigation. By late afternoon, we still had not been able to ascertain our position. The one poor sight we had been able to take through an overcast sky did not agree with Don's dead reckoning. To make matters worse, squalls were upon us. At dusk, there were still no stars for a sight, or to give us hope for a squall-free night. Were we too far north to miss the light completely and have to worry about trying to make a comeback into the head seas to find it? Or were we too far south and heading into the reefs? Either route was dangerous.

Don's plan was to sail north of our rhumb line at night, away from the area of reefs. The idea was also to put Svea in the southwest setting current clearly marked on the chart. Then the strong 20-knot winds could be utilized to best advantage. In other words, we were sailing two sides of a triangle, rather than the shortest route of a straight, ambiguous line. If we did not see the island before darkness fell we would carry on the northerly course until the depth sounder showed that we were over the 35-fathom line, the top of the triangle. Then we would stop and heave-to. Hopefully, we would drift down the back side of the triangle towards the light.

It was a blustery miserable night and although in theory Don's plan seemed sage enough, I could not help but wonder where we were. Don was up every 15 minutes to look for the light. An hour before dawn broke, he shouted, "I see the light!" He came down to check the sequence of the flashes with those marked on the chart and they did not agree. "Well, it just has to be Bramble." Don said with confidence. "What other light would be putting out a flashing signal? Come on. Get up. Let's get underway. The Torres Straits beckon!"

Not wanting to miss the first sight of Australia's outer reaches, I rolled out of my bunk to help get Svea moving in that direction.

Photo by Carl Moesly

Local craft off Samarai, China Straits, off Papua New Guinea

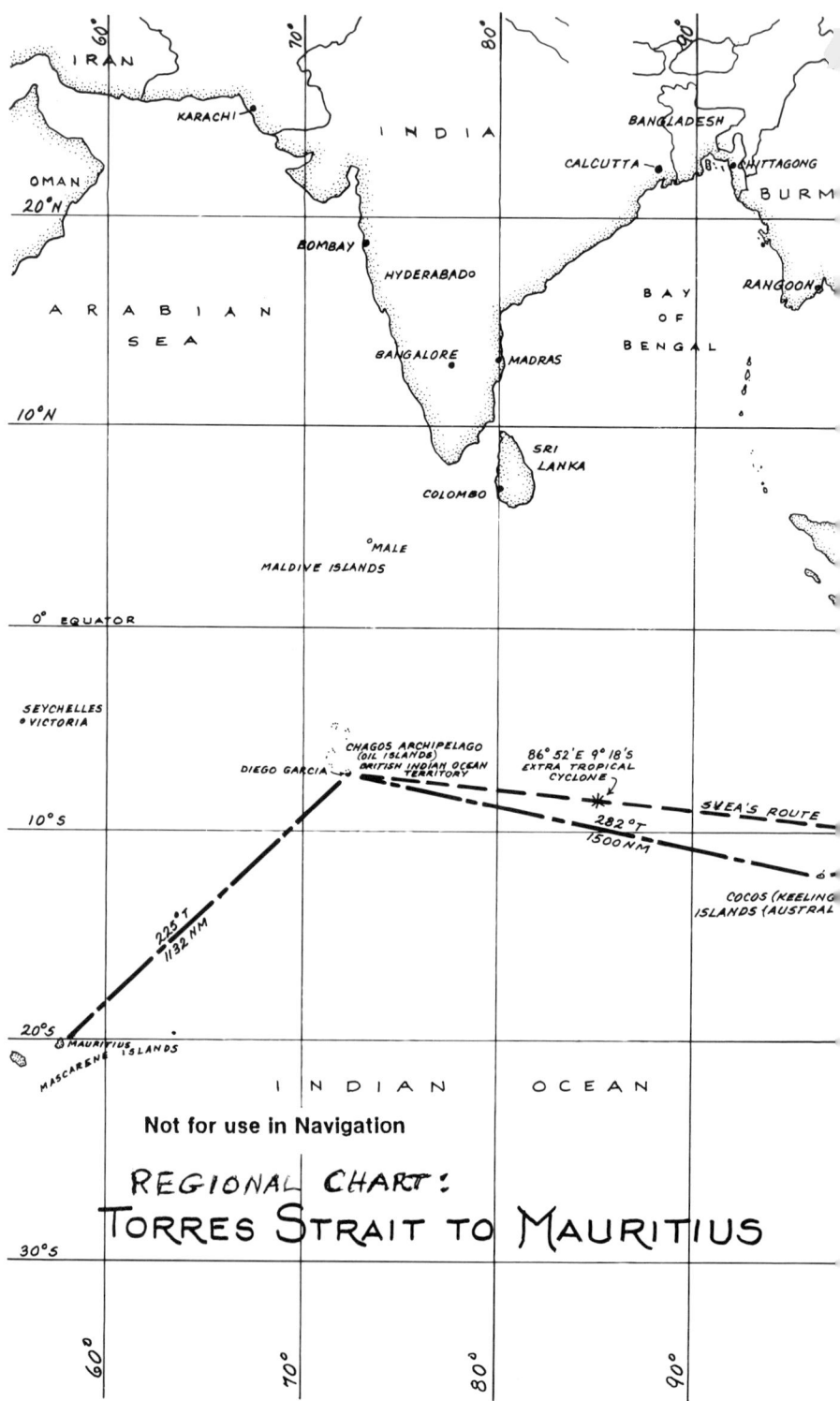

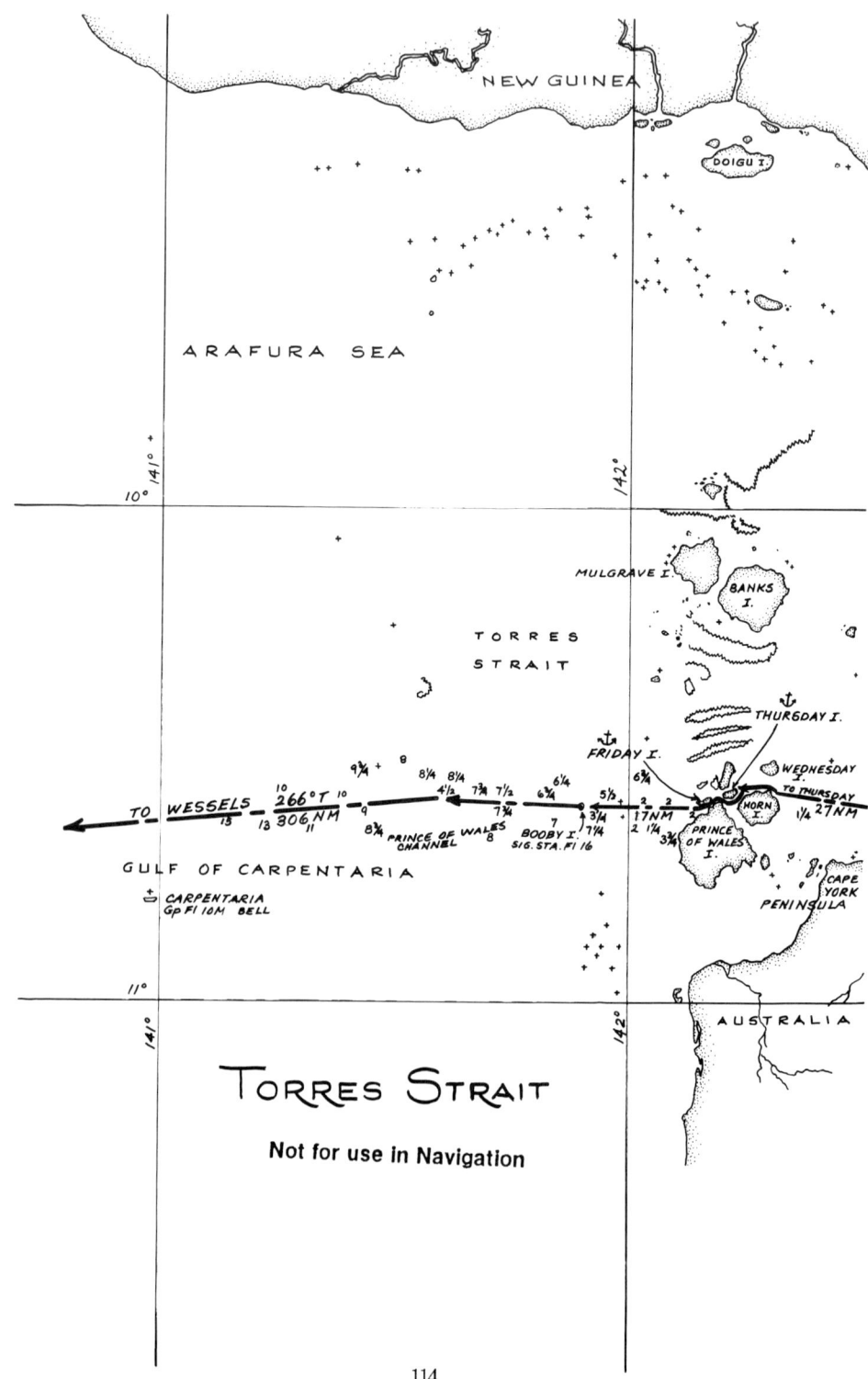

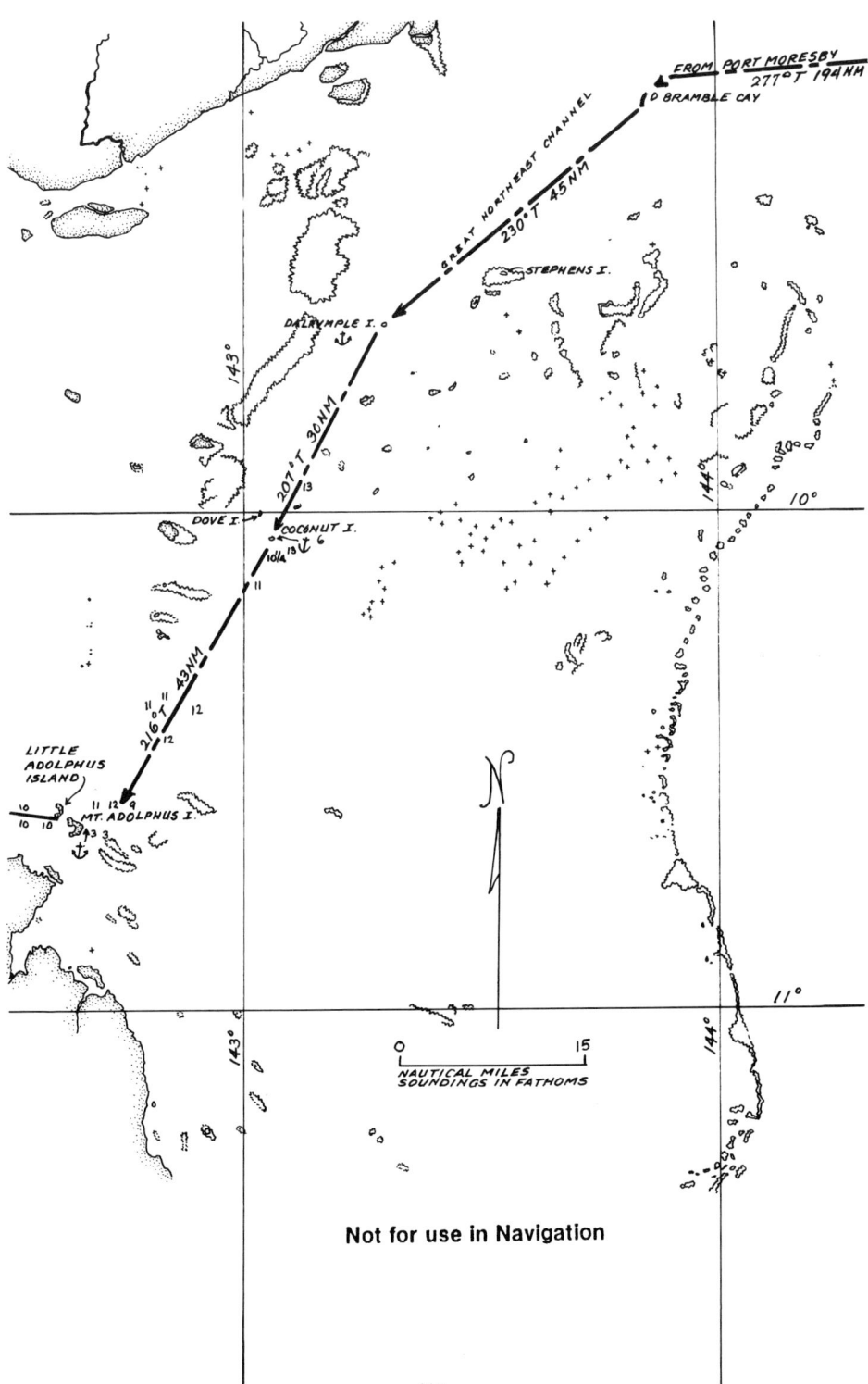

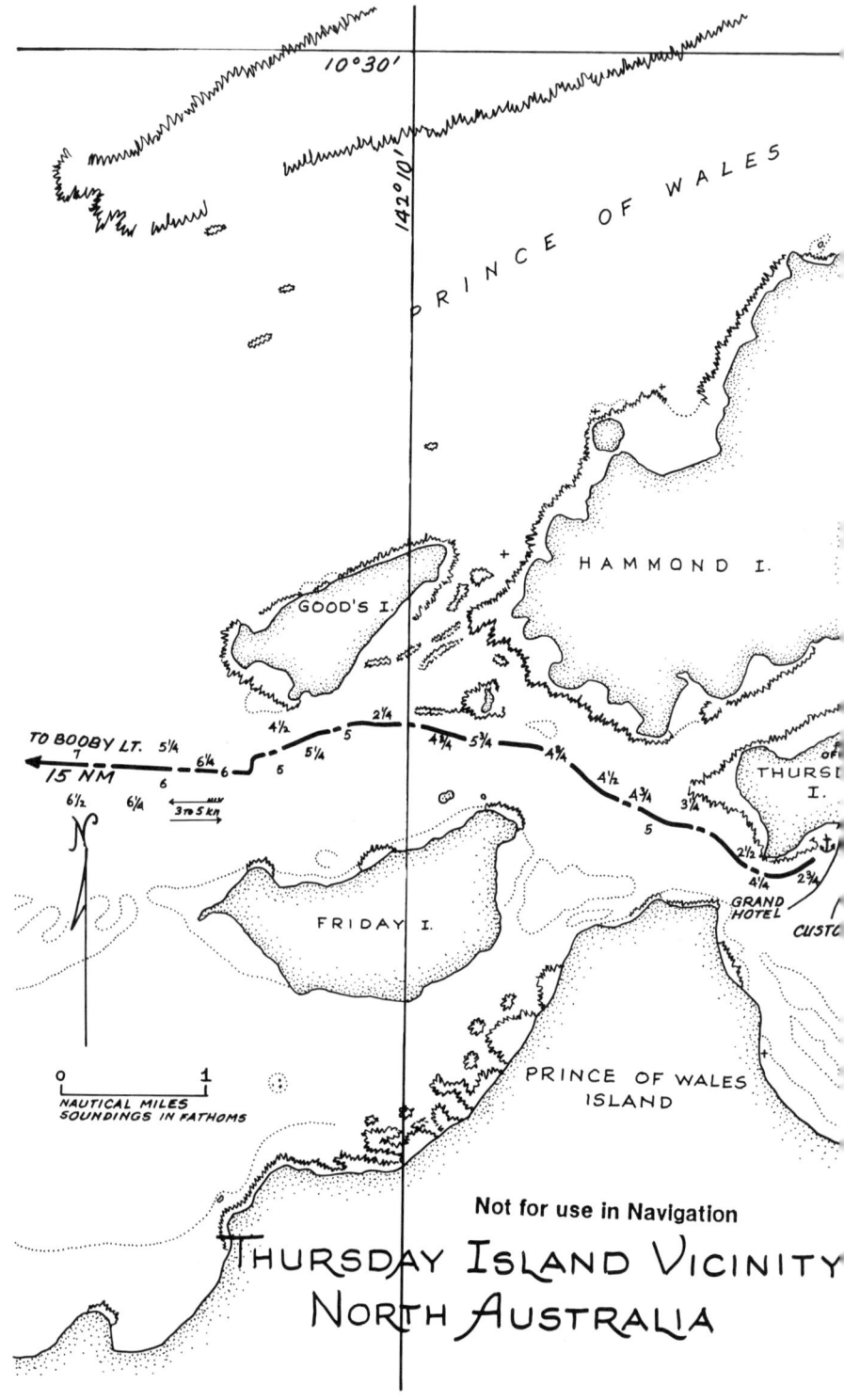

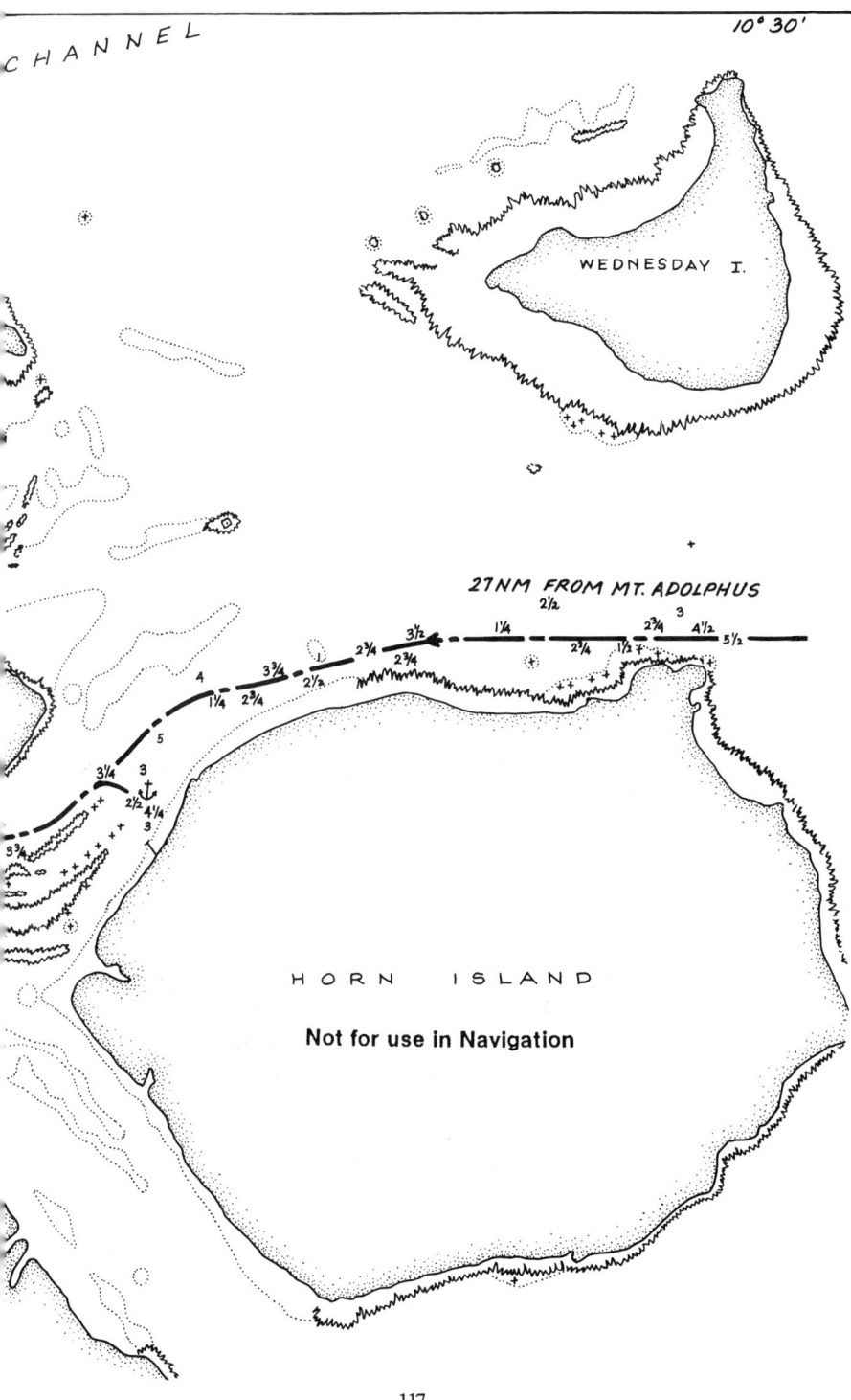

CHAPTER 10

ISLANDS and HARBORS, AUSTRALIA'S NORTH SHORE

Passage from Bramble Cay to Dalrymple Island, Cocoanut Island, Mt. Adolphus and Thursday Island, Australia

Small as it was, the lighthouse at Bramble Cay was exposed at dawn's early light, but a new problem arose to replace the old. "The pilot's not working!" Don shouted down to me as I started a pot of coffee brewing. I quickly put the pot in the sink for safety and grabbed my foul weather jacket.

"Take the tiller and I'll go down to check," Don handed the helm over to me and crawled back alongside the engine to examine the shaft. "Turn her into the wind," he shouted up. "The shaft is coming out the stern of the boat! Stop her!" He shouted louder. I quickly put the tiller over to starboard to pull *Svea's* bow up into the wind.

"Oh, my God," I gasped. "Now what has happened to the pilot?" *Svea* was slipping sideways in the small seaway that was skirted with reefs. Don worked frantically below to pull the shaft back into the boat and secure it, so the spinning of the propeller would not turn it back outwards again. It seemed so terribly long before he could give me an answer and then it was, "Okay, get her on course. The coupling joining the shaft to the reduction gear came loose. The lock washer broke." As our luck would have it, the lock washer was not one that we could replace from the spares we carried. It was a custom fit that had to be ordered from a marine store that could order it from the factory or a specialized mechanic. It seems like every time we go into a port, we have a work list of things to be done or items to be ordered. Thursday Island was going to be no different. It had been the starter at Madang and the injectors at Port Moresby, now the lock washer. What was going to be next?

We still had an engine, but no gears and no pilot, as the shaft had to turn to power the hydraulic pump. There would be no engine to get into anchorages and we had to become seat-of-the-pants sailors, not easy with the long-keeled sailboat that has a mind of her own.

Accompanied by heavy squalls and the blustery winds associated with them, we sailed into Dalrymple Island's western anchorage and dropped the anchor in front of the light structure. All afternoon Don worked on securing the shaft. When he came out from the tunnel alongside the engine he said, "I hammered the old lock washer into place and I know it will hold if we stay in forward gear, but for God's sake, don't try to reverse, or the whole thing will unscrew out the stern of the boat."

Thursday Island, Australia

When we finally reached Thursday Island after two other overnight anchorages in the Torres Strait at Cocoanut Island, then Mt. Adolphus, we found the paperwork boggling. The immigration official assured us that after it was all over, we could stay in Australian territories for up to a year. "But we only want to stay three weeks," Don countered. It was superfluous to ask a bureaucrat a question like that. They would not have a form for such a duration. We followed the rules set down in the little black book.

Thursday Island is much like Samarai in that both towns share memories of prosperity. Skeletons of the past came out of the old shops and warehouses that once were filled with pearling equipment and the fruits of their labor. The pearls and shells were used for making buttons, and other items of jewelry. The industry died when cultured pearls became abundant and plastics were substituted at lower cost.

Built atop a high hill, the town of Port Kennedy looks down on the harbor. A few old pearl luggers still remain afloat in the fast tidal waters that rip through the anchorage. Gone from the once-proud workboats are their sails. Many have chopped off their masts. Engines now power the derelict-looking craft. Gone, too, are the diving helmets and the heavy suits the divers wore to the bottom of the sea. The natural pearls are gone. At one time, pearl shells from Thursday Island were sent all over the world to propagate in foreign waters and perhaps seed new pearl beds. Some of the shells were sent to Suvarov Island.

On the streets of Thursday Island are black men, the men whose ancestors grew sturdy and strong to withstand rough sea conditions. Their chests expanded to allow them to dive deeply for the pearls. Like native craft being built to fit their environment, so did the different breed of the Thursday Island black man mature to large, muscular people with broad shoulders and thick, heavy legs, quite unlike their spindly cousins, the Aborigines of Australia, or their neighbors, the Papuans of New Guinea.

Thursday Island has had a rebirth of prosperity. Off-loaded at the long city docks are vast catches of prawns that are being harvested in the neighboring waters by adventuresome Australians.

The radio broadcasting station on Thursday Island never seemed to alter their weather forecasts for the marine area—always 20 to 30-knot winds out of the southeast. We could accept being caught out in winds like that, but to voluntarily leave an anchorage in bad weather was unthinkable, that is to everyone but an Aussie or a Kiwi, who know little better. We could well understand why our Aussie friend's wife was planning to plant her feet on terra firma when she reached her homeland. Of course, there are some sailors who defy the gods and leave on a Friday!

Eventually our needed lock washer for the gear box came in from Sydney and Don installed it. We were ready to go, but the weather worsened. We thought it foolhardy to begin a passage into the notoriously choppy Arafura Sea in such conditions. The anchorage was quickly becoming untenable as spray whipped across the decks and forced us to keep all of our hatches closed. In our five-day stay at the anchorage, the current sweeping past *Svea*'s hull caused the Sumlog to register a total of 45 nautical miles. That's pretty good mileage considering we were motionless behind *Svea*'s anchor! Running with the wind, the current put a tremendous strain on our ground tackle. Since the wind was on the increase, it was foolish to remain at the rough anchorage, even though it was our point of departure from the Torres Strait. We crossed the channel and sought a lee from the wind on the northside at Horn Island.

Anchorage off Northwest Shore of Horn Island

What a pleasant contrast it was from one side of the channel to the other! Away from the wind and current, we could open hatches and walk around the decks without foul weather gear. On one of the walks forward to check the anchor I saw a huge crocodile peering up at me. He was lolling around the anchor chain. We have had squid playing around the anchor chain, but never an 8-foot crocodile. I remembered what the Thursday Island sea captain had told us, "Do not swim in any of the coastal waters and look for crocodile tracks on the beaches! Always wear shoes because of the snakes!" Well, we were not yet in the Wessel Islands where he gave reference, but this introduction to Australia's marine animals made me a believer in "local knowledge."

Passage to Wessel Islands

Thursday Island radio finally gave an encouraging weather forecast. Despite our own gut feelings that the weather did not seem all that good, we departed Australia's northern outpost. Perhaps the attitudes of our Aussie friends had influenced our otherwise-prudent undertakings.

The arm of the Arafura Sea that marks the extreme eastern edge of the Indian Ocean and joins the Gulf of Carpentaria, is a shallow body of water. It has the reputation of being a rough and nasty patch of water. We encountered steep-to seas when we gained the open sea, but that sea was only 8-fathoms deep. We had 300 miles between us and the Wessel Islands, and we had a problem trying to figure out what sails to use. We needed the downwind twins, as the wind was aft, but which ones? We had to keep ahead of the following seas constantly knocking at *Svea*'s back door to come in. But, that meant more sail area and the worsening weather dictated a reduction in sail, not an increase.

"We have to stay ahead of that mess coming up astern," Don explained. "We've got to get the blues up."

"Both?" I questioned with not a little hint of anxiety.

"We'll try it with one," Don compromised and we hoisted the starboard twin. Soon afterward the wind increased further and we were forced to bring the big foresail down. The ride *Svea* had given us was exhilarating, but it was dangerously fast. Now with reduced sail, she swished and swayed like a matronly hula dancer. She defied the seas that slapped her fanny in teasing threats by breaking them in two with her pointed stern.

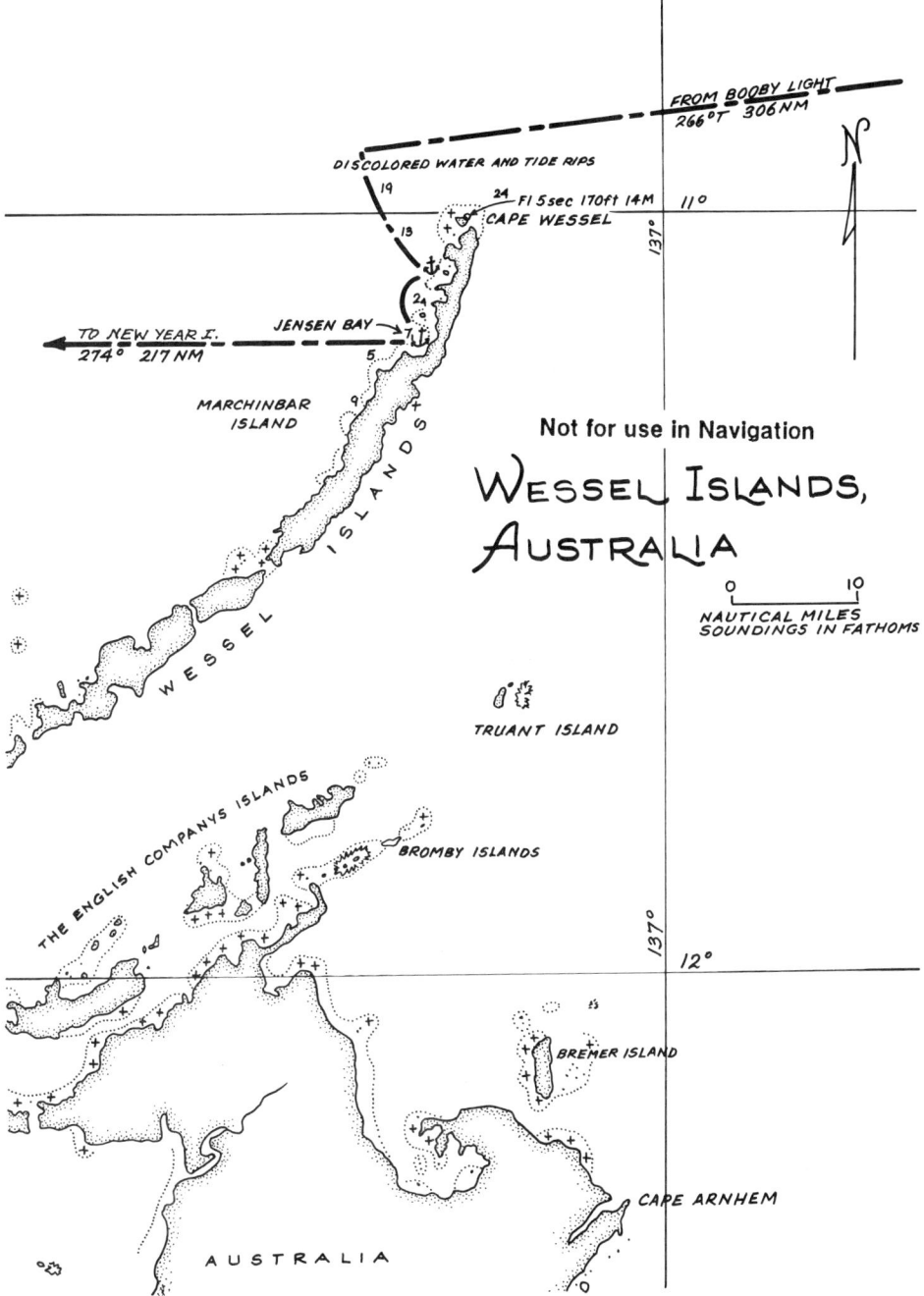

At midnight, we were abreast of the lightship *Carpentaria* and could then assume we had entered the northern edge of the gulf by the same name. Traffic was heavy enough to keep us alert. We wondered if the lights were coming from the prawn fishermen of Thursday Island. Unlike the heavily-built shrimper hulls used in our off-shore waters, the Australian version is much lighter in weight and has seemingly more horsepower. They do not look as though they were designed for extended days of offshore shrimping. It was a pretty messy sea in which to ply the shrimping trade in anything less than a sturdily-built trawler with a high freeboard.

Our noon sight put us 125 miles from the Wessel Islands. We were both down below when we heard a series of squeaks and chirps. "Must be a bunch of birds working an area of fish," Don surmised, but I went topsides and found the noises were coming from a huge pod of pilot whales. Their sonar systems were in high gear to tell their companions what a nice big toy they had found. Their pings and squeaks continued as they stayed with us for over an hour, doing crazy acrobatic antics in their favorite playground just forward of *Svea*'s bow wave.

It was growing close to dusk of the next day, when we spotted the lighthouse at the northern tip of Wessel Island. "We have only an hour left of daylight," I said to Don. "Can we make the anchorage before dark?"

"Remember what the old sea captain back at Thursday Island told us?" he questioned. "You know, the 5-mile area of tide rips?"

"We can't make the anchorage at Jensen Bay if we have to run out 5 miles and then back in," I conjectured.

"You're doing your own thinking now," Don laughed, for he never let me depend completely upon his decisions.

"Don't worry," he smiled. "I've checked the chart and the water shallows closer to shore and we'll be in the lee once we've cleared the point. We can anchor anywhere off the land. I think we can stand a roadstead anchorage for one night."

Anchorage off Northwest Shore of Wessel Islands

Like two inebriated sailors, drunk only from exhaustion, we fell into our bunks and slept a deep sleep. Australia's mainland protected us from the sea and its swells.

We awakened to a beautiful day and walked miles and miles of beach, bush and ruddy rugged cliffs that overlooked the Gulf of Carpentaria. Wearing long pants and shoes, like our old sea captain had warned us, we trod many paths laid down, not by man, but by beast. Embroidered in the beach sand were curlicues made by snakes, herringbone marks squiggled by lizards and the unmistakable swirls left by the tails of crocodiles. The telltale marks identified the creatures that walked the northern shores of Arnhem Land.

At one point high on a sandy knoll, we spotted the recent robbery of a turtle's nest. The eggs were broken and scattered, not a mess man would incur. The next nest we found was unmolested and we smoothed out the turtle's tracks and only hoped the predator hunted by sight, as we had, and not by smell. We were interfering with nature, but sometimes her survival-of-the-fittest tactics are a bit harsh and cruel to the victims.

Behind thick dunes we found the billabongs, the stagnant freshwater ponds whose flow to the sea has been stopped by pile-ups of beach sand. When a fresh rain falls again to swell the backwaters, the gates of sand will open like any other lock system, to dispell the flooded streams into the sea, sometimes finding the old channels and other times creating new ones. I recounted Banjo Patterson's song that made the billabongs so famous and became Australia's national anthem. I looked around for the swagmen who might be boiling his evening meal in his old billy, but the Wessel Islands neglected to include man in its inhabitants. What I should have been looking for was the origin of the many crocodile tracks that laced like a woven fish net to and from the billabong.

Don was so excited by the sight of the freshwater that he jumped into the pond, clothes and all, and I was right behind him. Then, I looked down and saw only reddish-brown water, stained so by the tannic acid of the leaf-covered bottom. I nudged Don, "You know, I really don't think we're too smart," I started a retreat to the muddy shore. "In this water you couldn't see a crocodile even if he bumped into your leg. You'd better get out of there." Don ignored my words of wisdom and continued his ablutions, fortunately free from the interruptions of any water-borne reptile.

Wallaby country was high rocky terrain that butted the sea then fell back into bushland. "If you could see what I do, you would not stand there," Don said. I walked back from the edge of the rock where I was gazing out at the sea. Off to an angle, I saw what Don had meant. Only a thin rock shelf cantilevered over the sea had supported me.

"There goes one," Don pointed to a quick sight of a reddish-brown furry wallaby. Very long in legs, but short in body, the kangaroo's smaller cousin skitted across the rocks in leaps and bounds to make the safety of his den tunneled underneath the boulders and partially hidden by a blind of small bushes.

At eventide, we were back at the billabong to take the laundry down from the clothesline I had strung between two trees. We reveled in the beauty of this man-forsaken scene and silently watched the different flocks of birds swoop down to the billabong for their evening nightcaps before retiring for the night. As if in predetermined pecking orders, each group took their turns at drinking, while the others waited patiently in the safety of the trees.

Passage to Croker Island and Port Essington, Australia

Like two legs of a crab extending outward from its shell, the Wessel Islands and the Coburg Peninsula jut out northward to form a half-moon

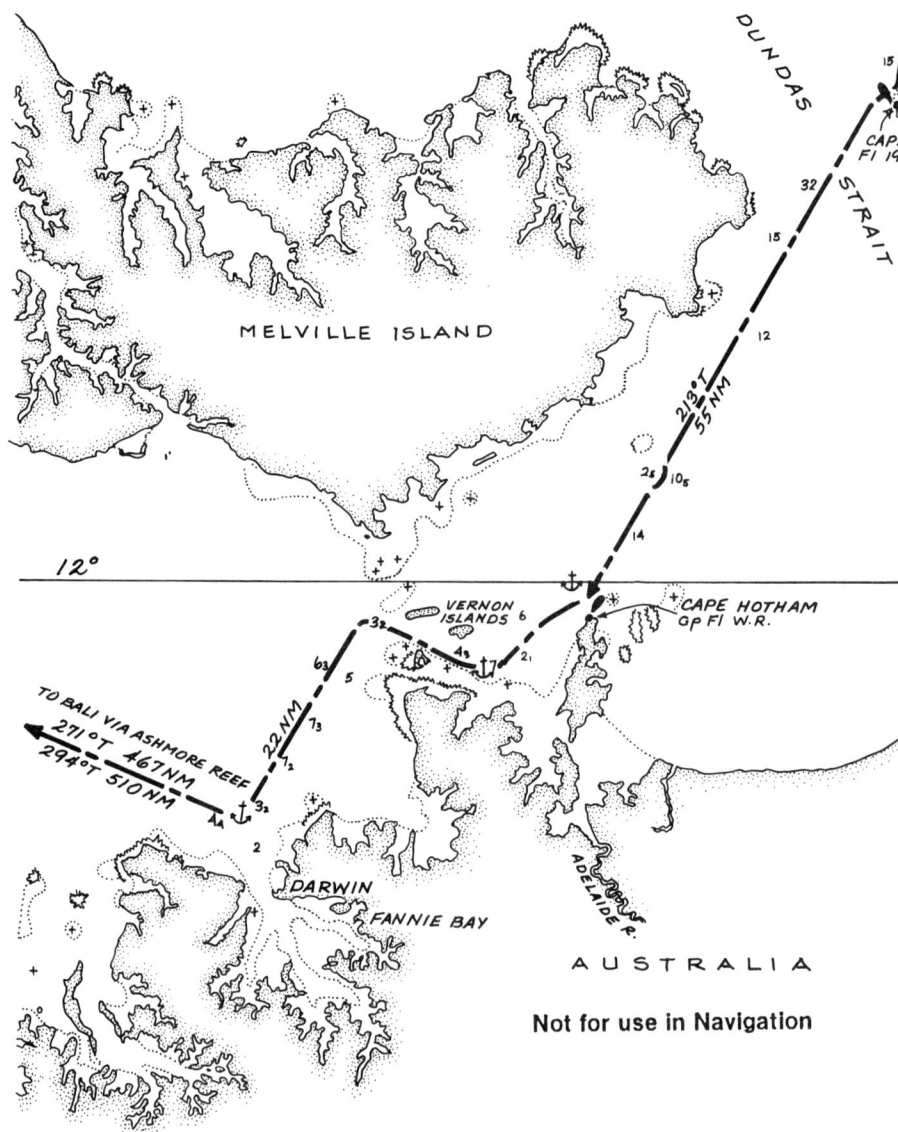

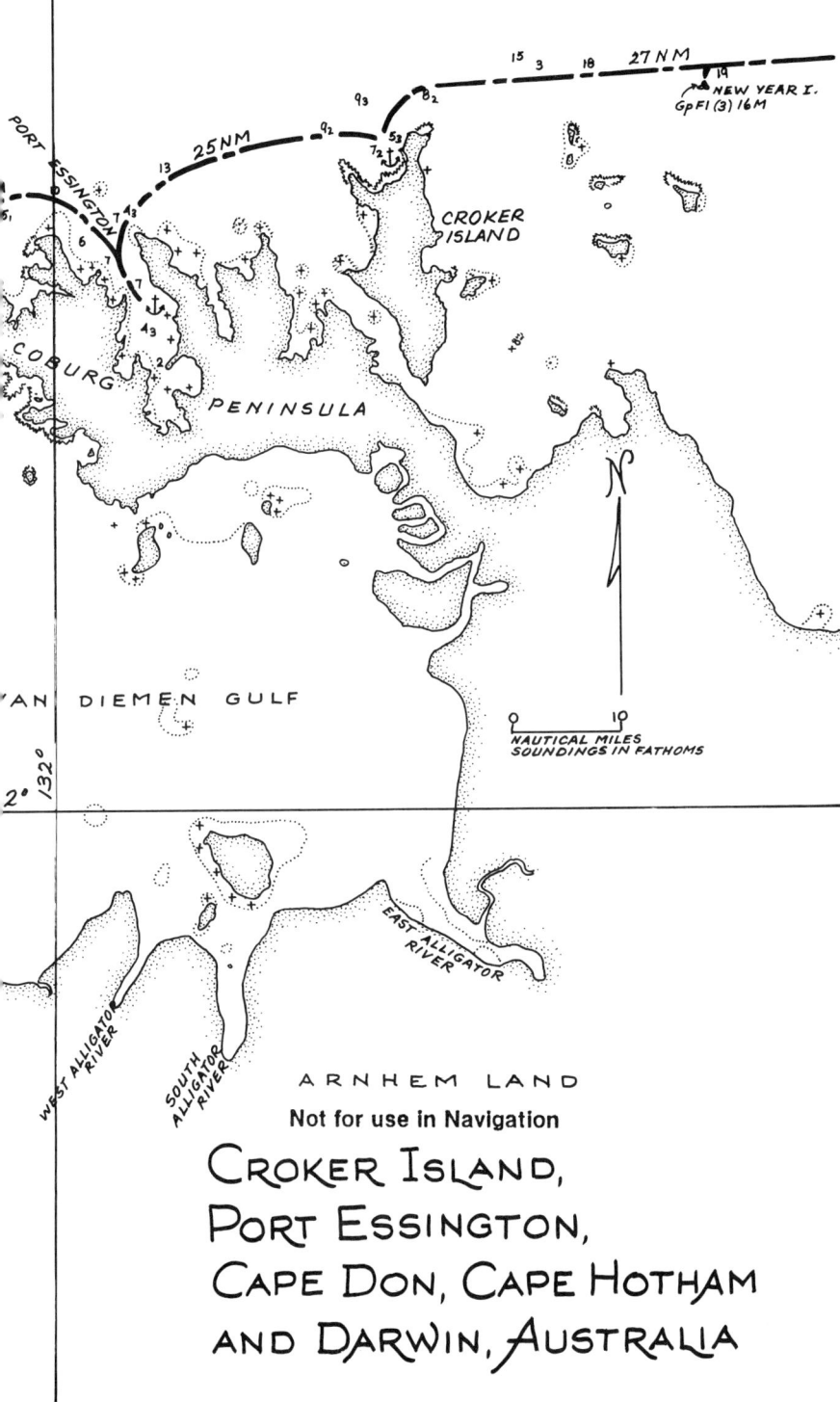

Croker Island, Port Essington, Cape Don, Cape Hotham and Darwin, Australia

shape north of Australia's Arnhem Land. We were underway across this 300-mile span bound for Cape Croker. South of us lay Arnhem Land where for hundreds of miles there is nothing but a sparse village of Aborigines way back in the bush. Australia's northern shores are desolate. Only the surviving Aborigines, who for years have roamed their lands and hunted the proliferance of wild game, call the upper reaches of the Northern Territory home. They are bothered little by the rangers who man the far distantly separated station outposts and protect the wild game. At night we welcomed the appearance of the Southern Cross adorning the starry skies. A fresh southeasterly wind maintained a steady airflow, as *Svea* passed through the quiet night on her way westward.

After a pleasant night tucked within the arms of the northwestern cove at Croker Island, we were eager to carry on for Port Essington. We hoped to meet one of the rangers who had befriended the *Rigadoon* crew on her first circumnavigation, but we found no one at home. Doors to sheds banged open and shut in the fresh breeze and curtains billowed out from the open windows. Tools were on the work benches and toys scattered across the sandy lawn, but not a man or a child was around to use them. We wondered what had called them away so suddenly, and we waited around for over an hour watching the funny brown bird with the big wide tail poking his strange beak in and out of the bushes. Quite disappointed that we had not made contact with the ranger, whom we had hoped would show us the wild game outback from the station, we returned to *Svea*.

Just before dusk, Don and I had watched two prawn boats come into the mouth of the bay. One dropped her anchor while the other tied alongside. That was not so strange, but two hours later when I got up to look around, I saw not two, but many more of these boats tied either stern-to or bow-to one another with only a couple of the boats having anchors down. With their rigging lights on, they presented a very strange sight, like a bunch of illuminated mating praying mantis. "It's Saturday night and I'll bet those prawn fishermen are having one whale of a good beer-drinking and poker party," Don laughed at the rafted shrimpers. I think he would have taken *Poco* to the Aussie fling if only I had enouraged him.

Passage to Anchorages at Cape Don and Cape Hotham

The following morning we made an easy run to an overnight anchorage at Cape Don. The following day we had a 50-mile sail southwestward in the Van Diemen Gulf to Cape Hotham on Australia's mainland. There at anchor we studied the tides to navigate the current-ridden Vernon Islands at slack water. From the anchorage we could see the first blinking navigational light leading into the channel. Once past those obstacles, we would have clear sailing in Beagle Gulf to Darwin.

Darwin, Australia

There were no green mountains to greet us as we approached Darwin's Fannie Bay. Everywhere we looked ashore there was nothing but mounds of red clay or long stretches of brown sandy beaches with a backdrop of modern high rise buildings crowded into the city. Later, we found the same red dust that covered Darwin's beaches surrounding her city. Bleakness and barrenness, and anything green, or thinking about turning green, was nourished and cherished.

The out-back environment was not easily erased from the modern city. The dust-covered "outbacker," donned in short shorts, faded flannel shirt and high-top boots swaggered incongruously through the doors of the modern shops. He behaved as if he were no different from the citified people who paid little attention to him, or to his weather-beaten spouse who always trailed a few paces behind him. He had a cowboy hat, equally as dusty as his shoes and clothes, set at a jaunty Australian angle on top of his dusty-blond hair. If my mention of dusty appears to be redundant I mean it to be so, for dust in Darwin was in the air as well as on the ground and on its people.

Aborigines also roamed the streets, but were found more often loitering around the public rest rooms and parks. I do not really know what I expected an Aborigine to look like, but it was certainly not what he did look like. I was surprised to see such slender brownish-black bodies being supported by legs that looked more like toothpicks than weight-bearing limbs. Their arms were just as skinny, but they had fairly large heads, which made them look quite top heavy. Their black hair was long and wavy, but thin, not at all the the thick tresses of the Polynesians. In fact, there was nothing about the Australian Aborigine that I could compare with anything else I had ever seen. Their pug noses flattened out to meet their chins and cheeks and their small eyes seemed clouded with despair.

Darwin found all of the cruising sailors scurrying hither and yon for provisions. Our next port for major supplies would not be until South Africa, with a few stops in between for periodic provisioning. Darwin also offered good medical services and we had our teeth cleaned, and we ladies had checkups with a local gynecologist. "I've never seen such a healthy lot of women as you cruising women," the doctor said after giving me a clean bill of health. "You Americans must really take care of yourselves!" How was he to understand that we had to take care of ourselves, for no one would take over our duties if we fell ill. The burdens would be put upon our mates.

Jim and Cheryl rented a car, which they shared with their friends to get the heavier provisions. Jim and Don found a source for new marine batteries, and Cheryl took me to the Casurina Shopping Mall on the outskirts of the city. For once, I did not have to lug all of my provisions in my back pack and walk a country mile to bring it back to the boat.

Darwin's 20-foot tides rather hampered our lightering supplies out to the boats. In the mornings we always had a wet ride against the wind to the beach, which was quite far away from the anchored boats. If the tide was in, we anchored the boats near the high water mark. On our return trip in the afternoons, the wind had switched around again so it would be on our nose. Now at low tide, our dinghies were stranded many yards up on the beach and we had to drag them down to the water. It was a case of damned if you do and damned if you don't. Some of the sailors became tired of lugging their dinghies back and forth and sought rides with those of us who had dinghies light enough to carry. Those sailors who had left their dinghies in on shore and hitched rides found their tenders the next morning quite full of sand brought in by the tidal breakers. Some were unfortunate enough to lose some gear when the breakers washed over them. Inflatable dinghies, called "rubber duckies" in Australia, were in for great abuse from the breakers pounding them against the many rocks that were on the beach. The heavier rigid dinghies were difficult to handle, but *Poco* fit the happy medium by being rigid, but lightweight enough to pick up and carry.

It was the Fourth of July and our Australian friends invited us to their "shout" of the American's Independence Day by hosting a barbecue in front of the Darwin Sailing Club. Our Aussie cruising buddies, Eric and Noel, toasted us with many tots of the good local brew bought in "stubby" sizes. We Americans talked about our heritage. I sang a robust and heartfelt rendition of "God Bless America," which prompted Eric to make a speech, "I have never seen, or heard, such a display of love for one's country. I toast you, Yanks, one and all. It's good to hear your praises and God Bless You all."

In a few days, we toasted a new celebration with champagne aboard *Wind'son*. Jim and Cheryl announced they were to be parents for the first time. Jim blamed the event on the primitive wood-carved fertility mask from New Guinea that they had put in their stateroom. The timing was providential, for in another hour we were talking through *Intermezzo*'s ham radio with *Rigadoon*, then in Bali. Jeanne told us she had just received a telegram from Carl and Don's sister saying their 90-year old father had just passed away.

Photo by Carl Moesly

Prawn (shrimp) fishermen leaving Thursday Island, Australia. Horn Island in background

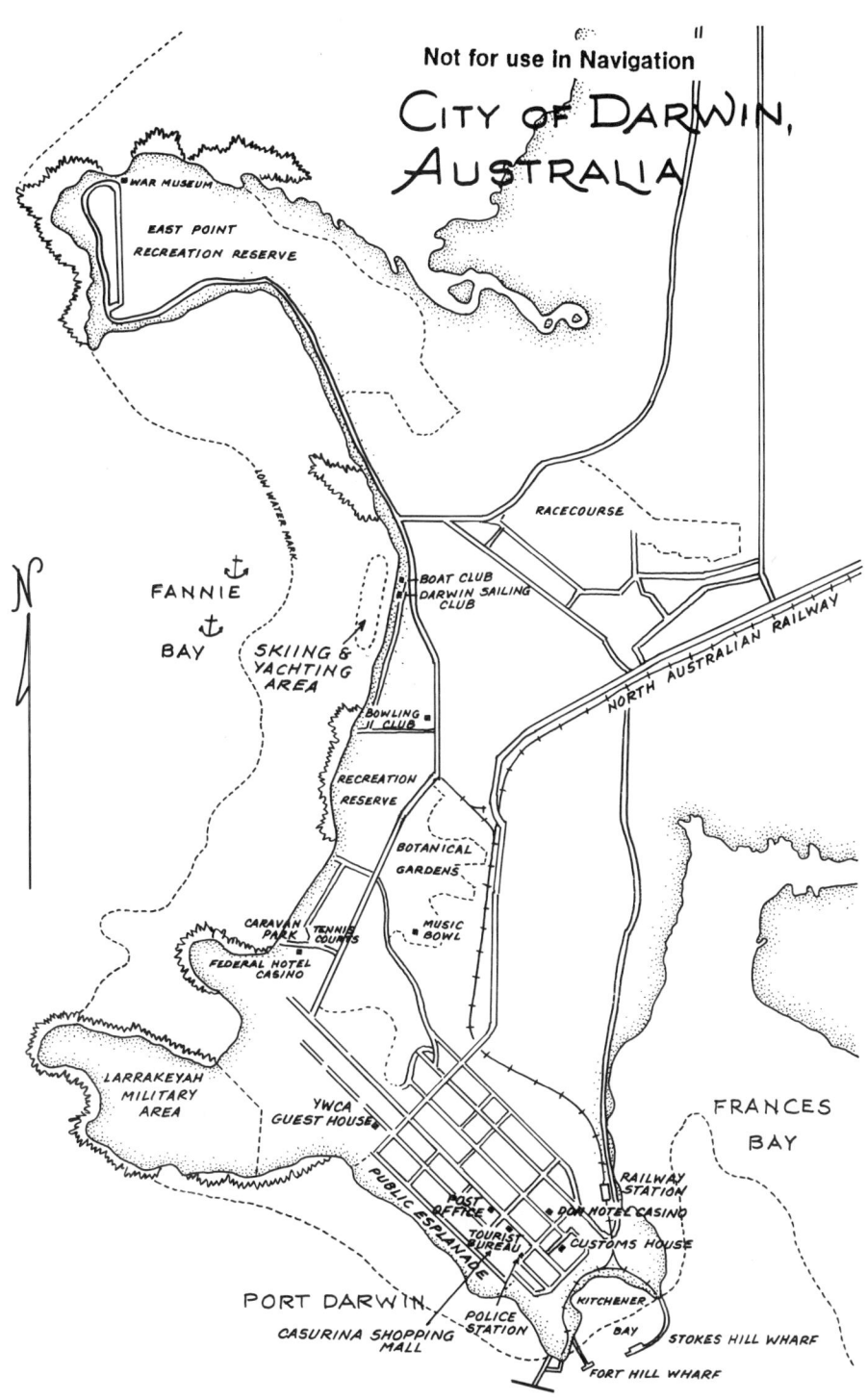

CHAPTER 11

BALI BECKONS

With a fanfare of ships' horns and friendly send-offs, we left Darwin's Fannie Bay and boomed out the big blues twin staysails before us. Our destination was Bali, 1,000 miles to the northwest. "We're due to have bad luck," I said with a frown on my face.

"What a thing to say at the beginning of a passage," Don scolded me.

"Well, it isn't a Friday," I laughed the frown away. The day was cloudless and there was little wind. The sails fluttered. In the lee of Australia, there was no sea. We opened the hatches to let in some air down below. The sun baked *Svea* against the griddle of the calm flat sea. "There's even dust out here in the ocean," I shook my head as I looked out upon the sea colored like a chocolate milk shake.

The depressing heat and the monotony of the sameness of the wind and sea was suddenly broken when the sail blossomed like a big blue dandelion poofing out in a gust of wind. The eyebolt that holds the port forestay to the bow piece gave way. In the light air, it was not difficult to bring the sail down and bag it, but the problem was to replace the bolt. We should also worry about the starboard bolt going, due to the fatigued metal that claimed its twin.

"Do you want to go back to Darwin?" I asked.

"We can't go back," Don answered. "We'll just have to carry on and hope we can find a machinist in Bali." I thought back to what Don's reaction would have been earlier in our trip, when a problem occurred and he became so frustrated at not being able to make a proper repair. Funny how time seems to iron out our wrinkles and makes one adjust to adversity with little stress. We made a jury-rig repair to replace the bolt by using chain and shackles. The sail went back up and we were again in business.

As the mainland of Australia fell farther astern, the water changed from its milky-brown to a blue-green. Separating the colors were clumps of yellow seaweed. Offshore in Florida, we would have fished that weed line for dolphin, but somehow we did not feel like fishing or cleaning up afterwards. Slithering in and out of the clumps were yellow and black sea snakes. "Remember, all sea snakes are poisonous," Don reminded me as if he were afraid I would bring them aboard as pets. Cats, dogs and birds, yes, but not snakes.

The wind changed from light to nothing at all and the blues came down. The sea looked like a great big dish of blackberry Jello with nary a flutter of wind to whip up a topping on the big swells. During the night, the wind came up and we hoisted sails. At dawn we had to change them when the wind shifted more astern. Furl the jenny, change the sheet lines and the position of the deck block, raise the port blue, raise the starboard blue, lower the main, but keep the mizzen to balance the roll, tighten the

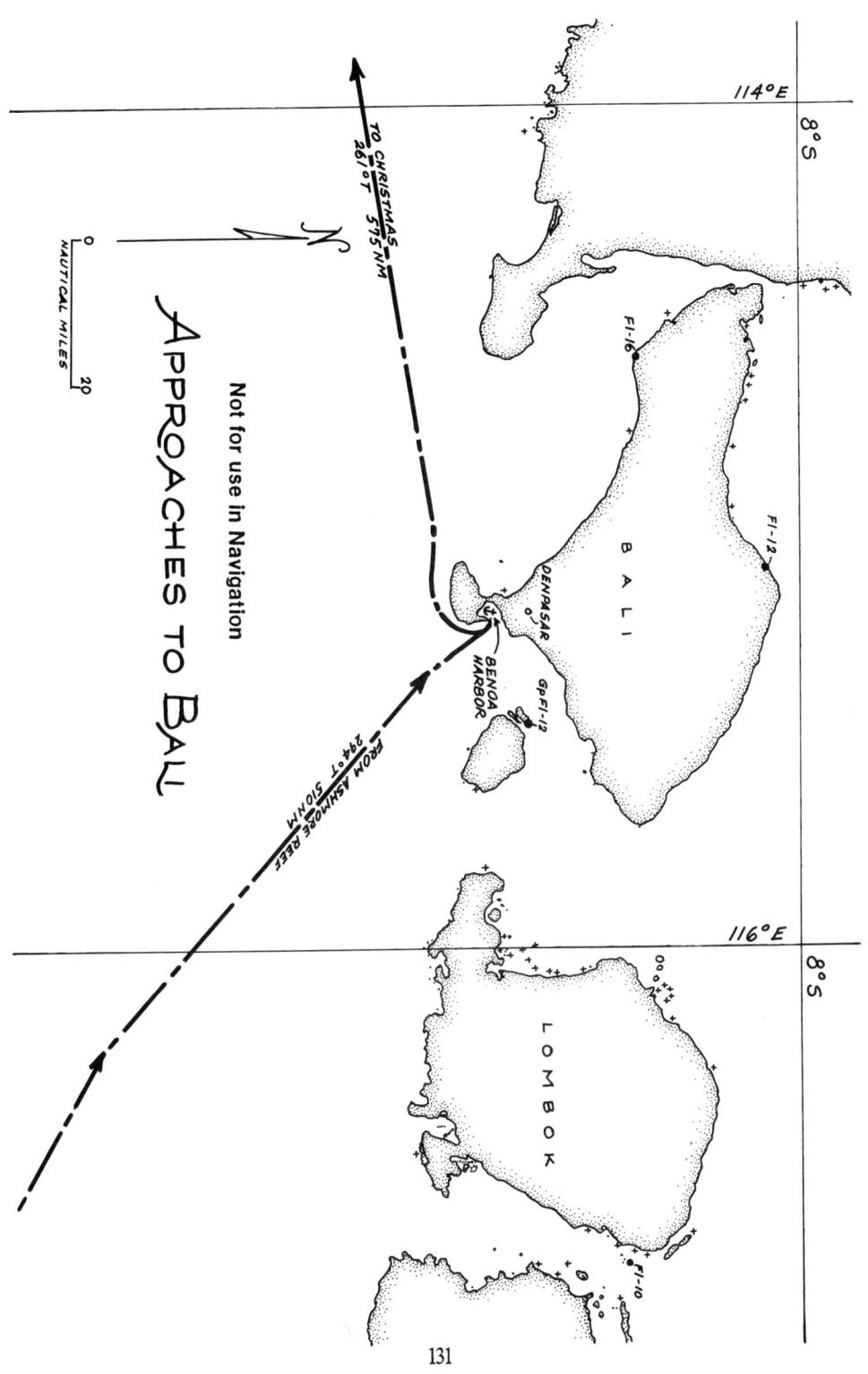

luff. "Have you fixed coffee yet, Susan E.?" Don asked when the sail work was done. And people ask what we do all day!

The miles logged each day were minimal—a snail's pace. No clouds in the sky, nothing to break up the density of the blue. Many nights we watched the sea capture the blazing red ball of the sun as it sank below the horizon to bring forth the flash of green when its top arc disappeared into the sea. We expected little or no wind, as we drew closer to Indonesia and the Equator, but there was hardly a zephyr from 13 degrees south latitude to 9 degrees south latitude where Bali rested.

We had wanted to stop at Ashmore Reef, with the hope of finding another delight like Minerva Reef, but we were in the wrong place at the right time, for when the reef bore ahead, it was too dark to contemplate a safe landfall. Heaving-to for so many hours would have set us way off course, so we continued on our way. We sailed from the Timor Sea into the Indian Ocean. Almost as if a line were drawn separating the two oceans, they acted like giant ping pong paddles, using *Svea* as the ball in the contest. Steep-to waves slapped one another and the spoils of their conflict sent dollops of spray dashing across the cockpit.

The salt accumulation on *Svea* began its build-up way back at Thursday Island. With no rain at Darwin or beyond to wash it away, the crusts of crystals glittered with the spectrum hues of the sun. A squall line appeared astern, but it was ill-defined and was heralded only by a small increase of wind. I ran below for a cake of soap to take a shower, but returned to the cockpit to find only driblets of rain falling. "He turned the spigots off," Don laughed at me, for he knew better than try to use soap and not have water left to rinse off the scum. The little rain did nothing but puddle the salt crystals.

"Maybe we'll end up with stalagmites growing on *Svea's* decks," I lamented to Don.

"Don't worry, a squall will stop their growth," he laughed and went below to see if he could pick up Denpasar's radio beacon at Bali's airport. There were no navigational lights on Bali's southern shores, so piloting by the seat of one's pants was the order of the night. Don also checked the depth sounder and compared the depths with those on the chart. Just before dawn, Denpasar's great loom of light beamed us in on a more direct course. With the light of day, the crest of Indonesia's unique island was well into view.

Soon we could see fast native proas with their lateen sails. They came from the harbor and from beaches on shore, setting out for a day of trolling for fish. By the number of huts and shacks along Bali's shoreline, Bali looked like the highly populated isle that it is.

Benoa Harbor, Bali

Maneuvering the intricate buoy-lined channel that leads into Benoa Harbor, *Svea* was greeted by one of the native boys who extended us a

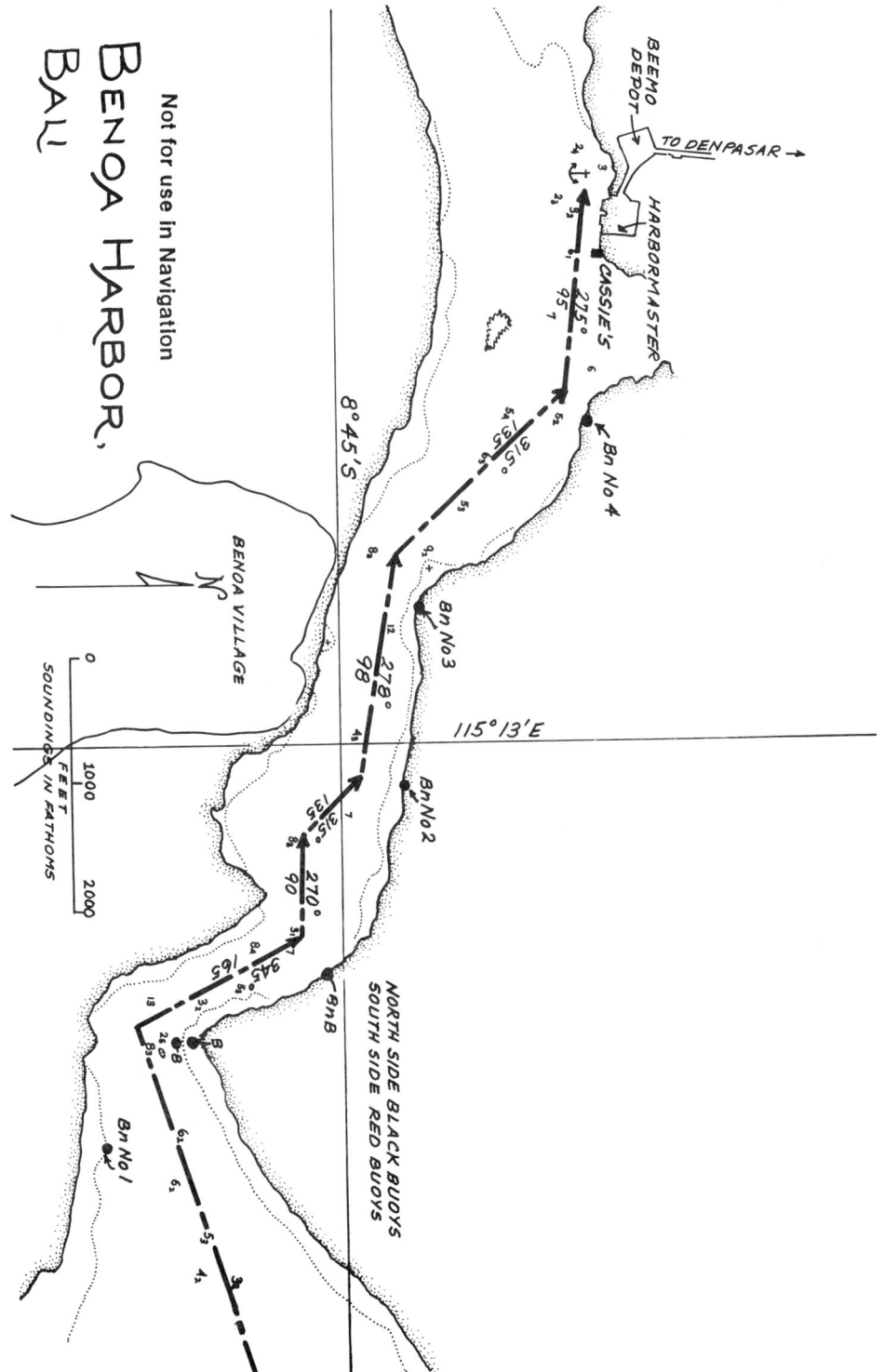

handshake of friendship and his business card, "Bali Yahct Services." I know the word "yahct" does not look just right, but that's how the card read. Madi told us he could help us with immigration, and anything else we might need. He and his brother Wayan ran the business and certainly did help all of the yachties. They found a machinist to repair the eyebolt on *Svea's* port forestay.

Once again, there was a meeting of the clan as *Sunflower* was there along with *Arion III*, after they had come down from the northern reaches of Indonesia. We had just missed *Rigadoon* as they had taken their New Zealand guests to Jakarta to catch a homeward-bound flight. Many times Carl wishes he had never made that trip and had stayed in peaceful Bali. *Rigadoon* was boarded twice by pirates and Carl's life was threatened. During the last encounter, the robbers stole their passports and expensive camera and climaxed the boarding with a severe blow to Carl's abdomen with a blunt object. Back on shore the pirates were received with great fanfare after their successful piratical attack of the American yacht. The next day when Carl went to the police, their reaction was simply, "How much will you pay to get your things back?"

All of the yachties knew to keep their boats away from Jakarta, Indonesia's capital city. Unfortunately, *Rigadoon* was put into jeopardy because of an airline that flew only into the city known for its pirates. Never will we be committed to any kind of schedule that says we have to be in a certain place at a certain time. Too many unexpected events arise that alter the best-laid plans, and the risks are sometimes to great to carry them out.

With Madi's help, there was little work to be done with the business of clearing customs and immigration. There were many visits to various offices. We wondered why all of the hoopla was necessary to obtain Indonesia cruising permits. Perhaps it was because Bali is unique. It differed from the rest of Indonesia where political, religious and social conflicts keep the kettle of discontent constantly in a stir and thievery a common occupation.

Al and Beth acted as our guides on our first day to town. We secured *Poco* on Benoa Harbor's shoreline that is supported by a high seawall. Then we boarded a "beemo." A beemo began as a small Japanese pick-up truck. Added to its bed was a box with seats astride each wheel. The beemo has a conductor as well as a driver. The conductor packs the little compartment with more than capacity. Each fare puts more rupiahs in his pockets. At one stop he squeezed an elderly woman and her daughter into the already over-crowded cab. The problem lay not with the women, but with their baggage of two quite-large uncovered buckets. One was filled almost to the rim with red-ripe blood, while the other contained the slaughtered animal's innards, not a pleasant sight. I visualized a bump in the road causing all of the passengers to look like victims of a massacre.

Denpasar, Bali's capital city, was all sights and sounds. Cassette players in the hands of the pedestrians or coming from the many keyhole shops along the road, almost overcame the din of the congested traffic that piled into the narrow streets. Mopeds with motors roaring and horns blaring zig-zaged between bicycles, beemos, pony carts and three-wheeled taxis. Pedestrians walked the sides of the road, seemingly unaware that death might lurk with each passing vehicle. On a pole between them, two men carried a poor pig encapsulated in a too-small woven basket, or maybe it was the men that were too small, for with every jogged-gait of the men, the squealing swine's backsides bumped along the roadway.

A bicycle adorned with brooms and feather dusters almost hid from view its driver who wore a hat looking much like an upturned lampshade. His vest was covered with pockets bearing brushes, spatulas and other kitchen ware. He was Bali's mobile answer to the Fuller brush man.

Shopping In Denpasar

We went in and out of the multitudes of shops, and were constantly amazed at the vast talents the Balinese have in the many forms of arts and crafts. To delight us further, Al and Beth took us to their favorite restaurant. For nine dollars the four of us ate like Chinese emperors and had seven varieties of dishes to choose from family-style servings. On the table were dishes of fried rice with shrimp, sweet and sour pork, fried noodles, a stir-fry melange of vegetables, snow peas and even frog legs. We washed it down with Pintang, the fine Dutch-tasting local beer.

"You hire the girls to do your haggling," Beth said when a couple of girls approached us. "To buy anything in Bali you must bargain." Beth knew the girls and hired them for a mere pittance for the rest of the day to go to the market. Quite unlike any other native market we had ever seen, Denpasar's shopping mall was a series of shops and stalls, bins and awning-covered tables drawn together in a mish-mash of buildings and street levels. Down well-worn steps that went at crazy angles, we were led into the catacombs, the basements that reeked of aromatic spices that the Balinese love to use in their cooking. Pungent odors of nutmeg and clove sent us reeling as we walked within the sanctum of the spice world. It was so dark there that I had difficulty telling a hunk of cinnamon bark from a nutmeg seed.

My girl Mada hustled me up and down crowded aisles and bartered with one vendor after another. At one point, she had me running through a confusion of eggplant, bananas and avocados to keep up with her and I knew Don had lost me in the race. I looked over my shoulder to see that Mada's friend, Mei Lei, had Don in front of her and was prodding him along with occasional thrusts to his backsides, as one would do to a mule.

After our bags were full, the girls insisted upon carrying them for us to the beemo station. I had also purchased some bottles of turpentine at the Chinese pharmacy stop, so I had a tangled lot to carry. Mada whipped her shawl from her shoulders, rolled it into a small circle and balanced the bun on top of her head, and on top of that my disarray of purchases.

The wee girl strutted down the rutted and crooked sidewalks with nary a misstep to spill a cucumber or a pineapple.

The Balinese are very religious and cling to their Hindu traditions, which were preserved for them by the Dutch who controlled their country for many years and refused entry to the Christian and Mohammedan missionaries alike. Temples are everywhere for Balinese to offer their prayers and thanksgivings. You had to be careful when crossing thresholds of the shops that you didn't step on the little flower and incense filled baskets that keep the evil spirits from crossing through their portals. We watched one young girl who set out her offering of rice on a banana leaf on the sidewalk and lit the stick of incense. Her offering was intended for her ancestors who were supposed to come down to earth and be nourished. Instead, a brown skinny dog got the sparse meal.

Benoa Village

Crossing the channel in *Poco* to go to the village of Benoa, we arrived at its shores the same time as the sailing freight boat. Their cargo was a boatload of green turtles. Don and I counted 40 turtles that had come from the ship's small hold and were forced to lie on the hot beach with their flippers holed and tied together to keep them from lumbering off. Pole-bearing matrons came down to haggle over prices, and then strung the poor beasts on the pole and carried them away. I still can not erase the terrible sorrow I feel for an abused animal. Part of American heritage is an instilled compassion for wounded or sick animals. However, in many foreign lands, animals are regarded strictly as a source of food or clothing, rarely as a pet that contributes nothing to the family in the way of income or food. If any compassion is expressed, it is saved for the human babies who are loved and the elderly who are respected.

Our Island Tour

Temples, monkeys, rice paddies, silver workers, batik designers, weavers, wood carvers, volcanoes and even naked Australians on Kuta Beach were crowded into one day when we rented a van with Jim and Cheryl to tour the island. The price of the van was so little, yet it included the tour director as well as the driver. Never have we had so much for so little expense as we had in Bali where a tourist is constantly fascinated with many things to do and see. The tour ended back at Benoa Harbor and Carrie's waterfront shack where we sat at the one communal table. We had her specialty of the day, a nasi goreng, fried rice with whatever she had bought from the local fisherman that day. For years, Cassie has catered to the cruising sailors who anchor in the harbor in front of her tiny establishment. She stored their oars in the corner of the small room to keep them safe, while they went into Denpasar.

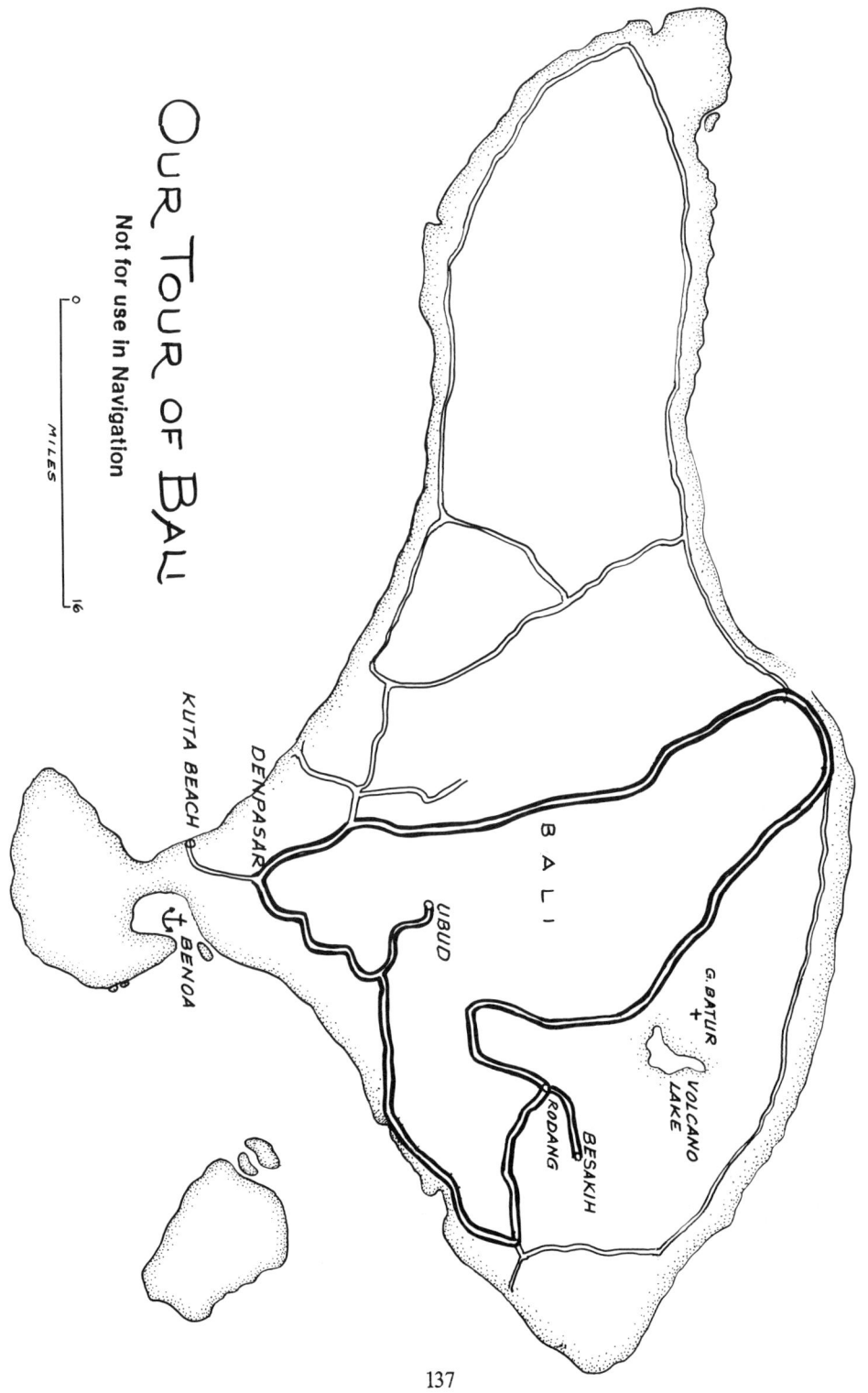

Preparations, Routes, Arrivals and Departures

"Hi, Noel, how was your trip?" we asked our Australian friend who had just arrived in Benoa aboard his sloop *Gillawaw*.

"Don't ask me, Sue. I'll never, ever have another crew! I had to play nursemaid and cook for two helpless and sick crew members who know nothing about sailing. I even had to do the steering!" Noel lamented.

"Sounds like you miss Jackie, Noel," I said cautiously. I hoped that Noel's single-handed days were numbered. I handed him a basket of fruit and a loaf of Bali's bread. "You'll like it here, Noel. Bali is a great place for R and R before tackling that Indian Ocean."

"Hmm, maybe so, but I don't know what I'm going to do for crew," he commiserated. "No, I'm just not going to fool with them at all. From now on I am a single-hander," said our confused friend.

Bali was indeed a beautiful pearl. It is protected by strong inherent customs and cultures. They refused to become entangled in outside political squabbles. Bali was also a pearl thrust in an ocean that was renowned for its sudden uprisings of bad weather. We were grateful for the interlude of peace before having to challenge the Indian Ocean.

We hoped that our experience of the last three years had prepared us to deal with the dread of all circumnavigators, the southern Indian Ocean. Coming to the forefront in most sailors' minds were the expected gales and unpredictable weather. The large waves off the South African coast are no cups of tea, either.

We were still innocents abroad, for real gales at sea had never tested our wits. We pondered apprehensively whether we would have to use the storm jib or sea anchor, or both. Tales of others who had gone through gales and survived were frightening to listen to, but those recountable stories were the experiences of others and they were in the past. How would we react to being in a real gale at sea, or worse, a cyclone?

Our plan was to avoid the gale-infested waters south of the large island of Madagascar. We would set our course to the waters north of the large island. We hoped to explore out of the way groups of islands like the Farquhars, Gloriosos, Aldabra and the Comores. From there, we would sail south down the Mozambique Channel to reach Durban, South Africa where we would be reunited with our friends. Then we planned to sail around the Cape of Good Hope at Cape Town in January, the best time of the year for the rounding.

Wind'son, *Intermezzo* and *Rigadoon* among others were headed for that area. Bound for Singapore were *Sunflower* and *Arion III*. *Arion III* would carry on through the Mediterranean after a lengthy stay in Sri Lanka. Perhaps that would be the safer route to get across the Indian Ocean through its northern reaches. However, it presented different problems, such as piracy, political squabbles, more time en route, and higher cost for marinas, food and anchorages. The worst part might be slogging to windward up the Red Sea to pass through the Suez Canal.

On *Arion III*, Didi had been in touch with *Rigadoon* on her ham radio and told us about their incidents with the pirates. Carl and Jeanne were now underway from Jakarta bound for Diego Garcia in the Chagos Archipelago, on their first leg of the Indian Ocean Passage. Didi rowed over to tell us Jeanne was due to call and invited us to come aboard when the call was expected.

"How are the seas, Jeanne?" I asked my sister-in-law.

"Oh, they're about 20 feet high and the winds are clocked at about 40 knots. Things could be better but we're all right and so is *Rig*," she answered, using the shortened name for their able vessel. My heart felt for them and I knew the anxiety they must be feeling. On their first circumnavigation, one of their cruising friends had lost her life when the boat she was on rolled over in huge seas off the southern tip of Madagascar. She was caught in her forepeak cabin and drowned when water rushed in that could not exit the closed cabin door. The Indian Ocean is not to be taken lightly.

All of us were taking on fuel and supplies. Like most everything else in Bali, diesel fuel was cheap. We paid only $20 for a 55-gallon drum. The container was delivered aboard a sailing proa. Her skipper sculled alongside and hand-pumped the fuel into *Svea*'s tanks. Another service of Wayan Kota's "Bali Yahct Services!"

"See ya down the line," we called out, as we made our way through the anchorage and called out our last farewells. It was then August and it would not be until November when hopefully, we would all be assembled in a new land, far across the sea. Geographically, we were only half-way around the world. The second half would be the shortest in time, for there were fewer islands to break up the long passages. It should take less than a year to complete our circumnavigation, or so we thought when we departed the peaceful shores of Bali.

photo by Carl Moesly

Bali local market

CHAPTER 12

GALES IN THE INDIAN OCEAN

Passage to Christmas Island

Southeast winds were so light when we left Bali's harbor bound for Christmas Island that we had to raise the lightweight twins to get moving. Outside the harbor, Don counted more than 200 sailing proas already at work trolling for fish in their coastal waters. A pod of pilot whales rushed towards us and I looked for them to start throwing leis of flowers on our decks to tell us we were welcome to return to beautiful Bali.

The wind freshened a day later and we changed to the big blue twin staysails everbent westward, *Svea* is served well by her downwind twins. Small stormy petrels, sailors call Mother Carey's chickens, came out of nowhere to dance upon the newly-formed white caps, like ballerinas in their tiny toe shoes.

Svea's log read 115 miles made good noon to noon, but when Don plotted the course on paper we actually had made only 92. A current was retarding our progress and Christmas Island still lay 500 miles away from us.

"Thar she blows!" Don shouted with glee when a very big whale surfaced and blew a geyser from his blow hole. Then, thrusting his giant flukes skyward, he sounded and left behind a huge swirl of water in his descent.

"He's coming towards us," I screamed and was ready to start the engine, but he went on his way with nary a nudge to scratch his back against *Svea's* hull. Don was disappointed that the huge mammal had not stayed around so he could have had a better look at him.

The southeast trades remained steady. Under clear skies we maintained our rhumb line course towards the west, the sun at our backs in the morning and in our faces in the afternoon. It was easy enough to keep our bearings knowing those two things. To sail around the world, all one has to do is head west, well almost, anyway.

There was no doubt as to our general position when the yellow-plumed tropic bird appeared above *Svea's* masthead. Christmas Island tropic birds are the yellow tropic birds found only in the waters of the island giving them their name. Our steady flow of southeast trades began to waver, but *Svea* sailed into the night with no sail changes. Our early morning ritual was to clear the decks from the many flying fish that had erred in their flight plans during the night. It was no wonder that the anchorage at Christmas Island was called Flying Fish Cove.

About 100 miles from Christmas Island, Don tuned in the radio direction finder and located the island's signal, "X M S." As we hove-to during the night, a current pulled us towards land and by morning, the island was well in sight. Gannets and boobies filled the air and the smell of their

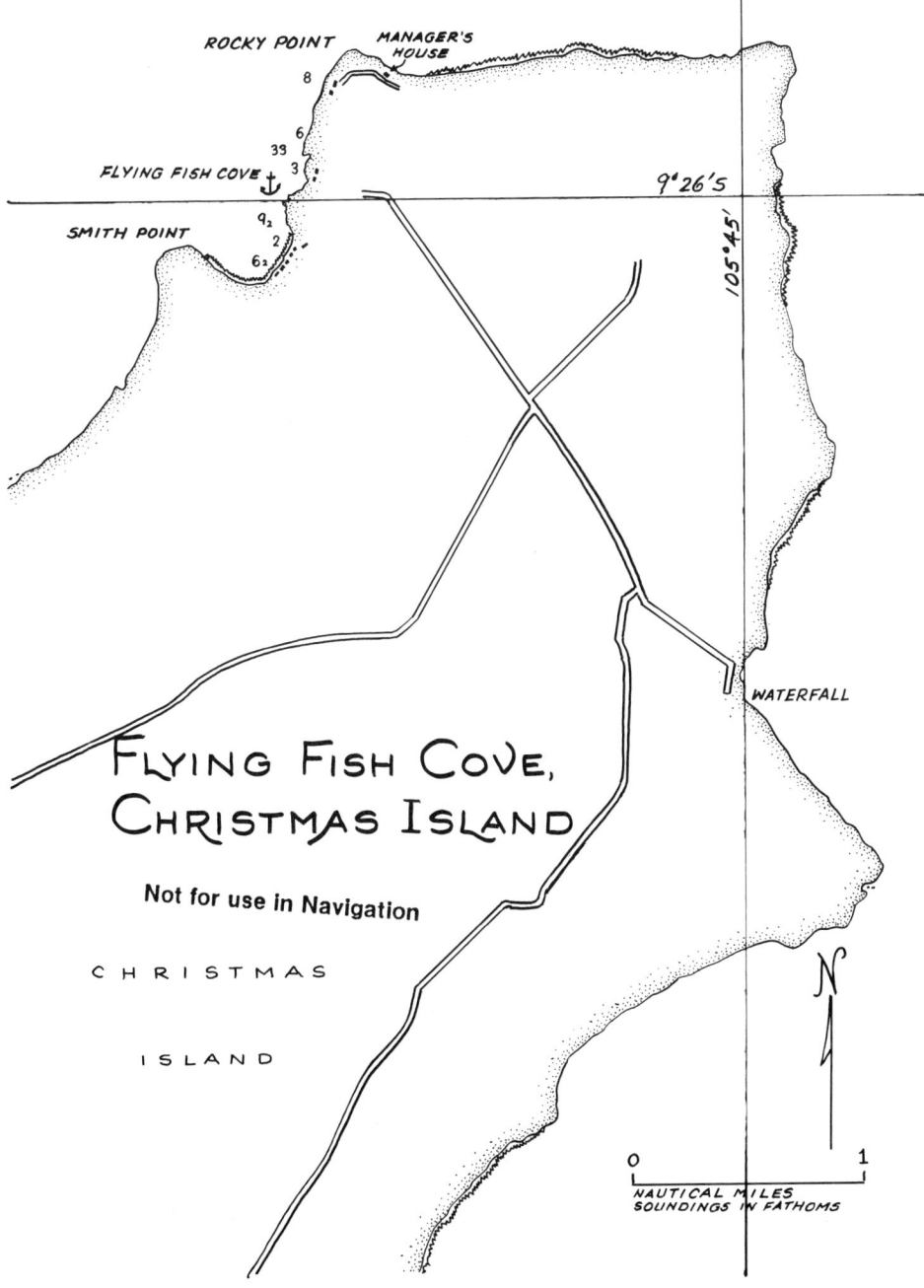

guano grew stronger as we closed with the very high island. Christmas Island is being mined for its rich deposits of phosphates by the British Phosphate Company. The labor force is a large contingent of Malaysians who have lived for years on the island, now a possession of Australia.

Flying Fish Cove, Christmas Island

A lovely female police sergeant greeted Don as he climbed ashore. Together they went to the immigration office where the paperwork was simple. The island is a company town. Just about everything is controlled by the mining company, from the yacht club down to the hospital and pharmacy. For free we could hop the company bus and take a tour of the island. The yacht club's bar is run on an honor service with a box to hold the chits. You pay these along with any other expenses incurred, at the company's office upon departure. We worried about the ease at which free-loading hippies could abuse the system. They could ruin it for cruising sailors who follow in their wake, as they did at Bora Bora.

"We're leaving on another Friday?" I asked when Don said it was time to bring *Poco* on deck.

"Isn't that our lucky day?" Don countered my question.

"One of these Fridays Murphy's law is going to catch up with us," I said. I was reluctant to leave. We had met some yachties we liked who were harbor-bound due to engine problems, and I enjoyed the friendly Australians ashore. One other yacht in the cove with a German couple aboard was loading supplies for their passage towards the Red Sea and back to their homeland. She was putting aboard vast quantities of low priced Australian beer.

"Oh," she said as we went by in *Poco*, "When I go to sea, I drink. I don't eat. I get seasick." Maybe I should have taken a lesson from her.

"We've got a long run ahead of us," Don explained as we prepared the bridle to hoist *Poco* on board. "Cocos-Keeling is over 500 miles away and it's another 1,500 beyond Cocos to the Salomons in the Chagos. Then, we'll have most of this ocean behind us."

"I know! I know!" I frowned. "Maybe I'll take an airplane, as our one Aussie friend advised me to do when you had the great idea to sail across the Tasman Sea."

"Are you being a reluctant mate?" Don, half-disgusted and half-understanding asked.

"Oh no," I answered untruthfully. "I like sailing in rough seas, the wind in my face and salt spray in my hair and scudding along with the lee rail under water!"

"I've never known you to lie before," Don laughed. "Come on, Susan E., let's get this turkey rolling and get on to those islands. You'll change your mind when you get your toes in that beach sand."

Of course my attitude would change. I am a woman and that is my prerogative, but I had to be honest with myself. I was no different from any other sailor who feared the Indian Ocean and I knew that Don shared some of my apprehension. He just did not give into his emotions, never had, never would.

Passage to Pass by Cocos-Keeling

Big swells were running up from the south when we left Flying Fish Cove and we pondered their origin. Damn this anxiety clouding the issue of getting the present work done. "Set them aside Susan E.," I talked harshly with myself. "The barometer is steady and *Svea* is scudding along nicely. No cause for concern."

By morning the swells began to crest and spew out clouds of spray. We had to reduce sail and we pulled down the twins. We raised our favorite combination, "the answer to all problems," the jenny and mizzen. I began to relax knowing we could easily alter the jenny by rolling in some of the sail and jiffy reef the mizzen.

The wind increased further, and breaking waves accelerated their momentum to assault our small boat. As the waves grew larger, *Svea* grew smaller, until I knew we were much too inadequate to contest this huge and angry sea. The waves waged war seriously.

"Get the door in," Don called down to me. "The waves are threatening to come aboard!"

I pulled out the lightweight louvered door we usually use to close the companionway and set it in place. At least I could see Don's shadow through the slots and air could come below. But seawater came through the louvres and over the hatchway to drip into the galley sink. We had never had water come below before. This was something new and I did not like it.

"We need the storm jib," Don shouted down. "We're going too fast with the building wind. Let's get it up while we can still function on the foredeck."

I went into the forepeak to grab the sail and the storm door for the companionway stared back at me. Why had I painted it black? The ominous black door leered at me as I grabbed for the small jib. "You'll be back to get me next," it said in silent warning. The door was solid with only a small, but heavy, portlight to allow a thin stream of light below. No, I did not want to be put below behind that door. I shoved the thought aside and carried the jib to the cockpit. The sea was churning and hissing, and its anger frightened me. I looked only to raise the small jib after we had rolled in the remaining small area of the jenny.

After the work was done, we went below and Don tuned in the radio direction finder and found we were right on course for Cocos-Keeling. "We're not going to attempt a landfall in conditions like these," he said. "We have to keep these seas behind us."

"What do you want to do?" I asked, for I knew the seas coming abeam put us in a dangerous position.

Onward to the Salomons

"Let's carry on for the Salomons," he suggested.

We took a more northerly course thereby putting the seas on the quarter. They still pummeled us, but the direct hits were split apart by *Svea's* pointed stern. Thank God for double-enders in following seas! It was difficult to gauge the speed of the wind without an anemometer. The wind was well over 30 knots, and the seas were over 12 feet high. We had none of that in the South Pacific except the time we were anchored at Raiatea. The Indian Ocean was indeed living up to its reputation and frightening *Svea's* crew of two who had little experience with gales.

The next day was August 20th, Don's birthday. My happy birthday ditty was drowned out by the moaning and groaning wind. We learned by the sound of the rushing waves which ones would board us and which would fall short, but shove us ahead with an added push as they crested and sent added momentum towards *Svea's* stern. A very large wave hurtled itself upon us like a battering ram, and *Svea* staggered under the blow. She shook violently to rid herself of the offender, then rallied and the pilot pulled her back onto course. Thank God for the pilot to save us from standing out in that water-soaked cockpit.

Don had to go out in the cockpit to start the engine for the daily charging of the battery. The angry seas spit at him with every breaking crest. "I think I see a break in the clouds," he shouted down with decided eagerness of hope in his voice.

"Maybe we can get a sun sight." I grasped for a chance to know where we were. It had been two days since we had taken a sun sight and plotted our position.

"We'll know soon enough," Don tried to pacify me, for I knew he would not jeopardize the sextant by taking it out into the water-drenched cockpit unless he absolutely had to. Perching on an upturned dinghy trying to maintain a balance, while at the same time trying to look through a small lens to bring the sun and the horizon together, is a feat for an accomplished acrobat. Don is not a nimble one.

By changing course for the Chagos Archipelago and its Salomon Islands, we had added another 1,500 miles to our passage. I guess there was no real reason to pinpoint our position. It was just that I liked to know every noon hour where we were. It was always cause for a celebration with our daily cold beer, but neither of us was in any mood for celebrating, and as far as the cold beer, we needed nothing to dull our senses. I pursued the matter of the sight no further.

The winds began to slacken and the violence of the sea waned. Now there was not enough wind for the small storm jib to keep us ahead of the still large seas and we had to raise more sail. We unfurled the jenny and raised the already reefed mizzen. "No sense getting foolhardy about shaking out that reef," Don said, but we did celebrate the end of the gale by having a decent meal cooked on a stove, that for a change, did not threaten to throw its pots at me.

The sun greeted us the following day and Don went topsides to look around. He found 21 flying fish in various stages of rigor mortis lying about the decks. He pulled the sextant from its wooden box and took a sun sight. After three days of no sights at all, we found our position to be 1,300 miles from the Salomons.

The gale was spent, but why did the milky overcast remain? Why had not the trade wind clouds replaced the cirrus ones? Why were the swells still so large and coming from the south? The answers began to fall in place when the misty rain fell with a decided drop in the barometer. We were in for another storm. According to the pilot charts, we were supposed to be free of gales in this part of the Indian Ocean. What went wrong? Of course, we were the rare statistic.

Rains continued throughout the night and each squall was prefaced by an added increase of wind. Thinking it might be the last chance to have a good hot meal, I fixed sausage and eggs for breakfast. The barometer read 29.81 inches and was falling. Its reading back at Christmas Island was a steady 29.88 inches. Now as the usual high diurnal time of day should show a rise in pressure, our glass was down and falling. Although the seas began to build, the wind had not, and we cautiously raised the starboard blue to keep us ahead of the seas.

The confusion of the seas made galley duty miserable. To save steps at lunchtime, I put both of our meals on one tray, rather than on individual trays as I normally do. Don's pent-up frustrations burst forth in a show of anger when he could not juggle the two meals on the single tray. He promptly threw the tray overboard, like a temper-wrought child would toss a toy out of his playpen. I chastised him, but my words only gave more fire to his anger. Damn this uncertain weather. Both of us sat on a tinder box waiting for someone to strike a match.

By mid-afternoon, the barometer had fallen to 29.67 inches and the wind was finally on the increase. We brought down the twin and lashed it to the lifelines. This was a foolish thing to do, but the winds had been so erratic we thought we might be raising it again. A few hours later, we were furling the jenny and hanking on the storm jib. On the last sail change, we donned safety harnesses, which we rarely used because of *Svea*'s high lifelines. We were in a new ball game now and took no chances of flirting with danger. Our decks were awash with swirling water and a sudden lurch could send us over the lifelines and into the foaming cauldron of white water. It did not take the sea long to become angry.

It was a miserable night as we huddled in foul weather gear on the cabin sole and stayed ready to run topsides should the need arise. Shrieking wind and charging waves did little to ease the anxiety as we passed from darkness into a new day of much the same weather. My mind was running away with itself as I visualized *Svea* being picked up by the exceptionally frantic sea and pitched into the tumbling and turbulent waterfalls. Strangely, the wind had not increased during the night and we were grateful for the small mercy.

Autopilot Kaput

Don had the engine running and we were down below when I felt a sudden shift in direction and I jumped up to look at the compass over Don's bunk. "Our heading is east, not west!" I shouted, and looked out the drenched portlight to see the waves coming off our bow, and not the stern where they should have been. "Something's happened to the pilot!" I screamed and grabbed for my foul weather gear on my way out of the companionway door.

"Don, it's not working at all," I cried as I pulled the tiller back to midcenter and then to starboard to bring *Svea* back on course. I switched off the useless switch to the pilot and disengaged the hydraulic system. "Oh, God! Please let Don find the problem. We have over eight days before we reach land. Please, let Don find the trouble!" I beseeched Him.

Meanwhile, Don had located the source of the pilot's failure. Debris had clogged a limber hole under the shaft. With the constant drip of the stuffing box adding water to the sealed compartment, it gradually reached a level to keep the V-belt to the pilot constantly lubricated with oily water. This caused it to slip on its pulley. "I've found it," Don shouted up to relieve my worries. "Just keep her on course. I've got to clean up this mess."

Svea fought my insistence to keep her head from turning into the wind. Without the pilot, I could not imagine hand-steering that obstinate vessel for miles on end. Lashing the tiller would not have worked in the quartering sea conditions, so I reached deeper into my reserves, swallowed hard and held fast to course.

It took Don two hours to clean up the mess and remove all of the oil from the shaft, pulley, V-belt and bilge. Restrained so long hunched over in the tiny space in which he had to work, Don's own reserves of strength were tested beyond capacity and fatigue raised its ugly head. The only cure is rest.

"How can I do that when *Svea* is in danger?" Don barked at me when I suggested he lie down on his bunk and rest.

"You've got to try," I talked as calmly as I could to convince him. He laid down on his bunk and nods of sleep overtook him.

I looked around our once cozy cabin. Water dripped over the galley sink from the constant dousings that the companionway hatch was taking. Splashes were thrown across the aisle to spray the contents of the shelves behind the head. Water sloshed around the sink and splattered the cabinets and shelves behind it. Beads of saltwater dripped from the overhead beams where they joined the cabin sides. Water was being forced under the bedded-down mouldings. Some of the portlights oozed drips from water forced through their sealed frames. The invasion of seawater had violated our privacy and I was angry. I wanted to scream to the heavens, "How dare you do this to us?" Instead, I looked at the one comforting note, our still-dry bunks, and cuddled up in my sheepskin until it was time to check the watch.

With dawn there was a hint of the sun and the wind had decreased to less than 20 knots. I mentally painted a smiling face on the glass of the barometer when I saw the pressure was on the rise. Don's face wore a smile as well when he rose, for rest and hopes for a better day had erased the frowns of fatigue.

Photo by Carl Moesly

Balinese girl at Temple with food offering (Chapter 11)

CHAPTER 13

EXTRA-TROPICAL CYCLONE

Water Below and Water Above

For the next two days, we were cloaked in grey. The ominous-looking leaden sky turned the sea the same color and the wind moaned only groans, not shrieks, just groans.

"What is the sky trying to tell us?" I asked Don as I searched through all of our books on weather and tried to match the clouds hanging so heavily overhead with the illustrations. Cirrocumulus clouds marched into altocumulus and left only a grey sky, but with a slightly different woven pattern.

"Gloom," Don answered simply, for there was no answer, not yet, not until the barometer began a steady decline and we knew we were in for our third gale. The pattern was set when the light misty rain began to fall with the barometer. No sun and no sights. Our last sight had put us 860 miles from the nearest island in the Chagos Archipelago, Diego Garcia, the island leased from the British by the United States as a Navy and Air Force base.

The barometer reached a new low of 29.75 inches, more than a 10th of an inch from the Christmas Island reading and the squalls came continuously. Each brought a stronger wind. "Why did we leave a house and the ground it sat upon?" I cried out as the last reading of the barometer sent shivers down my back. I wanted to take it off the wall and turn it upside down, hoping the mercury would go back up. I kept asking myself why we were out there and why in such a small boat? We simply wanted to see the world through rose-colored glasses, but those glasses were now fogged by clouds of fear.

"Come on, Susan E. It's time to get the mizzen down. It's blowing out there," Don said calmly. It seems the more unseated my nerves become the calmer Don reacts to balance my lack of emotional control.

Our foul weather gear was soaked inside as well as out, and my clammy sea boots smelled like something rotten. Wet and clammy as they were, they still afforded some protection from the elements. In order to furl the mizzen, I have to perch on the edge of the cockpit coaming. This time as I grabbed for the sail to bring it down, water swirling around the catwalk marched right up the coaming and into my boots. The sea was a maze of white water as three distinct wave patterns waged war. Rain and spray mixed to fill the air with brackish water. This was a far worse gale than the previous two. The tiny storm jib strained at its hanks to be set free. With the small sail, we were still doing in excess of 7 knots as we ran with the storm.

Waves slammed into us and the wind shrieked to new heights. We tried to get some sleep, but only dozed fitfully. *Svea* rose with the waves, swayed from side to side, then lunged into the trough. This was not a violent motion, for her heavy long keel dug deeply into the faces of the waves to keep her bottom down and her bow up. She handled the stern waves well, but she labored with those from abeam.

Svea was pounded relentlessly by the violent seas. The sounds down below were terrifying. A new sound! "What is that?" I asked Don, as if he had all of the answers.

"Green water is coming aboard. What you hear are the cockpit gratings sloshing back and forth each time *Svea* gets pooped," Don explained with no added inflections in his steady voice. I tried to look through the louvered door, but I could see nothing in the darkness. In the shadows cast by the masthead light, I saw only the tiller strenuously trying to keep *Svea* on course. The pilot doing the work no man could do for very long periods at a time. The clicking sound that the electronics of the pilot makes every time there is a course correction was coming in rapid-fire succession. Still, we were maintaining our desired heading.

With the light of day, we could see through drenched portlights what we had been experiencing, but could not see, during the night. White water of cresting waves continued to lay seige on us. I don't really know which is worse, to see the horrendous sea, or hear it in darkness and ponder its magnitude. Either way it was terrifying. Three wave patterns still contested one another and their battlefield was covered with white foam. Fountains of water exploded into the air as challenging waves met head on in their battles to overcome one another.

"We're into something bigger than a gale, bigger than those last ones. Aren't we?" I asked the question with little doubt as to the answer.

"Fraid so," Don nodded as he grabbed an apple for his breakfast. Just the sight of fruit sent twitches to my stomach.

It happened about nine o'clock. Kah-whoom! The violent explosive sound racked through *Svea's* heavily-timbered hull. I sat bolt upright in my bunk as water poured into my face. I had not recovered from the shock of water when I suddenly became the target for flying bottles, jars and the tea kettle. The Dutch oven, which had been on the stove, landed right-side up at my feet and the shattered chimney to the kerosene light above the table was inside. Ironically, the glass shade had remained in place. Utter terror seized me and I screamed, "What portlight has broken?" But there were no portlights broken, or any hatches. The water had come through the dogged-down hatch above the table and water tight ventilators. A wave had picked *Svea* up, tossed her violently on her starboard beam, then fallen on top of her. It's difficult to say at what angle she stopped and righted herself.

Don had been sitting on the aft end of the port bunk when the wave heaved our small boat over. As if shot by a cannon, canned goods exploded from underneath the port bunk and pushed heavy cushions and plywood boards out of their way to hurtle through the air, and end up in a heap near my feet. Books from behind Don's head flew past him to join the sodden pile of jettisoned debris. Don jumped up and ran back to the bilge pump. The automatic switch had cut on to announce that *Svea*'s bilges were taking on water. I could hear it sloshing back and forth, soaking everything it could reach.

Don crawled back in the tunnel alongside the engine and he saw a waterfall cascading down from the lazarette opening in the cockpit, an opening supposedly sealed off by battened-down boards and locks. The waves had hit with such a violence as to gain that impossible entry into *Svea*'s depths. Burdened with her load of seawater, *Svea* staggered from side to side, trying desperately to raise her bow to meet the seas. Failing, she plunged headlong into the waves like a floating, but mostly submerged, water-logged raft. Crippled as she was, she lay prey to another wave that could cause her to founder completely.

"Are we gaining on the water?" I asked, but Don could not hear me above the roaring wind and thrashing seas. Still stunned, I tasted vinegar on my lips and realized that somewhere between the shelf behind the stove and me the bottle had broken and spewed out its contents. Pieces of broken spice jars littered my bunk. The faces of my Toby mugs screwed down on the shelf behind me were ludicrously painted with dill weed and caraway seed, among others. Mace peppered my bunk sheet and sodden bedclothes. The wet pillow soaked up the red-orange dye to make a strange batik design. The pungent odor of damp spices reeked more than the spice catacombs of Bali's market. Pieces of broken glass were everywhere, and round dents had been hammered into the solid teak cabin side where spice jars had ended their flight through space. Edges of cabinets and the fiddles on top of the freezer had been knicked by the passing broken glass. I looked down at myself and saw a small trickle of blood oozing from a cut on my arm. Miraculously I had escaped serious injury. I was not important and *Svea*, at that moment, was in dire need of help. We had to purge her full belly of water.

I was about to grab for the handle of another manual pump, but I felt *Svea*'s position change. "My God! It's the pilot! Gone again!" I cried, as I grabbed for my foul weather jacket instead, and tumbled through the half-closed companionway door to reach the cockpit. I lunged for the tiller which was jammed to starboard.

"Here!" Don gained my attention. "Put this on and snap it to the ring on the coaming." Don shouted as he had taken time from his pumping to throw out my safety harness. The stainless steel arm that connects the tiller to the hydraulic ram had locked it in a turn to port. Quickly, I switched off the electric and the tiller came freely in my hand.

Svea was riding helplessly in a violently agitated sea. I could hardly tell from what direction the confused seas were coming. I braced the tiller between my body and upper arm and tried to sort out the worst pattern of waves and head *Svea* in front of them. Still, she had to contend with the waves abeam. I was too busy concentrating on steering to worry about the magnitude of my fear. The speed indicator crazily darted from 5 knots to 10, past that mark and back down again to 5, as *Svea* made her uphill pull on the back side of the waves.

A new and bigger wave crested astern and broke short of *Svea*'s stern, but threw out its fury in a roar of bubbling foam. *Svea* lifted slightly and settled into the sea. The only sail we had up was the small storm jib and it was hanging only on its bottom hanks. The top three had pulled loose and the freed piece of cloth fought fiercely to tear itself away from the hanks holding its bottom edge to the forestay.

"We have to get this jib down," I yelled to Don when he stuck his head out to check on me.

"No, we have to get this water out of her first," he shouted. "Look over the side now and see if water is coming out the through-hull for the bilge pump."

I released my hold on the tiller and ran to the side and looked over, but saw only a backwash of water coming out of the hole, "Negative," I answered as I grabbed for the tiller that was slamming back and forth. Years of dust and debris packed behind ceilings had washed down to the bottom of the bilge to clog the strainer on the pump. Don worked laboriously to clear the screen. After several trips out into the cockpit to dump out the gunk-laden bucket, he tried the pump again and it belched out black clods of dirt before it began anew to evacuate the seawater.

"We're winning," Don screamed at me.

"But are we?" I thought, though I answered his words with a weak smile. The angry seas were mountainous and cannonading *Svea* with tremendous thrusts that shook her. She was in their way and they tried to push her aside. I was drenched constantly by green water tossed into the cockpit. The heavy rains added to the deluge of water. I tried so hard to steer *Svea* downwind from the biggest waves, but to look behind me to pick them out was an awesome task.

When her bilge was finally free from water, *Svea* began to respond more easily to the assaults from the waves and rose to meet them, then followed them down into the troughs where she wallowed and prepared herself for the next staggering blow. She was now handling the situation far better than I was. I knew better than to erupt with any female histrionics that had no part in the serious role I was undertaking.

With his pumping completed, Don came out to bring down the jib. Snapping his lifeline to hopefully immmovable objects as he groped his way along the cabin side, Don gained the mast and took the line and made a secure bight around a cleat. Like a dog roped to a post, he reached out for the sail to bring it down. I could not leave the helm to help him on the plunging foredeck. Constant spray clouded him from my sight. I could see nothing but chaotic fountains of spray as they shot across the deck like firehoses. Don finally cajoled the sail into a mad nest of tie-downs, which he secured to the bow anchor roller, more under the water than out as *Svea* plunged into the seas.

Svea continued to charge down the faces of the waves. We were going far too fast under bare poles in the still-building seas. Spray mixed with wind-driven rain pelted us like hundreds of daggers piercing the heavy thickness of our foul weather gear. We had to use our hands to protect our faces. Don had returned to the cockpit after he had finished his work on the foredeck. As he watched the seas, Don realized that *Svea* stood a good chance of pitch-poling into the seas. We doubted the use of our storm anchor, which would hold *Svea* stern-to, or bow-to the waves. Nevertheless, the heavy canvas anchor stood ready in the cockpit locker.

"I think we should lie-a-hull," Don shouted to me as *Svea* slid down the face of another wave. It was unthinkable to heave-to into the wind as we normally did in more moderate sea conditions.

I looked behind as I mulled the thought and watched an extra big wave begin its death march towards us. I guided *Svea* down its front and into its trough. "Please don't dig your bow in, old girl," I pleaded with our matriarch of the seas. She shook the water from her decks, raised her bow and waited for the next wave to lift her stern.

"We can't continue like this," Don exclaimed.

"No," I said simply. Considering *Svea*'s deep keel, her heavy pitch-pine planking, which had withstood the last blow with no structural damage, plus her low profile, which offered little resistance to the wind, we chose to lie-a-hull. We only prayed she would stay upright and not somersault into the vicious seas.

We lashed her tiller hard over to starboard to point her bow off the waves and she seemed to find her own position as the sea moved her. There was nothing else we could do for her, so we secured the companionway door behind us and went below. Strange that we had not put in the storm door, but I guess we had been too busy with other things and I did not suggest we do it now.

We were pleasantly surprised to find her motion much easier than we had anticipated and attributed it to her heavy construction. The reek of spices filled the air in the pent-up cabin. I leaned over to pick up sodden books that had ended up in the fray on the floor and tossed them into my laundry buckets. My bunk was littered with pillows soggy with saltwater, broken glass, seeds and weeds, all sprinkled liberally with paprika, mace, cinnamon and nutmeg. Any other time I would have laughed at the storm's imaginative mix of curry, but seasickness struck with a vengeance. I had leaned over too many times to pick up the debris. I reeled towards the head, but I could bring nothing up, for very little had gone down in the last two days.

I rolled up the mess on my bunk in the stained sheet and tossed it in another bucket. The stateroom was in complete disarray with wet sails mingling with sodden towels, dripping foul weather gear, wet trash, paper towels and stinking soggy sea boots. Dangling safety harnesses added a grotesqueness to the jumbled chaos. I lay prone on my bunk and tried to fight off another upheaval of my stomach. Don too, had fallen victim to the first stages of the illness.

We pondered the immediate future, but the answer came when the barometer plummeted to new lows. I began taking the readings more often and could hardly keep up with the speed of the decline: 29.69 inches down to 29.63, down more and more to 29.55 inches. A new sense of horror flooded over me and *Svea* twisted and tumbled in the torturous seas. The gale had been blowing, and steadily increasing, for over 24 hours. That damnable Indian Ocean was really putting on a show for us.

When the barometer reached 29.50 inches, it stopped its descent, but the wind took on a higher pitch, like a soprano reaching for a high note that was well out of her range. Then, suddenly, oh so suddenly, there was silence. No shrieks, no moans, or even groans. Even the waves let up their battle cries. For 5 hours there was silence and a bottomed-out barometer. After the 5 hours the winds returned as abruptly as they had left, only this time from the opposite direction. We had just pased through the eye of a cyclone and were about to meet its other side, face to face.

Survival became uppermost in our minds. No life raft. Our transmitter still was not sending, since we had not been able to replace the burned-out transistors in Australia. But who would hear us anyway? We were miles from any land and we had been well out of the shipping lanes. The last sight was 860 miles from Diego Garcia! There would be no freighters to spot us should we have to take to the water. We would not last long in mere life jackets. No one would know we were missing, not until November when our cruising friends congregated at Durban and we wouldn't be there. It was August. The future looked more than bleak.

"Don, look! The barometer! It's going up!" I cried. "It really is!" The barometer was on a decided upturn and the wind subdued its shrieks and lapsed into dull moans and groans, its death throes. The rains let up too and the waves toned down their assaults. At dawn, a glimmer of light broke through the leaden sky and hope for a new and better day shone down upon us.

"We're going to survive. We're going to make it," I shouted in great exultation. Our mighty vessel, the matriarch of the fleet, with all of the odds against her, had overcome and won her contest.

There was no explanation for a storm to occur in that part of the ocean at that time of the year. Extra-tropical cyclones are known to happen spontaneously when the pressures and conditions are ripe for them to form. We just happened to be the target for that rare occurrence.

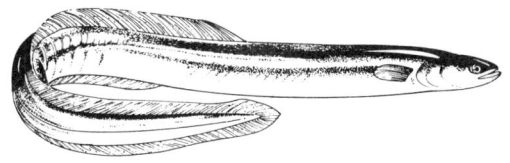

CHAPTER 14

THE TEMPEST IS OVER

Damage Assessment

We prepared to get underway after the storm had spent itself, and our terror diminished to vivid afterthoughts. Don went topsides to survey the damage. The lifelines were dangerously loose. One stanchion was ripped from the deck while another was loose. This damage was done when boarding seas kept filling the pockets of the sail that we had foolishly left lashed to the lifelines. The force of the water against the sail was more than the stanchions could bear. The base on the port side of the mizzen traveler was loose. "We can sail only on the port tack if we use the mizzen," Don said as he surveyed the base on the starboard side which seemed to be holding.

I was right behind Don as we continued our inspection. "Don, look at the mast! There's no varnish at all down the side behind the halyard," I cried, as I knew the laborious job in store for us to build coats of varnish on the barren and bruised wood.

"That wire acted like a rasp on the soft wood," Don ran his fingers along some of the chafed wood that he could reach. "Strange that we had never heard the steel halyard drumming against the mast. And for so many hours! Normally it's like being inside of a drum down below when that happens."

"We couldn't hear a thing above that shrieking wind," I answered. The wind was definitely dying, but not in silence. It groaned a few gasping sighs to remind us of its vengeance only hours earlier.

More inspections. More problems, but nothing structural was damaged or even moved around, as is often the case in wooden vessels when stress is brought to bear on their giving timbers. The main problem that confronted us was the failure of the pilot to respond to all of its signals. "It'll turn to starboard but won't return and go to port," Don called down to me. He had sent me below to listen for the clicking sounds coming from the electronics box each time the solenoid switches cut in to relay their messages.

"The little men in the box just aren't answering," I called up to Don who was working the switch and the remote control. Having to hand-steer *Svea* was no longer a fear, but a known fact.

Reluctant to get underway in the still-large seas, we remained lying-a-hull to sort out the problems. I sewed the piston snaps back on the storm jib and added extra seizings for good measure. We would need that sail when we got underway, for the wind was far from being a gentle breeze.

Passage to Diego Garcia, Chagos Archipelago

When the sun broke through the grey skies to stay awhile, Don took a sight. We were 600 miles from Diego Garcia. At least the storm had blown

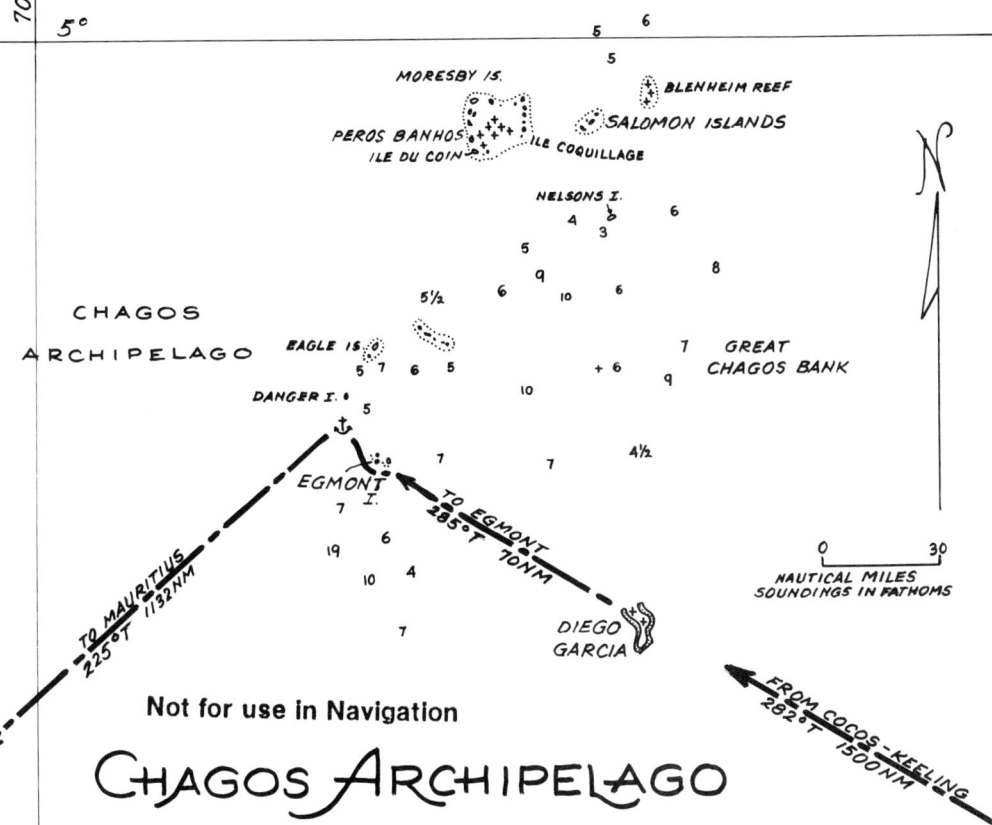

Not for use in Navigation

Chagos Archipelago

us in the right direction. "Let's get this turkey rolling, Susan E.," Don said when he plotted our course. "We've got lots of sea miles ahead of us and they're all to be gained by hand-steering."

After the main was up, we found we could set the pins to hold the tiller, that *Svea* could steer herself with only the one sail up. We were afraid to unfurl the jenny, for the storm had torn some stitching away from the sun shield. If we got it unfurled, the protective cloth might tear loose and wrap itself into a snarled mess. We had the storm jib for a foresail, but it was too small for normal winds. If we needed a working jib, I would have to dig through the sail locker to find it. We never used that sail as we relied so on the jenny.

Only the barometer remained steady for the next several days, for the wind played tricks with us, or games of hide and seek. We looked for enough breeze to get *Svea* rolling. We seemed to be in another pattern of doldrums, strong gusty squalls, then no wind at all. With so little wind, hand steering was miserable. When it rained as it often did, water came through my laced-down hood and ran down the middle of my back to puddle in the seat of my britches. Going below was not much different, for it was like entering a rain forest. Everything dripped from the moisture encouraged by the intrusion of saltwater and the lack of sunshine to dry it.

At one point, when the wind fell astern, we raised the big blues and were delighted to find that *Svea* could steer herself on the downwind course. The feeling was short-lived as the wind died and we were forced to bring down the sails. This was a difficult task even with the pilot, but without that help, the job seemed impossible and dangerous. I learned to appreciate that silent crew member more than ever.

When the sun decided it was going to stay awhile, I dragged out wet, soggy towels and clothes to try to get them dry in the sun. Nothing salty ever really dries and the claminess returned as soon as I took them below out of the sun. I thought of sailors who wash their clothes in seawater and knew it no wonder that saltwater sores broke out when they had to sit for so many hours in damp clothing.

The fickle ocean just wouldn't let us rest, not properly anyway. We were tired, tired from the storm, tired from what it left in its wake and miserably tired of hand-steering. The frustrations aggravated by the lousy weather often made us give up trying to sail *Svea* in windless conditions, and we opted for the chance to go below and crawl into our bunks and sleep.

If it were any consolation, we found we were not the only miserable creatures upset by the storm, for several spent birds came to visit and rest to gain strength before they resumed their flights. A large flock of gulls hovered over a disturbed patch of water. Above them soared a frigate bird who was waiting to steal their catches. A frigate bird, so far from land. Our last position put land 200 miles away. Poor bird, a real anomaly in the world of sea birds, like the sooty tern who also cannot land on the water to rest. Apparently the storm had diverted his course, as it had the other sea birds that came aboard. But the frigate would never come aboard, his safety was in the free airflows he needed to stay aloft. To get airborne, he needs a spring board to push him into space. His feet are far too small to give his body, with its wide wing span, the needed lift-off. Feeling sorry for the plight of the misguided birds took my mind away from my own self-pity.

Don was terribly tired. I had to watch out for fatigue. With the ever-changing wind, he needed his wits about him, and yet he unselfishly made sure that I got more than my share of sleep. "Don," I said calmly. "Let's both go below and rest. We can heave-to."

"Maybe tonight. Maybe tonight," he answered and stoically pulled *Svea* back on course. The anxieties of weather, broken gear and the dampness below were all taking their toll. We had sodden carpets, and gardens of mildew sprouting in overwhelming numbers. We were exhausted. Don was having trouble starting the once-faithful engine. It behaved erratically when it finally did start, and it poured out white smoke from the exhaust. The fluctuations in r.p.m.s also warned us that something was definitely wrong.

A bright note appeared when a storm-weary noddy tern paid a call. Definitely a land-based bird, the noddy was blown well off course and I was glad that *Svea* could offer some refuge. For a nest, the bird found a coil of rope on the cabin top. The noddy would go out fishing and always return to her coil of rope for a rest. Another visitor, a booby, came aboard. For awhile the noddy tried to show her seniority, but the booby's sharp beak put her back in the proper pecking order of sea birds. A second booby came to join the first. The two of them found their favorite perch on top of the mizzen boom. *Svea* was quickly becoming a floating aviary. Only the frequent rains that washed away their droppings saved the birds' homesteaded claims for them.

Don picked up a weak signal from Diego Garcia's radio beacon and for the first time in many days puffy trade wind clouds, like fleecy white lambs, scampered across the field of blue. To cancel our new-found glee, I found a sizeable leak in the exhaust riser and Don shut off the engine immediately. He had been running it to hasten our progress.

Don went below to check the leak and returned to the cockpit. "I don't think it's wise to carry on for the Salomons," Don submitted to the burden of our problems. "We're now getting fuel in the oil. I just drained a little oil into a cup and found it. Diego Garcia is a U.S. base and surely there will be some form of communication we can use to have parts mailed in from the States. I'm almost sure we need a new fuel injector pump. The spare we are carrying is only an emergency, and won't last long."

"You're probably right," I answered and immediately relaxed the tension that had been mounting with each newly-discovered problem emanating from the cyclone. It had taken us 27 days to make this 2,000-mile passage. Only 22 days had seen us 3,000 miles across the Pacific. We expected this passage to have been a typical passage within the trade winds, but the fickle Indian Ocean had made different arrangements.

When we were abreast of the atoll's pass to the lagoon, we knew we needed the engine to maneuver the channel. One compensation lay in the fact that had there been too many reef encumbrances in the pass, the U.S. would have blasted them away to make a clear passage for their own ships. "Will it start?" I asked Don as he hunched down in the cockpit ready to kick the starter button.

Diego Garcia, Chagos Archipelago

The engine did not start on the first kick, but did on the second. I knew I would never again complain about the noise of that diesel engine. To me the sound was that of a purring kitten, although one with a very sore throat. I was so excited about coming into an American port where we could expect friendly faces and a chance to repair our damages.

But I was wrong! Dead wrong!

"We have nothing to offer you," said both British security officers after they boarded *Svea* from a dreadful landing barge that had plowed into *Svea*'s quarter and smashed our fishing rod holder attached to the stern pulpit. They insisted further, "We are just a cement depot here. There is nothing, no one to help you, and you'd best leave."

"My God, we can't leave," I cried. "We hardly have an engine and we can't sail with only one sail." I looked beyond the shoreline and saw long rows of buildings, hangars for airplanes, housing for personnel and large fuel tanks, remindful of our own Port Everglades, but on a smaller scale. Yes, there were the other tanks closer to the dock that could have served as a concrete depot, but there was more to Diego Garcia than that. We were not to be fooled by the British officers who controlled the security of the atoll.

"We have to make repairs before we can carry on," Don said in his usually calm voice. "We've been in gales ever since we left Christmas Island. We can't use the engine and we can't use either the mizzen or genoa sails until we make repairs. Our lifelines are loose and dangerous. We have a serious leak in our stainless steel exhaust riser." I would have ranted, not kept my cool like Don, who laid the cards of our problems on the table. To add to our distress, a torrential rain was upon us. I can not express the utter disappointment I felt in having the door to assistance closed in our faces.

Finally, the officers realized the seriousness of our plight, that we were not an invasionary force and truly had storm-wrought problems. The one fellow asked, "Can you do the repairs yourself? We can only give you fresh water and only you, as captain, will be allowed ashore, but restricted to the water faucet at the dock."

"Yes, I'll try to make my own repairs," Don answered simply.

With the offer of fresh water from the dock and that given freely from heavens, I even washed the salt out of clothes and carpets, and everything else in sight that had been doused with saltwater. For hours, Don bent over the engine and straightened up only to go topsides and work on re-seating the stanchions and mizzen traveler. Another task was to build moulding strips to seal off the lazarette hatch in the cockpit. We would not go back to sea and give another boarding sea a chance to come below via the same route it had during the cyclone. Varnish on the mast would have to wait until a better place. We'd need more time to pull out still another locker of brushes, paints and varnishes. There were too many projects going at one time on a 38-foot boat. Only one can work below, so I kept my washing limited to the cockpit area. Everytime it rained I looked sadly at the mast, knowing that each raindrop was turning the barren wood black. There was no time at Diego Garcia to be spared on cosmetics.

The officials did allow us to stay in their lagoon, but we were under constant surveillance by the tower behind the dock. We did not go unnoticed by a young serviceman who was a diesel mechanic. He offered to us his three-day leave to see if he could help us. His three days would not

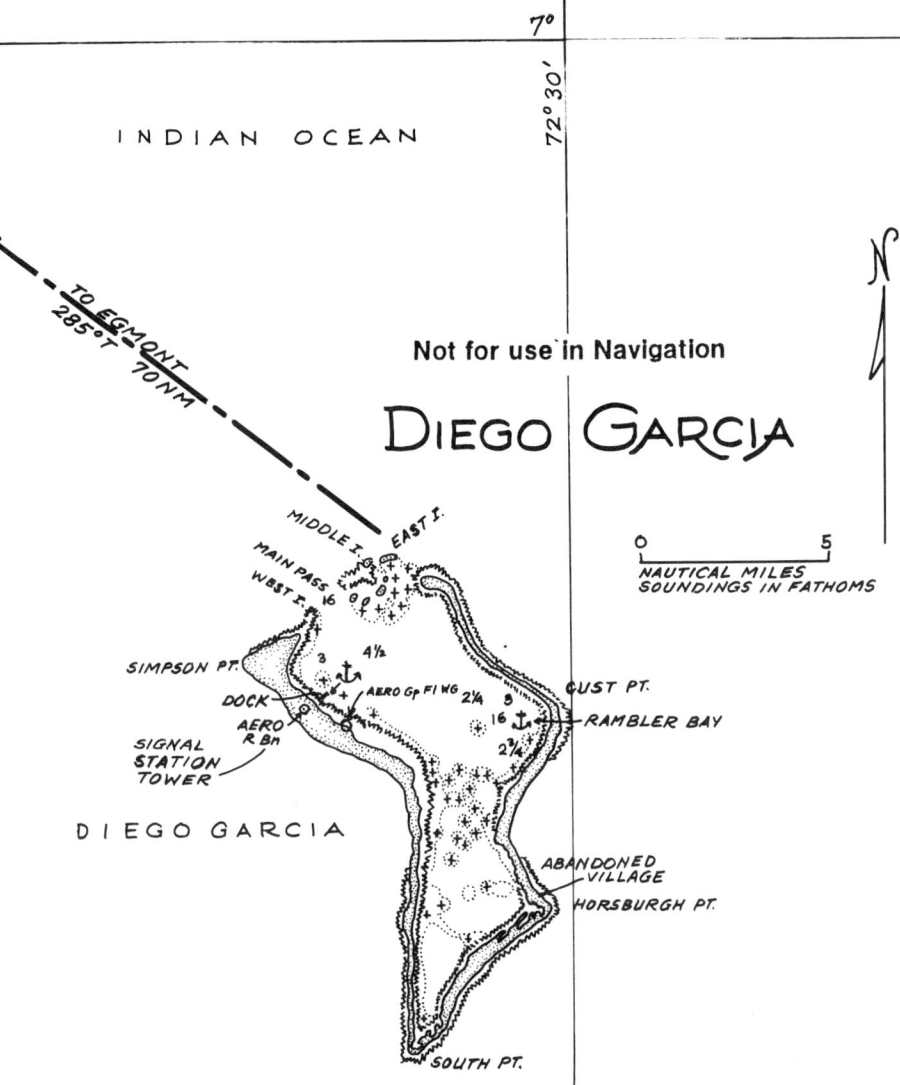

have taken him off the island, but would have put him on the pleasant east side of the atoll across the lagoon. On their free days the men do a lot of skindiving around the fringing reefs.

Unfortunately, Dave's hard labor did not solve our engine problem. He did manage to get the diesel started after the three of us all took turns at pumping up the hydraulic reservoir. It took 180 exhausting strokes to build up the pressure to 2,100 pounds. If the engine failed to start on the first attempt, then it was back to the pump handle and 180 more strokes. Don replaced the fuel injector pump and checked the timing, but that was not our problem either. We were not to find the answers until almost four months later when we had the engine pulled from the boat at Mauritius.

One day the officer came aboard by the same frightful steel landing barge that smashed the rod holder to tell us of their recent tragedy. Other than Dave, he was our only contact with the base. He began, "Four men went over to the other side of the atoll to look for crayfish and only three returned. The fourth boy was carried out to sea by an extra large swell that sent all of them awash on the coral reef. The other three were able to swim ashore."

"Oh, the poor parents," I immediately thought of the grieving parents, but also of our own past experiences when large swells knocked us off our feet on coral reefs.

"Well, the men were warned not to go, as the same cyclone that hit you folks caused alarmingly large swells on that side of the atoll, but they went anyway." The officer blamed the tragedy on the boys' disobedience. Whatever the cause or reason, a boy's life was lost and it had provoked a lot of paperwork for the bureaucratic hierarchy. We were asked again not to make any waves for their overworked clerical staff. Earlier, Dave had taken the co-ordinates of our position, when the cyclone came upon us, to the base's meterologist who had been tracking the extra-tropical cyclone. His position of the eye of the storm agreed with our own. Perhaps the real truth, that we indeed had been through a cyclone, registered on the security officers and they were less hostile.

"There's more strong wind forecast and you must seek better protection in the lee of Rambler Bay across the lagoon," our security guard called to us from the barge, which made me cringe everytime I saw it approaching *Svea*. "We'll put Dave on board to help you get the engine started, then get on over there."

Diego Garcia's lagoon has an 8-mile fetch, and there are no inner islands or islets to provide lees. This means it gets rough and a boat must be prepared to change from one side to the other as the wind changes. The lagoon is encumbered with scattered reefs and shoals, making the crossing dangerous in poor light conditions. Although frightened about the impending strong winds, I was relieved to leave the watchful eyes that always rained down on us from the tower. Also, on this opposite side of the lagoon I was free to go ashore, as it was not considered part of the base. It had been over a month since my feet had stepped on land. The freedom of an area larger than a 38-foot sailboat was wonderful. So was the taste of the fresh coconuts we found.

The bad weather system never materialized and we carried on with our work and went ashore in the late afternoons. Kicking over rocks to look for shells and peering under ledges seemed to ease the tension that we were constantly under in that security-controlled atmosphere. Even the automatic pilot relaxed its frozen state and began to answer more of its signals. Apparently, the moist salty conditions had affected the electronics, and once cleaned and dried, they attempted a recovery. Still, we were terribly frustrated by the inability to sort out the engine failure.

"You know," Don said. "It would not be safe for us to carry on towards the Salomons as originally planned. We've got to get this engine repaired properly."

"I know," I said. "What do you want to do?"

"It's not what I want to do," Don answered. "It's what I think we should do, and that's to get down to Mauritius where there is a dealer for our diesel and we can probably have spare parts shipped in. I think it unwise to sail around islands and reefs with a sick engine."

"I know you're right," I said sadly, for I had so wanted to go around the north end of Madagascar.

"We'll leave here and sail over to the next Chagos Island at Egmont, get some varnish on the mast and a few other repairs, then sail south instead of north," Don suggested.

As if the security guard had overheard our conversation, he came alongside the next day in a borrowed power boat and handed us already signed clearance papers. "I'm not rushing you," he almost blushed when he said it. "But I am sure you are about ready to leave and knew you would want these for your next port. Besides," he added, "I want to tell you that we have been in touch with your brother on *Rigadoon.*"

I stopped him immediately, "*Rigadoon*? Where are they? Have they been here? Do you know them?"

"They're over at Egmont and Carl has been radioing us daily weather information. He's anxious to see you and wants to help you with your repairs," the man said, but did not answer all of my questions.

"They talked about coming down here, but we've been out of touch. We last told him that we were heading up to the north end of Madagascar," Don said with surprise. "But that's great. We were just talking about going to Egmont to complete our repairs."

"Well, on my next radio sched' I'll tell him you are on your way, say tomorrow?" the Britisher asked.

"Yeah, I guess, maybe so, or the next day. It's only an overnight sail," Don answered. "Won't you come aboard for a drink? Thanks to Dave's help I can even offer you a little ice, as we run the engine a little each day to keep up the battery."

"Thank you," the Briton said and swung his legs over the lifelines and joined us in the cockpit. "I myself am leaving on the next plane for the U.K. Perhaps you might like to hear a funny story?" he paused and rubbed his finger alongside his nose. "That is, a funny story on us."

"Yes, go on," Don encouraged the subtle humor of the British officer.

"Did you see that sailboat come in about a week ago?" he asked.

"No, what sailboat?" Don countered.

"Well, a ketch under the Dutch flag sailed right into the lagoon, past the observation tower and up to the anchorage at the old settlement," he rubbed the side of his nose again. "No one even knew they were there until one of our aircraft reported seeing them. They've been here a whole week! I've just come from there now," he chuckled.

"A whole week, and in that time they never tried to attack the base?" Don laughed.

"Some security you guys have," I laughed. "Is that why you are leaving the island?"

"Oh, no," he laughed. "My time is up and I am more than happy to get off this rock."

The officer never revealed to us any of the secrets of the base. He did not have to. The number of airplanes that flew back and forth across the lagoon left little doubt about the traffic that was served at Diego Garcia. There were far too many day sailors who were out on the weekends in Rambler Bay to think they staffed a mere cement depot. We were not fooled by this British officer. Although part of the island is leased by the United States, Diego Garcia is owned by the British and they provide the security forces.

When the British took control of the archipelago away from Mauritius in 1965, they moved every native man, woman and child off the island as well as off the entire Chagos Archipelago. Many of them went to Mauritius, nearly 1,200 miles to the southwest. But other than a similar French-Creole patois language, the 419 displaced persons had very little in common with the city life the larger, over-populated island offered. The people of Diego and their neighbors were island people and copra plantation people. They had never before coped with city streets, walls of restrictions or halls of bureaucracy. Their new life was totally foreign and unacceptable. There was little they could do against those who caused their exodus.

With repairs done, we were eager to get on to Egmont and a rendevous with *Rigadoon*. With the possibility that the engine would not start to get us into Egmont's lagoon, Don had made certain that work had been done to insure the safety of the vessel, should we have to carry on for Mauritius. The cosmetics could wait, but not life-threatening problems.

Photo by Carl Moesly

Rigadoon tied to World War II concrete dock in Gavutu Harbor, Florida I., Solomons (Chapter 3)

CHAPTER 15

EGMONT AND MAURITIUS PASSAGE

Passage to Egmont Islands

With lighter hearts and a pilot that was trying to work, we left Diego Garcia, also leaving behind us the gloom that had surrounded us for so long. Egmont was only 70 miles away from the security-locked Diego Garcia, but it could have been a world away. When we arrived after a pleasant overnight sail, there was no one there, not even *Rigadoon*.

Egmont Islands Lagoon

"Don, I don't see *Rigadoon*'s masts," I said as I peered across the reefs and into the lagoon. Maybe somewhere, behind a cove or around one of the islets that circle the lagoon, would be Carl and Jeanne's 50-foot ketch. "Maybe if we go on into the lagoon and peek around some of the islands?" I asked with little hope of finding the tall masts hiding behind palm trees on the low-lying islands.

"They're not here and I doubted that they were when the British Rep' told us. They just told us a bunch of lies to get us out of Diego," Don said in disgust. "Come on now, we've got to see if we can get this engine started. We'll need it to get through the pass and across the lagoon to the anchorage," Don changed the subject. "If we don't have an engine we'll have to sail on for Mauritius. Might not be such a bad idea anyway, and then we'll get to the problem sooner."

"Come on yourself Gloomy Gus, the engine is going to start and we are going to enjoy these islands," I said with great confidence. When the engine fired on the first kick, the shock that my words may have triggered a miracle startled me. It would have been impossible to maneuver the pass and the lagoon itself without an engine. The lagoon was circled by five islands and smaller islets, and was peppered with reefs and coral heads.

"I'll bet there are fish around those coral heads," Don said as the pleasant thought brought a smile to his face. The sun was high and the fleecy trade wind clouds cast small grey shadows on the clear water. We nudged Svea towards a wide expanse of white sandy beach with profuse palms, within 100 yards of Ile Sudest. We dropped the anchor, and *Svea* fell back into a deep pool of blue water. We were protected on all but one side by land. In the monsoon season with northwesterly winds, our anchorage would be untenable. This was not the time of the northwest monsoons, and we were going to enjoy the beauty of the Egmont group of islands.

I relaxed under the spell of the peaceful scene, "Seems we're back to a life of beer and skittles."

"Beer?" piped up Don. "Did I hear you say beer?" His head peered down the companionway as I was fixing lunch. In my hand were two cold beers.

"You bet! I just had a feeling the engine would get us in here and I put two beers in the freezer and turned it on for the time it took to cross the lagoon," I smirked. Enough of fears, worries, gloom and doom. I ranted on out loud, "Damn you, Indian Ocean, you and your hexes and threats. Put your wrath away! We're going to enjoy this island and you go pick on someone else."

Don caught my words mid-air, "Remember, we get the work done before we play."

We did work in the mornings and into the afternoons, but a few hours of the day were saved for relaxing. The island was uninhabited except for hordes of wart-covered rats and zillions of hermit crabs. Rats have a way of surviving on very little, but on Egmont's islands they had a feast on the many coconut trees. These had grown quite wild since the population had been moved to Mauritius along with the people of Diego Garcia. We kicked over old bottles and came across stone-laid foundations of former dwellings and the remains of an old well. All gave silent evidence that the island was once a scene of life. Copra harvesting was their work. Now, the trees were overgrown and young plants starved out the fruit-bearing trees.

Hearts of Palm

By culling some of the younger trees, we did the older trees a favor as well as our own greenery-starved stomachs. We had not eaten fresh vegetables since Christmas Island. I devised many methods of cooking and serving hearts of coconut palm, a gourmet treat even for kings. We delighted in the abundant supply of coconuts. We ate hunks of sweet coconut meat as a child eats candy. On land we were amused at the hermit crabs who were always on the hunt for a new shell to house their growing bodies. Some of them were not very clever in selecting shells with inadequate dimensions or broken ones that did not travel well. The crabs lumbered along carrying their homes with them. We had little problem with the rats, for they skittered off for the safety of fallen logs and bush to escape us.

Turtles darted back and forth in the lagoon. It was great fun to chase them in *Poco*, that is, when they were not chasing one another. It was the mating season and Egmont Lagoon was their trysting place. Along the shoreline, young manta rays played and jumped in the shallow water as children would in a newly rain-swept street gutter. Their wings tossed up the water in animated attempts to douse their playmates. Don had been right about the coral heads yielding fish. We hardly had the lure down when a snapper grabbed it to provide us with fresh protein. At the change of tide, we cast for bonefish off the sand bores filling in with sand to bridge the islands. The fish hover at the bar waiting for water just high enough to get them across the sand, but yet not high enough to flood the mud flats. On these flats they feed on crabs coming out of their holes at low water to feed themselves. The cycle of life is evident in the man-for-

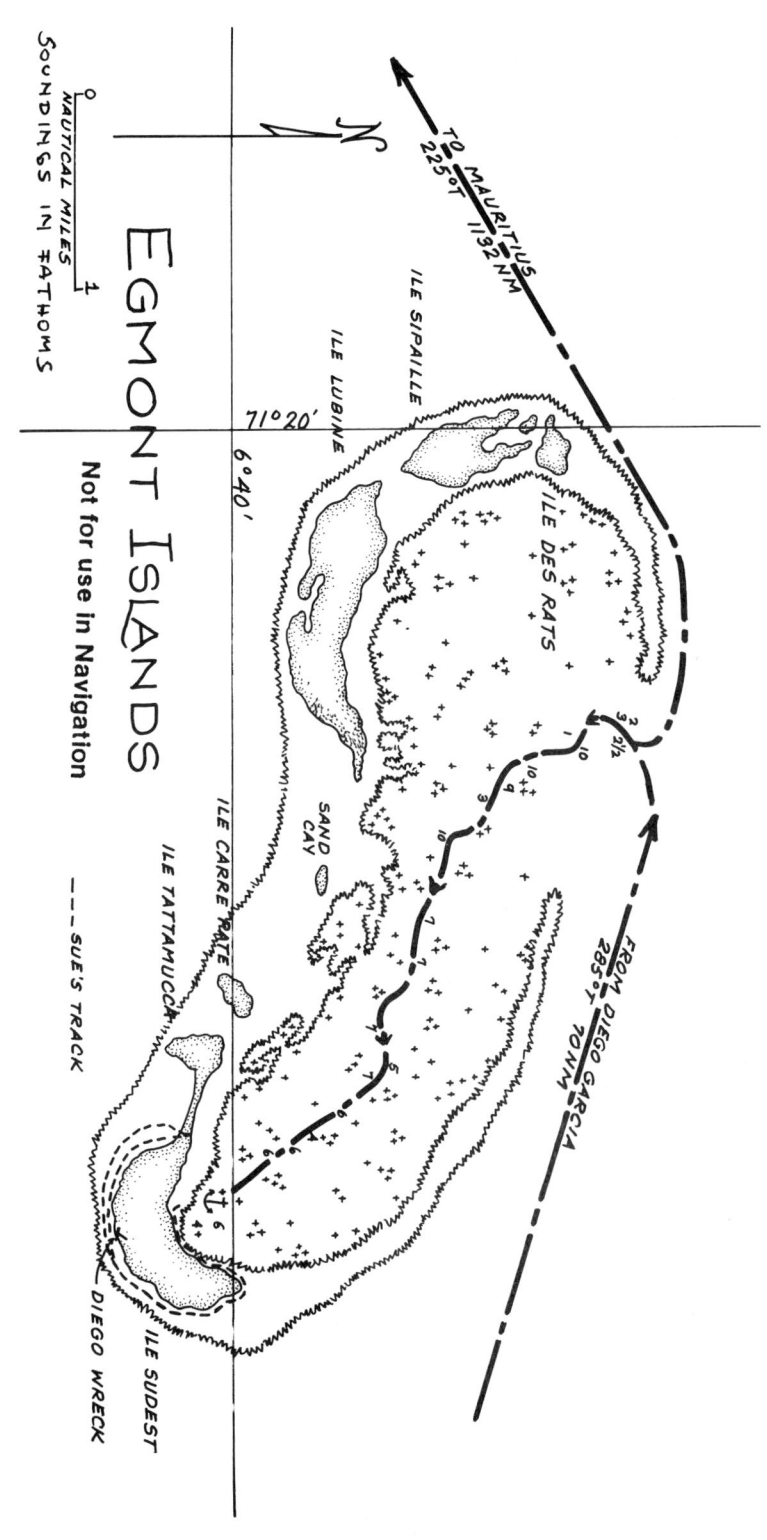

saken islands where the creatures are uninterrupted in their learned routines of survival.

The Beachcomber

"Miles and miles of white beaches," I said as I looked at the sloping shorelines of the scattered islets and islands, "almost like the Bahamas." I left Don with his spinning rod and began to meander down the beach in pursuit of seashells or anything else that strikes the interest of an inveterate beachcomber. Beachcombers do not always have to find a treasure to satisfy their pleasure. The pleasure lies in being able to set yourself apart from worldly cares and share those belonging to nature.

I returned to Don who was still fishing off the point of land. "Any luck?" I asked.

"I can't get these spooks to take the pink jigs that the bonefish in the Bahamas like," Don frowned as he cast out a different jig.

"Why should they take something artificial when they have so much food around them?" I said as I turned to go around the end of the island to search a different part of the beach.

"Hmm," he grumbled at my insinuation that he might be skunked as a bone fisherman.

One afternoon I finished my work a little earlier than usual and decided to do a little beachcombing towards the southeast side of the island where I had not been. As I began a brisk walk across the beach, I was invigorated with the return of the good things about cruising and decided to circumnavigate the whole of Ile Sudest. From memory, I recalled the chart and thought it not a very big island. But why did every cove I thought to be the west end of the island turn into still another cove and not bend around the island to its east side? I kept walking and now my eyes were looking forward for the hope of seeing the end of the island, rather than down looking for seashells. But the island continued without a break to announce its western side. The inner barrier reef also seemed to go in a long straight line, and not follow a curve.

"This is silly," I began to talk with myself. "I must have been walking for over an hour and I still haven't found the end of the island. I know it has an end. I saw it myself on the chart. Maybe I should go back the way I came?" I questioned the wisdom of continuing my exploration. "No, surely, the next cove will yield the bend to the lagoon and it will take me much longer to retrace my steps."

My route along the beach took me past a stone monument erected in the memory of the shipwrecked *Diego*. "Diego 1935," I read off the inscription of the tarnished green bronze plaque. I searched my memory for a piece of history that would connect with the *Diego*, but nothing came to mind. The mystery of the sailing freight boat would be solved when we reached Mauritius. There on Egmont Island only a rusting steel tank, resting on the shallow reef, stood as a mute memorial.

Seeing monuments in cemeteries or on the shorelines of islands always provoked a bit of interest for us. But now *Diego's* memorial provoked ominous misgivings about my venturing on an expedition alone and late in the afternoon. The sun seemed to be descending much faster after it had reached my eye level. I knew I had to turn around now, or I would not make it back before dark.

"Don will be worrying about me," I thought as I looked to the west and pondered the time of the day. I wore a watch only when I was harborbound in a land of civilization. "He'll think I've broken a leg, or something. We're not allowed to have accidents to cause one another concern. I've got to get back." Through the thick coconut groves, I could see a faint stream of light coming from the lagoon side of the island. I remembered seeing a narrowing strip of land on the chart. With great hopes of gaining the lagoon by an overland route, I left the beach and walked inland. I did not get very far before I had to climb over tree stumps and push my way through thorny bushes. I bogged down in marshy swamplands where I was attacked by mosquitoes. Clinging vines reached out to ensnarl me in their webs. Without a machete, I would not cut my way through the jungle that kept me from reaching the lagoon, Don and *Svea*.

Now I know what authors mean when they write about impenetrable jungles. In desperation, I threw myself against the unyielding bushes in aborted attempts to push them down and out of my way. I only incurred more scratches and bruises to add to those I already had over my entire body. Even my sunglasses had been ripped out of my pocket by a thieving branch. Another had dumped the contents of my shell bucket.

"You utter fool," I talked seriously to myself for the first time in hours. "You must get out of this mess and go back the way you came. You'll have Don so upset he'll be out looking for you in the dark. Then both of you will end up lost or in trouble."

The sun was sinking lower towards the horizon. The tide had risen to cover my former steps in the sand and in places I had to wade through pools of water up to my waist. The incoming tide disguised the more shallow route I had followed earlier in the afternoon. The sun was already beneath the horizon putting a pink glow across the lagoon, when I made my final turn and saw Don standing in *Poco* and scanning the shoreline.

"Here I am! Here I am!" I screamed. Don had already spotted my silhouette against the waning short twilight and was heading *Poco* towards me. He scolded, but not so much as I warranted, or that I had said in self-condemnation. I think he was glad to see his mate, although I was a bit worse for wear. The multiple bleeding cuts did little to convince him that I was really all right.

We gave ourselves a few more days to enjoy the island and to let my scratches reach a surface healing. The repairs had gone well and our spirits were happier. Don had completed his carpentry work of reseating the stanchions, and the lifelines were solid and stable. The hatch to the lazarette opening was sealed so tightly with moulding strips and sealant compound that even we could not break the seal. We didn't plan to until we reached Mauritius. I had gone over all of the sails and repaired the stitching on the jenny and helped with the clean-ups of spare parts. Tools were cleaned and oiled as well. Several coats of varnish were laid on to the bare wood of the mast and other pieces of wood below gouged by flying glass. Even the engine was working enough to allow us to recharge the battery and run the freezer. The wonder of all, the pilot was operating all of its functions. We blamed its malaise on dampness below affecting the electronics. Once the saltwater-soaked carpets and all were rinsed and dried, the pilot sprang to life. The freezer was stocked with fish from the lagoon and we were ready to put our thoughts towards the 1,100-mile passage to Mauritius.

Passage to Mauritius

The gales and the cyclone that we had experienced seemed to have vanished. The steady southeast trade winds had been in command for over two weeks. We left Egmont Atoll with a fresh breeze at our backs and big blue twin staysails in front of us.

"Looks like we're going to make Mauritius by way of a straight rhumb line," Don said when nothing changed. Wind stayed the same, sky the same, course and speed agreed with the balance.

"Wouldn't that be just wonderful," I answered. "Maybe the Indian Ocean is trying to make amends for all of the insult and injury it caused us with its nasty temper."

A few squalls came and went with just enough rain to wash away the salt spray, but not enough for showers or laundry. Winds remained constant from a southeasterly direction, varying little at times with the few squalls. We entered a new time zone at 67°30′ E longitude and set the clock back one hour. We would subtract another hour when we gained 15 more degrees of longitude farther west. We kept the chronometer, our quartz watch, set to Greenwich Mean Time to agree with time signals, but the clock on the bulkhead was changed to local time.

With the coming of cirrus clouds that streaked above the softer and lower cumulus clouds, we were not surprised when the wind increased and we were forced to reef the main. It became a bumpy ride, but *Svea* clung to her rhumb line and romped along putting the miles behind her. As long as the cirrus clouds were predominant, we had strong winds. When the soft cumulus clouds took over, the wind settled down to a more sedate 15 knots, and *Svea* relaxed her headlong sprint to Mauritius. For a pleasant change, we were enjoying the ride. *Svea* guided us across the gentle sea towards the island where we were to stay for nine months.

As we drew closer to land, the weather deteriorated and at dawn a heavy haze curtained the horizon. We were looking for Piton Rivière Noir, 2,711 feet high. Surely we should see the top of that mountain.

"We can't see anything through that haze," Don explained. At noon we took a sight that put us 53 miles from land.

"I can't believe that a current carried us that far away from land during the night," I said. Yesterday's noon sight gave promise of land in sight soon, and we hove-to to keep from hitting it. Now, a day later, we were almost as far away.

"If we had a reliable engine we could close that gap and still get in there today," Don said disgustedly.

Two more days under sail and heaving-to, we finally drew close enough to the island at early dawn to watch the fleet of native pirogues leaving their shores at Grand Bay for a day's fishing. We knew our anchor would be down in their harbor that night. Again the comparison between native craft and their local weather conditions was strongly evident. These boats are built of heavy planking with high freeboards to keep seas and spray out of their cockpits. "Those boats are pretty sturdy. Does that give us a hint that they might have stormy weather in this part of the world?" I asked.

"Remember the pilot charts," Don said. "Cyclones curl around this island in the season, and out of season the winds are always strong."

Some of the pirogues stepped their masts and unfurled their worn and tattered lateen sails to aid their diesels, while others were under sail alone. Several pirogues depended solely on diesel engines which poured out great puffs of black smoke. Their exhausts had colored their transoms a dirty black. "By the looks of those exhausts, I am not sure you will find a diesel mechanic," I laughed at Don. "I think they need a few injectors replaced, or at least cleaned."

"Maybe it's a 'mañana' island," Don laughed with me.

"No, silly, this is a French island. Mañana is a Spanish word," I said, "and I can't remember the French word for tomorrow."

Photo by Carl Moesly

Straw basket vendors at Bali (Chapter 11)

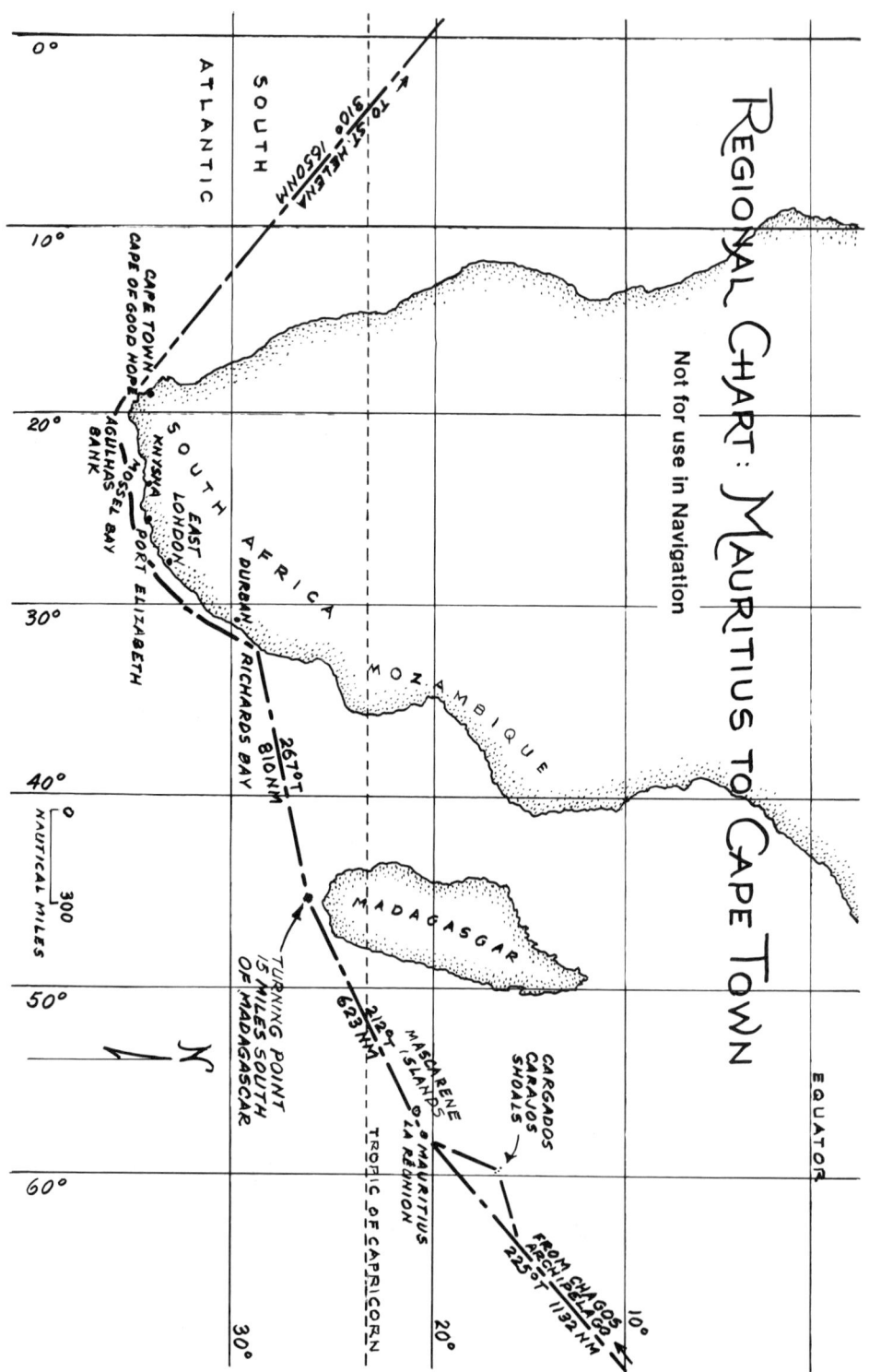

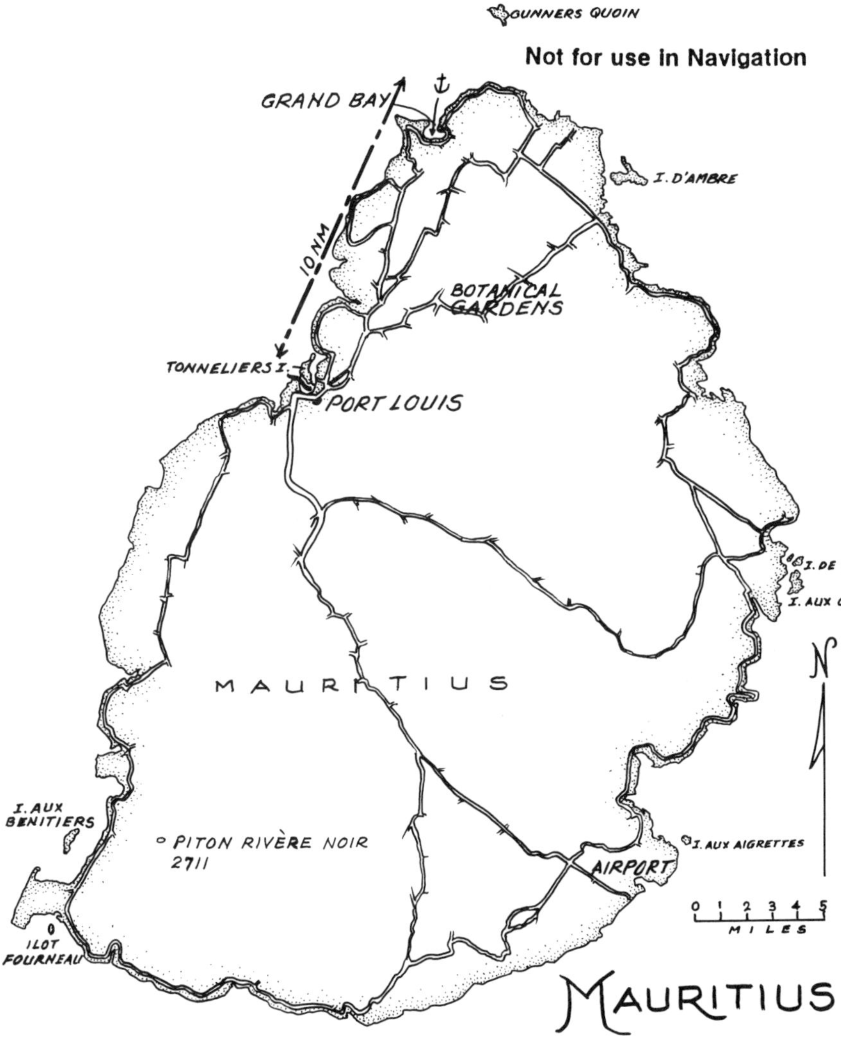

CHAPTER 16

LA BELLE MAURITIUS

Grand Bay Mauritius

"There they are," Don said excitedly. "There's *Wind'son* and *Rigadoon* and *Intermezzo*. We got here before they all left for Africa.

Carl hailed us and pointed out the best place to anchor. A very short time later, we were in *Poco* and headed back to *Rigadoon*. Jim and Cheryl came by in their dinghy to welcome us and I said, "Well, here we are, tail end Charlies again."

"We're just glad you are all right," answered Cheryl as she handed up a basket of fruit and vegetables for us. They were just about finished provisioning for their passage towards South Africa. "We were all so worried about you," she added.

"But how did you know to worry, for we were supposed to be up around the islands north of Madagascar?" I asked. Then we learned that Carl had been concerned about us and had contacted the American Embassy in Mauritius to try to locate us. They found we had been in Diego Garcia and the authorities had told them we had been through a cyclone, but we were not hurt.

"Those were lies then, that British officers told us? They said you were at Egmont and waiting for us. You never were in radio contact with them?" I fired the questions at Carl and Jeanne.

"Never," answered Jeanne. We did stop at Diego ourselves, and again at Egmont, but that was weeks before you were there. We certainly were not in radio contact with them and did not find out where you were until we contacted the embassy here in Mauritius."

We pushed that past behind us after we brought the news up to date. That night we celebrated our survival and arrival in Grand Bay with a big dinner aboard *Rigadoon*. Jeanne had made previous plans for dinner and had invited other guests. That was the night we met Yves Betuel, the grandson of the sea captain who lost his boat, the *Diego*, at Egmont. His tale unfolded when he learned we had stopped at the island. "Did you see a shipwreck on the south side of Ile Sudest?" asked Yves. He continued the story when I told him about seeing the monument and that only a rusting tank remained on the fringing reef. Yves always had a twinkle in his eye. He holds master seaman's papers himself.

"My grandfather sailed his *Diego* back and forth from Mauritius to the Chagos many times, but a storm put the sailing vessel on the reef. All of the men survived." But they were on the island 47 days before they were rescued."

We took to this French Mauritian immediately and he will always remain one of the bright stars that shone over us during our long stay in his homeland. As the days followed and our friends and family left for Africa, we welcomed the hospitality Yves Betuel gave to us so freely.

Tourists from all over the world come to beautiful Mauritius to loll on the beautiful beaches, and swim in the clear waters. There are multitudes of boutiques for them to shop in. Seafarers come to Mauritius for refuge from the savage sea and to replenish their supplies after the long passage across the Indian Ocean. Many of the sea captains come to haul their boats at the Taylor-Smith drydock in Port Louis. This yard has served freighters and sailing vessels since 1857 when the steam-powered pumps were first installed. The same old pumps continue to operate, but are powered now by diesel engines. It is not at all unusual to see ships in the large Port Louis Harbor flying the Greek flag moored next to those bearing the Russian flag. Mauritius is open to vessels of all nations, and wants to maintain its neutrality.

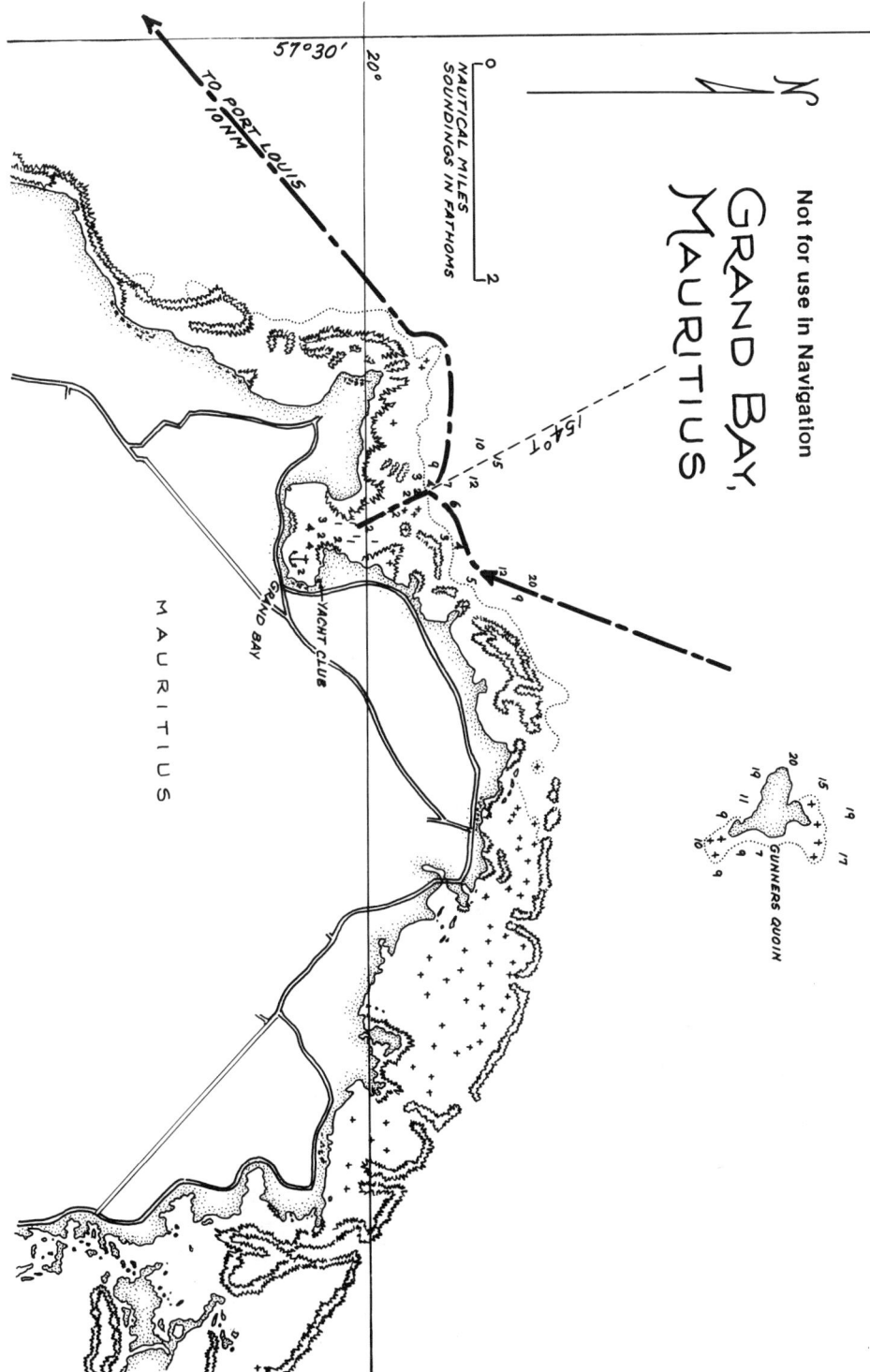

A small island of only 720 square miles, Mauritius supports a population of close to a million people. These include Hindus, Muslims, even Malaysians and Chinese. There is still a reigning minority of French aristocrats who produced the sugar barons, and are responsible for the success of the island's main industry, sugar cane. Like ships of all nations that mix in the harbor, so do places of worship that meld churches, temples, mosques, cathedrals and pagodas together all over the island. The mixtures of people have produced the Mauritian Creole who speak the common French-patois language.

In the last months before the beginning of the tropical cyclone season, Grand Bay at the northwest end of Mauritius gathers yachts from all over the world. Cruising sailors have come to lick their wounds and prepare for the 1,600-mile passage that will take them away from the summer cyclone tracks. These dangerous storms affect Mauritius and its sister islands of Reunion and Rodrigues, making up the Mascarene group. The passage will carry them on towards South Africa so they can round the Cape of Good Hope in the summer months of the southern hemisphere. Flags of many nations flew on the sterns of the boats anchored near *Svea* in Grand Bay. *Siddartha* from Holland, *Rainbird* from Australia, a small sloop from Germany and the large schooner from Italy were among those hosted by the Grand Bay Yacht Club. This hospitable club extends membership privileges to visiting cruising sailors.

"Don't you really think you should sail on to South Africa and get your engine repaired there?" asked Carl one night at dinner aboard *Rigadoon*. They had waited long enough to see if we still might be able to make the passage before the cyclone season locked us into Mauritius. Many of our friends had already left, and the anchorage was thinning out of foreign yachts.

"Carl," Don answered the question he had been asked before. "I just don't think it is wise to make that passage without electric power to supply me with any lights and the automatic pilot, not to mention the bilge pump. As you know, this can be the worst of all of the Indian Ocean Passages."

"Okay," Carl said. "Just thought I'd ask again. You know you stand a good chance of not getting away from this island for another six months, until the end of the cyclone season in July?"

"I am aware of that, but I don't consider *Svea* seaworthy in her present state. Anyway, how would I enter a South African port without an engine?" Don asked.

"You do have a point there," Carl conceded.

"I know if I don't get around the Cape of Good Hope within the next two months, I'll have to wait a whole year until the next season," Don put an end to the conversation.

Slowly as the boats departed, we were left with a sadness of not being able to follow them. By lagging behind waiting for us, Jeanne had been the envoy between the ham radio operators and the meterological station at Mauritius. She was on the air at regularly scheduled times to relay the

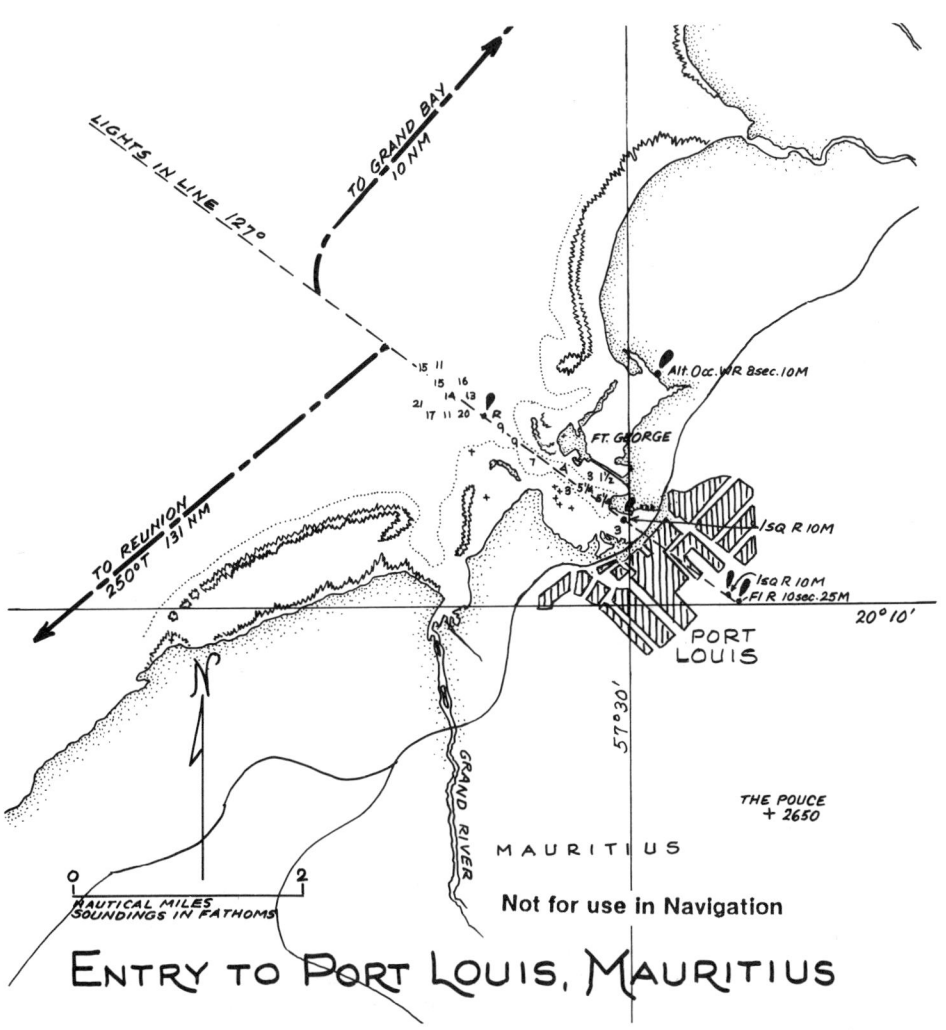

Entry to Port Louis, Mauritius

local weather forecasts to the cruising boats underway for South Africa. One time we overheard her conversation with Skip. *Intermezzo* was somewhere near Madagascar.

"When do these gales let up?" he asked. "We've had one right after another."

"You're in the heart of the gales," Jeanne answered and well-remembered their own experience on their first *Rigadoon*. She gave *Intermezzo*, and the others on stand-by, the local weather. She read off the official co-ordinates of weather fronts in the Indian Ocean.

And then it was time for *Rigadoon* to leave. December 1st, the official opening of the tropical cyclone season, was fast approaching. They had allowed themselves very little time to make the passage to Durban. With their departure, we were alone at Grand Bay, except for an occasional yacht that came south from Sri Lanka, or from other northern waters and had dodged the Southern Indian Ocean.

Don installed the new hydraulic head to the injector pump when it came in from the States. He checked the timing, which he found correct. The new part did not solve our problem. Yves often stopped by the club to see how we were progressing, after a day of supervising the Taylor-Smith Boatyard and its correlated businesses. He also brought any of our mail that had come to his office.

"How are things going?" our friend asked. When we told him not so well he repeated his long-standing invitation to bring *Svea* to the boatyard and let his mechanics take a look at the engine.

"We thank you Yves for your kindness. Perhaps that would be a smart move anyway with the cyclone season now upon us," Don said. We worried about being in Grand Bay without a reliable engine that we would need to maneuver, if a really big blow came into the bay.

"For that matter," Yves answered, "boats moored right here at Grand Bay have survived cyclones before but you know I open the drydock gates in the event of a cyclone. Local boats make their way into the basin and we close the gates and pump out some of the water to lower them out of the wind."

Being from Florida, we were no strangers to hurricanes and their vengeance. Don knew that the sandy holding ground was good at Grand Bay and that it was protected from wind on all but one side. But he doubted that any boat would hold to her anchors in this large bay if hit by winds of a strong cyclone.

Port Louis, Mauritius

We accepted Yves' invitation and sailed to Port Louis where we did have enough engine power to maneuver into the side canal adjacent to the drydock. Yves had told his yard crew to expect us. It was not long before two mechanics were on board to help us sort out the problem with the engine.

The diagnoses for the engine were as diverse as were the religions in Mauritius. First they suspected the valves and their clearance. They checked out correct. Then it was the injectors and we took those to the diesel shop in town and the mechanics found nothing wrong with them. Still, the problem with white smoke exhaust and hesitated startings existed. One mechanic said we had bad fuel when he learned we had taken on diesel at Bali. To them, the fuel was too cheap to be any good. Still, draining the fuel and replacing it did not solve the problem. Don again checked the timing of the injector pump, finding nothing wrong. About then, it was time for the work force to take off for their long holiday at Christmas time. "There is no major problem with your engine," said one mechanic for his parting diagnosis.

Meanwhile, we carried on with varied chores, and made friends with one of the mange-ridden mongrel dogs. With a little attention and food, she took it upon herself to be *Svea*'s guard dog and slept on the seawall alongside every night.

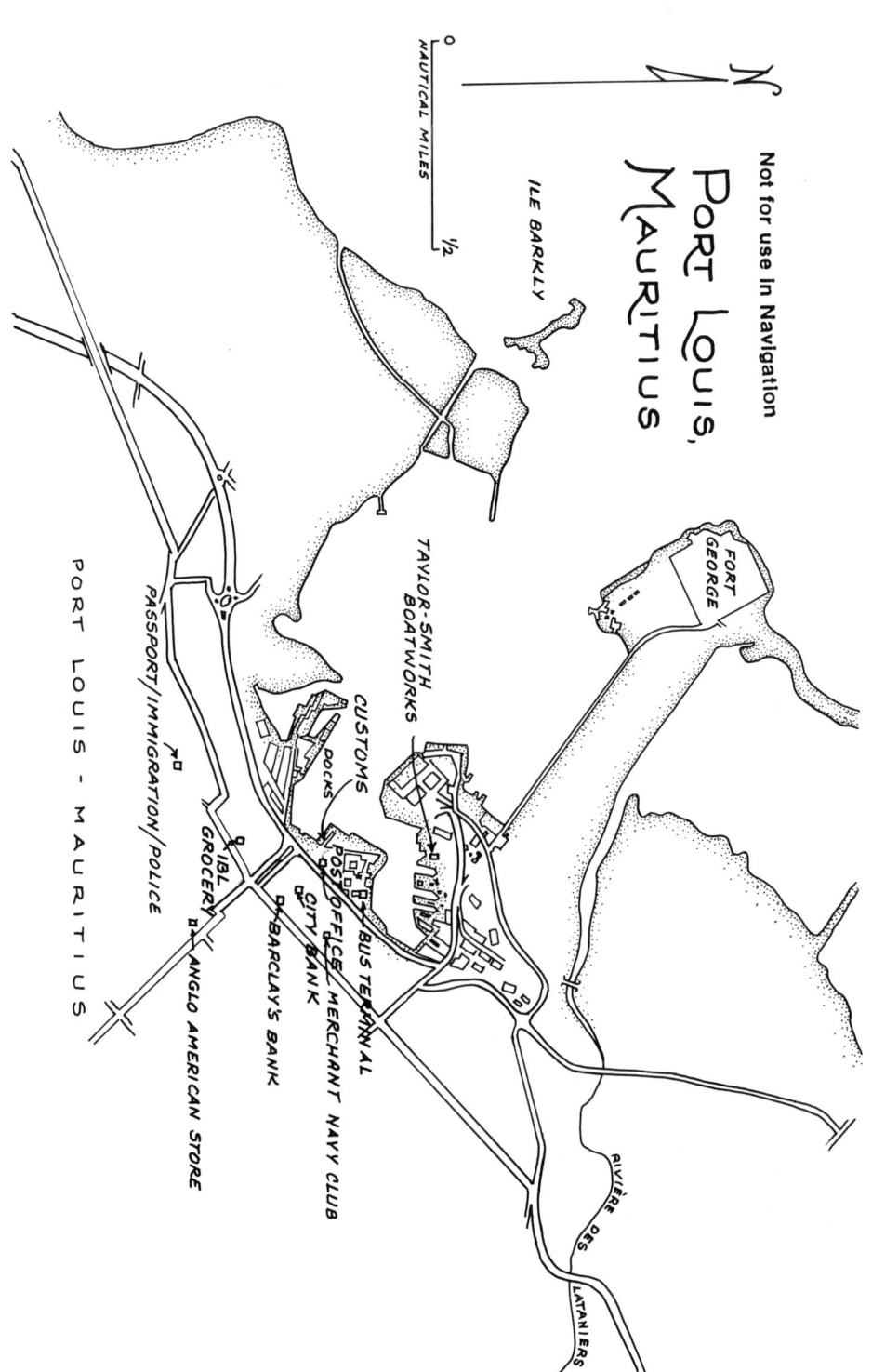

We enjoyed taking local bus rides that wound around the coastlines and through the hamlets where thatch-covered bungalows looked out over the sea. The ride from Grand Bay to Port Louis took us through the cane fields and up and around mountains. We crossed bridges spanning fast-moving streams where women were always seen doing their laundry. Our route carried us down into valleys planted with local produce and more sugar cane. Large piles of volcanic rocks, pushed away when the land was cleared, served as excellent fences. The strange peaks of the extinct volcanoes took on funny-looking shapes. They were aptly named, like Le Pouce (2,676 feet), which meant the thumb. It certainly looked like one and proved an excellent landmark for the sailor seeking a landfall on Mauritius.

The capital city of Port Louis was in sharp contrast to the beautiful white beaches and the greenery of the countryside. The ancient town was dirty and its broken sidewalks and gutters were cluttered with trash and sewage. Beggars were a common sight. One did not linger long in the marketplace where garbage was strewn about the mud-caked floors. I do admit to the delight of the spice section where I could sort through the open bins for anything from star anise to cumin seed. Creole curries are popular with tourists, but usually too spicy hot for cruising sailors who weaned themselves from exotic foods.

Cyclone Season

It was still before the work force left the boatyard for the Christmas holidays when we had learned about the first storm of the season that was spawned right on schedule. On December 1st, Albion was born 535 miles

Photo by Maurice La Coste

Aftermath of cyclone Claudette, Grand Baie, Mauritius

northeast of Rodrigues Island. As it made its route south-southeast, it slammed into a small steel sloop that had set out from Perth, Australia. The American yacht *Drambuie* was also out there somewhere as she had left Perth at the same time. Yves had come down to tell us about it.

"I was just on the radio and heard from Rodrigues," Yves said excitedly as he continued his story. "An Australian sloop named *White Wave* was hit just 300 miles from their island and will be underway soon for here. They are making jury-rig repairs there. They were dismasted, but managed to save their downwind booms and the boom to the main to make a temporary rig."

"But it's the cyclone season. What in the world were they doing out in the Indian Ocean this time of the year?" Don had asked. Yves just shook his head and added that there was no word from the yacht *Drambuie*.

"One thing is for sure, both boats gambled with the season and it looks as if they lost the wager," said our friend. Yves was more than familiar with the seas and the cyclone seasons around Mauritius.

About a week before Christmas, the yard crew had left for their holidays. Yves remained with a skeleton crew. Then the *White Wave* motored into Port Louis and Taylor-Smith Boatyard. Her crew had survived being knocked down twice and turned completely over and around another two times. Mastless and with all gear washed off their decks, including their life raft, they managed to send out a weak Morse code signal over their ham radio. Miraculously, their engine ran to give them some power. A freighter found them and gave them some fuel and food. Their foods had all been contaminated when a kerosene jug burst inside their galley locker. The sloop's survival was attributed to her steel construction and to the stalwart crew who stayed with her.

White Wave's saga was only the first of many to follow in what seemed to us a large anthology of sea tragedies, all having their origin in and around Mauritius. The cyclone Albion apparently missed the American yacht *Drambuie*. She was heard from later when her American couple put out a call on their ham radio that they were experiencing strong winds as they approached Mauritius. Those strong winds turned out to be the cyclone Claudette and *Drambuie* was never heard from after that. She was presumed lost at sea.

Later in the season, the raceboat *Kaleo*, involved in the spice race from Indonesia to Holland, lost her forestay short of Mauritius. She limped into Taylor-Smith Boatyard where Yves gave the captain his spare wire from his own sloop *Blue Shadow*. The *Kaleo* later met another disaster 130 miles off the African coast when she was hit by a freak wave and dismasted. It was reported from a Durban newspaper that the same freak wave tore into another raceboat and damaged her steering.

In the path of destruction was the 20,000-ton freighter *Devonshire*. Six men were severely injured when they were thrown into the ship's machinery by the force of the wave. We were convinced that cyclones revolving around Mauritius were dangerous. The freak waves off the South African coast were no less fearful. The Indian Ocean continued to keep us in awe.

Cyclone Claudette hits Mauritius

The cyclone that will long be remembered in Mauritius and implanted in our own memory is Claudette. She lashed into the small island three days before Christmas with winds gusting to 195 miles per hour. Sustained winds were over 125 m.p.h.

It was early morning when Yves came down to *Svea* with the announcement, "We have the first class warning on Claudette. This one could be serious. I'm calling in more of the yard crew. I think we'll be busy later on today."

The signs were not good as the barometer started vacillating. The skies were overcast and misty rains preceded the frontal attack of stronger winds. Big ships were already leaving the harbor to gain sea room, so Don and I did not wait for an upgraded warning of the storm to prepare for its onslaught. Years of Florida training in dealing with hurricanes set our steps in motion immediately after hearing Claudette's path. "Dig out the spare anchor line, then take the sails off the boom. We'll put them up in the shower room," Don began the first of his systematic orders.

With little panic, but lots of hard work for the next couple of hours in the increasing wind and rain, we had managed to turn *Svea* sideways in the canal and away from the seawall. We had six lines going to opposite shores and each line was carefully wrapped where it might chafe against the cement seawall. Two lines were carried fore and aft from the mast. After *Svea* was secured, we started working on the other boats in the canal, adding extra lines and chafing wraps to make sure they would not break loose and come down on *Svea*. We carefully checked *White Wave* which was unattended. Her crew had flown back to Australia and left her to await shipping home on a freighter. Meanwhile, the procession of local boats began to come into the drydock. Yves was directing traffic and securing the boatyard.

"Don, are you sure you don't want to bring *Svea* around into the drydock?" Yves asked.

"No, Yves," Don answered. "I feel safer where we are. We are going to stay on board so we can adjust lines as the winds shift direction. There are just too many boats packed in the drydock already, and I know I'd be asking for bent stanchions. I would not be surprised if one of these rows of boats broke loose and caused some damage. But Yves, I came to ask you if I could help you get *Blue Shadow* up here from Grand Bay."

"I'm too busy here, Don, and anyway it's too late, the seas are much too big. I'll just have to hope she can weather out the storm on her mooring," said the man who loved his sloop perhaps a little more than most men. She had been designed and built in Mauritius and had been an able contender in the Cape Town to Rio race. There was no doubt that the 44-foot boat built of teak was a beautiful vessel.

As the winds increased and the rains came with driving blows sounding sharply against *Svea*'s wooden hull, we hoped we had done our homework. Now it was impossible to do anything in the high winds. "I hear the tin roofs shaking loose from the sheds," I said as we crouched in our bunks with the weak kerosene light above the table flickering with each gust of wind.

"This is a mean one, and it's going to get worse," Don said as he watched the barometer dropping with increased speed. More strange noises of flying missiles as bits and pieces of equipment in the yard were tossed around and hitting tin sheds, and even the boats around us. A tremendous crack sounded when the transformer blew. The boatyard was locked into total darkness. Gusts were strong enough to heel us over, dip *Svea*'s caprail into the water and dump out the drawers in the stateroom.

"Time to blow out the kerosene light, Susan E." Don said calmly. "We don't need that fire hazard, and anyway I need my night vision."

Another gust tipped us, and the wind strengthened. "My God," Don shouted as we crawled out to adjust our nylon lines. "I can't understand how these nylon lines can stretch so much. Get a bight on that line," he screamed. "Don't let it get away from you!"

"Are you all right down there?" a voice called out from the seawall. Two of the boatyard crew were pushing into the wind trying to stay upright as they made their rounds with flashlights.

"Yes, we are," Don shouted back. Somehow the tension was eased a little by knowing the men were around. We did not know that the roof had blown off the mechanics' shed or that a line of boats had broken loose in the drydock and raised havoc with the boats downwind from them. Roofs had blown off many of the launches that carried crews back and forth to the freighters anchored in the harbor. Neither did we know that stanchions had torn loose from the sailboats and that their rigging had tangled. Flying bridges had blown off some of the sportfishing boats that had made it into the drydock from the resort at Black River. On shore, boats were lifted from their cradles and dropped against the support arms tearing gaping holes in their topsides. We could see none of this destruction, but we had our own worries; worries that the heavy water barges moored at the head of the canal would break loose and smash into us, and worries that flying debris would damage us.

"What was that?" I cried as I heard a crash hit *Svea*'s deck, a noise that was louder than the wind or the other noises. Like the noise each time the wind picked up a fender tied along the caprail and slammed it down on the catwalk. Don pried himself through the companionway door to look.

"Get on deck," he shouted. "One of the bow lines tied to shore has gone slack. Pulled the bollard right out of the ground. I've got to get another line ashore."

"You can't get off the boat," I screamed. "You'll never get back."

"Just do as you are told and I'll make it," Don shouted back as he took a bight on the Sampson post with another line he planned to take ashore.

"Take the port stern line and take a turn on the winch, and then slowly ease it out so I can take up the slack on the bow line. For God's sake, do not let it get away from you."

Miraculously, Don jumped ashore and secured the new line, then climbed hand over hand on another line to get back on board. At midnight, the wind stopped howling and the barometer stopped dropping. The eye of the storm passed over Mauritius. Near dawn, the wind was born anew from the opposite direction. It began ripping off the other sides of the tin roofs, but this side of the cyclone was not so strong and did not last long. In time, it spent itself and whirled back out towards sea.

At Grand Bay the tragedies were many and the beautiful white beaches were littered with Claudette's victims, *Prinz Gunther*, *Anaik*, *Yacouba*, and yes, *Blue Shadow*—all boats of the yacht club members. Many native fishing pirogues were wrecked as well, along with the Australian sloop *Symbol*.

"I watched the whole thing," Yves told us the next day. "I couldn't get home because of the downed trees and power lines. I went into the hotel at the head of the bay. I sat in the lobby as the waters rose above the seawall and over the swimming pool and patio, right into the hotel. I watched the waves tear at *Blue Shadow* until she could stand the strain no longer and broke from her mooring. I watched her wash up on the sandy beach, just missing the rocks. I hope her only damage is to her caprail," said the man who was missing the twinkle he always carried in his eyes.

After the storm was over, a sad parade of sailboats made their way on the backs of trailer beds to Taylor-Smith Boatyard. Some of the more fortunate with lesser injuries were able to come by sea. Yves had hired a large crane to lift the injured boats from the beach onto their makeshift stretchers to bring them to the yard for repairs.

Some would never sail again, like *Symbol*, whose Australian owner had been in South Africa trying to settle accounts regarding another sea tragedy which had involved him. Kim McPherson was the lone survivor of the freighter *Induna* when she sank in waters off South Africa. He was adrift on a leaking life raft for 33 days before he was finally rescued. Kim had left his *Symbol* well-anchored in Grand Bay, so he could go to South Africa and hire on as a merchant seaman to earn some money. Claudette left not only broken vessels in her wake; she claimed four lives as well.

Subsequent cyclones reaped more sorrow on Mauritius. Hyacinthe was blamed for the outbreak of 50 cases of typhoid. She was a very wet cyclone, pouring so much rain on the island that the city's water system was damaged and the water supply contaminated.

Engine Repair

In between cyclones *Svea*'s work progressed slowly. Her engine was pulled from the boat and found to have broken rings, bent connecting rods and one cracked piston. Prognosis was good, but time-consuming, as the parts had to be ordered from the USA. We had thought that the real damage was done to the engine by water from the storm. Not so, the damage was caused by the leaking exhaust riser, which had been leaking inside as well as out. Many pin holes in the heavy internal stainless tubing had allowed raw water of the cooling side to seep slowly down on top of the pistons.

Svea was also hauled out in the drydock to have her bottom cleaned and painted. Being in a drydock was another first for *Svea* and still another act of kindness from Yves Betuel. I had been reading Harry Pidgeon's book, "Around the World Single-Handed." On page 140 the author tells about the hospitality shown him when he sailed his *Islander* into Mauritian waters. Taylor-Smith back there in 1932 had hauled out his boat as an act of kindness. Fifty years later the tradition was still being carried on.

Back to Grand Bay

After six months and six cyclones, *Svea* was pronounced seaworthy. "There were times you doubted this day would ever come," said Yves as he helped us untie lines at the drydock canal. The work was done and we were heading back to the beautiful anchorage of Grand Bay.

"Oh so true," I answered and reached down to give a final pet to the little tan mongrel dog that I had finally cured of her mange by special ointments, baths and even pills. Yves had laughed when he heard about the last medication and said she was the only mongrel dog in Mauritius "on the pill." We said good-bye to the many mechanics who had helped us, the engineers, the guards and the pump house operators, who promised to take good care of the little dog we had named Mam'selle.

We had been in Mauritius so long that we needed special papers from the Mauritian government for permission to extend our visas. We also had our passports renewed at the American Embassy. It was then May and nearly the end of the cyclone season. Our problem was not in the immediate vicinity of Mauritius but in the waters towards Madagascar. Gales were still on the rampage there, where we had to go in order to make South Africa. Even though we wanted to get on with our passagemaking we would not take the gamble that a Mauritius sailor did when he challenged the 11th storm of the season.

"If I can run fast 500 miles to the north, and get outside the storm tracks and the 500-mile circle of Mauritius, I'll be safe," said the French Mauritian who was going back to France and his job as an aeronautical engineer. The edge of the cyclone Kolia caught him before he could escape the ambiguous circle. His ketch sustained a lost sail and a broken main boom. His three sons, his wife and he, escaped injury.

Still another tragedy was stacked on the pile of Indian Ocean capers. Yves still could not believe it as he unwound the new twist of fate. "The

Mauritius II went down yesterday," he said when he greeted us at the Grand Bay Yacht Club.

"What?" Don asked for he had gone aboard the brand new container ship with Yves only a month ago when she came to Mauritius from the Japanese shipyard where she had been built.

"The crew said they saw a 200-foot freak wave hit her, just 50 miles from Durban. It shifted her load of steel. She rolled over, couldn't right herself and started taking on water. She sank in less than an hour," our friend related. "The radio operator sent out the distress call. Then he had to crawl out a portlight that was under water to get clear of the ship. All of her crew got safely to their life rafts and were rescued by helicopters from South Africa."

The roll-on roll-off container ship was to be the staff of life for Mauritians. They had to import many of their goods from South Africa. The ship had made her maiden voyage to Australia to pick up a shipment of flour, but her second trip out was to be her last. The dream Mauritius held with her new ship turned out to be a nightmare that the sea rudely awakened.

The sea makes no reservations for big or small ships. There can always be a bigger wave to challenge the mightiest of ships. Prudent seamanship is the only weapon the cruising sailor has to contest it, and we were not about to gamble against the odds. We would enjoy our overhauled engine, perhaps take a side trip to an out-of-the-way island, and wait for the season to change before voyaging across the rest of the Indian Ocean.

Photo by Maurice La Coste

Yves Betuel's *Blue Shadow* off Grand Baie, Mauritius. She's now owned by Harry Anderson, Past Commodore of the New York Yacht CLub. The rock is Gunners Quion, landmark for Grand Baie entrance.

CHAPTER 17

SIDE TRIP TO CARGADOS CARAJOS SHOALS
(St. Brandons)

"Don," Yves became serious one night at the Grand Bay Yacht Club after he had delivered some of our mail that came to the boatyard. "I've been talking with some of my captain friends and they all agree that June and July are still too early for a safe passage to Durban. Even August is chancy. You're not thinking of leaving now, are you? It's only the middle of June."

"The pilot charts agree with your friends' advice, Yves," Don answered. "No, we'll not go this soon, but we have been talking about taking a side trip up to St. Brandons."

"Our harbor fever after seven months of being bound to Mauritius is becoming chronic," I laughed.

"I think you'll like it up there," Yves commented. "But there's nothing there you know, except for some Creole fishermen that go up there from here."

"Then I'm sure we'll like it," Don shared the same thought I was having of finding an off-the-beaten track hideaway.

"Do you need any charts?" Yves asked.

"No, thanks," Don answered. "We have them all, along with some of the local information. We were told that to find St. Brandons one must listen for the birds."

Passage to Cargados Carajos Shoals

Local sailors also told us the stretch of shoals was 26 miles of unspoiled islets, islands and reefs with long stretches of sandy beaches. They lay peacefully behind a large barrier reef. "Lots of fish and lobster," they added.

We waited for the ebb of a frontal system originating near Madagascar. With its lightweight southwesterly winds, we set out for St. Brandons, 230 miles northeast of Mauritius.

The same day marked the beginning of the annual sailboat race between Grand Bay Yacht Club and its sister yacht club in Reunion, the French island 131 miles to the southwest. In the light winds, the boats had their spinnakers flying. It was as if we were passing through a parade of colored parasols as *Svea*, with her newly overhauled engine, overtook the fleet to bid them adieu and good luck. What a wonderful sight it was to see the transformation of many of the local boats from a few months earlier when they lay crippled in the boatyard, victims of cyclone Claudette. Their injuries patched and healed, they were once again able contenders.

Once clear of the lee of the islands north of Mauritius, we gained a stronger wind and quickly hoisted the big blues and turned off the engine.

"What's the course?" I hollered down to Don who was bent over the chart.

"About 45 degrees magnetic, but we've got to compensate for that westerly current. Steer more easterly, say 60 degrees," he answered.

I started spinning the knob to the automatic pilot's compass control until *Svea's* bow pointed 60 degrees. The downwind twins were still holding the wind. With a slight adjustment to the starboard sheet, the leech stopped its fluttering.

A light misty rain began to fall and the wind switched more southerly. "Well doesn't that figure?" Don asked. "As soon as we get the sails set, the wind changes it's mind. But it agrees with that weather forecast we received earlier. We're in for another frontal system coming up from south of Madagascar."

"Ah, the joys of sailing are returning," I laughed as I began to hassle with the sheets to the twins to bring the big sails down and put the working set up.

At dawn, a lone bosun bird hovered above the mast. Perhaps he was eyeing the dead flying fish strewn across the starboard catwalk. The air was rather cold and the morning's hot coffee warmed me. The only English-speaking broadcast from Mauritius at 0800 confirmed the earlier weather forecast. The anti-cyclone system was brewing southwest of the Mascarenes, the name of the group of islands including Reunion, Rodrigues and Mauritius. It was heading northeast.

"Swells are starting up," Don said as he looked astern. "We'll be getting stronger wind later on."

Our noon fix put us well west of our rhumb line, even though we had been steering steadily east of it. The wind began to veer more southeasterly putting *Svea* on a close-to-weather course. She cut into the sides of the building waves.

At civil twilight the next morning, clouds obscured the stars. We couldn't take accurate sights to form the three points of the triangle that would enclose our position on the plotting sheet. We shot them anyway, but their plotted position put us 45 miles to the southwest away from the shoals. Don seriously doubted the accuracy of the sights.

We carried on with dead reckoning, but the growing wind and mounting seas spawned new pangs of anxiety. Perhaps we would not be able to find St. Brandon's and would have to return to Mauritius. Two cruising boats were unable to find the low-lying islands last season. Worse still would be our floundering around not knowing where we were, and be caught by darkness. Would we drift up onto the reefs, or would we drift away from them? The charts were dotted with shipwrecks whose captains had made fatal errors. No, we would be prudent sailors and sail south, away from them, but also away from the chance of finding them the next day.

By mid-morning, the skies began to clear enough to get a sight for line

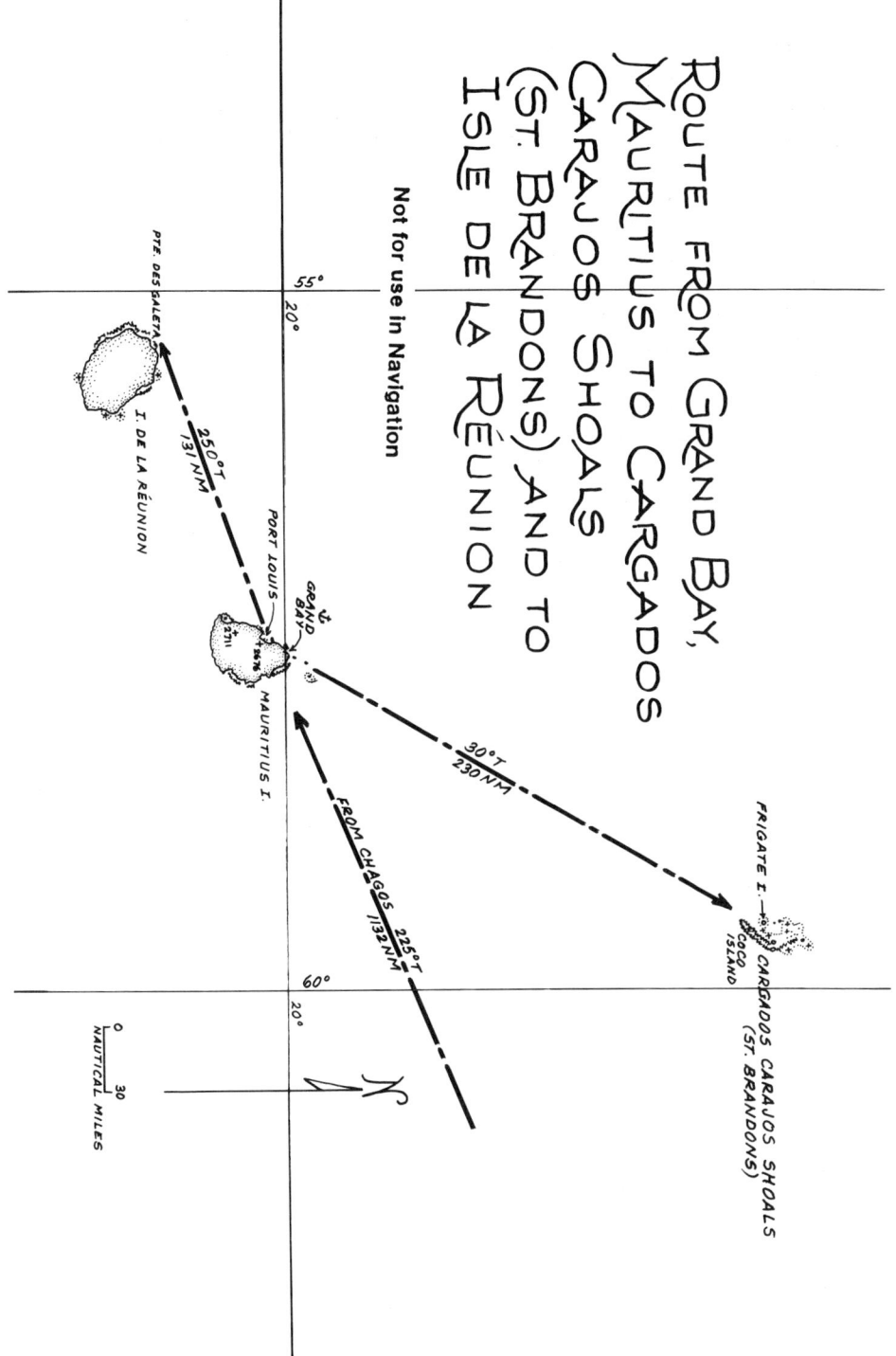

of position. We could be anywhere on that line. Since at that time of the year the sun was far to the north, the sight was closer to being a sight for latitude, because of the lack of a good angle. At noontime, we did get an accurate latitude sight, but should we go east or west of the position? The longtitude was dubious. When Don actually put the position on the plotting chart it placed us only 5 miles from St. Brandons. A seasoned sailor is not presumptuous enough to rely on a sun sight being that accurate. In fact, a good many cruising sailors take a series of sun sights and average them out. We did know that we would have to be within 6 or 8 miles in order to see low-lying reefs, or to see anything as high as a tree.

Not at all sure of our course, Don stayed in the ratlines and strained his eyes for a glimpse of a tree or a mound of sand. I happened to look over the side and noticed that the color of the water was more green than blue. "Don," I shouted upwards. "Look down at the water. It's changing color. We're over more shallow water."

"Turn on the sounder," he called down. "Looks like even lighter green water farther ahead. We're on the back side of the shoals."

Comparing *Svea*'s soundings with those on the chart, we located our position, but by now the wind was dead on the nose and strong. It was a rough sail to windward. As soon as the line of reefs afforded us some lee, we turned on the engine to make better time through the choppy seas. A very faint knoll of sand appeared off to starboard. "That'll be South Island," Don said. "We'll carry on for Coco in the crook of the shoals where we can have more protection from other points of the compass." Soon the scattered casuarinas that enclose the small fish camp on Coco Island came into view.

Coco Island, Cargados Carajos Shoals

St. Brandons is a dependency of Mauritius. The Mauritius Fishing Development has established fish camps on three of the larger islands. The main camp is at the north end of the shoals, at Ile Raphael. With so much sand surrounding us there was no doubt that *Svea*'s anchor would hold. We dropped the sturdy New Zealand plow anchor on the sandy shelf west of Coco Island.

Sandy beaches stretching out for miles beckoned us, but the steady 20-knot winds kept the waters choppy. This discouraged us from launching *Poco*. We found that the season in early June in the Shoals was far different from the previous October when other cruising sailors were there and had enjoyed more settled weather. I was most eager to walk those beaches and shoal waters in anticipation of finding the violet spider conch that is indigenous to the waters. Always the fisherman, Don wanted to cast off the points of the small islets at the change of tides. That is when the fish like to bunch up waiting for the current change to carry out small bait fish.

Sitting on *Svea*, we could not define the pass that led to the back waters

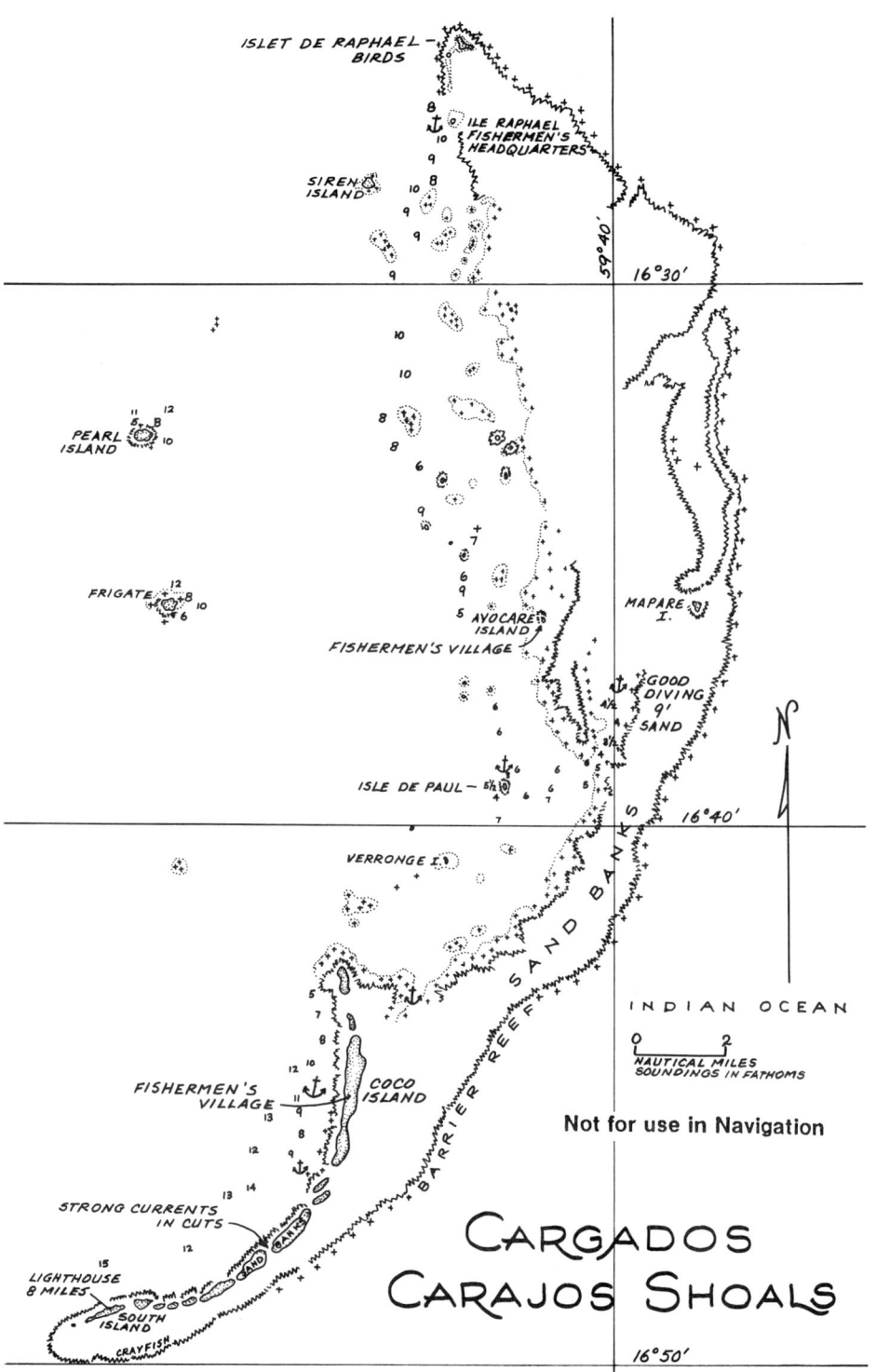

behind Coco Island. A line of reefs, topped with rows of breakers, seemed an endless chain from Coco to the next smaller island adjacent to it. Charts were not all that adequate. We were studying the charts when I looked up to see a man's head appear above the breakers. Then it was lost behind white water. Again, another head and it too, fell behind the breakers. The wind had dissipated and it was time for the fishermen to come out from their camp and get to work. Donned in capes of plastic tablecloths and tattered oilskins, two fishermen emerged from the frothing water. Their heavily-built wooden skiff of about 18 feet was tattered as well. Its low freeboard, which was good for rowing, gave them little protection from the flying spray. The boat was also rigged with a lateen sail, but the sail was furled around the unstepped mast and the fishermen came forward under power of the boat's small outboard.

Don had carefully studied their route through the reefs. Using sign language, a smattering of French, and a bit of Creole that I had picked up in Mauritius, I learned a few things about our new playground. Yes, they did have the violet spider conch, and they always had lots of fish.

Not long after they left, we put *Poco* on an identical route through the reefs and into the back waters of the lagoon. "That's a pretty far distance out to the barrier reef," I said as I looked out to the line of huge breakers charging against the buttress of coral rock.

"We'll make it," Don said confidently. Sometimes we had to walk *Poco* through shallow gardens of coral and plant life, and sometimes we had to pole her around coral heads. The going was far from easy, not like it had been to reach the barrier reef at North Minerva or any of the Society Islands, for that matter. Eventually, we just ran out of water for *Poco* and had to anchor her, while we carried on in the ankle-deep water. After all of the work in getting out there, we were disappointed to find the reef quite jagged and rough. Large crevices led to the sea and invited the huge breakers to follow their path back through the reef. The water rushed into the alleyways and cast their fury upon the rocks, where their surge was stopped by the rock walls. Everywhere we looked there were geysers of seawater. There were few places in the coral shelf that would appeal to a sea shell or even a crayfish for a home.

School for Terns

Defeated, we retraced our steps back to *Poco* and headed for the island south of Coco. Landing in the curve of a sand spit that faced the wind, we inadvertently interrupted a lesson being taught to a young group of roseate terns. The adults had their students gathered together and their lectures were as raucous as any marine drill sergeant. They only lacked swagger sticks to control their rank and file. Apparently the lesson for that day was how to take off into the wind. One by one the young birds took to the air, fluttered a bit on wavy patterns and landed back on the beach for added instructions. Other than announcing our presence to the young birds, the adults did not bother us and we carrried on around the small island that yielded nothing for the shell bucket or the skillet for dinner.

Anchorage Behind Reefs Northeast of Coco Island

To escape the swells from the western side of Coco Island, we upped anchor. With Don in the ratlines, we eyeballed our way northward. Dodging coral heads and going into neutral when overhead clouds shadowed our path, we made way to the north end of Coco Island. Then we bent southward to nestle between two reefs in 18 feet of sand bottom. After a couple of days checking out the underwater world around us as well as the beaches on the northeastern shore of Coco Island, we were once again bound northward.

Anchorage North of Ile de Paul

We were not at all welcome on the small Ile de Paul. When we landed on the beach we were suddenly surrounded by various terns that told us in no uncertain terms we were trespassing into their rookery. We had reached the anchorage near their island after carefully studying the chart and lacing *Svea* through many coral heads lurking under the surface of the inner lagoon's waters. Ile de Paul was to the south of us. Towards the northeast lay the barrier reef and to the northwest, a long stretch of coral heads that exposed their tops at low tide. Behind us were miles of shoals and scattered islets that shut out the swells which had rolled us in the exposed anchorage off Coco Island.

As we walked around the water's edge of the small island, little white terns, called "zozo lavierze" by the Creoles, hovered over our heads as if to land. Above them soared the frigates who displayed their vibrantly red inflated pouches to entice their lady friends into an act of courtship. Nesting noddy terns mingled with nesting frigate birds. It seems strange that the other birds accept the frigates into their rookeries. The robbers of their catches and robbers of their eggs make strange bedfellows!

Wanting a close-up picture of a young frigate, Don drew near to a downy-coated youngster who clung tenaciously to his nest. Don's threat to the young bird's safety triggered the only defense mechanism the bird knew. He regurgitated profusely, just missing the photographer by inches. Biologists have told us that birds often do this to lighten their loads before taking to flight.

Anchored in a focal point of activity, we found our next adventure on the reef that was now partially out of water at low tide. Somehow, swimming among the beauty of the underwater world mesmerizes one into its enchantment. While I was ogling the crevices and nooks and crannies for shells, I did not see the 6-foot white-tipped shark that was ogling me. My enchantment suddenly shattered and I quickly swam atop a mushroom coral that projected me out of the water. Bending down, I put my head under water and through my face mask searched the waters for Don. He too had spotted the shark. He found sanctuary amongst an array of coral surrounding a sandy plateau. The shark was merely patrolling his territory around the coral head. I don't take chances with these denizens of the deep, no matter how friendly they might be.

"The tide's changing anyway," Don said as he swam over to my refuge. "The current is getting too strong for you. We'll get on back to *Svea* with our gear, then go walk the beach." I was happy to trade my swim fins for reef shoes. The day ended happily with huge spider conchs filling my shell bucket. The previous storm had washed a number of them up on the beach and I was glad I didn't have to take a live shell. Even though a shell captured in the water may appear lifeless, there is a small creature, quite alive inside.

Ile Raphael

Having explored the small world around us, it was time to move on north up the chain of islets and shoals towards Ile Raphael, the main fishing station. We stopped once just in front of a sandy knoll. Off that point Don caught enough palomettas to keep us in fish dinners for several days. His one problem was dodging the small fairy tern who sat upon her lone egg. Apparently she had misjudged her birthing time. It was a most unlikely spot to drop an egg, right near the water's edge where an exceptionally high tide would wash her future family away. These small birds have little fear of man and yet, it is man, the fisherman, who frequently harvests their eggs on the nearby islands. We also found turtle nests molested by man. An outrage always brims over me when I see that man had meddled with nature. It hangs so precariously on such thin lines that any interference throws the scale dangerously out of kilter.

We watched as a small tern flew back to his rookery after catching his fish of the day. He was rudely interrupted by a frigate who was soon joined by another scavenger of the skies. The pirate zoomed in on the wee bird and after several assaults the tern fell to the sea. He fluttered and was once again airborne. He tried to continue his mission, but again was intercepted by the frigate. That time, he did not rise from the sea and the two frigates made magnificent dives from aloft to claim the bird's fish. I turned my head on who was to be the victor of the spoils. Survival is not always pleasant to behold.

Anchoring in the lee of Ile Raphael, we again watched a native craft maneuver the intricate path behind the reefs to show us the way into the back waters behind the island supporting the fishing station. Following the route taken by the skiff, we brought *Poco* up onto the beach where the fishermen off-load their catches. The smell was not one of roses as dried octopi were hanging on lines drawn between two poles. On a slab of rock pebbles, other fish were in various stages of drying. The fishermen were unloading large baskets of fish. Only one fish resembled anything familiar to us.

"We call them 'capitains', " said the Creole Mauritian who was the assistant manager. He came up to greet us when he noticed our pointing to red fish that were already split down their back bones and flattened.

"They almost look like our snapper back in Florida," Don said as we both looked around at the old-fashioned way they preserved their catches. Without refrigeration, they had to dry the fish. First they were put in vats of brine for 36 hours, then taken out to dry on pebbles of rock that reflected the hot rays of the sun. Afterwards, they were corded into large bundles and put in sheds to await the next boat from Mauritius, which was never on a set schedule. When the boat did come, the fishermen went in pursuit of lobster. Until the boat arrived there was no means of refrigeration to preserve them. Both the fish and the lobster brought very dear prices in Mauritius.

The manager, also named Raphael, told us they were considering refrigeration in the future along with other improvements. We wondered who would support it, and doubted the independent government of Mauritius would stand for the added expense. They did, however, support a radio weather station on Raphael Island. It was manned by two men who radioed us daily weather forecasts. Most of the predictions were of the weather we were experiencing at the time. This weather featured high winds and a continuous run of frontal systems.

Ilet Raphael

Wading, tugging and half-pulling *Poco* across the many sand bores that interlock the islets behind Raphael, we landed on Ilet Raphael that was carpeted with birds. Roseate terns and fairy terns, their eggs and their chicks and fledglings, all impeded our progress as we tiptoed around the island. A constant halo of fluttering birds encircled our heads. The cacophony of their twitterings drowned out our own voices. On this tiny island nature was parading her magnificent splendor before us. Never have we been so filled with awe over her accomplishment.

During the Napoleonic Wars, British fleets sought refuge at St. Brandons and took on eggs and fresh meat supplied by the birds. Since that time, the number of species have dwindled down to nine, and frigates and boobies are in danger of extinction. Rats, introduced by man, have whittled at the bird population as well. We wonder if man will continue to deplete the supply as he did the dodo bird of Mauritius. The Portuguese are blamed for that. Their seafarers ruthlessly killed dodo birds for sport as well as food. Now the only dodo bird left is one that was fabricated by man and is in the museum at Port Louis. The Portuguese were responsible for the name of Cargados Carajos Shoals. Translated from their language, it means "sea birds." This brings to mind what the Creole fisherman told us back in Mauritius, "To find St. Brandons, listen for the birds."

Passage Back to Mauritius

We waited for another frontal system to wane before we set out on our return trip to Mauritius. Rough seas built up by the passing front met us as we left the lee of the shoals, but the large waves fell astern. Regardless, we sailed under reefed sails as the weather was less than ideal. We were in no special hurry. A cruising sailor gets into trouble when he tries to hurry to meet schedules. Some sailors refute that statement, saying that the faster you go, the less likely chance you have of catching bad weather. I would rather arrive at our destination without ruffled feathers, even though we may have to alter course and change our estimated time of arrival.

"Whales ahoy!" Don shouted down the companionway. "Off the port beam!"

I scrambled topsides to see in the curl of the oncoming wave a very large grey, white and yellow body. As the form grew closer abeam, its full length fell just a few feet short of equaling *Svea's* 38 feet. The whale swam forward towards the bow and went on its way. Seconds later, another whale surfaced and blew. He too swam forward, crossed our bow and went on his way. A third whale, a much smaller one, surfaced, then fell back to cross *Svea's* stern.

"We're surrounded," I cried. "I'll start the engine."

Don replied with his usual glee at spotting whales, "But why do that? I've never seen whales this close up before. They're only on their migratory path and we probably just witnessed a family going by. They don't care about us, except that we were in their way."

And so our paths crossed. We went our way while the whales carried on more southwesterly. At 0300 the next morning the full moon outlined haystack-shaped Round Island north of Mauritius. By dawn we were entering familiar Grand Bay in time to wish the early departing fishermen a good and prosperous day.

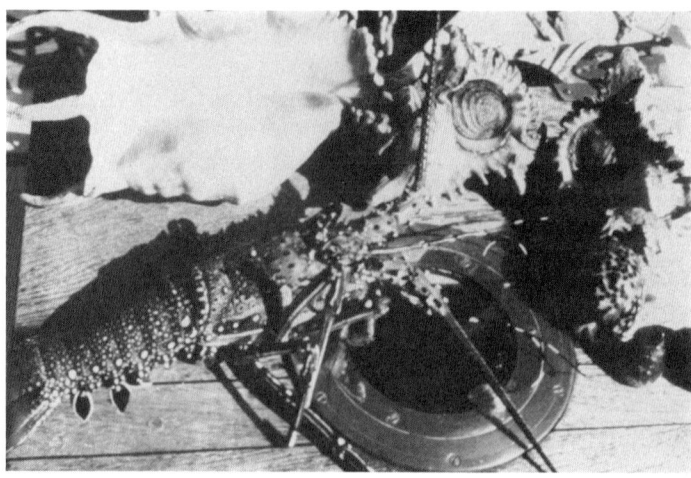

Fruits from the sea atop *Svea's* forward hatch at The Shoals, St. Brandon

CHAPTER 18

TO REUNION AND PASSAGE TO TURNING POINT SOUTH OF MADAGASCAR

Planning our Passage to South Africa

On our first night back at Grand Bay, we went as usual to the club for showers and a cocktail afterwards. When we saw Yves walk through the archway holding mail for us, we were surprised. "How did you know we were back?" I asked.

"Spies, my good people," he laughed. The twinkle he had lost to the ravages of the cyclones returned to his eyes. Yves missed very little that went on at Grand Bay and even less when it concerned a foreign yacht. We told him how we had enjoyed St. Brandons but also expressed that in more settled weather it would have been better. It was too rough to enjoy the dinghy.

"What are your plans now?" he asked. "Are you still thinking about going up around the north end of Madagascar?"

"No, I don't think so, Yves," Don answered. "We did a little homework with pilot charts and our navigational charts while we were up there. It seems that July and August would be the wrong time of the year to enjoy the islands. It would be too rough to get into the passes."

"I'm glad to hear you say that. My captain friends all agree that Mozambique Channel still has south and southwest winds," he said relieved. "Having to go south towards Durban could get difficult, especially if a good blow would counter that south-flowing Agulhas Current. You'll still have your share of gales going south of Madagascar."

The large island of Madagascar is an obstacle that cuts off a direct route to South Africa. Madagascar's submerged continental shelf extends southward more than 100 miles from the visible land. In this area, gales are common and the sea confused and extremely dangerous.

Currents South of Madagascar and Along the Coast of South Africa

To understand the danger further, when the westward flow of the Indian Ocean nears land, the current increases. As it hits the barrier of Madagascar, it deflects into two parts, one going north around the north end of the big island and the other going south, then across the continental shelf. This was the current that concerned us. After reaching the end of Madagascar's land mass, it resumes its westward course. Then the current meets the shallow water over the continental shelf, and steep seas with breaking crests result.

If a southwesterly gale comes up to oppose that current further, the resulting seas are horrendously dangerous. Years ago, *Rigadoon*'s friend lost her life over this continental shelf when the boat she was in pitchpoled into these heavy seas. Ironically named *Challenge*, the sloop was dismasted, and limped into Durban with a floorboard jury-rigged as a mast. The lifeless girl was consigned to the sea.

Our aim was to avoid Madagascar's 100-mile stretch of continental shelf. In case a southwester came up that could blow us towards the shelf, Don added an extra 50 miles for a margin of safety. For further safety precautions, he plotted two turning points to prevent our angling onto the bank unaware. Never have I seen a course plotted with such zig-zags and ambiguous marks! The seemingly drunken sailor who put down the marks was making sure we teetered not into the brink of known trouble. The Indian Ocean had taught us the hard way to respect her. The danger in that scheme was the addition of miles added to the passage, giving us more time to experience a gale.

The current going south around Madagascar and then bearing westward makes another split after it passes the island. One stream goes north and joins the Mozambique Channel where it turns and speeds southward. The other half continues in an almost straight line from Madagascar to Durban where it joins its split half coming down from the north. The combined currents produce a large body of warm water that becomes the Agulhas Current. The reinforced current picks up more speed as it flows southward skirting the South African coast, until it hits the Agulhas Bank at the southern tip of Africa. There, on Africa's continental shelf, it diminishes and is diverted northeastward back into the Indian Ocean.

At the junction of the currents north of Durban is also where the continental shelf bulges outwards. On its edge, the 100-fathom line that encircles the bulge, is the area where so many ships come to grief. Over the sudden rise of the continental shelf, ships engage the high seas wrought by a southwesterly gale opposing the strongest part of the south-flowing Agulhas Current. Such was the case of the sinking of the new *Mauritius II*, the roll-on roll-off freighter that Yves Betuel and Mauritius were so proud of. This is a prime area to encounter freak waves where the normal wave pattern suddenly meets with interference, such as the abruptness of the Agulhas Bank.

Advantages of Richards Bay, South Africa

We wanted to avoid this area the same as we did the continental shelf south of Madagascar, so we plotted our rhumb line northward towards Richards Bay where the 100-fathom line runs close to shore before the bulge of the continental shelf, and the current has not yet been reinforced by its split half coming across from the southern tip of Madagascar. Also, if we were unable to make Richards Bay as a port, the Agulhas Current would carry us south to Durban, the next port 90 miles farther down the coastline. We would still be inside the 100-fathom line and away from the strongest part of the current where it meets the edge of the continental shelf.

Perhaps the explanation appears redundant, but to understand the conflict between the sea currents and rises of land is to appreciate the fears sailors experience when they put their small boats into the oceans' battlegrounds.

Besides the fact that Richards Bay lay close to the 100-mile fathom line and lessened the chances of bad sea conditions, the area was closer to South Africa's game parks. This allowed us to visit them without having to leave *Svea* overnight. We had never left her for longer than daylight hours and we felt better keeping it that way. We learned from the S.S.C.A. bulletins that Richards Bay had haul-out facilities for visiting yachts. That knowledge encouraged us to make port north of the heavily-trafficked port of Durban.

Preparations for the Passage from Mauritius

To prepare *Svea* for an anticipated rough voyage, we did not fill our forward water tanks, in order to allow more lift in her bow. We did not fill the aft stern fuel tanks for the same reason, allowing buoyancy in her stern. We did not plan on much motoring and we wanted to conserve weight. I even rationed my canned goods to those I expected to use on the trip. I knew South Africa had fully-stocked supermarkets. I mainly counted on meals I had prepared ahead of time at Grand Bay and had stowed in the freezer for the rough days at sea.

We removed more weight from the bow when we dragged the 55-pound plow anchor below. We stowed it on the floor of the stateroom, which we use as a storage area while at sea. I stowed extra paper towels, napkins and toilet paper in boxes on the bunks so that underway I would not have to pull out the backs to the saloon bunks to get at my reserve supply. I also made sure that all of my cannisters of flour, rice, sugar and coffee were filled, so that I would not have to sort through the bilge to fill them at sea. The cookie jar and extra tins were overflowing with freshly-made cookies. I never went to sea without an abundant supply to munch on if the going got too rough to work in the galley. Besides pre-cooked meals in the freezer, were coffee cakes, buns and bread. I was as ready as I could get as we said good-bye to Mauritius.

The day we left from Port Louis, where we had gone to do the last minute provisioning, Yves came down to bid us farewell and brought some of his favorite French wine as a gift. He also had tomatoes hand-picked from his own garden in various stages of ripeness to last through the trip. The mechanics and boatyard crew left their jobs to say good-bye and wish us well. Out in front of the well-wishers was our little tan dog Mam'selle, who wondered if her boat was going to leave her again. Maurice, who had kept us in homemade ice while our engine was being repaired, left his busy job to bid us well. Maurice had gained the name of More Ice!

Passage to Reunion

As soon as we cleared the sea buoy, squalls began. We refused to turn back as we met the first near-gale storm of our passage to South Africa. It was then July 29th, two days ahead of our previously announced departure schedule. We knew that we were flirting a bit with chances of gales by leaving too early in the season. Most passagemakers plan to make this passage in October, or November, but nine months was long enough to be in Mauritius, or in any port for that matter. It didn't take long for the seas to build with freshening winds. When the rains followed, the mixture of salt spray and rainwater pelted us.

"Let's reef the mizzen and pull out the storm jib," Don called down to me. I was in my bunk trying to fight off a bout of seasickness. "We're going much too fast," he added.

Our old foul weather gear was really deteriorating quickly. Ribbons of yellow plastic peeled off in large amounts to leave only a thin layer of nylon tricot between me and the elements. "We've got to get new foul weather gear when we get to South Africa," I shouted out to Don.

"I know! I know! I have the same problem," he shouted back at me. "Just forget your comforts for a minute and let's get this turkey slowed down. Don't let out too much line on that jenny now, and give the wind a good balloon. I have to wind it up, you know."

"Just a minute," I screamed forcing down the upheaval rising in my stomach. "I have to throw up." I ran to the rail but in my haste picked the windward side. It really did not matter, for so much spray and rain was marching across the cockpit that everything was swept clean.

At least I felt better, although not in the best health. I carried on with the job at hand and we slowed the "turkey" down. All through the night, we lumbered into nasty seas, rain and spray. The motion was terribly erratic, like a runaway hobby horse. When we spotted the island of Reunion at dawn, Don was more than happy to suggest we stop. "I think we should turn in for a bit of rest, don't you?" he asked. I most heartily agreed. It was depressing and demoralizing to think our first day at sea we had managed to soak everything in sight with salt spray, get seasick and wonder whatever possessed us to take up sailing for pleasure. If this near-gale was trying to indoctrinate us for the seas ahead, it was convincing us that the Indian Ocean was not through with us yet.

Reunion Island

Stopping at Reunion meant the series of bureaucratic officials, as well as the anxiety of an unfamiliar port. We thought the rest worthwhile, and I could get some brown bread from the local French boulangerie that Yves had raved about.

After we had maneuvered the tricky entrance to the boat basin at Port Galets, friendly hands reached out to grab our lines and tie *Svea* alongside a boat moored to the quay. A broad smile beamed from the bearded

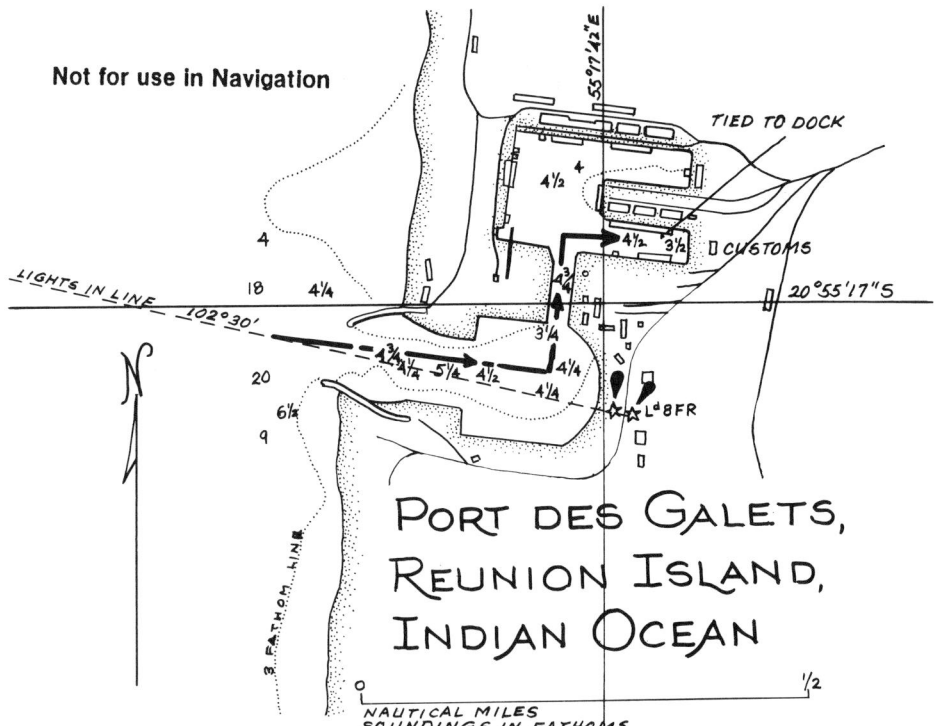

face. Topping the mop of grey curls was a royal blue Breton cap. "I don't think I'll have to call officials for you," said the thick French accent. "You have not gone unnoticed as you circled the island to make this port." He was right, for quite soon the parade of officials began.

Reunion is a typically French island. French francs are used, and we found familiar French canned goods in the supermarket. We sent Yves a card to let him know we had stopped at his favorite island, and that I had a loaf of the delicious brown bread he had recommended.

When we returned to *Svea*, the Breton-capped friendly fellow came by to see if there was anything we needed. His visit was soon followed by a young New Zealand girl who asked the same question. She and her friend Henri had sailed west to east from Durban. "You must have had to sail quite far south to pick up the westerlies?" asked Don who was impressed with the sail against the normal route.

"It was a bit rough," she laughed, but being a Kiwi, she probably thought the passage not unusual. "I'll have Henri call the met' office to check on the weather for you and to get a look at their synoptic chart," she volunteered. "Since he is French, it would be easier for him to understand the meterologists."

When Henri came home after work, he brought with him a wonderful report for the projected weather. "It looks as if we are under a ridge of high pressure and it's expected to last several days," he was happy to have the good news for us. We hoped the system would last long enough to get us around Madagascar.

Passage to Madagascar

The high pressure did indeed reign the skies as we left Reunion under power alone, for there was no wind in the cloudless sky. We did raise the main and motorsailed across the rumpled seas, leftovers from the previous blow.

Our first turning point at Madagascar's southeast corner was 623 miles away. We heartily welcomed the good weather that raised our spirits. We wanted to ask for more wind, but were afraid our request would come in too bounteous an amount, so we remained silent and were grateful for small favors. Swirls of water announced our companions, as a pod of friendly whales came alongside to wish us bon voyage. Above the masthead, a flock of terns joined the well-wishers. They were soon followed by a pair of bosun birds. Their presence sent a good feeling through us.

"With such a send-off, could there be anything bad in front of us?" I let the question hang in air. I went below to get our cold beers for lunch to celebrate the opening day occasion. Winds did increase somewhat, just enough to let us sail without the aid of the engine. Heavy freighter traffic made us glad that we had waited in Mauritius to make *Svea* seaworthy. We had power enough to keep the navigational lights and the autopilot going. I'll not deny the pleasure of knowing the freezer was full of easy-to-prepare meals, not to mention the cold beers and ice it gave us. So far, I was able to do galley duty without having to use the frozen meals.

We began to relax after the anxiety of a beginning passage diminished. The barometer held a steady high of 30 inches. The winds were more southerly than we wanted, for we had to steer north of our rhumb line. "We'd better get a wind change to southeasterly, or we'll have to tack off to keep from running into Madagascar's shelf," Don said as he plotted our position.

A small grey cloud appearing astern had heard his request, "Looks as if we're going to get that wind change," I said as I pointed to the mass of grey approaching us. "It just couldn't stay nice, could it?" I sighed and prepared for the squall.

By midnight with a descending barometer, we were rolling reefs in the main and the wind had switched away from the south to the southeast. When that squall passed, the moon came out in full adornment. Like a master of ceremonies running back on stage after a star's performance, the smiling face seemed to say," Ha! Ha! Thought you were going to get some rough weather, didn't you?" With a smirking grin, the moon continued, "Only teasing, only teasing. But there is a bigger and better performance to come right after this intermission."

The intermission began with an introduction of cumulus clouds at dawn, with gentle southeasterly winds. The barometer climbed back to a normal high of 30.02 inches.

The real show began 4 hours before midnight, trumpeted by gusty

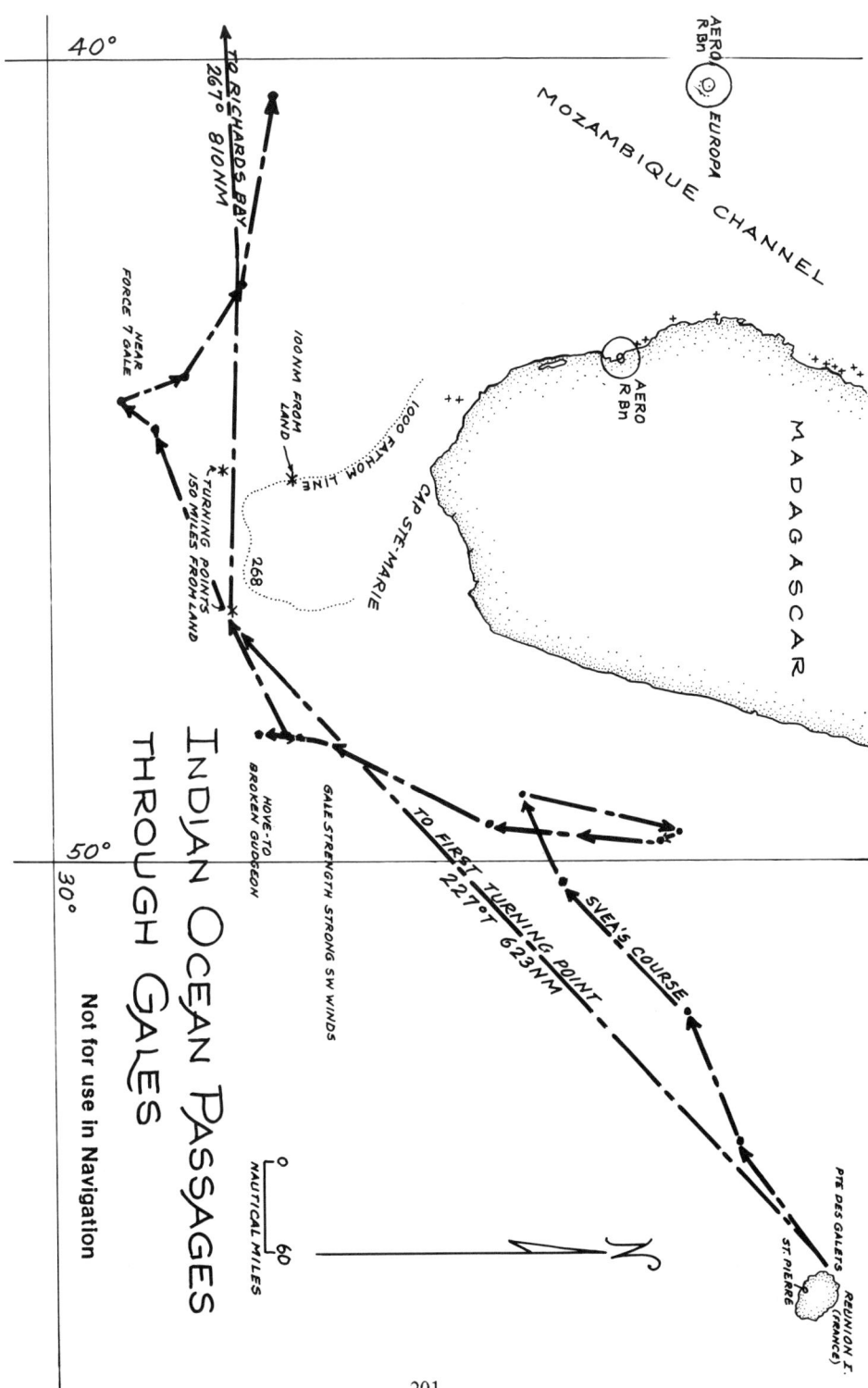

winds. We were only 92 miles east of Madagascar when *Svea* picked up enough speed to send us topsides to reduce sail. I didn't even bother to put on my useless foul weather gear, but did pull on my blue wool beanie and sea boots.

"The wind is turning southwesterly," Don shouted. "We'd better turn on the other tack and get some sea room. I don't know what we're in for."

We had already reduced sail with the gusty wind and with the new order shouted across the deck, we again had to make a sail change. We rolled in the jenny and jibed *Svea* around to face the large seas that had built up from the southeasterly winds. "This isn't going to work at all," Don said. "Let's just heave-to and wait this thing out, see what happens."

In the dark with only the spreader light to show us what we were doing, the main halyard fouled. "What's it grabbing on?" Don hollered as he tugged on the halyard to send the main aloft. The sail refused to go up the track.

About that time, a huge wave broke near *Svea*'s quarter and spewed out fountains of spray into my face, temporarily blinding me. "I don't know! I can't see!" I sputtered.

"Damn it! Get out of that cockpit so you can see!" Don shouted. He had not seen the boarding crest of the last wave.

I grabbed for the flashlight that we keep near the companionway door and I shone the beam on the mast. The halyard was caught on one of the flanges that holds mast steps we never use. Don walked the halyard off to another angle and flipped the steel line free. Other halyards had knitted themselves together as well. "We'll straighten out that mess in the morning. Get ready to reef."

I went back to the cockpit and pulled the crank handle out of the cockpit locker, then walked forward to take turns on the roller reefing gear. All in all the sail changes had taken us 1½ hours. We lashed *Svea*'s tiller to port and went below to grab fitful moments of sleep.

Backtracking in the Wrong Direction

By dawn, the barometer had climbed to a new high and the marvel of the last four beautiful days was only a lingering memory, not to be repeated. We had traveled from a high pressure system down to a low and back up again to an extremely high one. It became apparent that we were in for a gale. Winds were already exceeding 30 knots and were gusting to past 35.

"The main has to come down," Don called out to me. "We can't lie to these building seas. We'll have to run with the storm and keep the seas astern." We grabbed our safety harnesses to keep us inside the lifelines, as we worked at our stations to bring the sail down. The boom swung away from me when *Svea* lurched and it slammed back into my cheek, but fortunately did not pitch me overboard. After securing the boom into the gallows, I ran forward to furl the flapping sail and help Don get sail straps around it. I hated the restricting harness, but taking it off was not wise.

Tops of waves were now blowing off and seas were a confused maze of white froth. Under bare poles, *Svea* scudded along at 3 knots. We set the pilot so that it steered a course to keep the waves just off the quarter. We felt the seas much too large to lie-a-hull safely, as we had done earlier in the extra-tropical cyclone southeast of Chagos. We had to run with them. The pilot did the steering and saved us from having to sit out in that spray-swept cockpit. The wind strength was not as strong as the cyclone had been, but the waves were higher and the situation was none the less frightening. Our previous experience with the cyclone did nothing to quell our fears about this building gale. The barometer continued its ascent to reach an unbelievably high pressure and the seas continued to bombard us.

Water poured across the decks and coachroof, then rolled over the cockpit coaming as it rushed down the catwalks to exit at the stern. Green water came over the stern and filled the cockpit. Cockpit gratings were sent awash to bang back and forth like giant cymbals. Even Wagner in his wildest imagination never could have composed an operatic score to equal the noise of banging boards, crashing seas, and howling winds. No Wagnerian soprano could have screeched as high or as profound as that wind.

To try to tune out the sounds, we tuned in the Voice of America to learn that hurricane Allen was sweeping across the Caribbean, leaving 69 dead Haitians in its wake. We didn't have a hurricane on our tail, but we were traveling too fast under bare poles alone, and in the wrong direction. We should have been grateful for the small favor, for it took us away from the shores of Madagascar. After 40 hours of running backwards with the pilot doing all of the steering, we had run 120 miles in the wrong direction.

The storm spent its fury. When the sun wormed its way out of the leaden sky we took a sight, only to find that we were where we had been five days prior. But we were safe and no harm had come to *Svea* other than a brisk pelting with seawater.

"That was some show. I hope we just finished the finale," I said as I looked at the barometer over the galley sink.

"Don't count on it. We haven't rounded Madagascar yet," Don said glumly.

Photo by Carl Moesly

Grand Baie anchorage, Mauritius

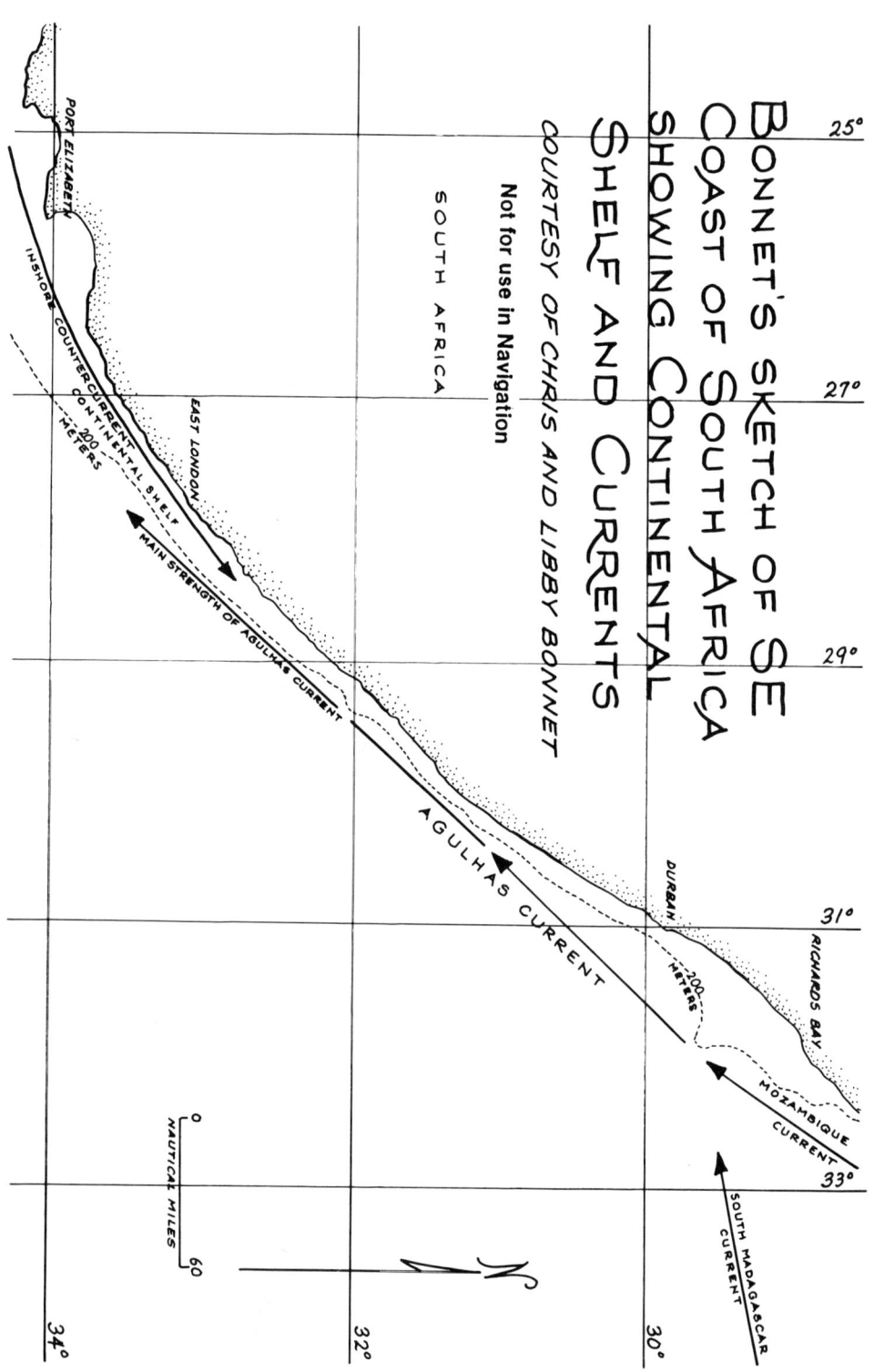

CHAPTER 19

PASSAGE TO RICHARDS BAY, SOUTH AFRICA

Towards Madagascar

The east wind that followed the storm was welcome. It put *Svea* on a broad reach towards our hypothetical mark south of Madagascar. We felt like the little engine in the child's story book that thought he could, thought he could make it up the steep hill. We hoped we could, hoped we could, make it around Madagascar. We truly hoped we could before another gale drove us backwards!

We picked up a radio broadcast of news in English, but from a Russian station. Stratus clouds streaked across the sky. "What does that mean?" I asked Don.

"I don't know," he answered. "You're the one who's always trying to match clouds with pictures in the books. You tell me. Stratus clouds can mean a clear night is ahead."

Don was right and we passed through the night in relative comfort. By morning, the wind was north of east and the mainsail blanketed the jenny. "Time to hoist the twins," Don decided.

"I don't really like this sky," I said as I set about to help with the sail changes. "There are too many stratus clouds and they're wearing a grey chiffon skirt."

"Barometer is still steady," Don, a man of few words, counteracted my concern.

The wind veered more northerly and the sky cleared off its grey skirt. Only harmless-looking cumulus clouds puffed their way across the clear blue sky. I can't help but think of the little lambs I bottle-fed in New Zealand when I see cumulus clouds scampering across a field of blue sky. We were 120 miles from our turning point. That still gave us a 20-mile margin of safety to avoid the edge of Madagascar's continental shelf.

"The barometer's dipping," Don said as he came out into the cockpit.

"Oh not now, not at this dreaded place! We could easily run up on the shelf if a gale comes up now," I said fearfully. "If the wind hangs in the northeast?" and I dropped my question mid-air, for I knew that would be a prelude to a southwester.

Don only nodded assent. Two more days and we would be around the southern tip of Madagascar, but it wasn't to be. We were to be dangled like mice before a cat's paw as the Indian Ocean flaunted the rounding of Madagascar before us, but wouldn't let us reach it.

As the winds veered anti-clockwise and increased in strength, we followed it around until we stopped when it came out of the southwest to blow a gale. We lied-a-hull and were battered and blundgeoned by great waves that tried to sit on us, then squash us. Angry seas spat at us as if they were trying to spit out a bitter pill, but *Svea* endured. By morning, that gale was on the ebb as the rising barometer came on its heels. At least we had been pushed in the right direction that time and had not retreated. This time the currents had control over us. But had we really won the battle?

Broken Gudgeon

"I need your help," Don called out to me from the cockpit. "I have to lean overboard to repair the rudder. You'll have to hold my feet."

"You have to do what?" I shouted back as I ran to the cockpit to see what he was talking about. I leaned over the stern and saw for myself the jagged piece of metal sticking out from the rudder. The top gudgeon, a more than adequate strap of stainless steel, had ripped apart as if it had been made of soft plastic.

"That must have happened after the lull last night when that big wave slammed into us," Don said. "It jammed the tiller arm over too, and pulled the pilot arm out of whack. I was able to straighten the pilot arm, but in the dark I couldn't see what it had done to the gudgeon."

With great difficulty, we pried the jagged strap away from the hull to allow the tiller to swing freely. Freely it did, for its weight fell upon the remaining straps and was at a most canted angle. Would the other straps hold it up? Had they been damaged as well, or had metal fatigue affected them too? I wanted to rig a bridle to harness the rudder. "But what if it falls off and we lose it?" I asked Don when he did not think too wisely of my idea.

"It just falls off," Don answered, but he too was just as apprehensive. We had so many miles to go with a damaged rudder, or maybe no rudder at all. Where would the currents take us? Would a freighter pick us up? Would they be able to hoist *Svea* up unto their decks?

The wind direction was still from the southwest. It was senseless to get underway. The barometer was rising: Surely the wind would swing soon to a more southerly direction. I went below and pulled out the flag bag and the "International Code Book of Signals." There was a set of three flags that read the message we might need: "I have damaged my rudder. I can not steer." I pulled out the three flags, the letters, M, S, and E. In addition I pulled out the letter F, for that signaled we had lost the rudder.

Winds slackened, veered a little south of southwest, and we started to get underway. Don attached the pilot arm to the weakened rudder and gave it some support. Still it wobbled like a young girl in her first pair of high-heeled shoes. Why the mirth at a time like this? I was exhausted, mentally. My thoughts ran from storm to storm, disaster to disaster. Why was the Indian Ocean picking on us?

The tricks were not finished yet. There were still some left in the bag. When the barometer started its downward plunge, and the winds switched around to east and began blowing 25 knots, we knew we were in for still another gale. The grey chiffon skirt returned to cover the stratus streaks and we had no doubts as to what was coming.

The sickening feeling that accompanies impending doom overwhelmed me, but this time I set my feelings aside and began to think about preparing for the new storm. I shoved towels in the ventilators and put the spice jars in a bucket before they were thrown at me. I renewed all of the paper towels I had squished against the overhead beams to soak up the oozing of seawater when it slams against the cabin sides. Don taped the glass chimney to the kerosene lamp. For the first time, he pulled out the ominous black storm door and set it into place in the companionway. The black door looked so foreboding, as if it were locking us in rather than the storm out. The tiny port light in the thick door gave little light and less view of the cockpit.

Two albatrosses appeared overhead as if waiting like buzzards to grab up the pickings should we founder. We were still running before the wind with full main. As the wind increased further, we had to reduce sail, for we feared too much strain on the rudder. We had to try not to burden it with a weather helm. We lowered the main and raised the storm jib. The wobbly rudder hung precariously to its remaining gudgeons to steer *Svea* down the big seas. We had been wise not to fill the water tanks forward in the bow and the fuel tanks aft. Without the added weight, her ends raised and responded to meet the seas.

When the barometer dropped to 29.94 and the wind veered to the north, we shook anew, for we dared not face another southwester so close to Madagascar. Waves were huge and crashed all around us. With the wind swinging from northwest, rains began with great violence. The wind seemed to be losing some if its punch after it had veered to the northwest. Surely it would swing down to southwest and blow harder.

Sunset approached and we watched the brilliant red sky as the horizon swallowed the sun. Was that a good omen? "Red sky at night, sailor's delight." Or, was it as our friend Janet Groene says, "Red sky at night, sailors take fright?" The barometer plunged more, down to 29.84 inches and the northwest winds gained further strength until they reached 30 knots.

"We're going to have to run with the seas, the waves are much too big," Don said. "Let's head southeast."

Wrong Way Again!

"But do we have sea room?" I asked. Having made our turn to avoid Madagascar's continental shelf, I thought we were dangerously close to the western side of the shelf.

"Just do as I say, don't argue now," Don said curtly. "We'll talk about it later. Just set the pilot for 135 degrees heading." We pulled down the storm jib and under bare poles *Svea* retreated in the direction from which she had come.

The darkened sky came alive with streaks of lightning and thunder rumbled across the water with moans of the wind to announce the oncoming rain. It fell in torrents, but the barometer started an upward turn.

Did that mean we were going to be free from the southwester? The wind did swing over to the west, and there it stopped and increased no further. "Let's lie-a-hull and see what it's going to do," said Don, discouraged that again we were stopped. Very carefully, we lashed the tiller to immobilize the rudder and went below to wait it out. We stayed that way for 12 hours while the wind teetered back and forth between west and southwest.

Passage from Madagascar to Richards Bay, South Africa

As the wind subsided, our fears lessened. Still it would not leave that southwesterly direction. The sky cleared and by morning a light southeasterly breeze set us on our way again. Richards Bay was 650 miles ahead and Madagascar was 90 miles behind us. At noon, we had our first cold beer in days to celebrate our survival from Madagascar's clutches.

Winds remained light and hung around the southerly direction. World news on Voice of America spoke of so many squabbles and political turmoils. Our little world was free from those problems, but our major battle dealt seriously with the weather, a win or lose situation that kept us fretful enough.

Later in the day we watched a strange-looking ship coming up astern. "It's a large tuna-fishing boat," Don said.

"No, it's a small warship," I conjectured. We were both wrong. When the ship altered course and ran abeam of us, there was no mistaking the markings on its smokestack. *Tepoebka* was a Russian whaling ship. She drew close enough to identify us, then carried on her northbound course.

Fleecy clouds commanded the sky and set our fears at ease. The steady barometer confirmed that a good day was in the making.

A bird, different from any of the others we had ever seen, appeared astern. Speckled like a herringbone tweed coat, the little fellow flew up to *Svea*'s quarter, plopped himself down alongside and drifted back in the wake until the distance between us became about 50 yards and he repeated the act. I got the message that this little Cape pigeon had done this begging routine before and had been rewarded by other sailors. He was quite happy to take our left-over bread, most unlike other sea birds that disdain anything but fish.

The bird-life population increased as albatrosses and fulmars came around. We still had our 400 miles separating us from South Africa's coast. Not to be outdone by the overhead wildlife, waterborne creatures made their appearance known, as a school of black and white porpoise swam around *Svea*. Again we wished for an identification book on whales and porpoise. We wondered if these fellows were the Dall variety, as their snouts were more slender and longer than the common bottle nose porpoise.

At dusk, when the sun sank from the cloudless sky into the sea, a green blip popped up on the horizon like a blob of toothpaste squeezed from a tube. It was calm, too calm and eerie. By morning, winds were still light,

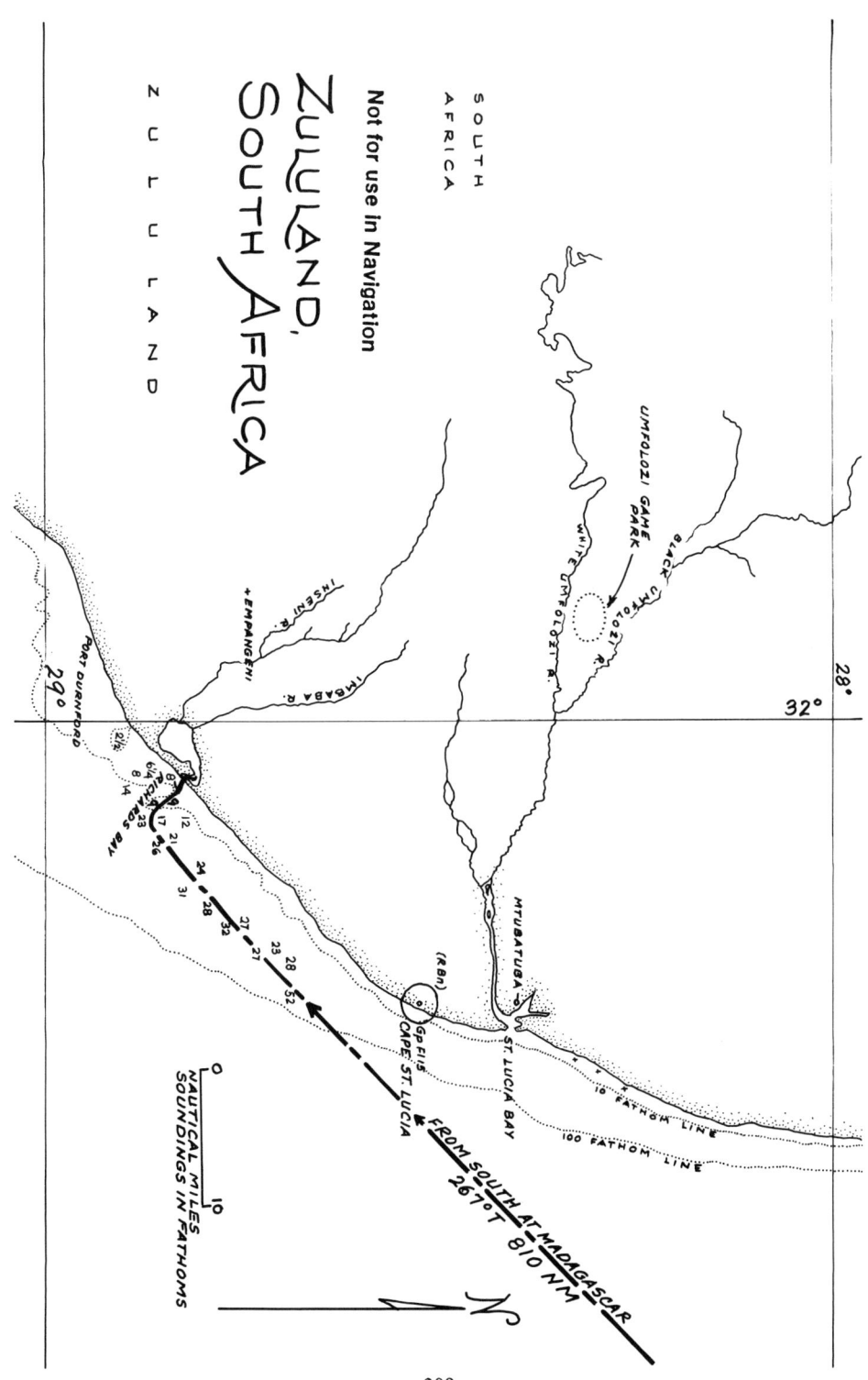

but the lightweight twins managed the airs and the fluctuating direction. It was Don's birthday, August 20th, and I made baking powder biscuits for him. The little Cape pigeon highly approved of the menu as well.

Richards Bay was 325 miles away at noon, only 33 miles made good noon to noon in the light airs. We had passed another time zone and set the clock back 1 hour, just 2 hours ahead of Greenwich.

Small white terns joined the other creatures still with us, the albatrosses and the Cape pigeons. They chirped and twittered so insistently that as we watched their show, we could not help but be amused at their antics in trying to land on *Svea*'s masthead. "Real simpletons, real dunderheads," I laughed at their play.

The barometer took an upward turn, and the high pressure produced a windless day. We turned on the engine to maintain our course. Still the Cape pigeon stayed with us. We saw a tanker in ballast going eastbound that agreed with our course. Our plotted position confirmed that we were in the shipping lanes.

Don took some time out to study the pilot charts as he felt our noon position was too far north of the course. We must have been set by that northbound current coming up from Madagascar that had control of us. At least that was better than going south, for when we reached the Agulhas Current we would be carried south. By going north, we had less chance of running up on the 100-fathom line that has its most dangerous edge outside of Durban. Still no wind after dinner, and we shut down the engine and lied-a-hull. "Maybe we should have taken on more fuel?" I asked.

The too-calm day should have been a warning to us that it preluded a blow. When the barometer started to drop, the northeast wind started up. All were signs that another gale was on its way. "Only 135 miles from Richards Bay and now another southwester to blow us away!"

"Let's ride this northeaster," Don said. "We just might make it into port if the wind holds in this direction. I don't think the remaining gudgeons will survive another strong gale. We've got to beat that southwesterly."

The wind was far too strong to keep up the big blues, so we pulled them down and replaced them with only part of the jenny. By reducing the foresail area and not the full mizzen, we put a strain on the helm, the weak rudder. We were trying desperately to outrun the inevitable southwester. Many times I looked astern to see if the rudder was still with us. Just seeing it wobbling, somehow reassured me that it was going to stay with us and get us into port.

A large supertanker crossed our starboard bow. We were in the heavier shipping lanes in the Mozambique Channel. Still the wind held northerly, but was intensifying. "I really don't like to use the jenny that way, but a sail change now would only slow us down and we have to keep moving," said Don. "The way it looks, we just might get into Richards Bay before this thing turns around to the southwest."

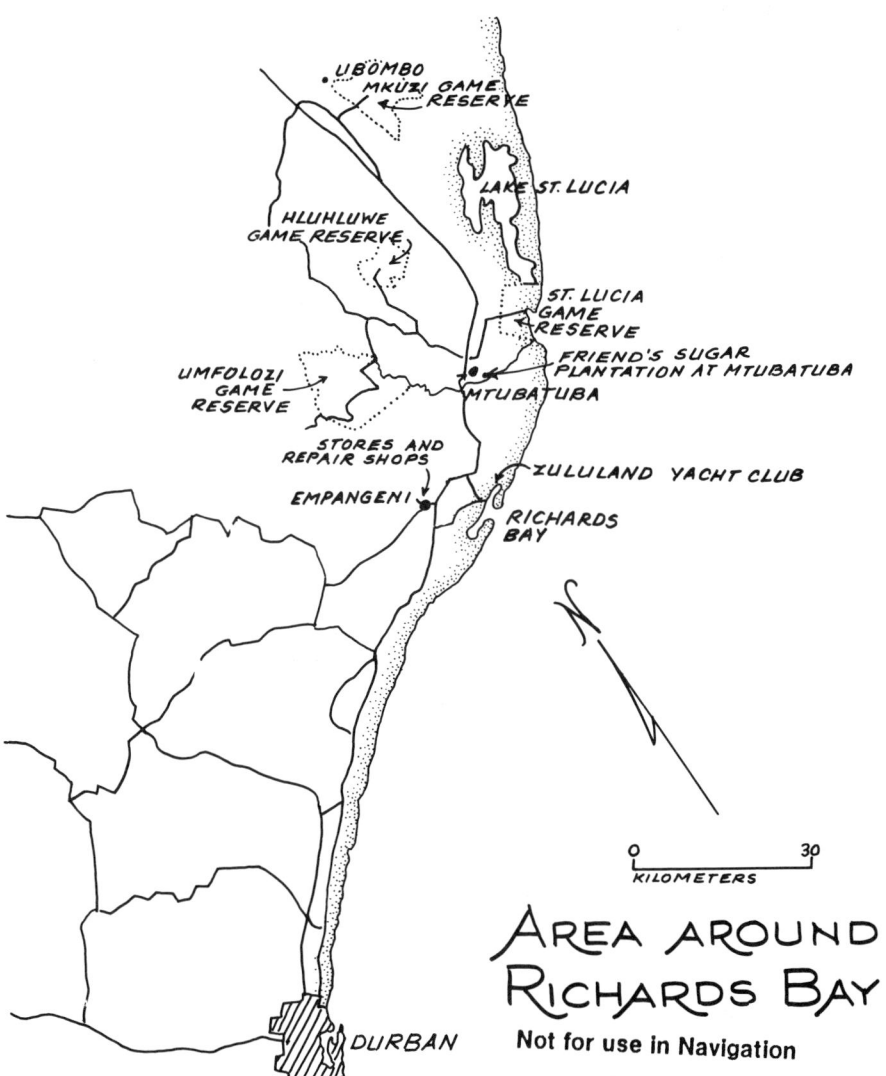

Land Ho!

It was midnight when I smelled land and Don picked up the light from St. Lucia, noted on the chart as having a range of 21 miles. We had to slow down, for dawn was more than 5 hours away. Speeding along at 6 knots we would arrive before the sun rose at 0500. Don needed rest badly and knew it. "Follow the 20-fathom line now. We've slowed down and we'll be following the coastline," he said. "Just don't get inside that 20-fathom line and we'll be safe from running into anything. Understand?"

I nodded and Don went below. The blinking shore lights from the largest coal bunkering station in the world beckoned me into Richards Bay, but I maintained course, or thought I had, until I looked at the sounder and found that it read 17 fathoms instead of the safe 20 fathoms.

I quickly altered course and turned out towards sea, then I lost sight of the lights. When Don came out at dawn to look for land and did not see it, he quickly turned on the sounder and found it read 20 fathoms.

"You dunderhead," he said angrily. "You let the sounder fool you again. The dial has spun around the 60-fathom mark and is starting on the next 60. We have 80 fathoms of water under us, not 20! I just can't leave you alone out here, can I?" Don was understandably angry, for now we had to head for shore against a wind that was northwesterly and bound to swing over into a southwesterly gale. Too, we had overshot Richards Bay and had to fight the current back north again. Don turned on the engine to help and when we did find the lee of Africa, we made better time towards our objective.

Richards Bay

The barometer was still falling when we reached the harbor entrance, but we were safely close to refuge. "We've cheated you this time, Poseidon, you old fool," I shouted and shook my fists at the imaginary figure. "You didn't get us with this southwesterly and you didn't get our rudder either." I quickly looked over the stern to make sure I had not told a falsehood.

After 23 days at sea from Reunion, we had arrived at a new land, a new continent, and made another milestone in our journey. Africa's dark continent was far from being shadowed in obscurity. The bright sun beamed down on undulating sand dunes rising in uneven knolls along the shoreline. Behind the dunes, long-necked creatures were not giraffes at all, but the steelwork of cranes moving back and forth loading the many freighters that come into Richards Bay. Until 1965, Richards Bay was a shallow estuary with a depth of only 6 feet that led the waters of the Mhlatuzi River into the sea. Lazy hippopotami lolled in the muddy river and the Portuguese in the 15th century visited the Riodos-Peixes, the name they gave to the river of fishes.

Svea chose a different route from the mariners that came to Zululand's shores centuries ago, for she followed the markers set along the dredged channel leading us into the boat basin shared by the many tugs working the bulk carriers in and out of the busy port. "There, Don, over there," I pointed to the high dock with the big sign painted on the cement wharf. "That sign reads 'Customs'." The high walls of the basin seemed to reach out and put their arms around *Svea* to let her know she was safe. The mean old Indian Ocean would never break through to get her, not yet, not for another five months when the southern hemishpere's summer was ended and it was once again time for passagemaking.

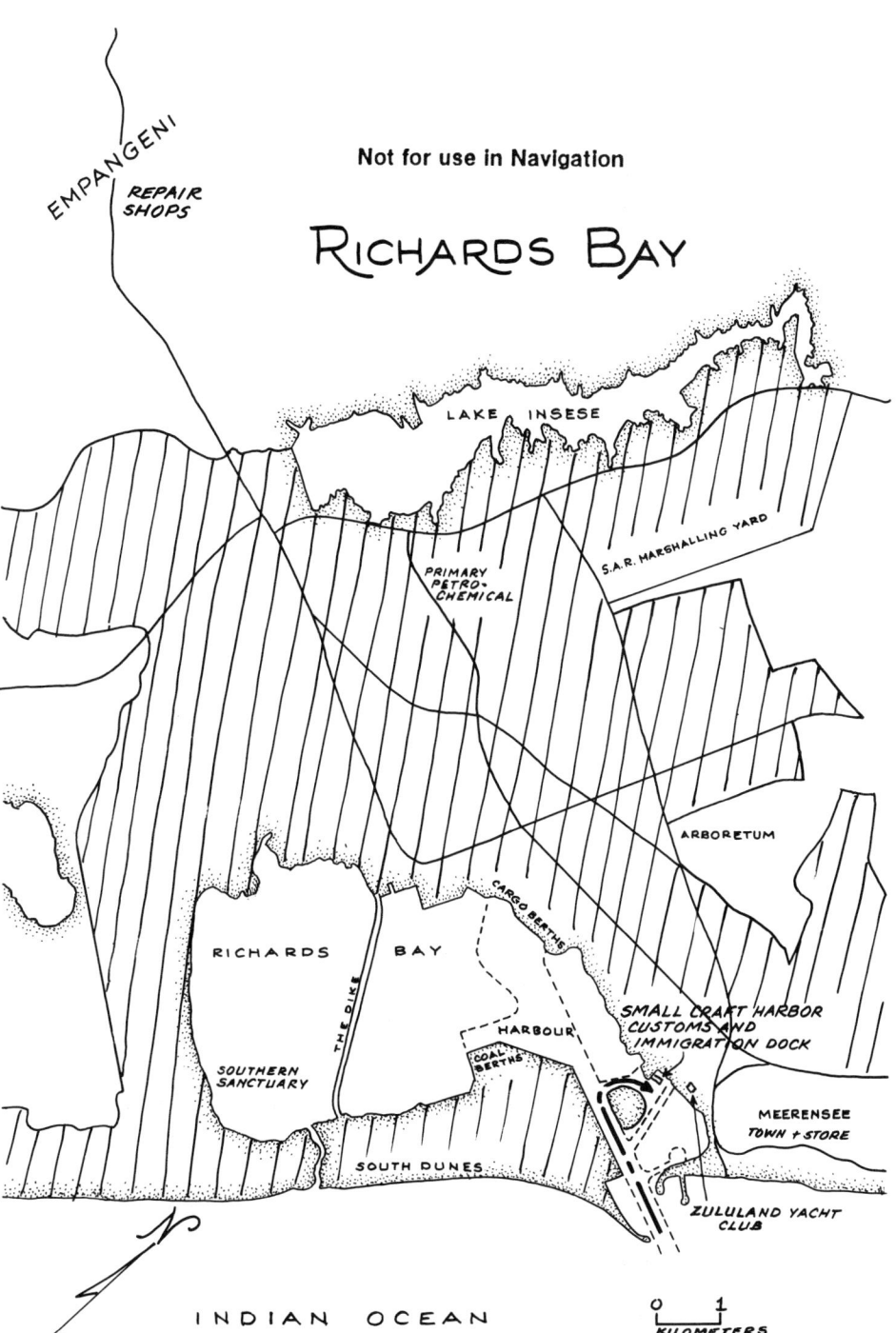

CHAPTER 20

ZULULAND

Richards Bay

"Where'd you come from, Yank?" asked the bewhiskered man who caught *Svea*'s bow lines as Don drew alongside the quay of the Zululand Yacht Club.

"We just came from the customs dock. We had a hard time finding the way to the club around all of these sand dunes," Don laughed. "We could see the masts of the boats but couldn't find the channel. We finally found a Dutchman who pulled up his fishing lines and showed us the way, but we darn near ran aground doing that."

"That must have been the *Albatross*," the gentleman grabbed his beard and a smile raised his red cheeks. "He's an Afrikaner and his boat doesn't draw as much water as yours! What did he do? Lead you across that shallow winding channel over there?" and our friend Basil pointed to the narrow strip of water behind us that was visibly quite shallow in the afternoon sun.

"Yes, Don answered. "I haven't put this boat aground since we left the States almost five years ago, but I came pretty close to doing it this afternoon."

"How long you been out?" asked Basil who was now joined by other club members who had come down to the quay to look at the new arrival.

"Started out from Mauritius about 27 days ago, and a northeaster blew us in here," Don relaxed in the company of the South Africans.

"Come on up to the club and have a beer; we'll talk about it," said Basil. "Most of the members are up there now, since it's Saturday and they come on weekends. I'm the only one living on my boat. She's over on moorings, the other side of the channel."

"What'll you have, Yank?" The fellow behind the bar asked, "A Castle or a Lion? Basil's buying."

Don, not very attuned to the accent of a South African, did not quite understand the word "Castle" and he repeated it like he heard it, "Kaas-ul."

Ernst Klaar

The members broke up in laughter and we were welcomed within the fold. Don wanted to reciprocate with a round for Basil and the bar, but we had no local currency. "Here, Yank yachtie," said a very thick German accent. "Take this 20 and when you get change, you can pay me back." A perfect stranger had given another perfect stranger a 20 rand note. From that day on, we never met a stranger at Zululand Yacht Club. We were so happy we had put in at Richards Bay rather than the busy, but more popular port at Durban 90 miles farther south. Here in Zululand, we could relax in the congenial atmosphere and not be caught up in the crowd of congested Durban with its more formal yacht club.

Hans and Alex Klaar's family junk at Richards Bay Yacht Club dock

The German voice had belonged to Ernst Klaar, a Swiss fellow who was gaining fame as a treasure hunter and diver. With his family of two boys, a daughter and his wife, plus Fritzie, their little dog, he had been sailing around the western part of the Indian Ocean for a number of years in his 50-foot junk, *Maria Jose*. Like a lot of treasure hunters, Ernst had the good days and the bad, but he was not about to tell you where he was when he had the good days. The club's commodore called him a lovable rogue and the bureaucrats called him something else. We called him our friend and enjoyed sharing the dockage next to him along the quay.

Ernst's oldest son, Hans, was quite fond of wildlife, particularly birds which he sketched. His drawings showed the love he felt for them. He was in a bird watcher's paradise at Richards Bay, for it was a bird sanctuary, and the town's planning board was careful to insure the protection of the wildlife. Although business was encouraged at Richards Bay for the industrialists who shipped aluminum, coal, and other minerals from the big bulk-loading port, the ecology of the area was not sacrificed in the name of progress.

"What's that noise?" I asked Hans early one morning when the sun was just peeking over the rise of sand dunes that kept the sea at bay from the tranquil early morning scene.

"Over there in the reeds on the opposite shore, Sue. You can't see him, for he's hiding from you," said Hans who knew without seeing the bird, what kind of crane he was. After his many early morning walks through the high grass fields skirting the yacht club, Hans would often share his finds with us. We enjoyed his tales of storks, pelicans, flamingoes and many other birds he identified, plus the mongoose, hippopotami and even the vervet monkeys that are happy inhabitants in the forest of trees that separates Richards Bay from the small town of Meerensee.

I must tell the funniest story of all and the laugh was not on Hans, but on his father. It seems that to appease the bureaucrats, Ernst had sold his treasured find of 12 bronze cannons to museums at a small profit. Breachloaders, they had come off Portuguese wrecks dating back to the 16th century, and were found somewhere off Madagascar. Another time in a separate negotiation, he gave the museum some earthen jars that he had found diving in the same vicinity as the cannons. A day or two after the bequeath, the curator of the museum stopped by *Maria Jose* to make sure Ernst was serious about his gift and asked him to sign papers to confirm the donation.

"Of course, why not?" asked the Swiss diver with the grey-peppered beard who without hesitation put his signature to the outstretched document.

"We just wanted to be sure. When we were cleaning the urns, we found a gold necklace packed in the sediment at the bottom of one of them!" they said and silently stole away.

For a minute, Ernst was speechless and then we heard him ranting, "Alex, Alex, you are the dummkopf," and the rest of his words were lost in the Swiss dialect. His younger son, who was the son responsible for cleaning artifacts brought on board *Maria Jose*, was seen hastily retreating from his father's wrath.

Umfolozi Game Reserve

Perhaps one of the greatest experiences we have ever had was thanks to a weekend sailor at the yacht club who took his Sunday off to take us to the Umfolozi Game Reserve, about 20 miles from Richards Bay. The day began with a blustery southwester, a typical day in that spring of the southern hemisphere, and we almost did not go when Leo came to pick us up. He convinced us that the gloomy days were the best days to see the animals, for they come out to feed and to play. We got to the park by traveling the national highway that took us up and over hills and through the lands where the Zulus have their kraals, their villages, built upon the tops of the knolls. Small circular mud huts, topped with conical grass roofs, stood on barren ground. Deep ruts of eroded soil marked the path water traveled during the rare times when it rained.

The plight of the overgrazed lands of the Bantu tribes is a problem not corrected by moving the tribes to another site, for wherever they exist, the problem exists. The wealth of a Zulu is measured by his number of livestock. Along the roadside, shepherds moved their cattle and goats, hoping that the few blades of grass of the road beds would feed their skinny animals. Women carried their babies in slings of bright-plaid blankets tied around their bosoms and waists. The infants rested on the buttocks of the black women.

We left the main highway at Mtubatuba and followed a smaller road, for about 6 miles, that took us through drier bush lands. As we neared the outskirts of the game preserve, we saw a herd of wildebeest mixed with a few zebra. I often wondered if a zebra's stripes were all the same pattern. I found out they they were as differently adorned as models in a fashion show, although their stripes ran in the same direction. Then the impala came with their graceful arcs of leaps and bounds. The magnificence of land and her creatures reminded us sailors that fur-covered animals could be just as majestic and beautiful as the creatures of the sea whose habitat we had been sharing.

Vultures were hovering over a recently killed wildebeest. To the side stood several marabou storks. We got out of the bakkie, the Afrikaner name given small pickup trucks, to have a look. The vultures were the last of the diners as they were cleaning up the sparse remains. Alongside the road in the gulley was a huge print of a lion's paw in the soft sand and farther up on the soft knoll, were pieces of fur where the animal had made his last stand against the king of beasts. Back in the bakkie, we thought in hindsight that perhaps our getting out of the safety of the vehicle had not been a very smart idea.

Around and up and down the small road we went. The sights of the animals made impressions upon us that would have filled a storybook full. Wart hogs traveled in the low bush with their young trailing behind in a single file. The beautiful nyala and the other antelope, like the kudu, were far

Photo by Carl Moesly

Giraffe in African Game Park

more exciting than I could have imagined. The ponderous rhinoceros looked rather silly munching on grass, rather than on the meat of an animal, but the beast is not a carnivore. Graceful giraffes poked their heads above the acacia trees, rather like little old ladies who strained their necks to look out of an upstairs window to see what was going on in the world below.

Zululand History

We were in the land of the Zulus, their hunting grounds of years before when their chief, Shaka, led his people into battles against the other Bantu tribes. He was a mean and victorious leader who saw nothing but a kingdom of Zulus. In 1879 the British had different ideas and although Shaka was now dead, his ancestors carried on the tradition of the Zulus. The first battle was heavily one-sided, 5,000 Europeans against 40,000 Zulus. What the British lacked in force, they substituted with pure dogmatism. Despite their first lost battle, they continued to fight the Zulu until they decisively defeated him in 1887.

Twelve years later, the British were engaged in the Boer Wars, fighting their kinsmen who had fought with them against the Zulus. As time had worn on there was little love lost between the two Europeans, that of the Afrikaner whose ancestors go back to the original Dutch settlers of 1652, and the British who conquered their opposition once again.

The Afrikaner did not go down in defeat, he only fell back to the more inland areas and regrouped. The Afrikaners' legacies continue. The signs in South Africa are a sign painter's delight. Every word is written not only in English, but Afrikaans as well.

In Zululand, the British influence is omnipresent. The offspring of the original colonists are still the landowners of the sugar plantations. One of these is our friend John Shire whose grandfather came from Somerset, England to start his farm at Mtubatuba from nothing but the land he stood on. Even the Zulus had made no claim to the land that was known to have malaria and the tsetse on it, the same reason given to the salvation of the white rhino at Umfolozi. The beast was not hunted in a land where the tsetse fly meant certain death from the sleeping sickness it injected or where malaria was rampant. Where the Umfolozi River splits and forms a section of land between its two streams is where the tsetse fly was most prolific and where the rhino found his stronghold. The legendary river runs through Zululand. Not far from the Shire's farm, in season, the banks swell to receive the rains, but there are years when droughts are cruel to the animals and the sugar cane.

Our Visit to a Sugar Cane Farm

John, his wife, Marilyn, and their two children were weekend sailors and kept their sloop *Suntan* next to Basil's ketch *Aldes* on the moorings. But on one Saturday morning Marilyn called up from the farm, which was about 12 miles from Richards Bay. "Sue," she said with a positive voice. "We're driving down there to get you and Don and bring you back

Photo by Carl Moesly

Zulu Queen and her children in front of their hut

to the farm for the night. We'll take you back on Sunday, so you won't be away from *Svea* too long.

"Away from *Svea*? Overnight?" I said aloud as Don and Basil were standing beside me. "We've never been away from *Svea* overnight!"

"Go on Yanks," Basil said kindly. "It'll do you good to get away. There are plenty of us around here who will look after your *Svea* for you."

Basil was so right, for the chance to see the Shire's farm was indeed a bright experience and another look into South Africa's wildlife, including Marilyn's domestic animals. Her pet geese, her tranquil chickens were especially raised not to cluck and squawk, and their four dogs had the run of the place. Their Zulu house boy, Genius, was part of the family as well. Marilyn talked with him in her best kitchen Zulu about preparing the evening meal.

John was like any other farmer, up before the crack of dawn to get his Zulu workers started in the cane fields. When he came back to the big house, we hopped in his bakkie to have a tour of his lands. Acres and acres of sugar cane waved in the light breezes. As we drove through the rows, John pointed out the small holes alongside the cane where small creatures made their homes. In the reed beds among the ponds, we watched the delightful little weaver birds hard at work. They were building nests attached to thin reed stems, winding and weaving strings of leaves through and around their basket nests.

Up the hills and over the undulating knolls we went. On the side of a high hill we stopped to watch a pair of migrating spur geese picking at the blades of tall dry grass. We came upon a cluster of trees where vervet monkeys swung from branch to branch, their tails balancing their high jinks. The monkeys are a nuisance to the cane farmers as they eat the new tender sprouts of the plant. "I have a neighbor who has an all-out war with these fellows," John said as he chuckled. "But I hope on my farm, there will always be enough room for all of us."

One day, John and Marilyn came down to Richards Bay with the trunk of their car loaded down with freshly-killed nyala meat. "The rangers are culling the herds now," Marilyn said. "And we thought you and Ernst could use some of the meat." We were delighted and Ernst took up the role as butcher. While he salted his down for lack of refrigeration on *Maria Jose*, we cut ours up into steaks and roasts and put them in the freezer. Nyala tastes like a tender venison and is really quite delicious.

Rudder Repair

When it came time to haul *Svea* and repair her rudder, we had help from everyone. Basil even hired a Zulu worker for us to do the hard work of scrubbing the hull and helping me with scaffolding. At least the Zulu used our tools rather than cane knives. One club member had his Zulus use cane knives to scrape the bottom of his 50-foot ketch. I gasped when I first saw Herman's three Zulus wielding their cane knives, like swashbucklers attacking their enemy. I was quite impressed with the efficiency of the tool, which whacked off the barnacles with little difficulty. Perhaps the marine trade should take a lesson from the cane farmers.

We had advice from everyone as to what we should do with our weakened rudder. With the help of the club members who worked in machine shops, we were able to get heavy stainless steel straps made. These reinforced *Svea*'s rudder and made it stronger than it had ever been. They also loaned us tools and gave freely of their time. They even loaned us their bakkies to take to Durban for other supplies. We were overwhelmed with their kindness, which seemed to soften the blows of the raging southwesters and angry northeasters that hampered our work.

Time to Leave

Meanwhile several foreign yachts were beginning to reach South Africa's shores in anticipation of rounding the Cape of Good Hope at the turn of the new year. Most of the yachts making landfalls at Richards Bay carried on for Durban and the excitement of the bigger city, but some preferred the smaller town and its country environment. They stayed to haul their boats and enjoy the cold beers on the weekends at the clubhouse. We remember well one German couple in a small 28-foot sloop. Quite adventurous and fond of cold climates, they had spent time in the Aleutians. Their destination when they left Cape Town was Nova Scotia. This was a large feat for a small boat. As we have learned through the years and especially in the cruising sailor's world, we all dance to different drummers. We prefer ours to be in areas around the warm climates of the Equator.

We have often been accused of not getting the full potential from *Svea*, but we answer, "Why?" Is there something more to be gained by pushing your vessel to her limit? Or pushing its equipment, or even yourself? We do not think so, for we all end up at the same terminals regardless of the speed of the race to get there. We have no desires to enter any competitions, for we feel the sea gives us enough of a challenge. Our strongest compelling ambition is to keep *Svea* seaworthy and all of her gear in working order without the costly expense of replacements. One of the biggest challenges was right in our foreground as 1,000 miles of Africa's coastline stood between us and the Cape of Good Hope.

It was now a year since we had parted from our old gang at Mauritius. We missed our friends with whom we had shared so many anchorages along the way. *Rigadoon* was back home in Florida where Carl was busy with plans for a new house. *Sunday Morning* was also in Florida and Jim and Cheryl had sold their *Wind'son* and were proud parents of a son. *Intermezzo* had been sold in Fort Lauderdale and Skip and Linda were in Cape Town having their new 62-foot aluminum boat built in a boatyard there. *Dreamtime* was back in Australia and *Arion III* and *Sunflower* were both in Singapore. Although all of us were now scattered across the oceans, our ties had bound us closely together and we would always remain in touch. In fact, we hoped to see Skip and Linda in Cape Town.

Christmas found us still in Zululand. We had stretched our stay, for we enjoyed the people of the sugar country who had taken us into their homes, as well as trips around the countryside. We were hesitant to move on south where we knew the weather could worsen. We had been at Zululand Yacht Club for over four months. We had shared all of the club's activities: the Sunday barbecues, called "braiflais" in Afrikaans, and the special occasions that called for extra kitchen duty on the part of the club women.

Atop *Svea*'s mizzen mast was a small tree that a small girl had picked especially for our boat. Sarah Kate and her daddy had walked through the woods until she had found the most perfect pine tree. We liked that little moppet who was the angel in the annual Christmas play at the club and whose tomboy antics were far from heaven sent. The New Year was just around the corner and it was time to tear ourselves from our new friends and begin our passagemaking.

CHAPTER 21

PASSAGE TO EAST LONDON, SOUTH AFRICA

Time to Leave Richards Bay

For the five months we were tied to the Zululand Yacht Club's dock, we learned well the general pattern of the weather systems that trounced the coastal waters with persistent lambastings. Northeasters brought forth strong winds and a falling barometer. When the winds veered more northerly, a slight lull in their strength heralded a rising barometer. That was soon followed by the sinister black cloud carrying the southwesters, which often reached gale force. Besides the blast at their onset, strong winds sometimes lingered for days to keep prudent sailors in port.

When the northeasters came, we were covered with dirt blown off the fields and when the southwesters raged, we were peppered with coal dust from the bunkers south of us. South African sailors were attuned to their lot. They employed the northeasters to sail south and the southwesters to sail north. To all of us, seasoned and novice alike, the true course either way was frightening. Ninety miles separated the two ports of Richards Bay and Durban. Often the wind changed direction midway, forced sailors to heave-to or run with the wind behind them back to their port of origin. There are few ports of refuge along the South African coast. Heaving-to in a blow was more common than not for the sailors who traveled the routes.

Like a volunteer fire department, young men from all walks of life volunteered their time to man the fast boats of the National Sea Rescue Institute to answer calls of distress and monitor the airways. Set up by the government, this organization, with their red and white boats, was a familiar sight at every port along the coastline.

One thousand miles of that dreaded coast separated us from Cape Town where we would round the Cape of Good Hope to leave Africa behind us and strike out across the Atlantic Ocean bound for home waters. It was a game of chance to sail that South African coast. Hometowners freely admitted that sailing off their shores was not a sport of gentlemen. Their boats were ruggedly built and the sailors that manned them had to reflect the same attitude. Rigid laws to maintain safety were enforced to keep the amateur sailors from causing harm to themselves or endangering the lives of others. Special clearance papers and float plans had to be filed before a boat could leave any harbor bound for another. This law included local sailors as well as the foreign visitors. One did not lackadaisically go out for a Sunday sail at the whim of their urgings. Signal stations were posted at every harbor entrance to monitor the traffic. Their main concern was to keep the channels clear for the freighters and bulk carriers. It was the commercial carrier that brought money into South Africa, not the cruising sailor or local yachtsman. All efforts were utilized to maintain that traffic.

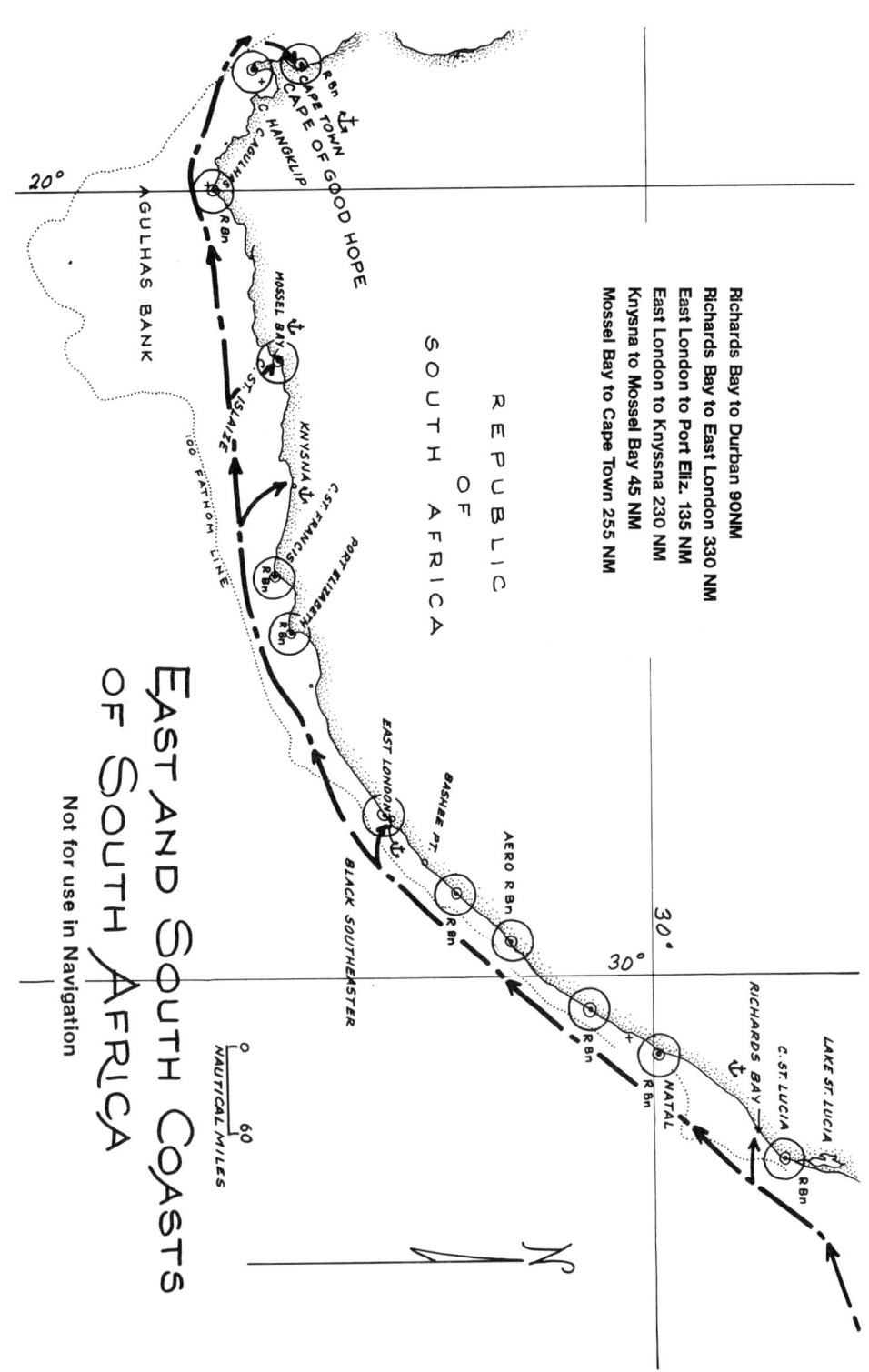

Off We Go

On January 10th, the middle of the southern hemisphere's summer, *Svea* was ready to go. Our bewhiskered friend, Basil, took Don in his bakkie to the offices of customs and immigration to fill out the seemingly reams of paperwork necessary to leave Richards Bay legally and enter our chosen ports along the South African coast. The waxed seals stamped on each of our clearance papers, needed for every projected port, were indeed impressive. More impressive to us was the send-off given to us by our new friends.

"See you down the line," we called out as Don turned *Svea* into a wide circle in front of the dock where our friends stood waving farewells.

"Don't forget to call us when you hit your first port," Marilyn shouted back.

The dying southwester had quelled its strength, but the riled seas took longer to diminish. We made way eastward and out to sea to gain the Agulhas Current that would speed us southward in its flow. We were careful to stay inside the 100-fathom line to avoid its edge where the freak waves occur.

"The barometer is falling," I said to Don as I glanced at the instrument over the galley sink.

"That figures," Don said as he glanced up at the sails. "The northeaster is on its way."

As the winds increased in strength from the northerly quadrant, we reefed sails and bent our way southward. We wanted to make as many miles as we could before the inevitable southwester forced us to heave-to or seek a safe harbor. The next morning Durban radio forecasted the southwester. In our earnest quest to put miles behind us, we had already sailed past her port of refuge and were committed to carry on.

Five Stormy Sou'westers

"We're going to have to stay out here and take our chances," Don admitted. "The chart shows some coves, but there isn't enough water for us. We'll get closer to shore to gain more of a lee."

Late afternoon blasts of thunder heralded the ominous black cloud preceding the sou'wester. The barometer fell to a new low. Lightning slashed through the black clouds hovering over the shoreline. *Svea*'s sails were reefed down where only a small area of the main remained. The southwest wind ripped across the cliffs and down upon the water to hit us with winds of hurricane strength. *Svea* bent to their force and her lee rail scooped up water that rushed back into the cockpit. I grabbed for Don's knee as the angle of heel nearly tossed us overboard. He jumped up to release the main sheet and spill the wind. Like an exploding umbrella caught by the force of the wind, the sail caught the edge of the spreader arm. Eight feet of the leech seam was ripped apart. The sail plastered itself against the shrouds to resemble a mummified ghost. We grabbed for the sail to bring it down, an arduous task in such wind. The lines to our safety harnesses tugged at us to keep us inboard of the lifelines. This was no gentle prelude to a sou'wester, for the wind continued its ferocity with the passing of the black frontal cloud.

"What are we in for? This isn't just a passing squall," I screamed to Don who was steering *Svea* downwind of the wind. "You're taking us out to sea. We can't get out there in this strong wind. The Agulhas current will be murderous against this wind."

"Just read off the compass to me," Don said. "I can't see it through this pelting rain."

Thirty minutes later, the wind subsided and the barometer was on the rise, but we were as wrung out as two very old dishrags. The sou'wester was still with us. Going south towards our destination was impossible. "We can't use the main, not until I sew it," I reminded Don when we considered heaving-to and waiting for a wind change.

Photo by Carl Moesly

Henri's *Challenge* after a gale on Madagascar's continental shelf. She was dismasted and limped into Durban with a jury rig

"No, we'll use the mizzen for the night, then in the morning, sort out the storm trysail," he said confidently.

"The storm trysail?" I questioned. "We've never used it!"

"We've never sailed the African coast before, either," said Don who knew we had to use a sail to claw off the shore if we were caught with the wind upon us. The storm trysail had a smaller area of sail than the main and should satisfy our need.

In the morning, I took my sail repair kit topsides and laboriously sewed up the torn sail as I braced myself against the boom, tied securely in the gallows. Durban radio reported extensive damage from the storm in which winds were recorded at over 62 knots. We were surprised when a fishing boat came alongside to see if we were all right and gave our position as being 10 miles north of where we thought we were when the storm hit us.

We've got the inshore northbound current going against us now," Don affirmed the situation.

With still another change of wind, this time out of the north, we got underway and headed again out to sea towards the Agulhas Current to gain its southward momentum. The sun came out to dry up the world.

The repaired sail was aloft and pulling nicely, the barometer was on the rise and so were our spirits. The happy scene was not to last. The next radio forecast predicted another sou'wester! A northbound freighter was in close to shore riding that current. We went in as well to stay out of the brunt of the wind and hopefully, gain a lee from the land. Our escape was cheered only by accompanying whimsical porpoise as they prankishly played around *Svea*'s bow.

The scenery was beautiful as we gazed beyond the high cliffs to see green rolling hills. Streams led haphazardly across the greenery and over the cliffs to reach the sea. Suddenly a shadow was cast upon the lovely scene when the approaching black cloud blotted out the beauty with still another forthcoming sou'wester.

That night we established our procedure for sou'westers as we sailed on the starboard tack that took us seaward until we felt the blustery wave action caused by the Agulhas Current countering the southwest wind. Then, we would switch tacks and drift back towards shore until the depth sounder showed that we were getting into shallow water. Back and forth, we continued and all the time to the wiles of whichever currents seized us. Waves charged us, rain pelted us and the winds terrified us. We see-sawed back and forth from Bashee Point. A camper who had pitched his tent on the high promontory wondered what in the world that foreign yacht was doing out there, as if we were sailing in circles in the intermediary stages of learning. Our hard-earned lesson was that sailing the South African coast is not for novice sailors. We would be glad when the Indian Ocean, with its surprises and hostilities, was behind us.

Drizzling, cold rain made us aware that we were deeper into the latitudes than our Equator-oriented bodies tolerated. Spray, tossed by riled seas, added to the misery. When the wind finally did swing around more northerly, we used the welcome change between northeasters and sou'westers to get underway and ride the rougher waters of the Agulhas Current southwestward in the right direction. Traffic was a constant problem. Freighters going north followed the in-shore current, while southbound vessels ran the mainstream of the Agulhas Current. *Svea* made her way between the routes of the big ships while her two lone crew members kept constant vigil.

After the fifth sou'wester, we were exhausted. Rather than struggle with tacking seaward and then coming back to shore on another tack, we just lashed the tiller and let *Svea* take us out to sea while we gathered some needed rest. We gained the Agulhas Current during the night. At dawn, I looked out the companionway to see the lighthouse off East London blinking a welcoming signal. What great luck! A free ride donated by the Agulhas Current. It was past time for our luck to change. In the one week since leaving Richards Bay, we had lopped only 330 miles off our projected passage. Those were the miles registered on the odometer. Lord only knows how many miles the currents had carried us. We would have been better off to forget about sailing and just stay in the Current, letting it take us southward.

East London

Again the contest between sailboat versus power boat reared its head when we had to make five tacks to make port. A power boat would have gone in a straight line, but the wind was dead on our nose when we turned to shore. Regardless of craft, the relief of reaching safe harbor in poor weather conditions is shared by all who ply the seas. We were no exception when the shores of the Buffalo River closed in to welcome us to East London.

"Where are you?" Marilyn Shire shouted over the phone when I finally got through to the Zululand Yacht Club and tried to talk over the din of the Sunday sailing crowd that was pushing at the seams in the small East London Yacht Club's cottage fronting the bay waters.

"East London," I shouted back and began to tell her about our trials and tribulations.

"We were so worried about you!" she cut in. "The sou'westers have really been on a rampage since you left."

"We've met them all, Marilyn, and one especially bad one that caught us south of Durban." I was unable to finish the rendition of our experience, for she knew the story already.

"It was you then," she gasped. "We had a friend on holiday at Margate and he told us about seeing a yacht out at sea that was heeled well over by the force of that strong wind that hit Durban." She took a breath. "When he described the boat, John told him it just had to be *Svea*, and it was! Are you all right? Is *Svea* all right?"

I answered yes to all of her questions and she made us promise to call her again when we reached the next port. The knowledge that a new friend cared so much somehow eased the anxiety we faced with South Africa's dreaded coast.

We were whisked away from the noise and its noisemakers by members of the small yacht club, who insisted we have a hot meal and even hotter bath. I reveled in the sweet-smelling bubbles in the typical South African bathtub that was long enough to immerse one's whole body. I wish American manufacturers would design their tubs to accommodate whole bodies, rather than halves at a time.

Back at the Fisheries dock where *Svea* was tied, we located showers used by crews for the nearby boatyard. Clearly visible were the signs above the separate doors that distinguished those used by "Blankies" and those for the "Coloreds." We were reminded of our friend back at Richards Bay who said a sign painter gets doubly paid in South Africa, for every sign had to display both the English and Afrikaner languages on them. We were now getting closer to the origin of the Afrikaner, or Boer, as he was known when the British first came to Cape Town to take possession of the Dutch settlements in 1806. Cape Town had been colonized in 1652 by an expedition led by Dutchman, Jan van Riebeck, under the auspices of the Dutch East India Company. The Dutch were joined in 1688 by French Huguenots and later by slaves from Madagascar and Java. In the mixture of languages Afrikaans was born.

We had heard about the East London Museum with its display of the rare prehistoric coelacanth that was caught off their shores in 1938. The fish dated back over 400 million years and its find was second only to one other found. The museum offered more than a stuffed fish, as life-sized mannequins stood in glass cages and depicted the peoples that walked through South Africa's history. Hottentots, Bantus and Bushmen seemed to step out from behind their glass enclosures to tell us how the white men came into their lands. Survival is not easy for those who stand in the way of progress. Progress? I wonder.

While we were in town, other poor souls, who had been floundering around in coastal waters, found East London as a port of refuge and had tied their boats alongside the Fisheries dock. When we returned, the sailors were comparing notes of their experiences with South Africa's dreadful coast. One boat had come all the way from Australia, while the other, coming only from Durban, had tales to match the long-distance sailor. East London succored their wounds. When the Durban boat reached Cape Town, we learned that the whole crew abandoned the projected plan to sail to the Caribbean. They left the captain alone to be commiserated by other captains who had experienced the same problem. The captain's crew was his own wife and two daughters. It's too bad that South

Africans cannot take their baby steps of sailing in the ideal conditions in the Bahamas. Their indoctrination to sailing leaves no room for any but the most stalwart of sailors.

The morning radio reported a raging flood at East London and strong gales ripping through Cape Town. The heavy rains were surely upon us. We realized that we were in for one of those rare southeast gales. The "Sailing Directions" call them "black southeasters that can be violent." We were not in the worst of it yet, as the weather forecaster warned all shipping to be aware of gales with winds 30 to 40 knots. At least, we had gained sea room but now there was far too much wind to carry any sail at all.

"The depth sounder records no depth," Don said. "We are well offshore and can safely lie-a-hull."

"Safely lie-a-hull," I muttered under my breath. What kind of safety is there in lying-a-hull? I donned dripping oilskins and went topsides to help lower the trysail that was straining to be released. Then we went below to wait it out. Both of us curled up on the floor in limp heaps of wet foul weather gear to try to get some rest.

Waves crashed against *Svea* and spewed out water to find the old places where they could penetrate the sanctity of our cabin. I was sitting on my starboard bunk when I looked up to see pulsating jets of water forcing their way through the hatchway above the table. The hatch over the stateroom floor was already sodden with wet sail bags, towels and clothing we had been wearing to keep us warm. Surely it was too cold for mildew to grow. I was miserable. Don was miserable and the problems of not being able to see the sun and utilize normal navigational aids compounded his miseries.

The morning after the gale was over, we were left with a windless sky and a thick covering of grey misty fog. The seas, still large, battered us as if they had to get in their last licks before they died. Sea became sky with no division. Everything was bleak and dismal. The gale had lasted for 48 hours. In its dying wake was a shroud of grey covering everything. Once so violent and then nothing, the sea became docile in its last death throes. Triumphant again, *Svea* had won the battle.

We went topsides to raise some sail, but where were we going without any wind? The fog thickened as if someone had added cornstarch to the grey soup.

"CHKK,CHKK." The sound continued. "Don did you hear that?" I called out. "Listen. I hear a ship's engine, as if it's in ballast, high in the water with its props spinning partially out of water. Don't you hear it?" I screamed. "We've survived a gale to get run down by a freighter."

"Be quiet," Don answered. "I want to see if we can tell what direction it's coming from." Then the ship's fog horn sounded like a muffled factory whistle. The sound came from astern and slowly worked abeam. We strained our eyes for a glimpse of the invisible, but highly audible ship. Where was it? How close was it? What was its route? There remained no answers, yet we blew our small horn hoping the watch might hear our weak but profound signal. Nothing but grey was visible. Only the sound was around and when it faded, we returned to the business at hand and

CHAPTER 22

AGULHAS CURRENT TO KNYSNA

Passage to Knysna

The next port of refuge down the dreaded coast on our route southward from East London was Port Elizabeth, 135 miles away. When we received a weather report that southeast winds were expected, we untied our lines from East London's dock and headed *Svea* out to sea towards the Agulhas Current that would take us south. Drizzling rain dampened our spirits and made running red rivulets out of the flakes of rust sifted down upon her from the railroad bridge spanning the Buffalo River right behind her berth at the Fisheries dock. "We've chosen better days than this to leave a port," I fussed at Don's decision as I coiled the wet mooring lines and stuffed them in the cockpit locker.

"At least it isn't a Friday," he laughed and tried to pay little attention to my anxiety, which I always felt upon leaving any port. "We really should put up the blues in this wind," he added. Just the thought of wrangling with those big downwind sails in doubtful weather conditions added more fire to my state of concern.

"What say we wait 'til the next weather forecast?" I pleaded. It was not long before we learned that a southwester was on its way, and fortunately, it came and went without too much ado. With our initial training on how to handle them, we passed through the night without incident, except for frazzled nerves waiting for the unexpected to happen.

By mid-morning the southwest wind was still with us and the barometer continued to descend. "Don," I called out when I looked ashore. "There's another black cloud advancing. What in the world does that mean? We already have the southwester now, and the winds are peaking out at 30 knots."

"I don't like the looks of this, either," Don answered. "Let's turn back to East London and wait this thing out."

"Splendid idea," I answered happily as I prepared to come about and retrace the few steps we had made through the night. But the cloud passed over with only a small increase of wind before it dumped water on us. The following radio forecast promised southeast winds and no gales.

"No gales," Don repeated. "Now, this is silly for us to turn chicken and head back for port. Let's carry on."

I learned back in the early days of our voyage that I was not to argue with the captain's decisions, mutter a little maybe, but on this decision I did have to agree. Above all else, I wanted to get this damnable coast and Indian Ocean behind us. We had a new problem confronting us, for the southeast wind put us on a lee shore. As the wind increased, we traded the mainsail for the smaller trysail. Neither one of us relaxed a muscle. Don stayed in his foul weather gear and slept on the floor to be ready to go topsides as the weather deteriorated rapidly.

tried to sail our vessel southward. But it was useless, no wind, no horizon, just endless grey. Dampness dripped from everything and we pulled down the sails, lashed the tiller and went below to wait for a clearing sky.

When the fog lifted, we caught glimpses of two big humps on the horizon. Don tuned in the radio direction finder and found our position to be off Cape St. Francis. Port Elizabeth was 45 miles behind us and we were sorry to have missed the port so happily visited by sailors before us.

Now the coast was bending more westward and we followed it. Although our magnetic heading was 310 degrees, which meant a more northwesterly direction, we had a 20-degree variation to add to the true course of 288 degrees. I previously had added the 20 degrees to 288 degrees and came up with 300 degrees. That's why I'm the cook and not the navigator. Another 40 miles farther westward and with another southwester chalked up on the log, we finally experienced better weather. It was confirmed when the wildlife came out to play. Cape gannets and albatross along with other smaller birds, turned the once bleak picture into one of hope and activity. The clear blue sky erased the former grey and 70 miles farther westward, the high bluffs of Knysna's heads appeared on the horizon.

Entering Knysna

The "heads" stand out like two massive monuments guarding the narrow channel running between them. The danger in entering the pass is the large outside bar with 17½ feet over it at low water. Breakers form very quickly against the tidal flows. The time to navigate the channel is just before high water. Never try to leave or enter on an outgoing tide or the waters will spit your vessel out as a child would a bitter pill. An inrushing tide could easily swamp your vessel or cause it to broach.

From the tide tables, Don had figured the slack water would be just as we arrived. We made two passes with sails down and the engine running for more positive control of the helm and to line up the range markers on the magnetic heading noted in the "Sailing Directions."

The churning waters were far from child-like as crashing breakers criss-crossed the channel in erratic patterns to threaten us. Don followed the narrow ribbon of blue water leading past the gates of stone and into the lagoon where the contrast to tranquility was startling. Dwarfed by the massive heads, the Victorian-style houses looked more like a Lilliputian village as they tumbled down the high hills overlooking the lagoon.

Weaving around the channel and past Leisure Isle, we joined the other anchored local sailboats. We dropped *Svea*'s anchor where it would stay for 10 days while we cleaned up and set about to enjoy the town and the surrounding countryside.

Knysna

Leisure Isle is dotted with quaint little houses with names like Mudeford Cottage. Most of the townfolk who lived there were retired. They enjoyed the leisurely life that Knysna offered its residents and tour-

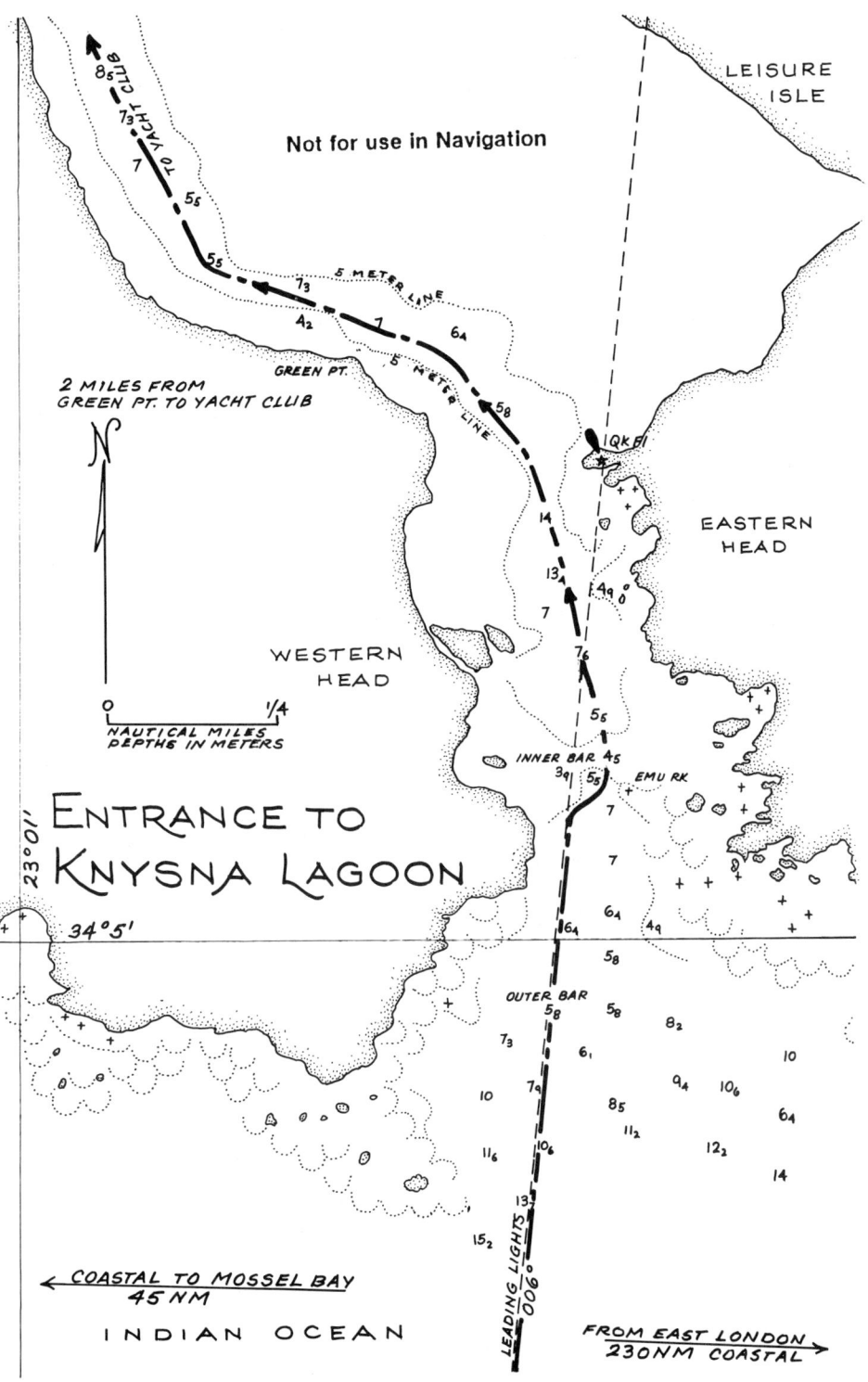

ists alike. Knysna is a favorite holiday place for the South Africans who flock to the comely village to enjoy the scenery. This historical town was built upon mountainsides overlooking a placid lagoon. Legends surround Knysna as do her mountains, and forests enclose her into a special place.

The town was founded by George Rex, the so-called bastard son of King George III of England. It was his town, his church, his roads and his descendants that carved Knysna's history. The town's streets are in staggered layers to accommodate the sharp inclines of the mountainsides. The shops are definitely tourist-oriented. You can find custom wares, such as yellowwood carvings that have made Knysna famous. The lagoon offers protected sailing to the novice sailor. The countryside offers beauty of nature's bountiful gifts to those who roam her forests. Her cliffs overlook magnificent beaches, and views across the Indian Ocean; beautiful only when looked upon and not challenged by trying to outwit its forces.

We were heartily welcomed to join the circle of events that revolved around the life at the local yacht club. The clapboard building sat out over the water perched upon rows of piling that supported it and the wide veranda encircling the frame structure. A long boardwalk led from the shore to the door, which opened to a large dining room. Paneled walls were adorned with pictures and trophies of days gone past and days present, when sailing events marked the highlights of the club's activities. Second to those events were the Friday nights when the members gathered in the bar fronting the harbor. They bantered about anything and everything, including the latest women's fashions seen on the last visit to Cape Town. One woman said aside to me, "I don't know why we talk about fancy clothes so. The only social events are here at the club and slacks are more the mode than dresses."

A couple gave freely of their time and proudly showed us their town. Knysna was something special to those who lived there and to those who visited. At night as we nestled comfortably and secure in the hollow of the lagoon, the lights of the village loomed like a million sparkling Christmas trees peaking to the tips of the mountainsides where they reached for heaven's blessings.

One day when we peered out *Svea*'s portlights, we saw a small group of ostrich feeding on a marshy bog out of water with the low tide. Later at the club, we learned they were an offshoot from a larger group farther south. They were classed as Knysna's pets. Perhaps in time, they too would dwindle as did the Knysna elephants that roamed the adjacent forests. Giant yellowwood and magnificent stinkwood trees still remain majestic in their wooded acres. They are protected by laws, which assure Knysna's heritage being saved. The laws came too late to save the elephants. Nature too, dealt an unkindly blow when the southeast gale that we were experiencing at sea, also ravaged and flooded parts of the little Karoo. Hundreds of cattle and ostrich were caught in the raging waters

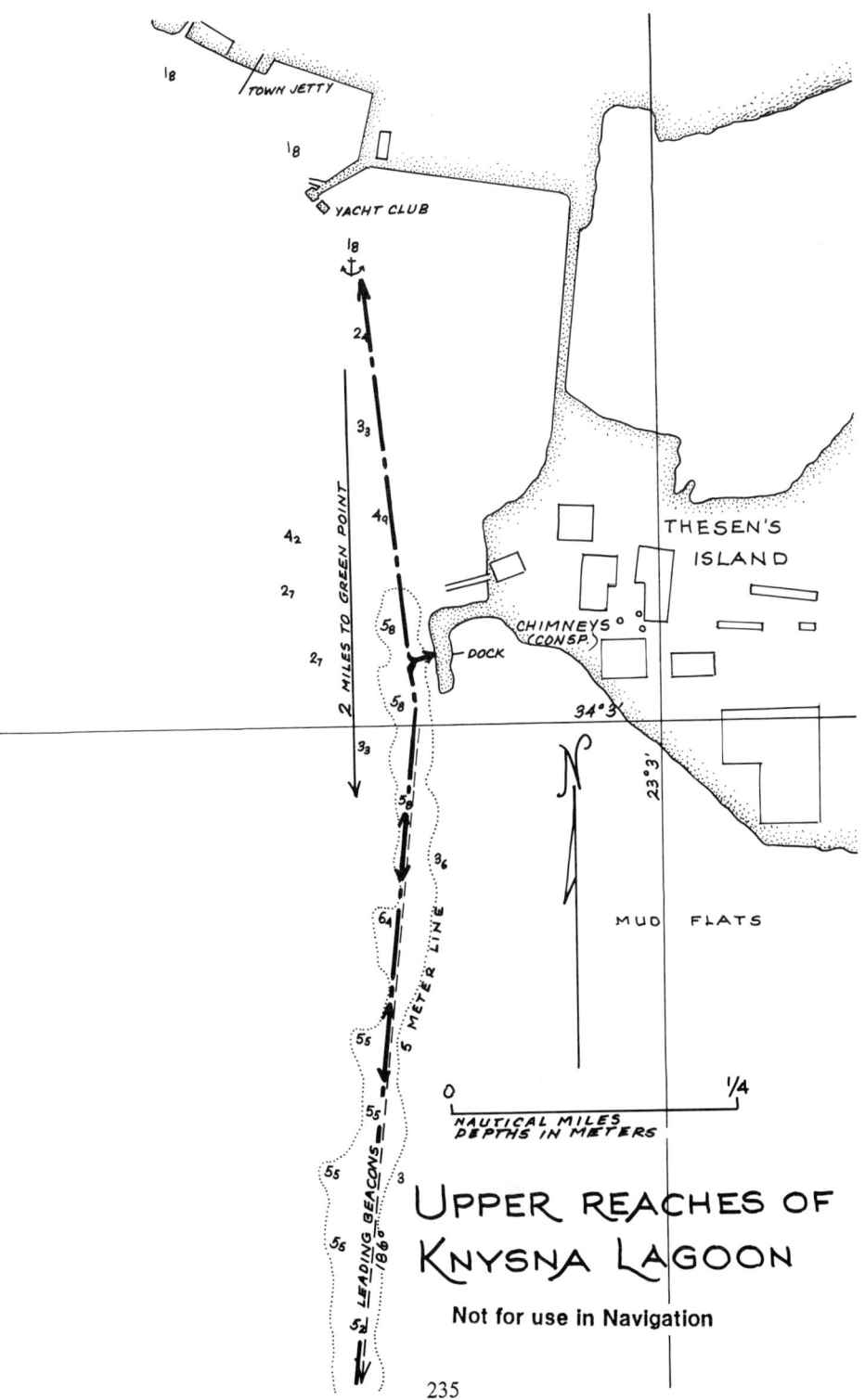

and washed out to sea, or were stranded on the once beautiful beaches where their bodies rotted in the returning sun. The same gale claimed 200 people from the inland town of Langsberg when it was completely inundated by flood waters. Nature's acts are not always kindly and they can happen on land as well as at sea. The land had offered us shelter and now it was time to return to the sea.

George Rex III Church at Knysna

The "heads" of Knysna

CHAPTER 23

CAPE OF STORMS

Passage to Mossel Bay

"This is a passage known for its viciousness. You're doing this just on purpose to frighten the wits out of me," I shouted to Don who had given the command that we were getting underway, then started to walk up to the foredeck to weigh the anchor. I didn't want to leave the nest we had found in the placid Knysna Lagoon flanked by its quaint houses and gentle people. I knew we had to go sometime but not that day.

"We don't want to miss the slack water time for getting out the pass," Don said as he proceeded forward to take off the snubbing line, completely disregarding my outburst. Years of marriage had dulled his attention to what he called my desires for creature comforts.

"But Don," I insisted, "It's not only a Friday, but the 13th of the month besides."

"Pay attention now, to my signals on the deck. It may take some doing to get the anchor out of the sand and we'll probably have to break it out," Don again ignored my words and continued to hoist the anchor chain with the electric winch. His main concern was to get *Svea* headed through the treacherous pass and out to sea. The weather was good and everything was right, except for Friday the 13th. Seasoned sailors would frown upon our choice of departure days.

As it turned out, we were too early for the slack water time, but Don methodically studied the pattern of the breakers and the winding channel. This time, he took the tiller and safely-guided *Svea* through the churning water and past the high cliffs. The "heads" seemed to look down to bid us farewell as they parted like curtains on the last act of the show of shows, the Indian Ocean and its finale, the Cape of Storms.

Winds were southeasterly but gentle. When the proliferation of wildlife appeared, we felt at ease and more ready to tackle the job at hand. Huge albatrosses flew overhead, dipped their wings to bank the arc of a wide turn, then hovered with the free airflow to look down upon their grocery store. Small fur seals popped their heads up like bobbing corks, then flipped a loop and sounded once again. Cape Gannets joined the albatrosses in their search for food. The area was similar to what we experienced off the coast of Panama with the nutrient-rich Humboldt Current. Here we were in the waters where the ebbing Agulhas Current meets the colder Antarctic waters coming up with the Benguela Current. Food abounds for the predators who feed off the teeming fish stock and plankton killed in the collision of the cold current with the warm. Birds were not the only hunters, as fishermen in their coastal trawlers were also out in pursuit of the bountiful offerings.

Mossel Bay, the home of the many fishing trawlers that work the local waters, was only 45 miles from Knysna. We hoped to make port before an inevitable southwester rained down upon us. Sailors before us had sought shelter there to wait for better weather to round the Cape of Good Hope. It was at Mossel Bay where Bartholomew Diaz first set foot in Africa after rounding of the Cape in 1488. South Africans attribute the legend of the Flying Dutchman to this Portuguese who named the Cape, the Cape of Storms.

Other chronicles of legendary data say it was the Dutchman Van der Decken. Richard Wagner set his opera, The Flying Dutchman, to the story about the captain who was lost at sea and forever committed to remain sailing in his phantom ship off the Cape of Good Hope in punishment for his blasphemous swearing at the winds. They always blew against him when he attempted to double the Cape. Back and forth he sails never to reach the shore. Legend also adds that if any mariner should see the spectral ship he will die.

But unlike the Portuguese navigator who is sailing through eternity, we had no intention of following his example. When Mossel Bay appeared abreast of us, we gladly turned into the beckoning harbor. Winds had veered more easterly and were quite strong. We knew them to be the prelude to the southwester that was forecast on the last weather report.

Mossel Bay

A sudden gust of wind caught *Svea* by surprise and she bent to its force. We quickly released the sheets and happily lowered the sails. We were close enough to the harbor for the engine to take us the rest of the way in. The harbor was designed for husky fishing trawlers, not for yachts with tender topsides easily marred by rough pilings. The docks were so high that it was difficult to get off low freeboard boats.

We were fortunate to find another sailboat tied near a steel ladder reaching down to the water. We called out for anyone aboard for permission to tie alongside. No one answered our call. We learned later that the owner had abandoned the boat as soon as he reached the port. He has been in some very rough weather on his passage from Durban and the boat sustained extensive damage to her rigging. It was not difficult to understand the man's decision to abort his sailing and put his vessel up for sale, but it was sad to hear the end of another man's dream.

After *Svea* was properly secured, we climbed the steel ladder to the dock, covertly homesteaded by huge colonies of grey-headed gulls. They challenged our footsteps, not only with their raucous squawks, but also by their vast deposits of slimy guano. This made us tiptoe along the length of the dock until we reached the safety of the shore. A change of wind would certainly send unwanted scents down *Svea's* open hatches.

"Do you think we could find some fish 'n chips?" I asked Don as we headed up the high hill that brought us into the main street of the small town that overlooked the sea.

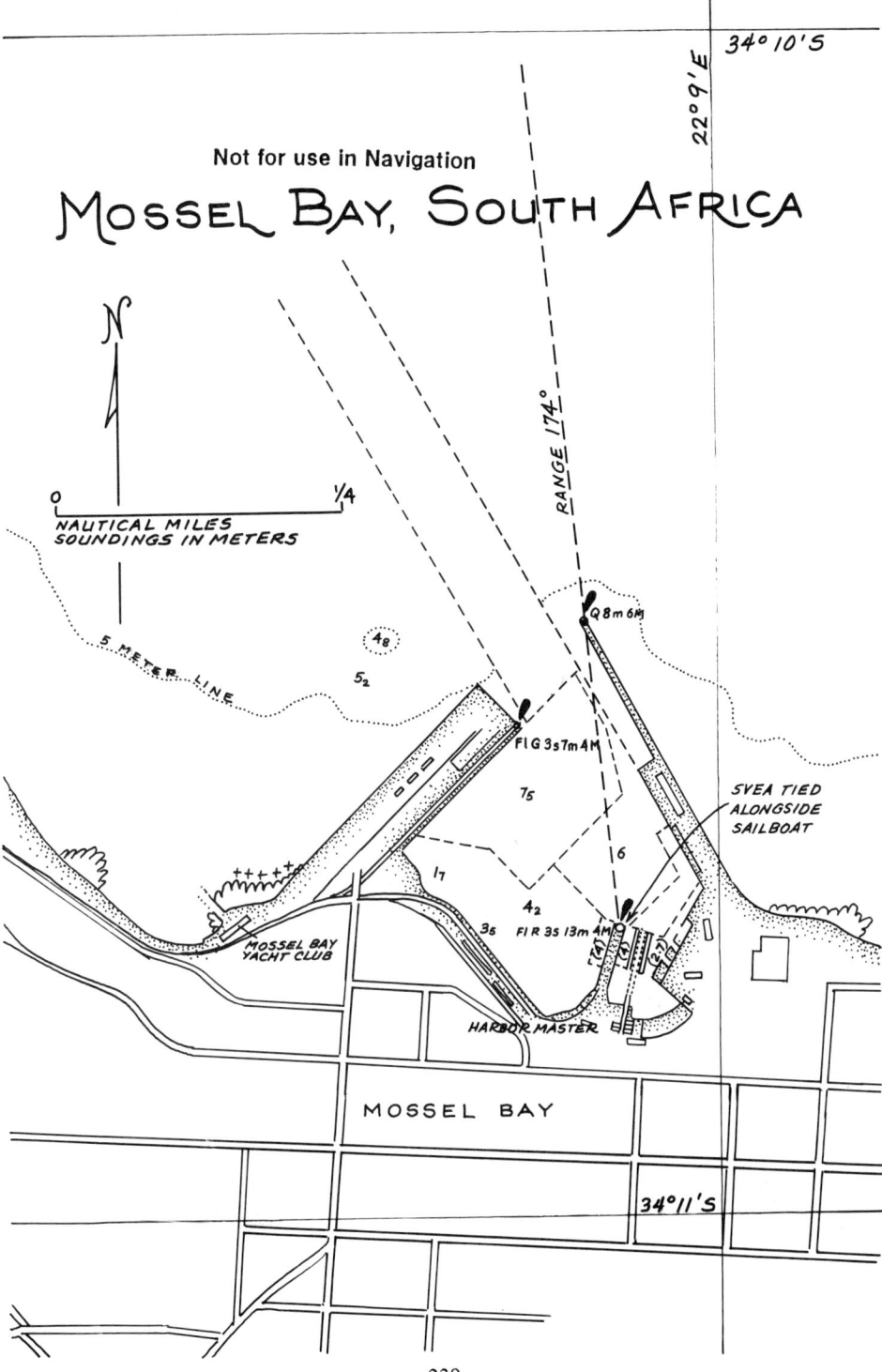

"In a town with all of these fishermen and trawlers?" Don laughed at my question. We found a take-out grill that filled paper bags beyond their brim and mounds of freshly-fried fish and French-fried potatoes. Finding the cold beer to go with the food, or even a place to sit down, proved to be a problem. We could find the bars, but signs above their doors made it emphatic that "Men Only" were welcome past their portals.

"I understand now why South African women sip their wines and brandies at home. They would be social outcasts in this man's world," I laughed as we headed back to *Svea* where we knew we had ice cubes in the freezer for our private imbibing.

On Sunday, we found the local yacht club. It was in the same spot where Diaz had come ashore to get water from the freshwater spring located at the head of the beach. Members proudly showed us the pipe that still trickled a small flow of water. They were not proud of the lack of concern the town gave to its piece of history, which was then covered by undergrowth. A viaduct carrying the city's drainage had been built over it. Only the yacht club members seemed to care about preserving the spot for posterity. One member wanted to buy the land along with its small cottage when he had heard the land was to be used for a high-rise complex. As everything else is destroyed in the name of progress, we will often wonder if girders of steel were really painted over Bartholomew Diaz' watering place. We also wonder whether Mossel Bay lost the homespun, hometown fishing-village environment that attracted us so much.

Photo by Carl Moesly

Mossel Bay, South Africa

Passage to Cape Town

The southwester promised by the forecaster never materialized. *Svea* put out to sea to face the Cape of Storms, the most southern point of Africa and the etheral home of the legendary Flying Dutchman. Many sailors dispute the fact that the Cape of Good Hope is the actual division between the Indian and the Atlantic Oceans. Looking at the topographical chart you can easily see that the end of Africa is not at the Cape of Good Hope, but at Cape Agulhas, whose point is the farthest south on the continent. Geologists argue that the nature of the sea changes only at the Cape of Good Hope some 80 miles farther west, where the barrier of the African continent reaches its true end, and therefore is the real separator of oceans.

Dots of cumulus clouds and gentle southeast winds with the barometer holding steady augumented our desire to renew our passagemaking. It was under these conditions that we left Mossel Bay behind us. It was cold as we worked our way farther south. One did not have to tell us that the Benguela Current of the Antarctic was under us. We could feel it, and so could the freezer, for it took less time running the engine to pull down the temperature in the box. The cold seaweather, circulated around the condenser, worked quicker and more efficiently than hot stilled waters in the tropics.

When an overcast sky replaced the blue one and the winds increased, we became apprehensive and started reducing sail. Usually the sight of the birds has a tranquilizing affect on us, but when numerous birds appeared so suddenly and were silhoutted against the leaden grey sky, they gave us an eerie feeling. They seemed to soar in limbo as if waiting for something to happen. They were too high to be working the waters looking for food. They were just idly hanging there getting a free ride from the airflow produced by some land configuration and playing like human gliders that love to soar above high cliffs.

At dawn on our second day out from Mossel Bay, we spotted the light at Cape Agulhas bearing 310 degrees. Don had plotted our course to give the Agulhas Banks a 15-mile margin of safety. A ship before us had not taken that precaution and would remain as a monument for others until the seas obliterated it.

We were drawing close to False Bay, the very large half-mooned shaped body of water that is notorious for spawning gales. At its eastern tip lies Cape Hangklip. Eighteen miles west across its wide mouth lies the peninsula that juts the Cape of Good Hope out into the sea. Winds increased further and the radio forecasters told of heavy rains in the Cape Town area, but there were no reports of gales. I couldn't help but think of the Flying Dutchman and wonder if he were looking down upon us. Don interrupted my thoughts as he turned on the radio direction finder and tuned in the radio beacon at the Cape of Good Hope. The signal "Z S H" came in loud and clear and Don made a fix on our position. "So far, so good," he smiled and the tension eased, but why didn't the wind? Was it going to get stronger? Again my thoughts were broken when Don hollered down to me from the cockpit, "Come on out. We've got to come about on the other tack."

Without donning full foul weather gear except for my light weight jacket, wool beanie and sea boots, I ran out to help with the tack. Just as I was about to release the sheet line to allow the jenny to swing over on the port side, a huge wave came out of nowhere, slid up *Svea's* backsides and thoroughly baptized me with its full load. My boots were full of water and I was livid with rage, "Damn you Flying Dutchman, just because you're out there fooling around with nothing to do is no reason to pick on me," I just shouted to the heavens, or whoever would listen. That Indian Ocean just had to get in its last lick before it would let us go. It has been so calm with no large seas, especially since rounding Cape Agulhas, that had afforded us a lee from the former seas.

"Come on. Come on," Don shouted. "Stop worrying about your comforts and let's get this turkey moving and get out of here!" Cold and angry, I did what was required of me and then retired to the warmth of the cabin. I washed away the saltwater and put on clean clothes. The Atlantic Ocean accepted us with calm seas and a promise of better things. Except for that last boot-filling incident, our passage beginning on Friday the 13th, had been one of the best passages we had along that dreadful South African coast.

At midnight, we were becalmed, but behind us was the anxiety of rounding the Cape of Good Hope and there was nothing else to do but shut down and get some rest. At dawn, a light northerly breeze came up and we got underway. As daylight appeared, a grey misty blanket of fog came with it. A large container ship broke through the veil to starboard, but it passed harmlessly by and left us locked behind the grey curtain of fog. Don began to work his fixes with shore-based radio beacons. It was impossible to see anything. I could hardly see my hand before my face. A fog horn sounded and I froze with fear. Don grabbed for our small horn and answered the signals given every minute, 60 seconds without deviation. The sound grew closer, passed our bow, then carried on westward. We had seen nothing.

"Get up on the bow and look out," Don said confidently as if I could possibly see a collision before it happened. I didn't argue and went forward as I was told, but I could see nothing ahead, only a glimpse of frolicking porpoise just beside us. I had to laugh and think of them as pilots coming out to show us the way in.

The fog began to lift and we caught a quick glimpse of an outbound ship that was apparently leaving Cape Town's harbor by its bow-on position. Don took a bearing on the ship before a new blanket of fog rolled in to cover it. Ever so slowly with the jenny and engine, we moved towards what we thought was shore. Again the fog lifted for seconds to show us we were dead on course, then as if a magician were playing games, the land

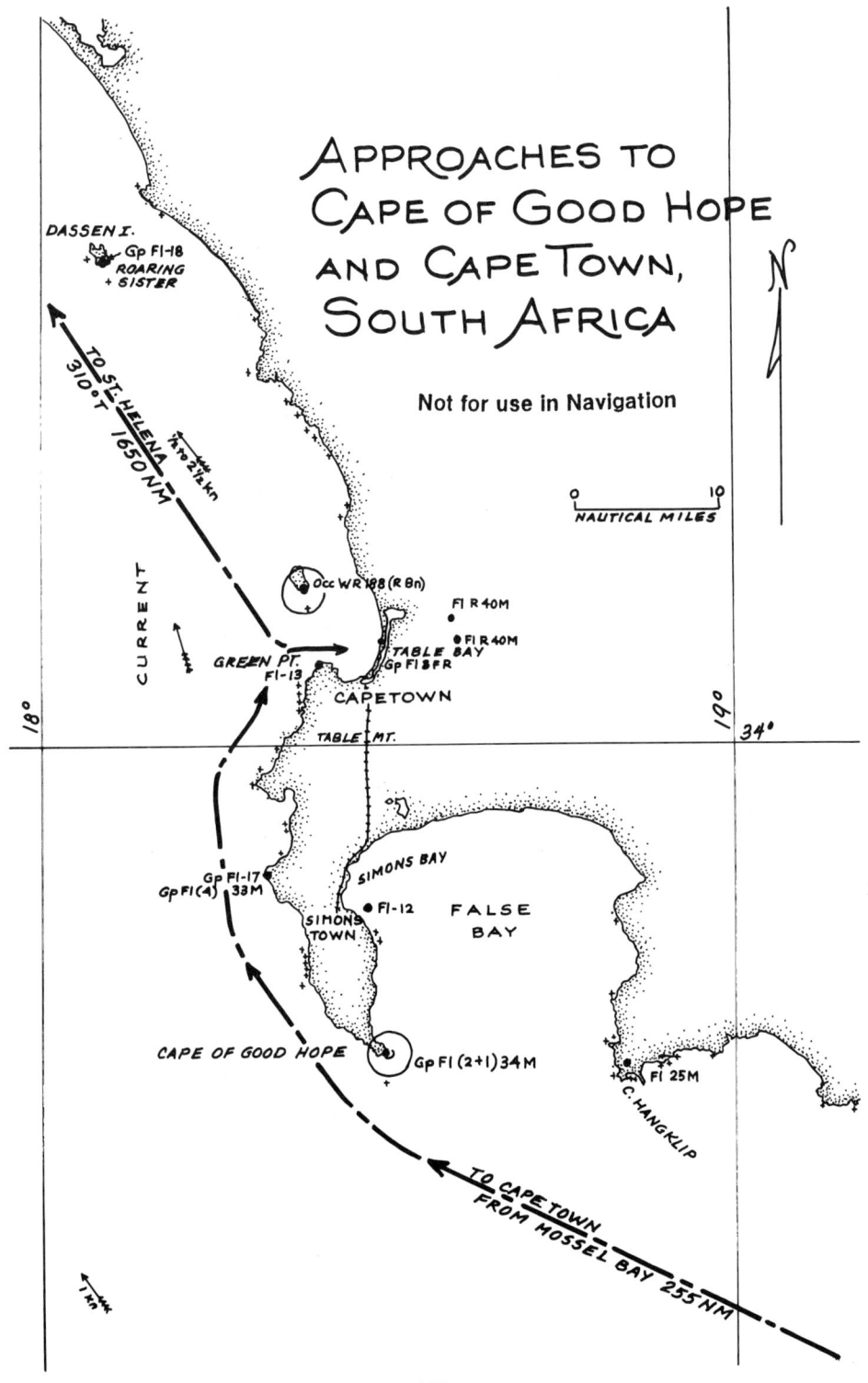

disappeared behind the cloak of grey. We were committed to the land. We were too close and if we turned seaward we would surely lose our way in the adverse currents, or easily become targets for the many ships that call into Cape Town harbor. At least being close to land, they would have lookouts for local traffic. Oh how we wished for radar.

"Stay up there and look out," Don shouted at me when I started to walk back towards the cockpit. He was beset with worry, for we were going against everything we had learned about approaching land in poor conditions. Land was the enemy in most cases, not the open sea.

Another fog horn pierced through the still air. It sounded again, "That sound is constant," I screamed back. "It's coming from land, not a moving ship. It's coming from right over there," and I pointed right in the direction of the sound. Again the fog lifted and a ray of sunshine ribboned a path on the land and crossed over the lighthouse that had been sounding fog signals. Now there was no mistaking Table Mountain. We could be no other place in the world but Cape Town, whose landmarks have guided sailors for centuries. The flat-topped mountain was created more than 150 million years ago when silt deposits from the African continent dropped into the sea and burdened the sea bed until it collapsed. The sides of the trough it formed bent inwards and squished up the top layer of silt which rose above the sea. That top layer became Table Mountain.

With sun to guide us, we skirted the coastline and made way for the harbor which we still could not define. Then it happened again. The magician waved his cape and the land disappeared behind a new layer of fog falling as quickly as a window shade. Not even an outline or a shadow of a building was seen behind it.

Don switched on the depth sounder and told me to take over the cockpit. "I'm going below to examine the charts. Just hold her on this course until I get back."

He was back in seconds to check heading and the sounder's recordings, then he went back to the chart for only a second and was back with his report, "We're going to follow soundings into the harbor. We're on the 10-fathom line and it leads us right on in."

"If you say so," I said meekly but I was not sure. I should not have doubted the decision. He has an innate talent of weighing all aids and putting them in their proper perspective to come up with a sense of direction. "He found Bramble Cay when no one else did, didn't he?" I reminded myself of our approach to the Torres Straits when only dead reckoning navigation enabled Don to find that small spot in the Coral Sea.

"I hear birds," I screamed as I most certainly did hear the raucous calls of seagulls. They were too close as they perched on the stone breakwater. "Look, Don, right off the starboard, the breakwater! We're going to hit it!"

"Relax, Susan E.," and his voice was calm. "Look now and see if you can see a green light. It should be right off the starboard bow to your

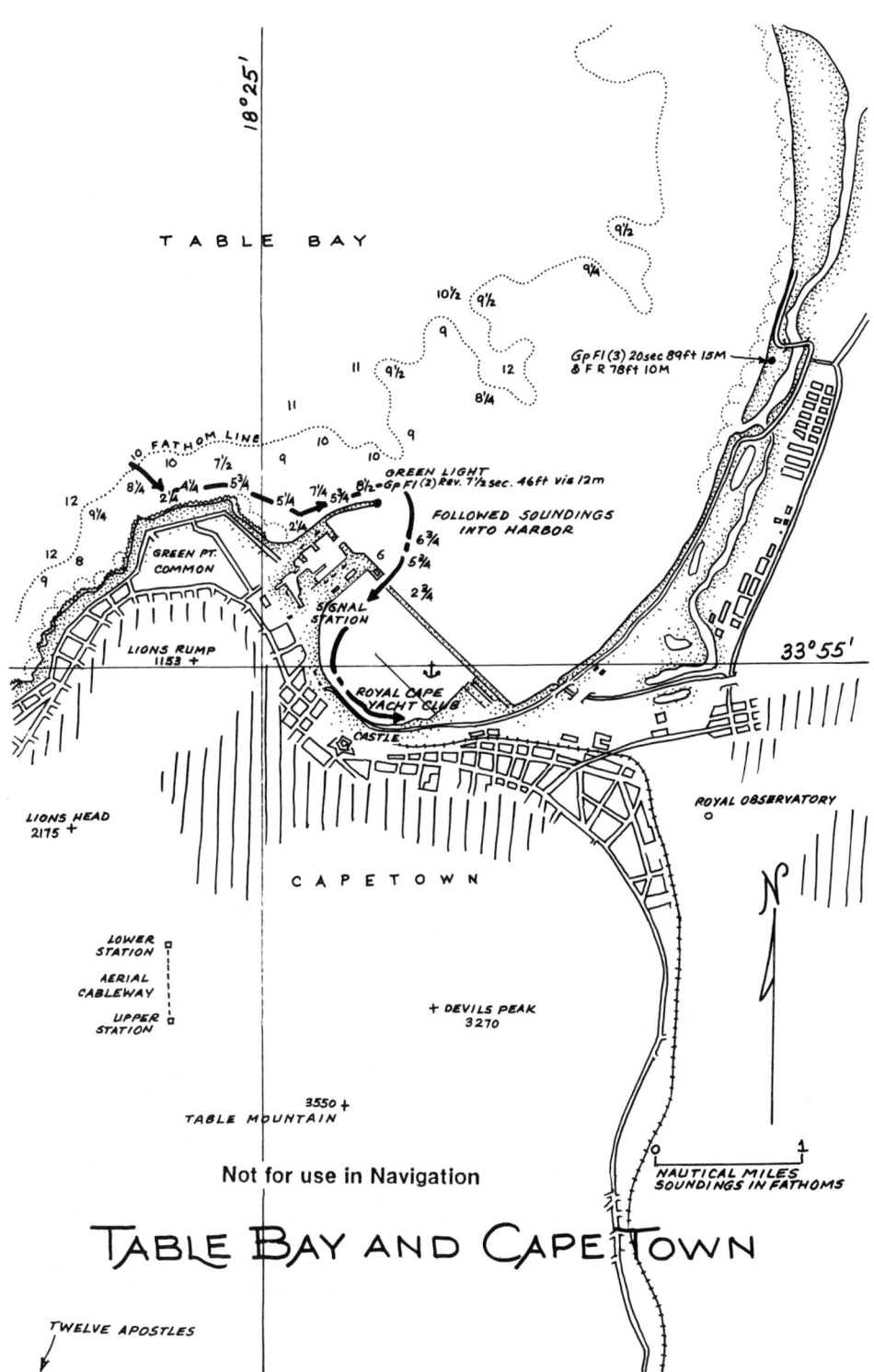

right, for it marks the end of the breakwater. I think we're right where we want to be."

Cape Town

Don was right. It was at the end of the breakwater and slowly we crept around its edge. Don turned *Svea* on the new heading which led us right into the center of the harbor. As the fog lifted, we saw other sailboats and we followed them back into the cove that marked the home of the Royal Cape Yacht Club. This club has graciously hosted foreign yachts for many years. Ian, our Australian friend from Richards Bay, was at the fuel dock to take our lines. Not far behind him were Etienne and Nicole, also Richards Bay friends. Their lovely *Here Moana Tea* was tied to the club's floating docks. Able hands in all had *Svea* secured. We were no longer alone with the sea. The camaraderie of cruising sailors is unequalled. The feeling of reaching a port and seeing a friend is often overwhelming.

In the morning when the club was open we met Joan Fry, the secretary who remembered our *Rigadoon* family from their first circumnavigation and welcomed them again on their second voyage. She handed over our mail and told us about the club's welcoming privileges to foreign visitors.

"They're all talking about you, the Yank, who came into Cape Town during that fog last night. You're some kind of a hero," Joan smiled. We didn't tell her that it was really a matter of survival, that seafarers before us encountered far more than we had in finally reaching Africa's southern tip.

The Royal Cape Yacht Club is a rather formal club. Ladies are expected to dress and act like ladies. If they step over the threshold of the men's bar to attract their mate's attention, the man sitting there must "treat" the house. We ladies were allowed to sip our beer on the patio.

We made a phone call to Skip and Linda Dashew who were still in Cape Town having their new 62-foot aluminium boat completed at Anchor Marine. Despite their busy schedules, Linda came to the club and whisked us away to their rented home. What a delight for us to enjoy their full-size bath tub, their laundry facilities, dinner at home, but mostly to renew old friendships. While Skip was with the new boat, Linda took me on provisioning shopping tours. Their daughters were in the local school where learning the Afrikaans language is part of the required curriculum.

"It's really beautiful here, the flowers, the buildings, and even the people" I remarked, as we drove in and around the town nestled beneath Table Mountain.

Cape Town reflects its Dutch ancestry in the many white-washed buildings with their noble dark brown arches. These are vivid contrasts to the stark straight lines of modern, high-rise commercial buildings holding the executives of South Africa's "Mother City," founded in 1652. This is the name fondly given to Cape Town by her country's people. Though this is an underground conglomerate of modern shops, restaurants and markets, it is quite unlike the catacombs of Bali's native market. There are many excellent restaurants and interesting bars.

Cape Town is a mixture of colors and heritages. There are charming old buildings, and the city has a beautiful setting between the sea and Table Mountain, 3000 feet flat-topped. The influence of the Dutch blends with that of the French Huguenots, British and Malaysians. Mosques share the same streets with the Dutch reformed churches. They all make up Cape Town's amalgam of cultures and societies. One of the city's attractions is the friendly polygot population, a mix of race, creed and color. Archbishop Desmond Tutu called Cape Town the Rainbow City. The varied colors are also seen from the flowers. South Africa boasts 320 species of their indigenous proteas, a large flower with feathery tips on its petals. Flower vendors an Adderly Street in downtown Cape Town are anachronisms in a modern city.

A lot of Don's time was taken up with chores to prepare *Svea* for the more than 5,000 nautical miles we would undertake. One example is trips to town to have the fuel injectors cleaned. Work on the boat is never ending, and much of it has to be done before you put to sea.

Photo by Carl Moesly

Cape Town docks

A strong southwester changed our minds about when to depart Cape Town. Rather than waste the day, we decided to take the train to Simonstown, the naval dockyard on False Bay at the end of the rail line. As we passed through the gates at the large station to board the train it was rather like climbing aboard a Long Island commuter train. Following the tracks through the city and across the peninsula to False Bay, the train led us down the shoreline past Fish Hoek and into Simonstown. Looking from land at False Bay with its maze of white water was far different from looking at the opening from seaward. There we knew a gale could spawn any minute, one fearsome enough to shiver the timbers of the most stalwart boat.

The resulting following southeaster was forecast by the arrival of Table Mountains's "table cloth." With the advent of wind from this quadrant, a heavy mist floats across the high plateau and settles like a frothy lace tablecloth graciously laid upon a banquet table.

With the next southwester, but a predicted gentle one, we decided it was time to leave. Ahead of us lay, 5695 miles of the Atlantic Ocean until we reached the Caribbean, the sea that bade us farewell five years before. Linda came down to the docks to say good-bye.

Photo previously published in Yachting World

Provisioning at Cape Town

CHAPTER 24

ACROSS THE ATLANTIC

Passage to St. Helena Island

As we untied our lines from the floating docks at the Royal Cape Yacht Club's front door, the receptionist called out over the loud speaker, "Goodbye *Svea*, Sue, and Don, and God Bless!"

Stern-to the waving farewells, *Svea* left the docks and proceeded to the harbor, busy with ships coming and going. Past the breakwater, past Table Bay and Robben Island, the same route taken centuries back by the Portuguese, Dutch and British seafarers, our double-ended ketch headed out to sea. This began the longest passage we had ever attempted, 5,695 miles of the Atlantic Ocean ahead of us before we could enter Caribbean waters.

With Table Mountain in the background, penguins and fur seals played in our wake to bid us more farewells. It was cold there on the 34th south latitude, and we had our thermal underwear on underneath our sweatshirts. In that southern hemisphere, March was the beginning of autumn. I shivered, but blamed it not entirely on the weather, but on the anxiety I always faced at the start of every passage. "We're on the homeward bound track, Susan E., back in our ocean," Don called out as he watched my gazing back at the clowning creatures behind us. We both felt sadness. Neither one of us looked forward to going home. Home was *Svea*. Fort Lauderdale was only a place on the chart where our friends and family still lived.

When Don called the Cape Town meterological station, they had told him that a weak southwesterly frontal system should remain in the area for a few days. They suggested we stay close to shore to get the land breezes and stay out of the influence of the South Atlantic anticyclone high that was offshore at that time of the year. We could expect little wind from it. At 30°15′ south latitude, we could expect the beginning of the southeasterly trade winds and could then leave the coastline to find better sailing winds.

The "Sailing Directions" noted that north of 25 degrees south latitude we would be free from gales. Once past the Equator, and after crossing the bank of doldrums, we expected to find the northeast trades. Our plan was to sail on a northerly course to be at a better angle to utilize the northeast winds when they came in. Many sailors choose to reach the South American coast at a more direct angle, then they sail close to the wind to reach the Caribbean. In their favor is the north-moving current. In the belt of low pressure that divides the northern and southern hemispheres and separates the southeast trades from the northeast ones, we knew to expect the doldrums. Don figured at that time of the year we should experience the Intertropical Convergence Zone around 2 degrees north latitude.

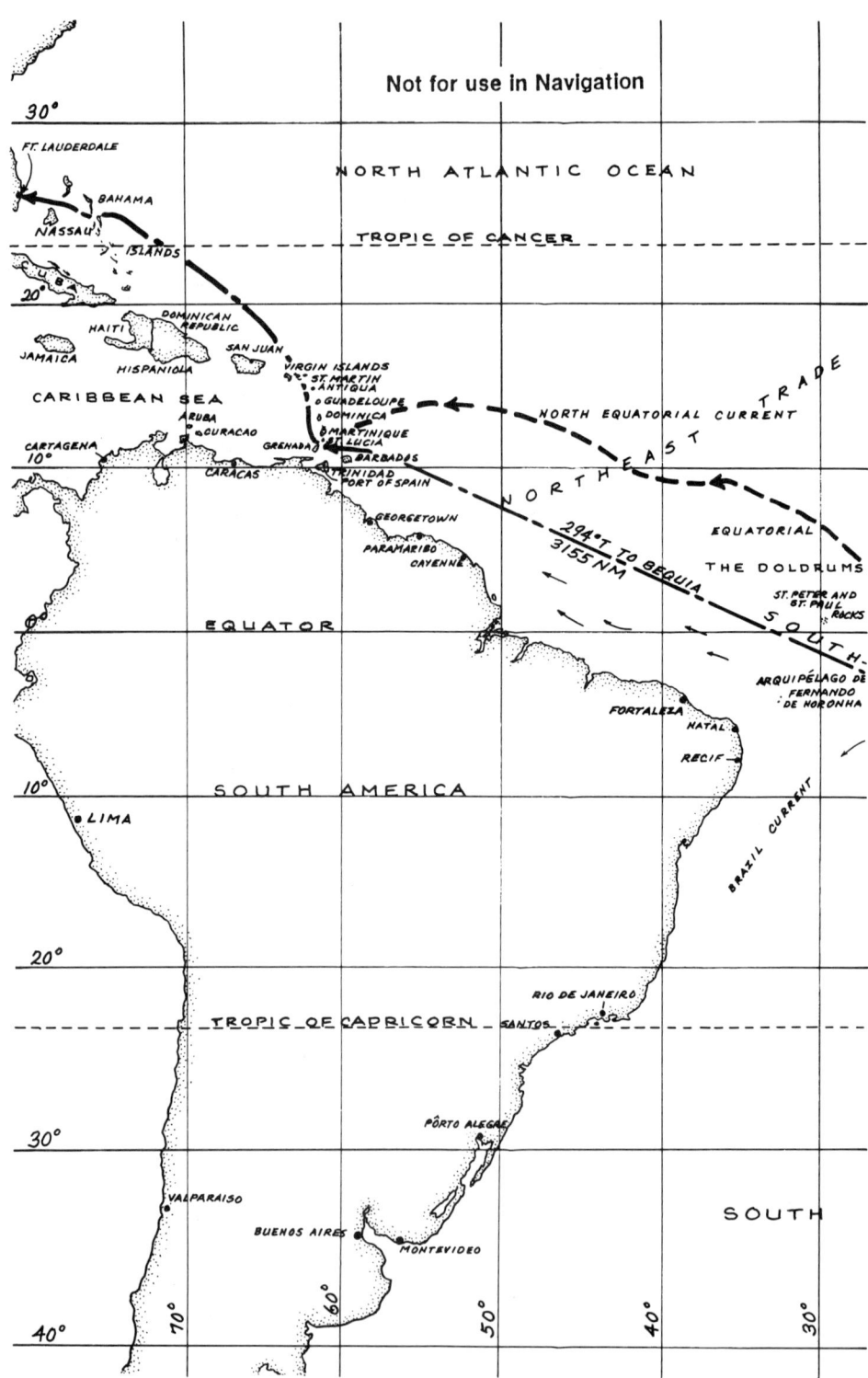

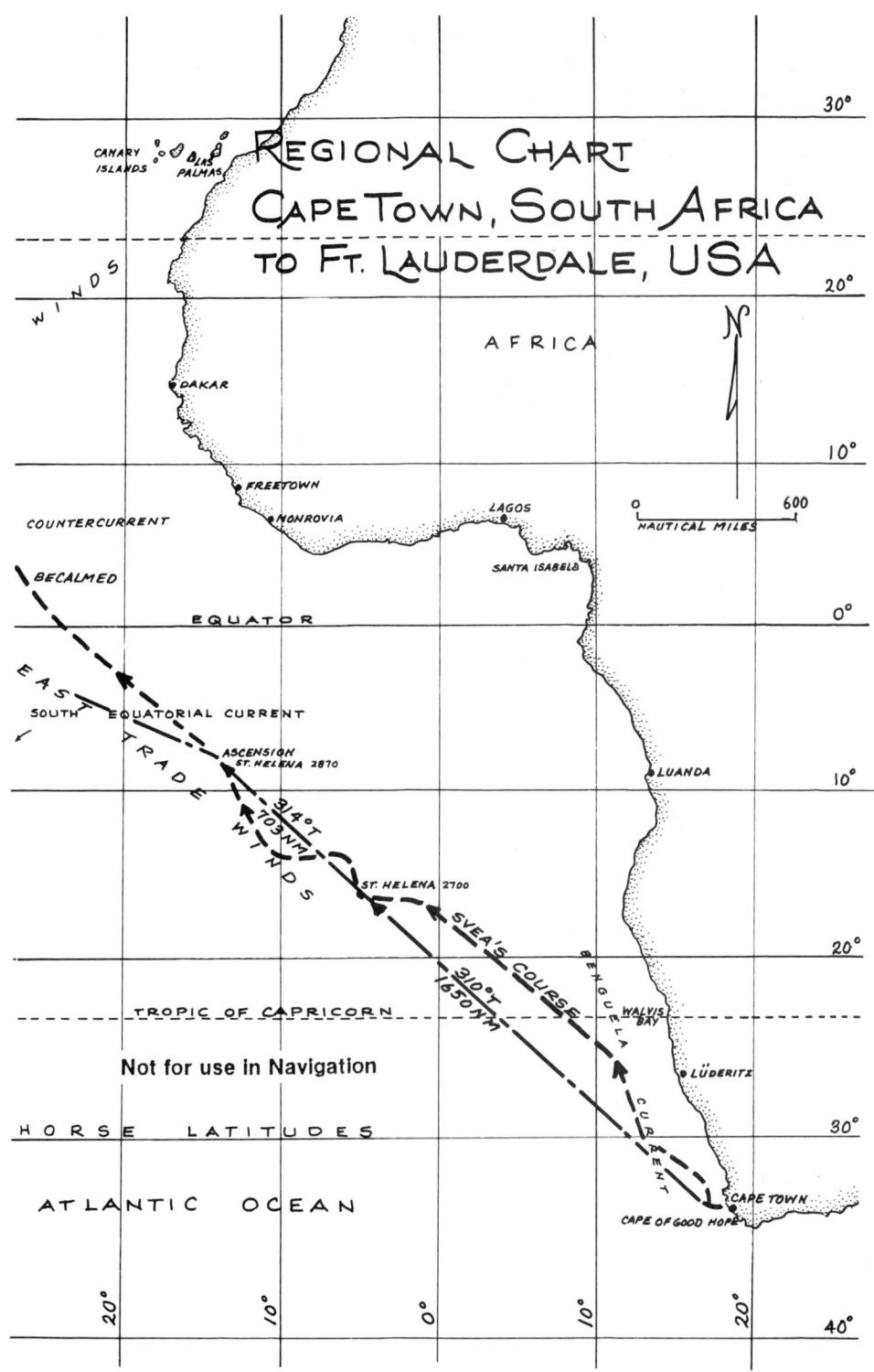

March 11th we were really underway. Had we waited two more days we would have had our favorite departure day of Friday the 13th, but the winds were right on the 11th. Sailors don't ask for particular favors, but take whatever help they can. The southwesterly winds were light, but *Svea* made way with all three of her working sails pulling evenly. At dusk, we renewed our anxiety about what to expect for the night. An interlude with playful porpoise and roly-poly fur seals took our worries away and brought forth the happiness of watching the whimsical antics of the seaborne creatures.

We had really wanted to make an overnight anchorage at Dassen Island to see the principal breeding grounds of the jackass penguins and other wildlife. This offshore island is described by naturalists as the eighth wonder of the world. However, due to the combination of light winds and our late start from Cape Town, we couldn't get there before dark and were forced to remain at sea lying-a-hull. We were delayed at Cape Town waiting for fuel to be delivered to the club's docks. Traffic was a problem off that southwest coast, for many fishing trawlers were working the offshore waters. We had to stay alert to stay out of their way. The lighthouse was a comforting sight throughout the night.

When the northern edge of the frontal system passed, southerly winds increased to 30 knots and *Svea* took off like a scalded dog. "It's okay, girl," I actually laughed. "You don't have to make up for lost time. We have plenty of miles ahead of us."

When that system left, light southeasterlies returned and we put up the big blue downwind twins. The coast of Africa soon disappeared behind us. Sadly, we left as well the creatures that had kept us company: the seals, the penguins, and even the gannets.

All was not beer and skittles, for the weather never seemed to make up its mind just what it was going to do. After a few days of constantly changing sails to match the whims of the fickle winds, we quit trying to get the most out of the different wind changes. We let our favorite combination of jenny and mizzen do the sailing for us. We still had to consider the possibility of gales, so there was no complete relaxation. The winds blew, then stopped, then blew harder than ever to die again. It was so frustrating to know we had so many miles to go, yet we piddled along so slowly.

A sudden violent squall sent both of us running out into the cockpit to tend sails and have a look around for the cloud or clouds, that caused the problem. Nothing in the skies indicated anything severe. The dreariness of the sky matched the bleakness of the horizons.

"It's all because we didn't leave on Friday the 13th."

Still in the area of gales on our fifth day out, the winds and seas did get serious and increased enough to send huge waves crashing down upon us. We were both in the cockpit when we watched an extra big one charging up astern. "Stand in front of the companionway door," Don shouted. "Don't let that wave hit with full force or it will crash in the door!"

I obeyed the command, as I lacked time to utter an argument about the poor pay and the kind of jobs a first mate is expected to do. The wave broke short of *Svea*'s stern but spewed out its fury across the cockpit. I sputtered and spumed, "You're a real buddy," I said to my captain who used to be my best friend. To add to the miseries, the toilet handle broke inside its porcelain bowl and we were forced to use a bucket.

The seas and wind remained confused and *Svea*'s path was an erratic one. "I think we'll be the first ones to corkscrew ourselves across the Atlantic," I screamed when a stern wave pushed us ahead, only to have one from the beam slap us and throw spray into the cockpit. Slowly we drew past the area of gales south of the 25th latitude. On the ninth day out, when our noon sight put us 600 miles from St. Helena, I was delighted to look up to the sky and the the fleecy white cumulus clouds of the tradewinds scampering across a field of blue. "The trades are here!" I shouted with joy. Don ran from the cabin to see for himself. By that night,

Photo by Carl Moesly

Jamestown Harbor, St. Helena

the sky had returned to the leaden grey. Spits of rain dampened our spirits and puddled the coal dust given to us so freely by the coal-fueled trains that went back and forth near the yacht club at Cape Town.

Latitude 16 degrees south, and we pass from the eastern hemisphere into the western. We are now in our old part of the world and right on the same local time as Greenwich. When he worked the sights, Don would have to be careful to add, rather than subtract, the figures he had been computing. We celebrated the night with a roast chicken dinner and a bottle of South African wine, a bon voyage gift from our friends back at Richards Bay.

As we drew closer to St. Helena we also drew closer to shipping lanes. We had been away from the freighter routes in our more northerly course and therefore had been able to get more uninterrupted sleep. Now, we would have to stay alert and keep better watches. The rains finally came upon us as we approached St. Helena's Jamestown Harbor, as if the Gods willed that *Svea* and her crew should take their baths before meeting the public. Huge swells were running into the harbor which would make it very difficult to launch *Poco* to get a line to the mooring buoy. There was no room to anchor.

"We can stop if you like," Don said as he looked at my downcast eyes. For I did want to see Napoleon's exiled home, but not at the cost of something happening to *Svea*. "But I don't think it is wise to launch the dinghy in these swells," he added, "let alone leave *Svea*, and how in the world do you think we can get ashore without being swamped by those big waves?"

"No, anyway I guess I can see it from picture books," I answered like a sullen child who has been promised something only to have it not happen. It was foolish of me, I know. I saw the crashing breakers where docks, or wharfs, should have been. Still I was not convinced that we shouldn't try to make a landing.

Passage to the Equator

Sadly, we made a wide circle, waved a greeting to some of the cruising sailors we had met in previous ports and left behind the chance to see the lovely high island, but also escaped a possible injury to us, *Svea*, or *Poco*. Following in our wake, and nearly grabbing *Svea's* rudder with its outstretched wings, was a huge manta ray. He seemingly had discovered a fond attachment to our small vessel. "Some sailors have whales that have love affairs with their vessels, but we have to be different and find a manta ray," Don laughed as he leaned over the tiller to set the pilot arm.

"Next stop Bequia!" Don called out when he turned on the pilot and headed *Svea* back out to sea. "Only 3,800 miles to go! Unless we want to stop at Ascension Island 700 miles away."

"Thirty-eight hundred miles is like saying we're going to cross the United States and come part-way back again, so put on your hat and let's go." I did put on my hat, the old straw one from Panama that keeps the sun off my face. The sun had come out for a couple of hours before it hid behind clouds, turning us back into the same old weather pattern beseiging us all along. Squalls, misty rain, and no wind at all. We just could not seem to shake this kind of weather until we got closer to the Equator and the belts of the doldrums. We were only on 11 degrees south latitude. Don did not expect the doldrums until we reached 2 degrees north latitude.

The only thing steady was the barometer. That consoled us along with the knowledge that there are never any cyclones in the South Atlantic. As we gained latitude, we also gained higher temperatures. We replaced our thermal underwear and sweaters with T-shirts.

Still no rain to amount to anything. We took saltwater baths on the catwalk, then rinsed off with precious freshwater from our own tanks. "Linda said they filled their water tanks when they passed through the doldrums," I told Don as he fussed at my seemingly wasteful use of freshwater.

"Don't count on it, unless you want to bet your life on it. We can't be assured of getting rainwater. Remember they also said they had the sailor's typical 'milk run' passage," Don reminded me about *Intermezzo*'s classic passage across the same Atlantic Ocean that we were in.

"Yes, and like Al Fox told us he never changed a sail on *Foxtrot* for 22 days," I added.

We reached our half-way mark at 5 degrees south latitude and were right on our rhumb line. The Voice of America kept us informed of the world news and we wanted to stop sailing to civilization. Perhaps we should stay adrift like the Flying Dutchman, only choose a better place than the Cape of Good Hope to wander aimlessly. Stormy petrels and a bosun bird came by to pay a call and then a very tired noddy tern came aboard to rest. They do not range far from coastal waters. The nearest land was Peter and Paul Rocks, nearly 500 miles northwest. What storm or wind change caused his navigation to malfunction?

Hooray! 24 degrees west longitude and the Equator! Salute King Neptune! Too bad the toilet was not working for I wanted to see if the swirling water actually did do a complete turn-around in the change of hemispheres.

The heat in the cabin was stifling. Don's prediction of the doldrums rang true when at 2 degrees north latitude we found them. We experienced the first real rain we had since the little cloudburst at St. Helena. Winds were so light that we were nearly becalmed. We rigged the water catcher on the foredeck. These doldrums were nothing like the ones we had experienced off Panama with their bursts of lightning and blasts of thunder. This was all so innocent, so calm. So was *Svea* as we lied-a-hull and rolled for 13 hours while waiting for wind to propel us onward.

Passage to Bequia, St. Vincent, Windward Islands

The winds returned and this time from the northeast as we expected but we did not expect the same weather as we had experienced in the southern hemisphere. There was no difference, only the direction of wind. Squalls and calms with spitting mists of rain continued to plague us. Sights were not easy and often doubtful.

"What was that?" I shouted as the loud **pop** sent me bounding from my bunk to see what was the matter.

"The jenny's in the water. Hit the deck!" Don called down.

The wire halyard holding the sail had parted where it runs through the sheave and the big sail was bent on going overboard. We tugged and pulled, bringing up gallons of seawater in the bags of cloth, but eventually we brought it inboard. "What are we going to do? We need that sail!" I said as we looked aloft to see the naked sheave which once held the jenny's halyard.

"We'll have to use the rope halyard, but I don't expect it to hold for very long and I can't get the luff tight enough to allow the sail to do its job," Don said as he set about to re-rig the foresail.

Don was right as the rope halyard chafed through in another day and we had not one, but two naked sheaves up the mast. The only thing left to do was to send Don aloft in the bosun's chair to rethread the halyards. "I'm not sending you up there in this lousy sea condition. You'll never be able to hold on to keep from swinging, let alone do the job," I said with determination.

"Don't worry. I'm not about to go up there in this," Don said. To confirm his decision a wave broke abeam and splattered us with its frothy crest. With only the main up, our speed was reduced to 4 knots. Not long after that we encountered some very confused seas and strong winds, then pondered the use of any sail at all. Don figured we had sailed into the equatorial countercurrent with its erratic sea pattern.

Strong winds continued for another day. After a routine check around decks Don came below and said, "You won't believe this, but we have just been through a Sahara Desert dust storm."

"You're right. I don't believe you," I said with concern for I knew this weather was getting to both of us and was Don hallucinating?

"I'm serious. Go topsides and see for yourself," he shook his own head in disbelief. A thin film of light brownish-red dust was coating everything. The windward side of the rigging, upturned *Poco*, just everything!

"But we are 1,000 miles from Africa!" I exclaimed.

"If we look like this, you can imagine what the Arabs and camels look like," said my friend whose wit had returned.

Misty rain fell to puddle the dust and dribble red streaks down the cabin sides. The dust coated the sails and outlined the seams, as if they had been stitched with the ickish brownish-red thread. When the haze bringing the dust lifted, the wind stopped completely. *Svea* sat like a fallen bird with her sails fluttering in the last attempt to get airborne.

"Time to get me aloft," Don saw the chance to get the halyards woven through the sheaves and was getting the gear ready. He even had an audience for his aerial acrobatic act. A pair of dolphins was lying in *Svea*'s shadow. They thought *Svea* served as a perfect blind for them to lie in wait to prey on the smaller fish. The sea was a maze of slicks, like a million mirrors reflecting the undulating swells. These same swells rolled Don back and forth against the shrouds and stays as he worked aloft. He used cable clamps to make new ends for the wire halyard and threaded that through the open sheave and replaced a new rope in the other sheave. *Svea* was back in business.

April 15th we celebrated my birthday with a can of Dinty Moore stew. It was too rough to prepare the roast beef I had planned for the festivity. We even forfeited the happy hour martinis and had Scotch highballs instead to toast the occasion. Fourteen hundred miles to go and 4,400 behind us. Over a month underway from Cape Town.

I was convinced by now that I did not like long passages. I did not like the restrictions that the winds put upon us, dictating with authority which way we could go and how fast. If only I could have lavished in our South African friends' big bathtub, I knew I would have felt better. I know it is only a matter of conjuring up a positive mental attitude, but I was doubting the mental part and the positive part was definitely negative. The attitude? Lousy and befitting the weather.

Easter Sunday, Don came below after his stroll around deck to say, "The bunnies are having a terrible time hiding their eggs under the wave tops." My friend brought a smile to my face and I prepared our own eggs sunny-side up to match my new attitude.

Eight hundred miles from Bequia, and the skies take on a new look, one with promising flecks of white clouds set upon the blue. The problem now was not the weather, but the angle of the sun. It was traveling northward at the same rate of speed we were and remained overhead. Perhaps that sounds good, but not when it is directly overhead. We could not get enough of an angle with our sun sights to get a good latitude. We could not sail out of this problem and the only alternative was to take star and planet sights. Just the mention of star sights set Don's feathers to rise. He hates to perch on top of *Poco* in a rolling sea to get all of the shots necessary to fix that triangle on our position.

The wind switched to southeast, giving us a downwind run, but we were still apprehensive about raising the big twins in uncertain weather. They are not the best behaved lot in the sail locker, but when you need downwind sails, you put up downwind sails, and so we did. But we kept better lookouts for changes, and certainly monitored the barometer more frequently.

At 12 degrees north latitude and 57 degrees west longitude, we were 225 miles from Bequia. When I looked aloft to check the sails and follow them down, I noticed the clew of the starboard twin straining to let go. "Don," I shouted, "We've got to get the starboard twin down. It's about to go."

"We're getting them down anyway. We've a wind change coming up.

Look, see how those ripples are changing," he pointed astern. Again, he was right and with the wind came the rain, just like it had as we approached St. Helena, when it was time to prettify ourselves and our vessel for our public appearance. The rain lasted long enough to get showers and shampoo our hair. I even had enough water left over to wash away some of the Sahara dust that lingered in nooks and crannies on the decks and in the cockpit. Like Tillie, Mrs. Clean, I got out the scrubees and polished the stainless steel. I was proud of our sturdy ship and I wanted her to look her best.

The next morning Don took a sight from the moon. He knew he needed a better position than we had been getting with the sun directly overhead. We were north of our rhumb line. It was still a tremendous thrill when we spotted our landfall, even though Barbados was not our primary objective. We passed north of it and altered course for Bequia, where we arrived later that same afternoon. After 47 days and 5,700 miles, at sea, *Svea*, like a grand old lady, majestically waltzed into the open arms of Admiralty Bay. She was justly admired by the local audience.

Don taking a sight with *Svea's* "big blues" staysails flying aloft behind him, wind astern

Admiralty Bay and South End of Bequia

Not for use in Navigation

TAKEN FROM "YACHTSMAN'S GUIDE TO THE WINDWARD ISLANDS"
BY JULIUS M. WILENSKY, WITH PERMISSION FROM PUBLISHER
WESCOTT COVE PUBLISHING CO., BOX 130, STAMFORD, CT 06904

SCALE IN MILES
0 ½ 1 ½ 2

CHAPTER 25

THROUGH THE EASTERN CARIBBEAN

Bequia

Elizabethport, Bequia's waterfront town was not yet stirring when I awoke from a sound night's sleep. I poured my first cup of coffee and went out into the cockpit to wake up with the new day. An early morning rain had rinsed away some of the salt from *Svea's* decks and cleaned everything in sight. The mountains, the white houses that speckled the knolls of green and the cottages that flanked the water's edge, made Admiralty Bay a pretty anchorage.

With the coming of the freight boat from the neighboring island of St. Vincent, the town stirred and slowly came awake. So did Don, who sleepily walked out to join me in the cockpit. "We're surrounded by boats," was his first comment of the day, but an understandable one when all you could see on the water were boats of all sizes, even a small freighter. Amongst us all were the small Bequia dinghies with their native boy captains curiously scanning the fleet as they rowed nearby each one.

"They're selling papayas and pineapples," I answered Don's silent question when he looked across one of the small boats to see if the boys had been fishing and what they had caught.

"At bargain prices, I suppose?" he questionned.

"I wouldn't really say that, but you know we are spoiled by the natives in the South Pacific who gave us their papayas," I reminded him.

"Everything in the South Pacific spoiled us," he mused backwards. "In fact, that South Pacific was the whole trip." I did have to agree with him. It was true that everything seemed so good from the Marquesas on through New Guinea. Then the pleasures stopped and the fight for survival began when the Indian Ocean fell under *Svea's* keel.

Later in the morning, we found mail waiting for us at the Frangipani Hotel. This was the central meeting place for yachties who come to spin their yarns over a cold beer on the open terrace. The hotel graciously handles the cruising sailor's mail, and we thanked the pretty receptionist for holding ours. Then we walked down the beach to the customs house and made our legal entry into St. Vincent: Bequia, located in the Grenadines, is governed by St. Vincent, the independent island to the north. That political situation was not at all odd, for all of the Windward and Leeward Islands are a mixture of countries and cultures. They weave a scattered chain some 400 miles northward to reach the U.S. Virgins. St. Martin is even split between French and Dutch.

We left Bequia bound for whatever port was available when we wanted to stop. Sailing in the lee of the curving arc of islands protecting us from the rolling swells of the Atlantic was a delight for we had wind but not the seas to accompany it. The delightful sailing stopped when the wind died

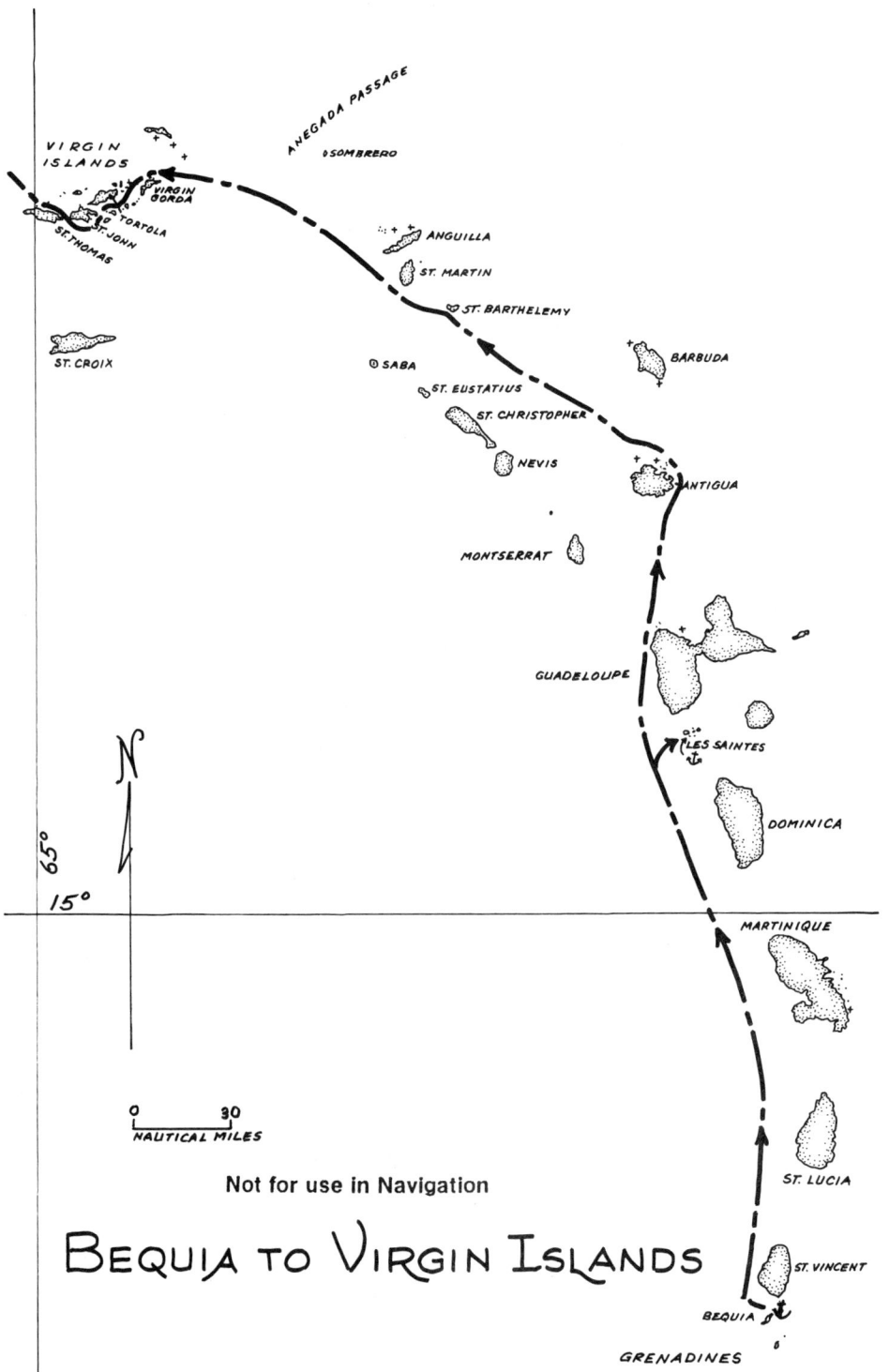

and left us stranded so we stayed at sea and lied-a-hull until the morning breeze came up to send us on our way.

Lying-a-hull would probably seem a terrible waste to the many bare boat charterers who were thick as flies on a honey doughnut in those Caribbean waters. They were all bent to reach nightly ports to begin their rounds of parties. Towards dusk they would all come home to roost like chickens to reach a nest for the night. We learned at Bequia to avoid the more populated anchoring places in Admiralty Bay that the bareboat sailors liked. At least one or two of the charter boats would not be properly anchored. They either dragged down on the other anchored boats, or their captains had not allowed for ample swinging room. At the change of tides, boats drifted together.

We rather envied these beginning sailors, for the greatest fun in cruising is the anticipation of it all. Everything new that is learned is exciting. When the accomplishments are weighed at the end of the cruise, the feeling is thrilling. Not that new adventures stopped being thrilling to us, for they will always continue to do so, but the basics were old hat. We could see beyod the luster of the cruising life and know how very many hours it took to make those varnished surfaces shiny and how many hours of routine maintenance were needed to keep our vessel seaworthy.

Harbor Hopping to Antigua

The same weather plaguing us across the Atlantic was still around to haunt us as we carried on northward. Squalls, rains and then calms were constant companions. We stopped at the French Iles Des Saintes anchoring off the west shore of Terre D'en Haut. The following night we anchored at Deshayes on Gaudaloupe's western shore.

It was then on to Antigua's English Harbour where the race week had just ended. The participants and spectators remained to continue the revelry. Boats of all nations, sizes and varieties packed English Harbour, where centuries ago Lord Nelson had come to rest and repair His Majesty's ships.

When we arrived, the sport had changed from sailing to girl watching. Topless maidens pranced around decks. Don did not complain one bit about the free shows, but I wondered about the ghosts from Lord Nelson's English gentry, who seemed to haunt the old buildings restored in the former Nelson's Dockyard.

St. Bart's

We left the very British surroundings. Eighty-four miles beyond on our northwestward trek, we were in the very French surroundings of Gustavia Harbor on St. Barts. This small anchorage is a haven for yachties who enjoy active shoreside activities. The relaxed immigration protocol was high on the lists of aimless wanderers. The high prices of goods and food, however, discourage the type of free-loaders we found throughout the Pacific.

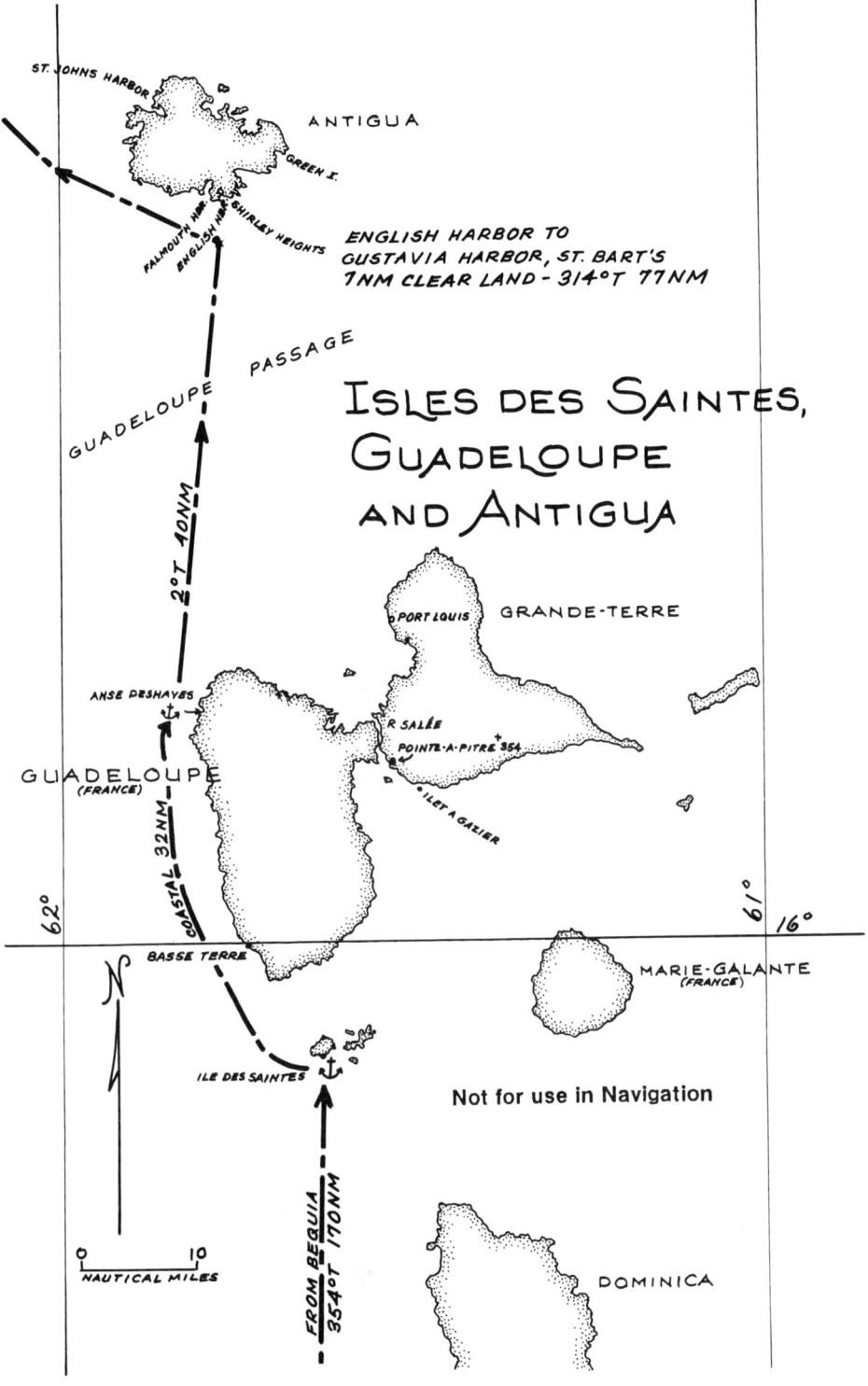

St. Maarten

Only two hours after we left St. Barts we anchored in the Dutch surroundings of St. Maarten's Philipsburg Harbor. A day later we proceeded to the island's Simson Bay Anchorage. My change purse was filled with French francs, East Caribbean currency, Dutch guilders and internationally accepted U.S. dollars. Courtesy flags of the different nations went up and down *Svea*'s starboard yardarm. They never stayed aloft long enough to fade in the afternoon sun, that is, when the sun did come out. The lousy weather refused to leave us.

Anegada Passage

Anegada Passage separates the Leewards from the Virgin Islands, and is often nasty. Heavy swells rolling into the passage from the open Atlantic bear down upon currents already confined within the small area between the islands. Steep-to waves build very quickly in some wind conditions, making it extremely dangerous to small boats sailing through.

As we approached the passage after numerous passing squalls, we found the waters quite choppy, as if a giant egg beater had been hard at work. But when the wind died, so did *Svea*, and in time, so did the waves. We were becalmed in the Anegada Passage! We laughed at the comparison with our being becalmed in the Windward Passage five years prior. "Neptune must be smiling down upon us to calm the seas so much," I smiled as we pulled down the sails and set up our learned routine of lying-a-hull.

"I don't think I would exactly call being becalmed in the Anegada Passage a fun event," Don smirked. Three hours later with a new wind we were once again underway at a plodding speed of 3½ knots.

Rendezvous at Trellis Bay, British Virgin Islands

After rounding the northern tip of Virgin Gorda, we headed south to anchor at Spanish Town off the west shore. Although we were anxious to sail on to the U.S. Port of entry at Cruz Bay on St. John, we were more ea-

Don returning to *Svea* with provisions, Gustavia Harbor, St. Barts

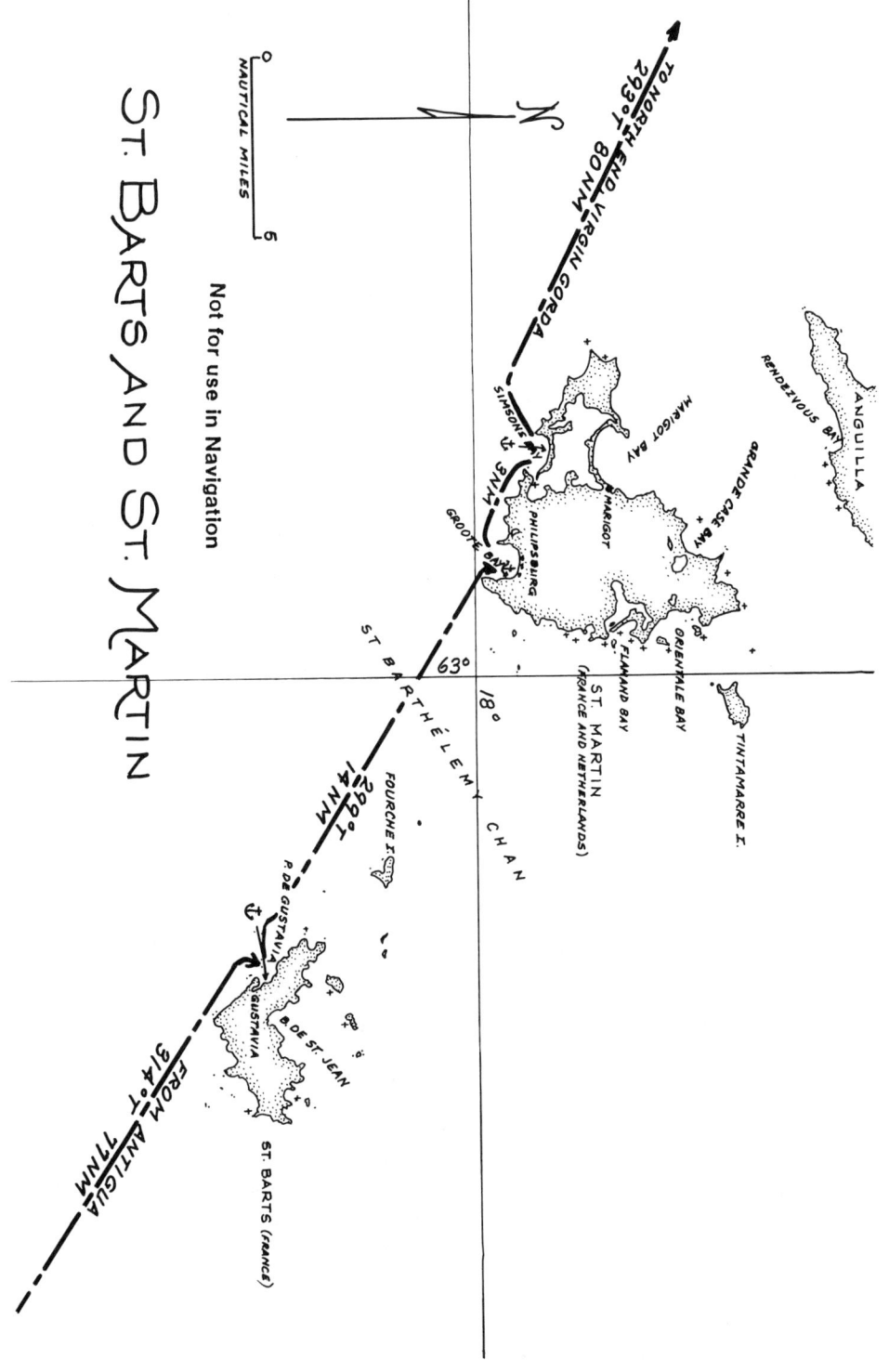

ger to stop at Trellis Bay on Beef Island in the British Virgins 5 miles away, just to see our New Zealand friends. Ross and Minine Norgrove had moved there and built their new home overlooking Sir Francis Drake Channel.

"Hi there maties," Ross said with a grin as wide as a Cheshire cat's when we walked through the front door of the lovely house they built by the sea. Waters lapped at the rocks on the beach just outside their terrace door.

"We couldn't go back to the sea, so we brought the sea up to us," Minine's accent, left-over from her days as a youth on the island of St. Croix, peppered her talking laughter. She went out to the kitchen to mix us all some drinks and start dinner.

St. John

We left the next day for St. John to take care of our legal entry into the U.S. Urging us to return, Minine gave us her shopping list for St. Thomas.

The island of St. John was our first American port since we had left Pago Pago in American Samoa. To land in home waters after such a long time, and with so many miles between ports, seemed to us like a great event. But we were greeted just the same as if we had casually sailed down from the States. Customs clearance was relaxed and uncomplicatd. Officials thought nothing at all unusual about a U.S. documented vessel returning home after being gone for over 5 years during which she encircled the globe. We really did not expect a ticker-tape parade, but I do admit to being disappointed at their lack of acknowledgement. What I should realize is that only to the participants are some events worthy of importance. **Editors note:** *U.S. Customs officials have become blasè because they frequently greet U.S. and foreign sailors who have crossed oceans and/or circumnavigated. Hundreds of boats circumnavigate every year. Sue performed a great service to future circumnavigators by keeping a careful log and marking sketch charts.*

St. Thomas

The abrupt return to civilization came when we arrived in St. Thomas. We were greeted by indifference, rudeness and hostility. We were not at all comfortable in Charlotte Amalie Harbor. We were eager to leave and find a more hospitable island, that perhaps was not so overpopulated with tourists. But where was it going to be? We were past the areas where humble natives give freely of their hospitality and enjoy doing so.

Rendezvous with Jeanne Moesly

"This is what we came home to?" I asked Don as we prepared to weigh anchor and head back to Trellis Bay. We stopped overnight at St. James Bay off the east shore of St. Thomas. Then we anchored overnight at West End, Tortola, where we checked into customs for the British Virgins. We anticipated the arrival of our sister-in-law who had sailed the same route

US and British Virgin Islands

Not for use in Navigation

on *Rigadoon* and had returned home a year earlier. Jeanne was coming down to cushion the cultural shock she knew we would experience. When we called her Stateside from St. Thomas, she said her plans were to fly down to look for property in the British Virgins. This just happened to coincide with our arrival. We think her trip was twofold. The property was secondary to her desire to welcome us home.

Minine and Jeanne met us at the landing when we anchored back in Trellis Bay. Their laughs and welcome hugs, along with the constant flow of dry mirth from Ross later, erased the depression we had felt upon leaving St. Thomas. Now we were back again in the folds of cruising sailors and we bantered our conversations back and forth. Even Minine's many cats didn't have a chance to get a meow in edgeways.

Jeanne's goodie bag for us included so many items we had not seen in over 5 years. These ranged from needed spare parts to charts, smoked hams, yams and biscuit and gravy mixes. "The airline steward looked at me kinda funny when I got on the plane with my big bag, which I insisted stay by my side. I knew he suspected something, but I wasn't prepared for what he really did say, 'Hmm,' he looked at the suspicious bag. 'Going to meet a yacht, huh?', " Jeanne laughed at the aborted hoax she thought she had been playing.

Jeanne's reindoctrination program eased us over the hump we knew we had to hurdle when the last few miles and the end of the passage lay before us. She flew back to the States and we prepared to get underway. Ferrying jerry jugs from Norgrove's cistern, we filled *Svea*'s water tanks. It was not easy saying good-bye to the couple who had kicked some of the rocks out of the way on our path home.

Passage to the Berry Islands, Bahamas

It was then the last day of May. Since June 1st heralds the onset of the hurricane season, we were most apprehensive when the same old weather pattern refused to leave us. From years past, we knew the systems that we were experiencing could be preludes to hurricanes. Although squalls, rains and calms were quite familiar by now, we could not help but think the conditions were ripe for spawning a hurricane as we faced the last 1,000 miles of our voyage. The sun kept its vigil directly overhead when it did come out. Getting good sun sights for latitudes was not always possible.

We made our way north, dousing sails in sudden squalls and flying everything when weather permitted. Each time a new radio broadcast came from local sailing areas, we realized we were drawing closer to home. When the Fort Lauderdale station came in loud and clear, we knew there would be no others to replace it.

The Berry Islands

Our plan was to stop at San Salvador in the Bahamas, but winds did not allow it. We made for the northern tip of Eleuthera where we turned

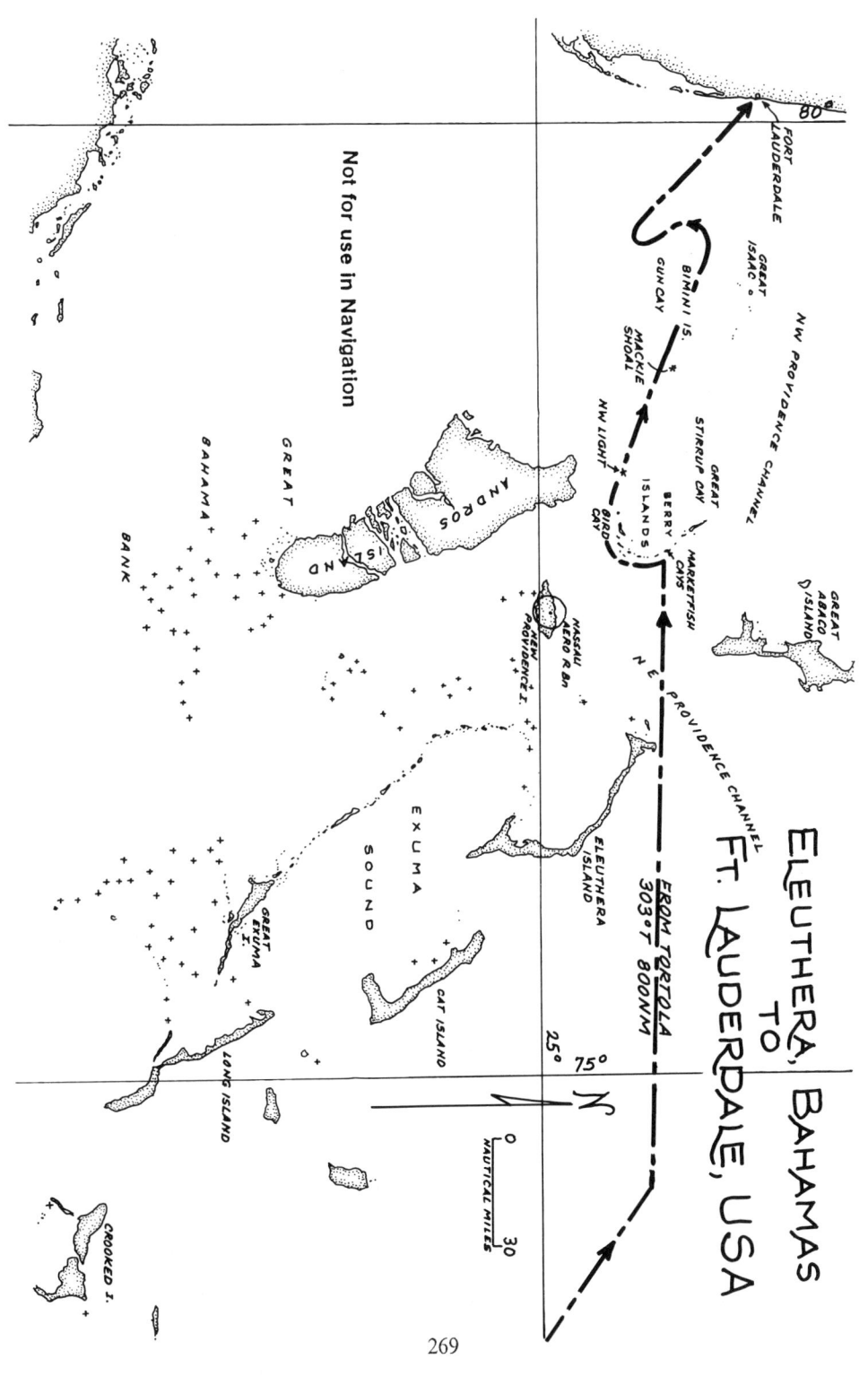

west, then south again to our favorite Berry Islands. We anchored at Market Fish Cays. From there we witnessed small fast boats running to their mother ships. The drug dealers were in action. "Yep, we're getting closer to home," Don shook his head as he knew the mother ship had a destined port on the U.S. mainland.

Making our way southward towards the southern end of the Berrys, we stopped at some of our former favorite anchorages: Alder Cay and Bird Cay. We left there for Northwest Light, then on north through Northwest Channel. We had another overnight stop, a rough one in 13 feet depth on the Great Bahama Bank east of Mackie Shoal and west of North Rock. We saw yet another drug transfer that night.

After rounding North Rock at the top end of North Bimini, we were greeted by a southwest wind. "You know it's quite foolish to try to sail into the wind, and with the Gulf Stream, we just might end up in Bermuda," Don said when we met the blue waters of the Atlantic.

"It looks as if we're going to make an unplanned stop at Dollar Harbor," I said with a big smile. I wanted desperately to keep the end from coming. Don was eager to get home, to get started into something, even though that something was still as nebulous as an unidentified ship on a foglocked sea.

"I know you," Don laughed. "You wanted to stop anyway at Dollar Harbor, didn't you?"

"How come you know so much, my friend?" I asked. I had felt a wave of relief sweep over me, like a sudden reprieve.

"You get to know each other after being so close for so long," he smiled. "We're going home, Susan E. Think we can handle the return?"

"Of course," I said with confidence. "We broke away from conformity when we left, but we can build a newer and better way of life, using the tools of love, compassion and humility, all things we found along the way to make anything worth doing."

See you down the line, when you grab your chance!

Svea tied alongside old drydock at Taylor-Smith Boatyard, Port St. Louis, Mauritius. That is laundry running up her halyards. Chapter 16

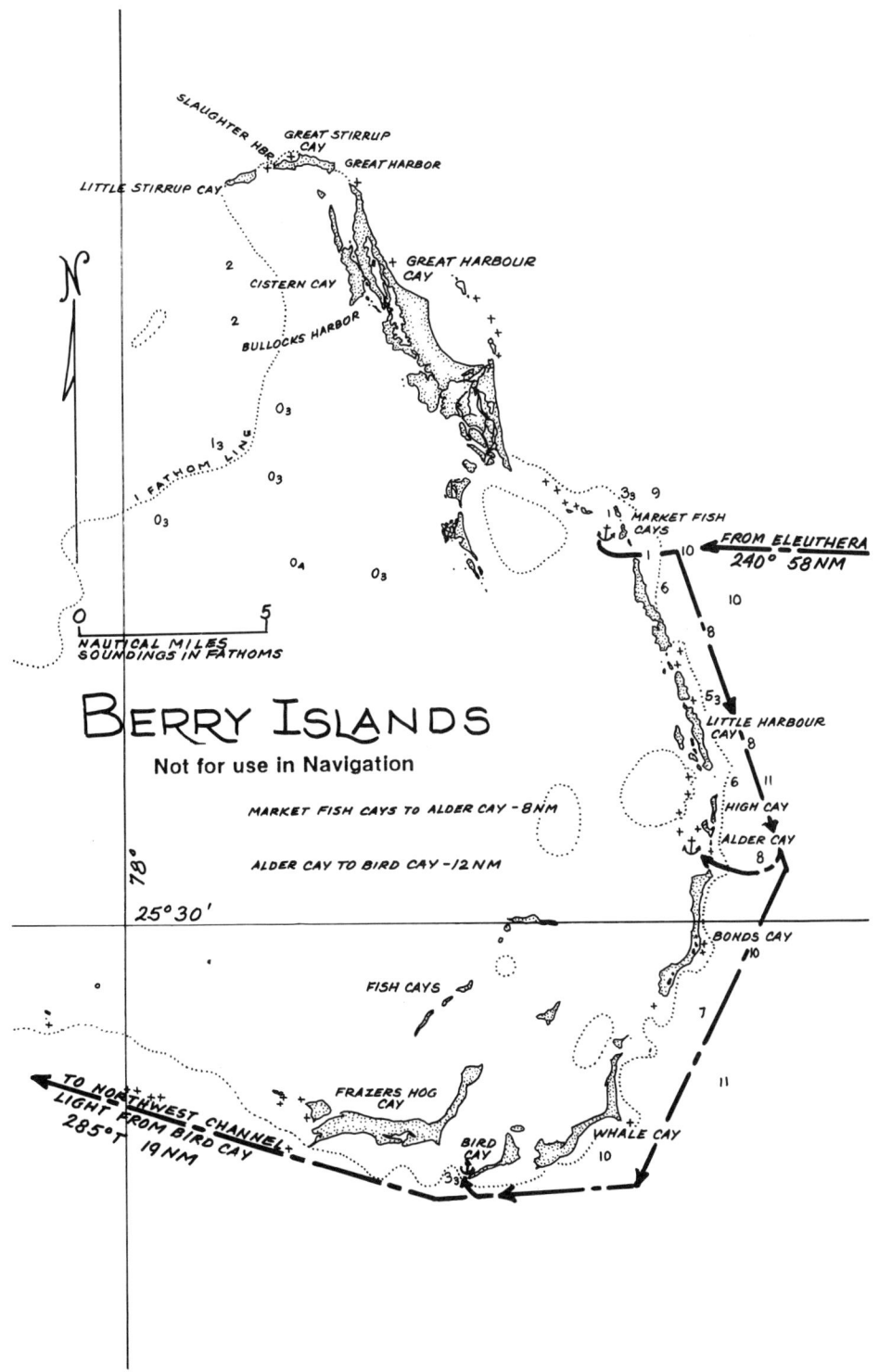

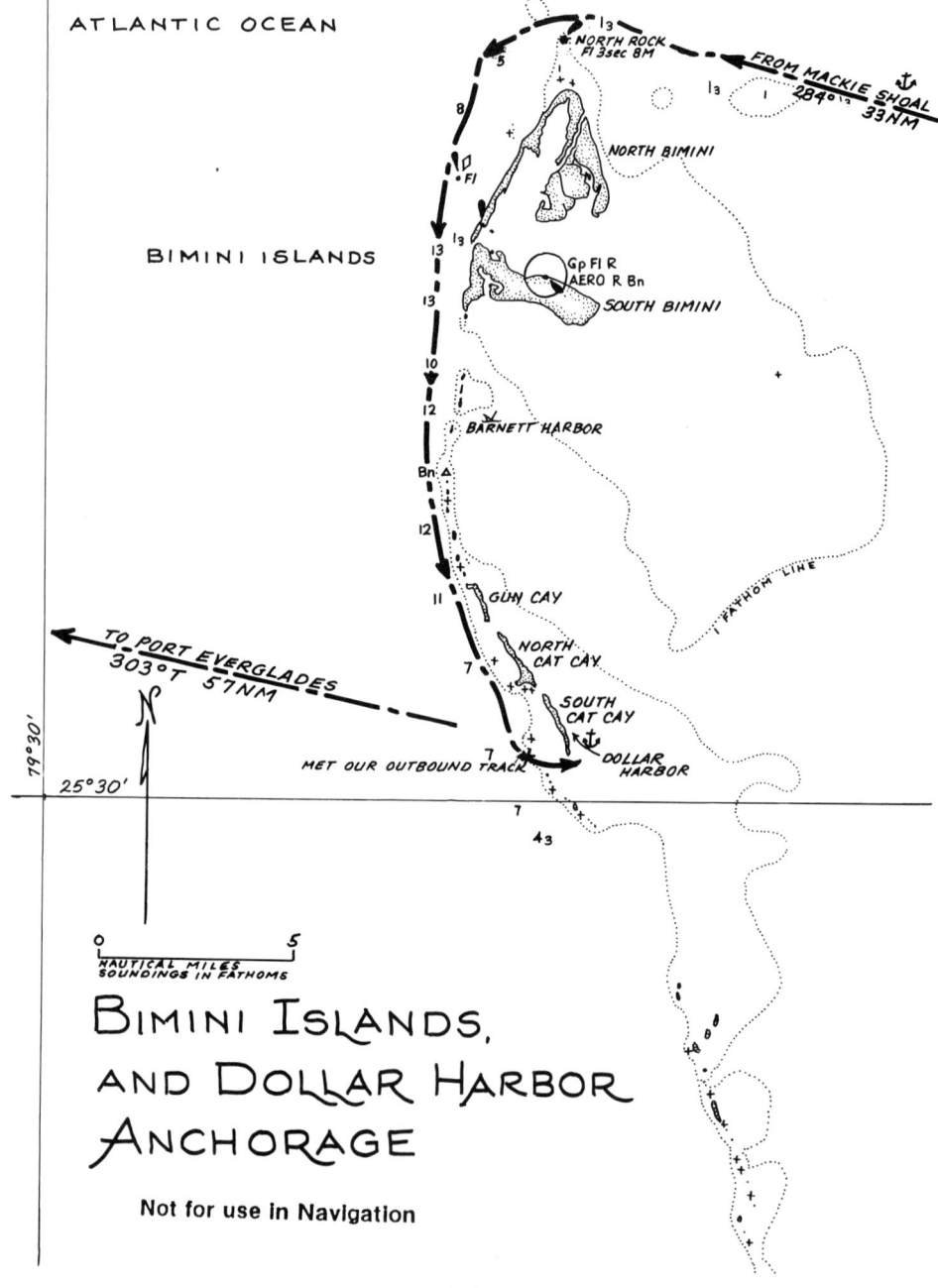

APPENDIX I

TRUE COURSES AND NAUTICAL MILES

Fort Lauderdale to Miami	181°T	20NM

BAHAMAS

Miami to South Cat Cay	108°T	48NM
South Cat Cay to Browns Cay	155°T	10NM
Browns Cay to Sylvia Light	070°T	11NM
Sylvia Light to Northwest Light	090°T	46NM
Northwest Light to Nassau	118°T	50NM
Nassau to Highborne Cay, Exumas	169°T	12NM
Then	110°T	19NM
Highborne Cay to Cape Santa Maria, Long Island	127°T	102NM
Cape Santa Maria to Clarence Town	154°T	41NM
Clarence Town to Fish Cay, Bight of Acklins Island via Long Island	138°T	51NM
Fish Cay to Castle Island	195°T	25NM
Castle Island to Matthew Town, Great Inagua	153°T	80NM

HAITI

Great Inagua to Cape Mole, Haiti	168°T	70NM
Cape Mole to Channel east of Navassa Light, Windward Passage	220°T	110NM

PANAMA

Navassa Light to Isla Grande, Panama	205°T	600NM
Isla Grande to Porto Bello	Coastal	10NM
Porto Bello to Colon	Coastal	17NM
Colon to San Blas	Coastal	60NM
Panama Canal Transit, Colon to Balboa		50NM
Balboa to Perlas Islands	116°T	34NM
Perlas Islands to Piñas Bay	153°T	38NM
Balboa to Taboga, Panama	182°T	11NM
Taboga to Isla Bona	190°T	13NM
Isla Bona to Punta Mala	200°T	70NM

COCOS ISLAND

Punta Mala to Cocos Island	255°T	440NM

GALAPAGOS

Cocos Island to Genovesa Island, Galapagos	210°T	360NM
Genovesa to James Island: (route to Equator)	250°T	60NM
(route from Equator to James Bay)	168°T	14NM
James Island to Guy Fawkes Islands	127°T	28NM
Guy Fawkes Island to Academy Bay, Santa Cruz Island	Coastal	28NM
Academy Bay to Barrington Island	100°T	16NM
Barrington Island to Floreano Island	230°T	35NM
Black Beach, Floreano Island to Pta Essex Isabella Island	285°T	60NM
Pta Essex to Tagus Cove	Coastal	50NM

MARQUESAS

Galapagos to Hiva Oa, Marquesas	259°T	2,845NM
Hiva Oa to Tahu Ata	Coastal	10NM
Tahu Ata to Fatu Hiva	145°T	40NM
Fatu Hiva to Hua Pou	307°T	108NM
Hua Pou to Nuka Hiva	002°T	28NM
Nuka Hiva, Marquesas to Manihi, Tuamotus	226°T	485NM
Manihi to Ahe	298°T	9NM
Then coastal to pass	253°T	8NM

FRENCH SOCIETY ISLANDS

Ahe to Papeete, Tahiti	215°T	52NM
Then	227°T	210NM
Papeete to Moorea	270°T	11NM
Moorea to Huahine	299°T	84NM
Huahine to Raiatea	265°T	21NM
Raiatea to Tahaa	295°T	17NM
Eyeball navigating through reefs separating islands		
Tahaa to Bora Bora to SW edge Then to pass	Coastal	4NM
Bora Bora to Maupiti	272°T	27NM
Maupiti to Mopelia	256°T	98NM

COOK ISLANDS

Mopelia to Suvarov	293°T	570NM

THE SAMOAS

Suvarov to Ofu	262°T	391NM
Ofu to Pago Pago, American Samoa	262°T	59NM
Pago Pago to Apia, Western Samoa	Coastal	8NM
Then	304°T	69NM

TONGA

Apia to Vava'u, Tonga Islands	Coastal	20NM
Then	200°T	320NM
Tonga to Minerva Reefs	223°T	410NM

NEW ZEALAND

Minerva Reefs to North Cape, New Zealand:		
To mark at 500 NM north of North Cape	252°T	455NM
Then	180°T	500NM
New Zealand to Minerva Reefs	22°T	788NM

FIJIS

Minerva Reefs to Suva, Fiji	339°T	365NM
Suva to Tradewinds Hotel anchorage	Coastal	2½NM
Suva to Yanutha Island	Coastal	26NM
Yanutha Island to Vunanui Harbor	Coastal	10NM

VANUATU

Vunanui to Port Vila, Efate Island, Vanuatu	273°T	570NM
Port Vila to Havannah Harbor	Coastal	26NM
Havannah Harbor to Emae Island:		
To island	12°T	30NM
To anchorage		3½NM
Emae Island to Epi Island	325°T	26NM
Epi Island to Malekula	291°T	20NM
Port Sandwich, Malekula to Vao Island	Coastal	42NM
Vao Island to Malo Killi Killi	Coastal	12NM
Malo Killi Killi to Santo, Espiritu Santo	Coastal	14NM
Santo to Palikulo Bay anchorage	Coastal	14NM
Palikulo Bay to Hog Harbor, Espiritu Santo	Coastal	25NM
Hog Harbor to Sakau Island Coastal		10NM

BANKS ISLANDS

Sakau Island to Lakona Bay, Santa Maria Island	020°T	45NM
Lakona Bay to Vanua Lava—Rigadoon Falls	358°T	28NM

TORRES ISLANDS

Rigadoon Falls to Hayter Bay, Tegua Island, Torres Islands	307°T	60NM

This is as far as Volume I takes you, but we're including the rest of the trip here, so you'll have a complete picture.

SOLOMON ISLANDS

Hayter Bay to Santa Ana, Solomon Islands	301°T	285NM
Santa Ana to Star Harbor, San Cristobal	Coastal	12NM
Star Harbor to Wanoni Bay	Coastal	29NM
Wanoni Bay to Kira Kira	Coastal	9NM
Kira Kira to Ugi Island	302°T	15NM
Ugi Island to Marau Sound, Guadalcanal	302°T	57NM
Marau Sound to Honiara	Coastal	60NM
Honiara to Gavutu Island	037°T	25NM
Honiara to Tamimbo Bay, Cape Esperance	Coastal	20NM
Tamimbo Bay to Russell Islands	292°T	29NM
Russell Islands to Tongoro Passage, Marovo Lagoon, New Georgia	294°T	61NM
Gizo, New Georgia to Baga Island	309°T	25NM
Baga Island to Treasury Islands	296°T	59NM

PAPUA NEW GUINEA

Treasury Islands to Cape St. George, New Ireland	314°T	218NM
English Harbor, New Ireland to Put Put Harbor, New Britain	294°T	31NM
Put Put Harbor to Rabaul	Coastal	30NM
Rabaul to Cape Lambert	Coastal	55NM
Cape Lambert to Madang, Papua New Guinea	258°T	360NM
Madang to Sio Lighthouse	115°T	105NM
Sio Lighthouse to Kiriwina, Trobriands	124°T	264NM
Kiriwina to southern tip of Vakuta	351°T	30NM
Southern tip of Vakuta into anchorage	Coastal	6NM
Vakuta, Trobriands to Wamea Bay, Amphlett Islands	211°T	26NM
Wamea Bay to "20" mark between Fergusson and Sanaroa Island	173°T	24NM
"20" mark to Scrub Island	Coastal	4NM
Scrub Island to Ebega Point	243°T	9NM
Ebega Point to anchorage, Gomwa Bay	Coastal	2NM
Gomwa Bay to Sewa Bay, Normanby Island	Coastal	31NM
Sewa Bay to Nuakata Island	166°T	17NM
Nuakata Island to "20" mark on chart	181°T	5NM
"20" mark to entrance to China Straits between "1" & "18" Dorasi Shoal	241°T	18NM
Dorasi Shoal to Belesana Slipways, mainland Papua New Guinea	Coastal	5NM
Belesana to Samarai		3NM
Belesana to Suau Island, South Cape, Papua New Guinea	Coastal	30NM
Suau Island to Hood Point	285°T	145NM
Hood Point to Port Moresby	Coastal	50NM

TORRES STRAIT, AUSTRALIA

Port Moresby to Bramble Cay	277°T	194NM
Bramble Cay to Dalrumple Island	230°T	45NM
Dalrymple to Cocoanut Island	207°T	30NM
Cocoanut Island to Mt. Adolphus Island	216°T	43NM
Mt. Adolphus Island to Thursday Island	284°T	24NM
Thursday Island to Booby Light	279°T	17NM

AUSTRALIA

Booby Light to Cape Wessel	266°T	306NM
Cape Wessel to Jensen Bay	Coastal	7NM
Jensen Bay to New Year Island	274°T	217NM
New Year Island to Croker Island	Coastal	27NM
Croker Island to Port Essington	Coastal	25NM
Port Essington to Cape Don	Coastal	25NM
Cape Don to Cape Hotham	213°T	55NM
Cape Hotham through Vernons	Coastal	21NM
End of Vernons to Fannie Bay, Darwin	Coastal	22NM
Darwin to Ashmore Reef	271°T	467NM

INDONESIA

Ashmore Reef to Bali	294°T	510NM

INDIAN OCEAN

Bali to Christmas Island	261°T	575NM
Christmas Island to Cocos-Keeling	260°T	530NM
Cocos-Keeling to Diego Garcia, Chagos Archipelago	282°T	1,500NM
Diego Garcia to Egmont Island, Chagos Archipelago	285°T	70NM
Egmont Island to Mauritius, Mascarenes	225°T	1,132NM
Mauritius to Cargados Carajos Shoals, Mascarenes	030°T	230NM
Mauritius to Reunion Island, Mascarenes	250°T	131NM
Reunion to 1st Turning Point south of Madagascar	227°T	623NM

SOUTH AFRICA

South of Madagascar to Richards Bay, South Africa	267°T	810NM
Richards Bay to East London	Coastal	330NM
East London to Knysna	Coastal	230NM
Knysna to Mossel Bay	Coastal	45NM
Mossel Bay to Cape Town	Coastal	255NM

SOUTH ATLANTIC

Cape Town to St. Helena	310°T	1,650NM
St. Helena to Ascension	314°T	703NM

EASTERN CARIBBEAN

Ascension to Bequia, Grenadines	294°T	3,155NM
Bequia to Iles Des Saintes, Guadeloupe	354°T	170NM
Iles Des Saintes to Deshayes, Guadeloupe	Coastal	32NM
Deshayes to English Harbor, Antigua	002°T	40NM
English Harbor to Gustavia Harbor, St. Bart's	Coastal	7NM
Then	314°T	77NM
Gustavia Harbor to Philipsburg, St. Maarten	299°T	14NM
Philipsburg to Simson Bay, St. Maarten	Coastal	3NM
Simson Bay to north end of Virgin Gorda	293°T	80NM
North end of Virgin Gorda to Spanish Town	Coastal	7NM
Spanish Town to Trellis Bay, Beef Island, Tortola	Coastal	5NM
Trellis Bay to Cruz Bay, St. John	Coastal	19NM
St. John to St. Thomas	Coastal	10NM
St. Thomas to St. James Island	Coastal	4NM
St. James Island to West End, Tortola	Coastal	6NM
West End to Trellis Bay, Beef Island	Coastal	13NM

BAHAMAS

Trellis Bay to north end of Eleuthra, Bahamas	303°T	800NM
North end of Eleuthra to Market Fish Cays, Berry Islands	274°T	58NM
Market Fish Cays to Alder Cay	Coastal	8NM
Alder Cay to Bird Cay	Coastal	12NM
Bird Cay to Northwest Channel Light	285°T	19NM
Northwest Channel Light to Mackie Shoal	259°T	31NM
Mackie Shoal to North Rock, North Bimini	284°T	33NM
North Rock to Dollar Harbor, South Cat Cay	Coastal	18NM
		18NM
Dollar Harbor to Port Everglades, Fort Lauderdale	303°T	57NM
	Total Voyage	31,579NM

APPENDIX II

RADIO COMMUNICATIONS
by
Julius M. Wilensky

The Moeslys are both ham radio operators, as are many other circumnavigators. This allows them to stay in touch with other cruisers, who can give them weather and sea conditions ahead. You need a Single Sideband Radio, standard with circumnavigators.

Ham Nets

While I was in New Zealand last fall, I visited one of their two "ham nets," and listened to reports from boats coming south from Fiji and Tonga. Some were encountering heavy weather, not unusual in these passages. The ham net operator at Opua received these reports, and was able to answer queries from other boats. He had access to weather satellite reports, and could make sense out of the reports he received and his weather map.

There has been a proliferation of ham nets, now numbering more than 900, and covering nearly every nook and cranny of our world. A listing of these is a book in itself. There may be others, but the best listing I've seen is published by Tiare Publications, P. O. Box 493, Lake Geneva, WI 53147, USA. Titled "The World Ham Net Directory," this is updated periodically. I have the Third Edition, published 1991, which I bought in 1993. It only lists one of the two New Zealand nets.

The book is divided into three sections, listing the nets by name, by frequency, and by air meeting time. Mike Witkowsky is the author. He also edits the ham band section of the monthly bulletin of the Association of DX Reporters, and he publishes his own ham DX newsletter. You can send information to Mike at 4206 Nebel St., Stevens Point, WI 54481.

Many of the nets are useful to circumnavigators, but the listing also includes special interest nets like railroad fans, retired persons, and people who enjoy talking to one another over long distances (DX'ers and/or "rag chewers"). You can judge from their names whether they'll be helpful in the manner of the New Zealand nets. For weather in your area or ahead of your course, you wouldn't want the Southern California Old Timers Net or the International Police Net, but you might want the Southeast Asia Net, or the South Pacific Cruising Net.

Single Sideband Radio

This is what hams use, but they are useful for anyone making long passages. Marine SSB charges to talk to a phone via a marine operator costs $4.95 per minute. You can receive government produced weather forecasts, ship observations, routing advice, as well as "net" observations and forecasts. Ships generally call in their observations at 0000, 0600, 1200, and 1800 GMT. Newer sets have weatherfax capability, decoders and printers, which will let you receive weatherfax charts and rebroadcasts of satellite photos.

You can also receive WWV, the National Institute of Standards and Technology from Fort Collins, Colorado. They broadcast continuously updated tropical depression and storm center information for the North Atlantic west of 35°W, including the Gulf of Mexico and Caribbean at 8 and 9 minutes after every hour. They cover the North Pacific east of 140°W at 10 minutes past each hour. WWV's frequencies are 2500, 5000, 10,000, 15,000 and 20,000kHz.

WWVH is the National Institute of Standards and Technology station at Kauai, Hawaii. They broadcast the same kind of information as WWV, but for the north and south Pacific. These broadcasts are on the same frequencies as WWV at 48, 49, and 50 minutes after each hour.

Both stations also give time ticks that let you calibrate your timepiece, accuracy necessary for sextant sights. With worldwide coverage by GPS, who needs a sextant? You do, if you sail around the world. Your GPS could conk out.

Imarstat (International Marine Satellite)

This is another way to communicate long distances from your boat. There are eight satellites over four ocean regions. This has been in use for large vessels for many years but because of power and antenna requirements, has not been practical for circumnavigators in small boats. More recently, Imarstat C has been introduced for 12 volt use with a small fixed omni-directional antenna. You can send or receive messages via laptop computer at 600 bits per second. Imarstat C can send to a fax machine but cannot receive fax messages. The only problem is the high cost, presently $8000 and up for the terminal and the laptop computer. Imarstat C service costs $1.12 per kilobit.

Imarstat M service is voice transmission, recently made available. It only costs $5.50 per minute but needs an antenna that's too big for small sailboat masts, and the equipment presently costs $15,000 and up.

While Imarstat C or M may be too expensive now, keep an eye on these prices. Look what happened to the cost of GPS. Greater demand and competition brought the price down to where even I bought a Magellan GPS last year.

High Seas Direct

AT&T has started a service that provides direct access to their telephone network without operator assistance. You hook a modem and a handset into your SSB, enabling you to bypass the marine operator. The call only costs $3.50 per minute. The handset and modem now cost about $1500, available from marine electronics dealers. Calls can be billed to an AT&T calling card, or a local phone company credit card, or the AT&T Universal Card, or to a third party number.

Comsat

Comsat Corp. has announced a new satellite phone service with global range. At present, it's voice only, no data or fax, but these enhancements are being developed. It's a private call, direct dialing from your boat. It requires a 24 inch antenna. See Comsat's new sets, called MobileLink at your electronics dealer.

VHF

Because of limited range (normally 25-40 miles) and line of sight transmission that can be blocked by high mountains close to you, VHF sets are useless on long passages. However, long passages frequently result in destination anchorages, like the French Society Islands, the Eastern Caribbean, the Bahamas, Maine, Southern New England, Chesapeake Bay, the Florida Keys, the Mediterranean, New Zealand, USA west coast, Hawaii, Alaska—you name it. Most boats in these locations have VHF sets and use them to talk to each other and to land-based stations. The Coast Guard monitors channels 16 and 22, and in USA, you need channel 13 to open bridges. Marine operators can patch you into any telephone system, local or long distance.

These sets are economical to buy, easy to install, and require little maintenance.

How can they help a circumnavigator? For a few instances, by letting him communicate with other boats in heavy coastal traffic. By determining before you go ashore, whether a marine supply store has what you want, whether a shoreside restaurant can accommodate you, by letting customs or harbor masters know that you are nearing port and want information on procedures or anchoring directions—let me count the ways!

One of the more important uses of a VHF set that I hope you never need, is to get advice on coping with a medical emergency. You can accomplish this on the high seas with your SSB radio, but in popular cruising areas, few boats have single sideband. Charterers all use VHF, and it always amazes me how quickly I hear doctors respond to calls for help when I'm cruising in popular areas. There is nearly always a physician cruising within the limited range of VHF sets, in popular cruising areas.

Most VHF sets have the seven designated weather channels WX1 through WX7. The first three are currently in use all over USA coasts. They broadcast continuous NOAA weather forecasts, updated every few hours, and include weather warnings and weather watch conditions. These forecasts are tailored to the station's local area, and are usually the best near term forecasts that you can get. Canada has a similar system using VHF Channels 21 or 83.

Other Possibilities

Whitbread and BOC Challenge round-the-world racers have been putting aboard electronic wizardry that not only enables them to be tracked for position, but includes VHF, SSB, shortwave radio saatellite telephones, computers for sending and receiving E-mail, satellite weather information, EPIRB's radar, and GPS.

You can add as much of this as you want, and/or can afford. You should have a separate battery to operate all this, and you need solar panels and a wind generator to replenish battery power.

•

A salt water atmosphere is the enemy of electronics. I've seen various methods used to keep electronics dry. Plastic covers, silicagel, but most unusual was Jamie Bryson's electronic stowage that he proudly showed me when I came aboard at Opua, New Zealand. Jamie converted the quarter berth on his Rawson 30 into an electronics stowage. He enclosed it with ventilated doors, and says it works well. He has an impressive array of sets.

Other Helpful Publications

"Weather for the Mariner" by William J. Kotsch, U.S. Naval Academy, Annapolis, MD 21402

"Selected Worldwide Marine Weather Broadcasts," National Oceanographic and Atmospheric Administration, Riverdale, MD 20737-1199

"Mariners Guide to Single Sideband" by Frederick Graves, SEA, Inc., Mountlake Terrace, WA 98043

Send for Tiare Publications' Catalog, address above, under Ham Nets.

Drydock at Taylor-Smith Shipyard, Port Louis, Mauritius. See Chapter 16

APPENDIX III

MAIL FORWARDING SERVICES
by
Julius M. Wilensky

Many round the world sailors have all their mail diverted to a relative or trusted friend who will deposit checks in a pre-arranged manner, pay bills, throw away junk, and forward the other mail. This forwarding is done when the sailor phones an address where the boat will remain for a couple of weeks. This is a lot of work for the person selected, and this person has to be sure that they can differentiate between true junk mail and some that may interest you (marine catalogs, boating magazines, annual reports etc). This person also has to act fast on your phone call, because two weeks is little enough time for delivery to far-away places.

Another way to handle these necessary chores is to hire a Mail Forwarding Service. They all charge a monthly fee, and they require a postage deposit that they can draw upon. Some require other fees, such as a percentage of the postal cost as a handling fee, or an extra charge for a different person. Check out **all** costs to be sure there will be no suprises. Some Services will take phone messages, find parts for you, or track you down if there's an emergency at home.

Try to get a Service with a fax number. A fax is less expensive than a phone call from foreign countries. Try to arrange for them to send you a "no mail" card when you call so you know that none is missing.

Following are a few Mail Forwarding Services that have been recommended by users, and have been reliable.

Travelers Remail Association
6110 Pleasant Ridge Road
Arlington, TX 76016
(800) 666-6710 or (817) 476-9466

Travelers Mail Express
Box 10121
Eugene, OR 97440-0121
(800) 843-7282 or (503) 344-4869

Cruising Services
Box 11778
Hialeah, FL 33011-1778
(800) 326-1023

Home Base
Box 65656
Lubbock, TX 79464-5724
(806) 794-9644

There is a "Directory of U.S. Mail Drops" published by Loompanics Unlimited, Box 1197, Port Townsend, WA 98368, $14.95 plus $3.00 shipping costs. It lists hundreds of USA Mail Forwarding Services.

Some other Mail Forwarding Services advertise in the classified sections of boating magazines.

Photo by Carl Moesly

Rigadoon Falls, Vanua Lava I., Banks Is. See Chapter 1

PLACE NAME INDEX

Admiralty Bay, Bequia 258-260, 262
Aldabra I., Indian Ocean 138
Agulhas Current, Bank, Cape,
 South Africa 195, 196, 204, 210,
 224-227, 230, 237, 241, 242
Alder Cay, Berry Is. 270
Amphlett Is. 94, 95
Anegada Passage 264
Antigua 262, 263
Aore I., Espiritu Santo 22
Arafura Sea 89, 119, 120
Arnhem Land, Australia 122, 126
Arundel, New Georgia Group 65
Asaro, Papua New Guinea 84
Ascension I., Atlantic Ocean 254
Ashmore Reef, Indian Ocean 132
Atlantic Ocean 222, 241, 248, 249,
 255, 260, 262, 264, 270
Australia 72, 75, 78, 88, 89, 93,
 102, 108, 111, 116, 118-121, 123, 126-
 128, 130, 153, 174, 179, 180, 184, 221

Baga I., New Georgia Group 67
Bahama Is. 32, 166, 229, 268
Bainings Mts., New Britain 76
Bali 108, 130-132, 134-140, 247
Banika I., Russell Is. New Georgia Group 55
Banks Is. 13, 26
Baranago Harbor, Florida I. Solomon Is. 51, 53
Beagle Gulf, Australia 126
Beef I., British Virgin Is. 266
Benguela Current 237, 241
Benoa Harbor, Village, Bali 132-134,
 136, 138
Bequia, St. Vincent, Windward Is. 254, 255,
 257, 260-262
Bermuda 270
Berry Is., Bahamas Is. 268, 270, 271
Bimini, Bahamas 27, 272
Bird Cay, Berry Is. 270
Bismarck Archipelago, Papua New Guinea ... 68,
 70-72, 74
Black River, Mauritius 181
Bloody Ridge, Guadalcanal I., Solomon Is. 50
Bonkovia, Vanuatu 20
Bora Bora, Society Is. 142
Bougainvillae, Solomon Is. 38, 59, 68
Bramble Cay, Torres Straits 80, 110,111,
 118, 244
British Virgin Is. 264, 266, 267, 268
Buffalo River, East London,
 South Africa 227, 230

Cape Don, Australia 125, 126
Cape Hangkip, South Africa 241
Cape Hotham, Australia 125, 126
Cape of Good Hope 138, 174, 220-222,
 241-243, 249, 255
Cape St. George, New Ireland 70
Cape St. Francis, South Africa 232
Cape Town, South Africa 138, 170, 180,
 221, 222, 228, 231, 234, 241-248, 251,
 252, 254
Cargados Carajos Shoals (St. Brandons) 185-
 189, 193, 195, 203
Caribbean 203, 228, 248, 249
Chagos Archipelago 89, 144, 148, 154,
 155, 157, 162, 172
China Straits 90, 96-99, 101, 102
Coburg Peninsula, Australia 123
Coco I., Cargados Carajos Shoals
 (St. Brandons) 188, 190, 191
Coconut I., Australia 118
Cocos-Keeling, Indian Ocean 142, 143

Comore Is., Indian Ocean 138
Coral Sea 244
Charlotte Amalie Harbor, St. Thomas 266
Christmas I., Indian Ocean 140, 242,
 145, 148, 158, 164
Croker I., Cape, Australia 123, 125, 126
Cruz Bay, St. John 264

Dalrymple I., Australia 118
Darwin, Australia 108, 125-130, 132
Denpasar, Bali 132, 134-136
DesHayes, Guadaloupe 262
Devils Point, Efate I. 13
Diamond Narrows, New Georgia Group ... 63, 65
Diego Garcia, Chagos Archipelago,
 Indian Ocean 139, 148, 153, 154,
 157-160, 162-164, 172
Diamond Passage, Espiritu Santo 26
Dobu I., Amphlett Group 94
Dollar Harbor, South Cat Cay, Bahamas 270,
 272
Durban, South Africa 138, 175, 184,
 185, 195-197, 199, 210, 214, 220-222,
 224, 226-228, 238

East London, South Africa 222, 227-231
Efate I., Vanuatu 13, 14
Egmont Is., Lagoon, Atoll, ... 161-166,168,172
 Chagos Archipelago
Eleuthera, Bahama Is. 268, 269
Elizabethport, Bequia 260
Emae I., Vanuatu 16, 17
English Harbour, Antigua 262
English Harbor, New Ireland 70, 72
Epi I., Vanuatu 16, 17
Equator 70, 88, 227, 249, 254, 255
Espiritu Santo, Village, Island, Vanuatu 13,
 21, 22,24, 26

False Bay, South Africa 241, 248
Fannie Bay, Darwin, Australia 127, 130
Farquar Is., Indian Ocean 138
Fergusson I., Amphlett Group 94, 95
Fiji 13, 53, 62
Fish Hoek, South Africa 248
Florida 176, 180, 193, 221
Florida I. (Gela) 50-53, 65
Flying Fish Cove, Christmas I.,
 Indian Ocean 140-143
Foreland Anchorage, Epi I. 16
Fort Lauderdale 221, 249, 251, 268, 269

Gavutu Harbor, Florida I., Solomon Is. 51, 52
Gizo, Solomon Is. 65-67
Glorioso Is., Indian Ocean 138
Gomwa Bay, Dobu I., Amphlett Group 94, 96
Grand Bay, Mauritius 169, 171-176, 178,
 180, 182-184, 187, 194, 195, 197
Great Bahama Bank 270
Greenland 72
Grenadines 260
Guadalcanal I., Solomon Is. 38, 45-50, 54,
 55
Guadaloupe 262, 263
Guam 79, 89
Gulf of Carpentaria, Australia 120, 122
Gulf Stream 270
Gustavia Harbor, St. Barts 262

Hathorn Sound, New Georgia Group 63, 65
Hayter Bay, Tegua I. Torres Is. 30, 31
Havannah, Vanuatu 13, 16
Hele Bar, New Georgia Group 62, 64

285

Henderson field, Guadalcanal I.,
  Solomon Is. 50
Hog Harbor, Espiritu Santo 22, 26
Hood Bay, Lagoon, Papua New Guinea 102,
  103, 150
Honiara, Guadalcanal, Solomon Is. 38, 45,
  47, 49, 50, 53
Horn I., Australia 120
Horse Island, Penobscot Bay 69, 70
Humboldt Current 237

Ile de Paul, Cargados Carajos Shoals
  (St. Brandons) 191
Ile (Islet) Raphael, Cargados Carajos Shoals
  (St. Brandons) 188, 192, 193
Iles de Saintes 262, 263
Ile Sudest, Egmont Group 163, 166, 172
Indian Ocean 83, 88, 89, 120, 132,
  138, 140, 142, 144, 145, 153, 157, 168
  172, 175, 179, 180, 183, 184, 195, 196, 198,
  201, 206, 212, 215, 226, 230, 234, 237, 241,
  242, 260
Indonesia 89, 108, 132
Iron Bottom Sound, Solomon Is. 38, 51

Jakarta, Indonesia 134, 139
Jamestown Harbor, St. Helena 254
Jensen Bay, Wessel Is., Australia 122

Karkar I. Madang 87
Kavieng, New Britain 79
Kirakira, San Cristobal I.,
  Solomon Is. 36, 38, 39, 41, 42, 47
Kiriwina I., Trobriands 90
Knysna, Lagoon, South Africa 230, 232-235,
  237, 238
Kolombangara, New Georgia Group 62
Krankett I., Madang 87, 88
Kula Gulf, New Georgia Group 67
Kuta Beach, Bali 136

Lakona Bay, Santa Maria I., Banks Is. 26-28
LaMap, Malekula I. 21
Lambeti Harbor, New Georgia Group 65
Lambon I., Village, New Ireland 72
Langsberg, South Africa 236
Leeward Is. 260, 264
Leisure Isle, Knysna, South Africa 232
Le Puce, Mauritius 178
Lever Plantation, Banika I.,
  New Georgia Group 55

Mackie Shoal, Bahamas 270
Madagascar, Indian Ocean 138, 139,
  161, 172, 175, 183, 185 186, 195, 196,
  199-203, 205, 207, 208, 210, 216, 228
Madang Village, Harbor, Papua,
  New Guinea 44, 75, 79, 82-86, 89,
  90, 100, 118
Malaita, Solomon Is. 28, 58
Malapa I. 45
Malekula I., Vanuatu 13, 18-21
Malo Killikilli, Vanuatu 21, 22
Malo Strait, Vanuatu 21, 22
Marau Sound, Solomon Is. 45, 48
Marovo Lagoon, New Georgia Group,
  Solomon Is. 54, 55, 59, 62
Market Fish Cays, Berry Is. 270
Marquesas 260
Mascarenes, Indian Ocean 186
Matupit, New Britain 76
Mauritius 89, 112, 161-164,
  166, 168, 170-172, 174, 176, 178-180,
  182-186, 190, 193, 194, 196-198, 200,
  214, 221
Mbaeroko Bay, Enogai, New Georgia I. 65
Meerensee, South Africa 216

Melanesia 13
Mhlatuzi River, South Africa 212
Mindi Mindi, New Georgia Group 59, 62
Mono I., Treasury Is. 67
Moso, Vanuatu 16
Mossel Bay, South Africa 237, 238-240, 241
Mt. Adolphus, Australia 118
Mt. Vulcan, New Britain 76
Mozambique Channel, Indian Ocean 138,
  195, 196, 201, 210
Mtubatuba, South Africa 217, 218
Mundi, New Georgia Group 65

Nelsons Dock Yard, Antigua 262
New Britain, Papua, New Guinea 35, 71,
  72, 74, 76, 77, 80
New Caledonia 25
New Georiga I., New Georgia Group,
  Solomon Is. 55-56, 65
New Guinea I. 77, 88, 89, 96, 100,
  105, 110, 119, 260
New Ireland, Papua New Guinea 35, 71,
  72, 77
New Zealand 64, 75, 83, 92, 134, 188,
  205, 266
Normanby I. 97
North Minerva Reef, South Pacific 190
North Rock, Bahamas 270
Northern Territory, Australia 126
Northwest Channel, Bahamas Is. 270
Nuakata I., Village 96

Ontong Java I. 53

Pago Pago, American Samoa 266
Palekula, Espiritu Santo I. 26
Panama 237, 254, 255
Papua, New Guinea 35, 71, 72, 75, 76,
  79, 80, 83-86, 90, 101, 102, 107-110
Pavuvu, Russell Is., Solomon Is. 55
Pawa, Ugi I., Solomon Is. 43
Pepesala Channel, Russell Is. 55
Peter and Paul Rocks, Atlantic Ocean 255
Philipsburg, St. Maarten 264
Pinas Bay, Panama 76
Piton Rivière Noir, Mauritius 168
Plum I., Solomon Is. 65
Point Cruz, Yacht Club 47, 50
Point Hood, Papua New Guinea 105, 106
Port Elizabeth, South Africa 230, 232
Port Essington, Australia 123, 125, 126
Port Everglades 158
Port Galets, Reunion I., Indian Ocean 198,
  199
Port Kennedy, Thursday I., Australia 119
Port Louis, Harbor, Mauritius 172, 175-
  179, 193, 197
Port Mary, Santa Ana, Solomon Is. 33, 36
Port Moresby, Papua New Guinea 75, 79,
  88, 90, 102, 105-110, 118
Port Sandwich, Vanuatu 18, 20, 21
Port Vila, Efate I. 13, 15, 20
Put Put Harbor, New Ireland 73

Rabaul, Harbor, New Britain, Papua,
  New Guinea 59, 62, 65, 68, 72-75,
  77-80, 84, 86, 87, 89, 102, 103
Raitea, Society Is. 144
Rambler Bay, Diego Garcia 160, 162
Red Beach, Guadalcanal I., Solomon Is. 50
Red Sea 138, 142
Rendova Harbor I., Solomon Is. 64, 65
Reunion I., Mascarene Group, Indian
  Ocean 174, 185, 187, 195, 198,
  199, 212
Richards Bay, South Africa 196, 197,
  205, 208, 210-216, 218, 220, 222, 224,
  227, 228, 246 254

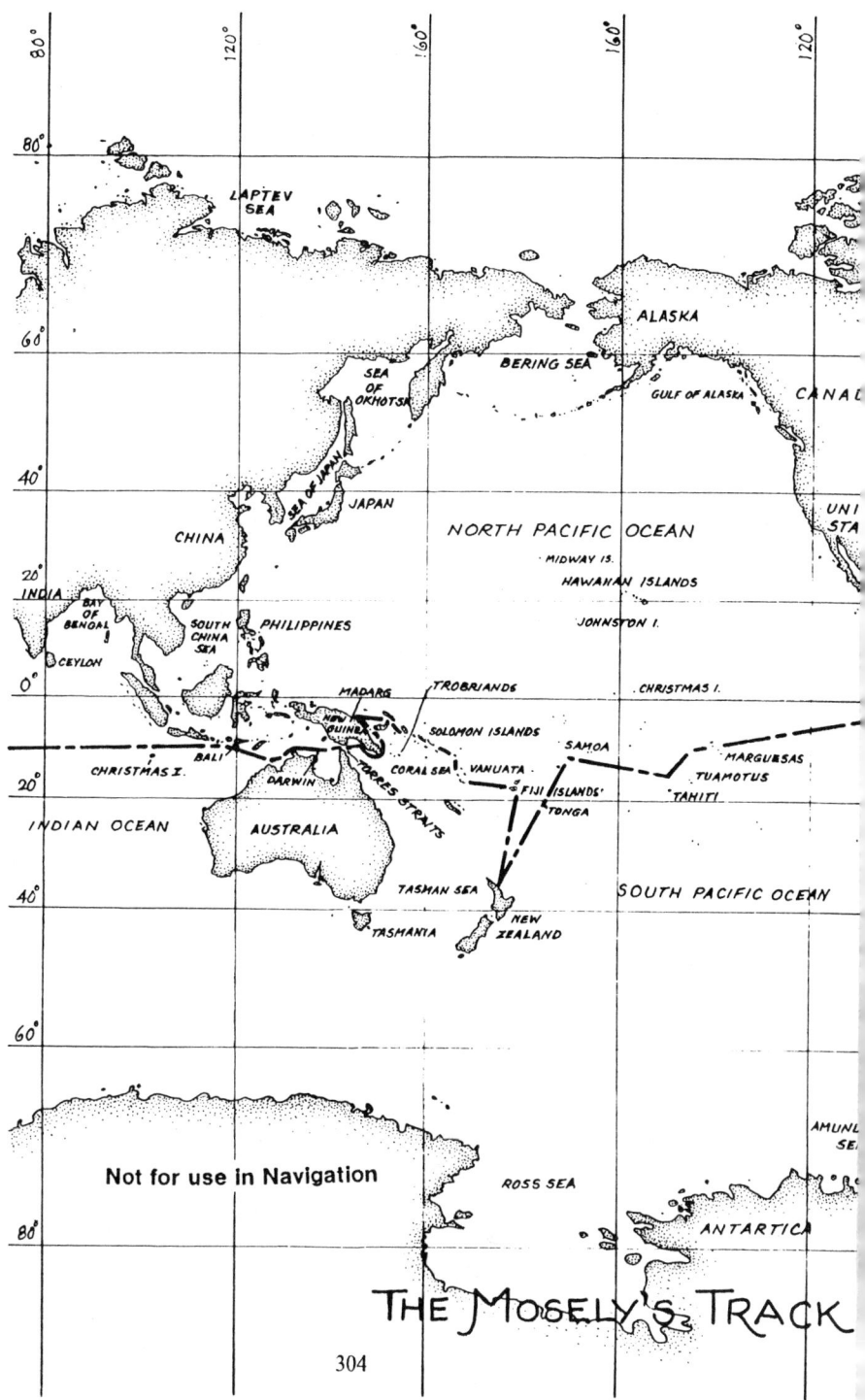

Rigadoon Bay, Vaua Lava I., Banks Is. 28-30
Robben I., South Africa 249
Rodrigues I., Mascarene Group, Indian
  Ocean 174, 179
Round Head, Hill, Papua New Guinea ... 103, 107
Round I. Indian Ocean 194
Russell Is. New Georgia Group,
  Solomon Is. 55, 60

St. Barts 262, 264, 265
St.Brandons—See Cargagos Carajos Shoals
St. Croix, U.S. Virgin Is. 266
St. Georges Channel, New Britain 72
St. Helena I., Atlantic Ocean 249, 253-255, 258
St. James Bay, St. Thomas 266
St. John, American Virgin Is. 264, 266
St. Lucia, South Africa 211
St. Martin (St. Maarten) 260, 264, 265
St. Thomas, U.S. Virgin Is. 266, 268
St. Vincent 260
Salomon Is., Chagos Archipelago,
  Indian Ocean 142, 144, 145, 157
Samarai, Papua New Guinea 89, 90, 97-100, 119
San Blas, Panama 21
San Cristobal I., Solomon Is. 37, 41, 42
San Salvador, Bahamas 268
Santa Ana I. 37
Santa Cruz Is. 32, 26
Scrub I., Amphlett Group 94, 96
Seqhe, New Georgia Group 62
Selwyn Bay, Ugi I., Solomon Is. 43
Sewa Bay, Normanby I. 96
Simonstown, South Africa 248
Simpson Bay, St. Martin 264
Simpson Harbor, Rabaul, New Britain 73
Singapore 138, 221
Sir Francis Drake Channel, British
  Virgin Is. 266
Society Is. 55, 190
Solomon Is. 13, 30, 32, 33, 35, 38,
  39, 42, 50, 62, 64, 67, 68, 70, 72, 93
South Africa 83, 138, 174, 182-184,
  195-198, 204, 218, 220, 222-224, 226,
  228, 242, 243, 246, 251, 252, 256
South America 249
South Cape, Papua New Guinea 101, 102
South Island, Cargados Carajos Shoals
  (St. Brandons) 188
South Pacific 260
Sri Lanka 138, 175
Star Harbor, San Cristobal I.,
  Solomon Is. 36, 37, 39

Stirling I, Treasury Is. 68
Suau I., Papua New Guinea 102
Surundu Bay, Espiritu Santo 22, 26
Suvarov I. 119

Table Mountain, Bay, Cape Town 244-249
Tahiti 13
Tasman Sea 142
Tavanipupu, Solomon Is. 45, 47, 55
Tegua I. 32
Terre d'en Haut, Ile de Saintes 262
The Slot, Solomon Is. 47, 50-52
Thursday I., Australia 116, 118-120, 122
Timor Sea 132
Tongoro Passage, New Georgia Group 55
Torres I., Straits 13, 26, 30, 32, 90,
  102, 110, 112, 114, 115, 118, 120, 244
Tortola, British Virgin Is. 266
Treasury Is., New Georgia Group,
  Solomon Is. 67, 69, 70
Trellis Bay, Beef I., British Virgin Is. 264,
  266, 268
Trobriand Is. 90-92
Truk 79
Tulagi, Solomon Is. 38, 50
Tupuselei, Papua New Guinea 106

Ui I., Vanuatu 18, 20
Ugi I., Solomon Is. 41, 42
Umfolozi Game Reserve, River,
  South Africa 216, 218
U.S. Virgin Is. 260, 261, 267

Vakuta I. , Village, Trobriands 90, 92, 93
Van Diemen Gulf, Australia 126
Vanququ I., New Georgia Group 62
Vangunu I., New Georgia Group 55
Vanuatu 13, 26, 67, 72
Vao I., Vanuatu 18, 21
Vernon I., Australia 126
Virgin Gorda, British Virgin Is. 264
Viru Harbor, New Georgia I. 64
Vovohe Cove, Kolombangara I. 67

Wamea Bay, Amphlett Group 94
Wanoni Bay, Solomon Is. 38, 41
Wessel Is., Australia 120-122
West End, Tortola, British Virgin Is. 266
Windward Is. 260
Windward Passage 264
Wolverine Entrance, Papua New Guinea 106

Zululand, South Africa 209, 212, 214,
  218, 221

Photo by Carl Moesly

Zulu Kraals, Zululand, South Africa. These are small circular mud huts, topped with conical grass roofs. See Chapter 20